Global Heritage

Blackwell Readers in Anthropology

This series fulfils the increasing need for texts that do the work of synthesizing the literature while challenging more traditional or subdisciplinary approaches to anthropology.

Each volume offers seminal readings on a chosen theme and provides the finest, most thought-provoking recent works in the given thematic area. Many of these volumes bring together for the first time a body of literature on a certain topic. The series thus both presents definitive collections and investigates the very ways in which anthropological inquiry has evolved and is evolving.

1. *The Anthropology of Globalization: A Reader*, Second Edition
   Edited by Jonathan Xavier Inda and Renato Rosaldo
2. *The Anthropology of Media: A Reader*
   Edited by Kelly Askew and Richard R. Wilk
3. *Genocide: An Anthropological Reader*
   Edited by Alexander Laban Hinton
4. *The Anthropology of Space and Place: Locating Culture*
   Edited by Setha Low and Denise Lawrence-Zúñiga
5. *Violence in War and Peace: An Anthology*
   Edited by Nancy Scheper-Hughes and Philippe Bourgois
6. *Same-Sex Cultures and Sexualities: An Anthropological Reader*
   Edited by Jennifer Robertson
7. *Social Movements: An Anthropological Reader*
   Edited by June Nash
8. *The Cultural Politics of Food and Eating: A Reader*
   Edited by James L. Watson and Melissa L. Caldwell
9. *The Anthropology of the State: A Reader*
   Edited by Aradhana Sharma and Akhil Gupta
10. *Human Rights: An Anthropological Reader*
    Edited by Mark Goodale
11. *The Pharmaceutical Studies Reader*
    Edited by Sergio Sismondo and Jeremy A. Greene
12. *Global Heritage: A Reader*
    Edited by Lynn Meskell

Global Heritage: A Reader

Edited by

Lynn Meskell

WILEY Blackwell

This edition first published 2015

Registered Office
John Wiley & Sons, Ltd, The Atrium, Southern Gate, Chichester, West Sussex, PO19 8SQ, UK

Editorial Offices
350 Main Street, Malden, MA 02148-5020, USA
9600 Garsington Road, Oxford, OX4 2DQ, UK
The Atrium, Southern Gate, Chichester, West Sussex, PO19 8SQ, UK

For details of our global editorial offices, for customer services, and for information about how to apply for permission to reuse the copyright material in this book please see our website at www.wiley.com/wiley-blackwell.

Library of Congress Cataloging-in-Publication Data applied for.

Hardback 9781118768860
Paperback 9781118768549

A catalogue record for this book is available from the British Library.

Cover image: Photograph taken in Angkor, Cambodia by Lynn Meskell

Set in 10/12pt Sabon by SPi Publisher Services, Pondicherry, India
Printed and bound in Malaysia by Vivar Printing Sdn Bhd

1 2015

For Sherry, Lila, and Sylvia

Contents

Notes on Contributors

Christoph Brumann is Head of Research Group at the Max Planck Institute for Social Anthropology, Halle, and Honorary Professor of Anthropology at Martin Luther University Halle-Wittenberg in Germany. He is the author of *Tradition, Democracy and the Townscape of Kyoto* (2012) and co-editor of *Making Japanese Heritage* (2010) and *Urban Spaces in Japan* (2012). He has published widely on urban anthropology, the concept of culture, globalization, utopian communes, and Japanese gift exchange. Alongside his ethnographic study of the UNESCO World Heritage arena, he is currently preparing a new project on Buddhist temple economies in urban Asia.

Denis Byrne is Senior Research Fellow at the Institute for Culture and Society, University of Western Sydney, Australia. He has worked in both government and academic spheres of heritage conservation and has contributed to critical debates on heritage issues in Southeast Asia and indigenous Australia. He is author of *Counterheritage: Critical Perspectives on Heritage Conservation in Asia* (2013) and *Surface Collection: Archaeological Travels in Southeast Asia* (2007).

Chiara De Cesari is an anthropologist and Assistant Professor in European Studies and Cultural Studies at the University of Amsterdam. Her research focuses on heritage, memory, and cultural politics and how these change under conditions of globalization. She has published articles in *American Anthropologist*, *Memory Studies*, and *Studies in Ethnicity and Nationalism*, among others. She co-edited *Transnational Memory* (2014, with Ann Rigney) and is currently finishing a book entitled, *Heritage and the Struggle for Palestine*. Her most recent project explores the making of a new European collective memory in relation to its blind spots, particularly the carceral heritage of colonialism.

Chip Colwell is Curator of Anthropology at the Denver Museum of Nature and Science. He has written and edited ten books, and more than forty articles and book chapters. His research has been highlighted in such venues as *Archaeology Magazine*, *Indian Country Today*, the *Huffington Post*, and the *New York Times*.

Rosemary J. Coombe holds the Tier One Canada Research Chair in Law, Communication and Culture at York University in Toronto, where she is cross-appointed to the Departments of Anthropology and Social Science. Until 2000 she was Full Professor of Law at the University of Toronto. Her award-winning book, *The Cultural Life of Intellectual Properties* was reprinted in 2008. She publishes in the fields of anthropology, cultural studies, and legal studies on the politics of cultural property and heritage management at the intersections of neoliberalism, informational capital, and human rights.

Alfredo González-Ruibal is Staff Scientist with the Institute of Heritage Sciences of the Spanish National Research Council (Incipit-CSIC). His work focuses on the archaeology of the contemporary past and the negative heritage of modernity (war, dictatorship, colonialism). He has recently co-edited the collection *Ethics and the Archaeology of Violence* (with Gabriel Moshenska, 2014). His recent book, *An Archaeology of Resistance: Materiality and Time in an African Borderland* (2014) deals with his other research interests: resistance, egalitarianism, and the material culture of indigenous communities.

Peter G. Gould is a consulting scholar at the Penn Cultural Heritage Center of the University of Pennsylvania Museum of Archaeology and Anthropology and an Adjunct Professor of Archaeology at the American University of Rome. After a career as an economist and business executive, he received his Ph.D. from University College London, for which his research in Belize, Peru and Ireland concerned the governance features of sustainable community economic development projects associated with heritage sites. He is a founding director of the Sustainable Preservation Initiative, which supports community economic development projects associated with archaeological sites, initially in Peru.

Martin Hall is Vice Chancellor (President) of the University of Salford, Manchester and Professor Emeritus at the University of Cape Town (UCT). He was previously Professor of Historical Archaeology, inaugural Dean of Higher Education Development, and then Deputy Vice-Chancellor at UCT. He is a Fellow of the Royal Society of Arts, a Fellow of the Royal Society of South Africa, a Life Fellow of the University of Cape Town, and past President of the World Archaeological Congress. Martin Hall has published extensively on pre-colonial, colonial, and historical archaeology, and on the representation of the past in the present.

Michael Herzfeld is the Ernest E. Monrad Professor of the Social Sciences in the Department of Anthropology at Harvard University. Over his long career, he has authored ten books – including *A Place in History* (1991), *Cultural Intimacy* (2nd edition, 2005), and *Evicted from Eternity* (2009) – and numerous articles and reviews, and has also produced two ethnographic films about Rome. A former editor of *American Ethnologist* (1995–1998), he is Senior Advisor to the Critical Heritage Studies Initiative of the International Institute for Asian Studies (Leiden). His research in Greece, Italy, and Thailand encompasses historic conservation and gentrification, crypto-colonialism, nationalism and cultural intimacy, and artisanship and apprenticeship.

Charlotte Joy is a Lecturer in Social Anthropology at Goldsmiths College, University of London. She carried out fieldwork in Djenné, Mali, and at UNESCO in Paris and is the author of *The Politics of Heritage Management in Mali* (2013). Her research is concerned with developing an ethnographic approach to understanding the politics of cultural heritage and the links between cultural heritage, rights, and the ethics of the uses of the past in the present. Her new research documents the destruction and rehabilitation of cultural heritage during the current conflict in Mali.

Morag M. Kersel is Assistant Professor in the Department of Anthropology at DePaul University and affiliated faculty with the Center for Art, Museum, and Cultural Heritage Law at DePaul College of Law. She co-directs the archaeological and ethnographic "Follow the Pots Project" in Jordan (http://followthepotsproject.org/). She is a co-author (with Christina Luke) of *U.S. Cultural Diplomacy and Archaeology: Soft Power, Hard Heritage* (2013) and a co-editor of the volume *Archaeology, Cultural Heritage and the Trade in Antiquities* (2006). Her research interests include the prehistory of the Levant, cultural heritage policy and law, and the trade in archaeological artifacts.

Sophia Labadi is a Lecturer in Heritage and Director of the Centre for Heritage at the University of Kent. She has a Ph.D. and a Masters in Cultural Heritage Studies from the Institute of Archaeology, University College London and graduated from the Institute of Political Sciences in Grenoble (France). Since 2001, she has worked for a number of regional and international organizations. For UNESCO, she has worked in the Secretariat of the 1972 World Heritage Convention and the 2003 Intangible Cultural Heritage Convention. She was a Getty Conservation Guest Scholar in 2006–2007, the recipient of the Cultural Policy Research Award in 2008, a Senior Research Fellow at Durham University in 2012, and a fellow at the National Gallery of Denmark in 2014.

Kathryn Lafrenz Samuels is an Assistant Professor of Anthropology at the University of Maryland, whose research examines cultural heritage in the transnational sphere, in the ambit of international economic development, democracy promotion, human rights, and global climate change. In 2013–2014 she was a Fulbright fellow in Tromsø, Norway with the Norwegian Institute for Cultural Heritage Research (NIKU). She is co-editor of *Cultures of Contact: Archaeology, Ethics, and Globalization* (2007) with Sebastian De Vivo and Darian Totten, *Making Roman Places: Past and Present* (2012) with Darian Totten, and *Heritage Keywords: Rhetoric and Redescription in Cultural Heritage* (2015) with Trinidad Rico.

Ian Lilley is a Professor at the University of Queensland. He has worked in Australasian and Indo-Pacific archaeology and cultural heritage for thirty-five years. He currently does fieldwork in Australia and New Caledonia, and has just begun a major project examining Indigenous issues in World Heritage management. He is Secretary-General of the ICOMOS International Scientific Committee on Archaeological Heritage Management and also serves on two IUCN Commissions. His most recent books are a heritage management volume on *Early Human Expansion and Innovation in the Pacific* (2010) and the university textbook, *Archaeology of Oceania: Australia and the Pacific Islands* (2006).

Christina Luke teaches at Boston University, where she also serves as editor of the *Journal of Field Archaeology*. She works closely with US embassies and foreign ministries in various countries to explore the pivotal place of heritage in social life and personal experience. Her recent publications include *U.S. Cultural Diplomacy and Archaeology* (2013) and several articles focused on cultural policy and sovereignty.

Her current research focuses on heritage studies, international development, and geopolitics in Turkey, the Balkans, and Latin America.

Lynn Meskell is Professor of Anthropology and Director of the Archaeology Center at Stanford University. Before coming to Stanford in 2005 she was Professor of Anthropology at Columbia University in New York. She is Honorary Professor at the University of the Witwatersrand, Johannesburg. Some of her recent books and edited collections include *Cosmopolitan Archaeologies* (2009) and *The Nature of Culture: The New South Africa* (2011). Some of her new research involves an institutional ethnography of UNESCO with a particular focus on heritage rights, sovereignty, and international politics.

Webber Ndoro is currently the Director of the African World Heritage Fund based in Johannesburg, South Africa. He is also Associate Research Fellow at the University of Cape Town. He was Project Manager at ICCROM in Rome, where he worked on the Africa 2009 programme. His recent books and edited collections include *Great Zimbabwe: Your Monument Our Shrine* (2000), *Cultural Heritage and the Law: Protecting Immovable Heritage in Sub-Saharan Africa* (2009), and *The Archaeological Heritage of Africa* (2014). He has published several articles on heritage management in Africa.

Noel B. Salazar is Research Professor in Anthropology at the University of Leuven. He is author of *Envisioning Eden* (2010) and numerous articles and book chapters on the anthropology of heritage tourism. He is chair of the IUAES Commission on the Anthropology of Tourism, founding member of the AAA Anthropology of Tourism Interest Group, and editorial board member of *Annals of Tourism Research* and *Journal of Heritage Tourism*. In addition, he is registered on UNESCO's and UNWTO's official roster of consultants, an expert member of the ICOMOS International Cultural Tourism Committee, and the UNESCO-UNITWIN Network "Culture, Tourism and Development."

Gamini Wijesuriya is currently a staff member of ICCROM in Rome. He was Director of Conservation in the Sri Lankan Department of Archaeology from 1982 to 2000, and then a Principal Regional Scientist in the New Zealand Department of Conservation from 2001 until moving to ICCROM in 2004. He is engaged in a variety of international level training and capacity-building activities related to conservation and management of heritage, including World Heritage. He has published several articles on conservation and management of heritage.

Gro Birgit Ween is Associate Professor and a Keeper of the Arctic and the Australian Collection at the Cultural History Museum at the University of Oslo. She has done fieldwork on indigenous issues, such as rights, heritage, and nature practices in Northern Australia, Sápmi, and Alaska. She is a member of several research projects: Anthropos and the Material (University of Oslo), Arctic Domus: Human–Animal relations in the North (University of Aberdeen), the CICADA project (McGill), and Arctic Domestication in the Era of the Anthropocene (Norwegian Centre for Advanced Study at the Norwegian Academy of Science and Letters).

Lindsay M. Weiss recently completed a postdoctoral appointment in the Department of Anthropology and the Stanford Archaeology Center at Stanford University. Her current research explores the dynamics of heritage and history in the postcolonial context of South Africa. She is currently completing her manuscript on the relationship between liberation heritage and liberation history in South Africa, examining the role of national, corporate and, informal urban heritage in mediating social tensions in post-apartheid landscapes.

Yujie Zhu is currently a Postdoctoral Research Fellow in the Australian Centre on China in the World at the Australian National University. His research on the heritage cities of China explores heritage politics, cultural consumption and production, romanticism, and practices of everyday life. His work has appeared in leading tourism and anthropology journals, including *Annals of Tourism Research* and *Current Anthropology*. As part of his work in UNWTO, he co-edited the book *Sustainable Tourism Management at World Heritage Sites* (2009). Since 2013 he has served as the Vice Chair of Commission on the Anthropology of Tourism in International Union of Anthropological and Ethnological Sciences (IUAES).

is cultural heritage being preserved for in this instance, and on what basis are we sacrificing the present for the future through the protection of things?

Moving from the international to the intranational frame, Colwell looks to the American Southwest to trace how ethics have become infused with heritage management, particularly amongst descendant and indigenous communities seeking to exert greater control over historical objects and places. These developments have emerged on a number of fronts. Some archaeological projects are training the next generation to work more ethically and effectively with communities. Other research projects have used multivocal methodologies to incorporate the viewpoints of multiple stakeholders about the past. Moreover, Native communities have established their own museums and used them as vehicles to preserve, promote, and perpetuate their traditional cultures. In the arena of repatriation, new conversations and projects seek to overcome the colonialist histories of museums as sites of power over heritage, and museums now regularly seek out the participation of descendant communities. In sum, Colwell asserts that the implementation of ethics has enabled issues about who has control over heritage, whose voices are heard, and who benefits from heritage to come to the fore.

Ndoro and Wijesuriya ask pointedly whose heritage is it that we are managing and conserving? Through an examination of historical developments in conservation across Asia and Africa, they remind us that heritage management was practiced in these regions long before European colonization. Throughout Asia, Buddhist, Hindu, and Confucian worldviews influenced how the remnants of the past were perceived and commemorated. Across Africa, traditional religions and later Islam and Christianity guided how heritage places were used and managed. Traditional systems of care have evolved through time and still have established approaches: in some instances the custodianship of culture and nature pre-dates or was parallel to Western methods. Yet the methods introduced in both continents under colonial rule still have lasting legacies that are further reinforced today by the efforts of international heritage agencies. Their chapter takes up the challenges and contradictions that arise from the historical impositions of those colonial heritage management systems today in a globalized world.

Ndoro visits the case of Tsodilo Cultural Landscape in Botswana to demonstrate how the concept of a protected areas management system has influenced the governance of World Heritage sites across Africa. Like Byrne and Ween, he questions the validity of a natural science model of conservation for living communities. Tsodilo was the ancestral home of the San and Hambakushe who have subsequently been marginalized in its conservation and management. After World Heritage inscription these groups were considered a threat to archaeological and heritage work and to site conservation, due to their traditional subsistence practices of hunting and herding. Underlining again the problems associated with the nature–culture dualism, Tsodilo's protected areas management plan has been readily exported throughout Africa as exemplary, whether for natural or cultural heritage places. Ndoro argues that site trajectories like Tsodilo are dynamic and their management cannot be standardized through international instruments that are narrowly constituted from one part of the globe. Moreover, heritage professionals need to address and support "community-based systems" that have been marginalized by state-based systems and Western conservation discourse. Such state frameworks are incapable of providing a holistic and sustainable management of local cultural heritage in isolation.

Wijesuriya describes the legacy of French colonialism and conservation interventions by the École Française d'Extrême-Orient into the vast World Heritage site of

Introduction: Globalizing Heritage

Lynn Meskell

The international conflicts in Iraq and Yugoslavia in the 1990s and the concomitant destruction of cultural property had profound effects for the study of archaeology and heritage. Archaeologists became more politically attuned and more self-reflective by seeing their materials deployed as targets or shields and connected communities deeply affected by the cultural cleansing, destruction of memory, and erasure of their material pasts. The shelling of Dubrovnik, the destruction of the Mostar Bridge, fighter jets stationed at Ur, the looting of the Baghdad museum – all of this collateral damage unfolded before our eyes. For the field of heritage something had irrevocably changed. The world watched live the wholesale and often targeted destruction, in some cases perpetrated by the liberators themselves as they trenched, bombed, and looted their way through years of conflict. For nations like Iraq and Afghanistan, this externally wrought destruction was immediately followed by international condemnation of their local inhabitants and then calls for salvage and assistance, leading to what might be seen as a cycle of internationally sanctioned destruction then reconstruction. Cultural commentators often expressed more grief over the loss of antiquity than the loss of life, leading many to question the ethical priorities of international preservationist initiatives.

Many of us came to realize that the creation of heritage is also the creation of heritage conflict. It is commonly said that heritage is history with a point or history that matters. However, history as a discipline is the account that gets authorized after conflict rather than that which is bound up in the midst of things. And while it is true that only select fragments of the human past, in particular places and times, are reified for their cultural significance and value, heritage is deeply enmeshed with materiality. Therefore it is not simply historical accounts or narratives that have salience for living populations, but rather tangible places and objects are necessary to mobilize identifications, significations, and memorialization. The post-9/11 world has only reinforced these observations (Meskell 2002). Whether for the social performance of memory, trauma, protest, or uplift, a material past is discursively assembled to serve as a physical conduit between past and present. Since sites and objects bear witness to particular pasts and have those histories woven into their

Global Heritage: A Reader, First Edition. Edited by Lynn Meskell.

very fabric, they physically embody and instantiate the past in the present in a way that no textual account can fully achieve. That being said, we have increasingly come to see what many indigenous communities have long realized and indeed practiced: that these physical landscapes, monuments, and objects cannot be separated from intangible beliefs and resonances. The artificial separation of these traits is itself a symbolic violence. And when the immaterial connection that people experience disappears, the significance of those same sites and objects may also decline in the public imaginary.

Heritage, one could argue, is a supplement to history. It completes and elaborates upon what is missing from the past in the present, serving as an accretion and a substitution. Heritage is then a dangerous supplement (Derrida 1976) since our understanding of the past is always vexed by presence and absence, indeterminacy and determinacy, thereby dislocating the substance of heritage by its very construction. The slippery, mercurial nature of heritage allows it to be endlessly reinterpreted for personal and political possibility. There is no unmediated past. Our negotiations and endless iterations reveal that the past is always already a representation of a representation. Moreover, the constitution of heritage, rather than just history, often suffers from an over-burden of meaning that resists containment in any one particular location. Heritage sites thus become sites of contestation over meaning and practice, entreating obligation and responsibility, and further requiring ongoing symbolic attention and maintenance.

Heritage places and practices also require managing, governing, translating, and capitalizing, such that new political economies have developed around heritage that entail a new generation of interdisciplinary scholarship, as the contributors in this volume evince. The particular focus on materiality with which archaeology is synonymous, and which anthropology has more recently adopted, provides an appropriate methodology for taking heritage seriously. An ethnographic sensibility has also emerged around heritage work as a methodology to connect the lived experiences of these new heritage economies with broader international processes and politics. Today we may best be served if we also incorporate the technics of other disciplines: politics, law, economics, sociology, tourism, geography, ecology, and conservation. As the authors in this volume demonstrate, only by having an interdisciplinary approach can one hope to trace the capillary networks surrounding heritage from its precise local embeddings, radiating out to national arenas, and into the global circuits through which such projects gain traction and leverage.

Global heritage, I would posit, is not a thing per se, but a set of politically inflected material practices, whether one is talking about a World Heritage site, for example, or its governance through a set of international legal framings, translated and enacted at a national level and having devolved concrete effects for local residents. There are many things that remain from the past in the present that have never attained the status of heritage. Yet it would be difficult to mobilize the full swathe of heritage practices without some connectivity to the spaces, sites, objects, or practices of the past. While not underestimating the intangible aspects, it is the material dimension and its ramifications that scholars, particularly those with archaeological training, are adept at tracing. The material constitution of sites, their management, conservation, insertion into tourist economies, mobilization within national and global imaginings, and their many connected communities are all processes in which archaeologists are well versed.

Over the past decade, a great many texts have been produced that claim the title of heritage or heritage studies, many of them unmoored from any particular discipline, methodology, or approach. This volume is different in that it explicitly brings together scholars primarily trained in archaeology and anthropology, while the collaborative authorship broadens the theoretical and geographical scope of the individual contributions. Heritage scholarship divorced from any archaeological, ethnographic, or other particular disciplinary grounding is likely to remain intellectually thin, and it is debatable whether there currently exists a cohesive discipline of heritage studies in practice (though something approaching it may be emerging). Without the methodological and intellectual commitments that disciplinary training affords, studies of heritage tend toward the descriptive and momentary, relying more on modes of representation rather than the results of long-standing fieldwork or analysis.

Developing Heritage

I have suggested here that heritage assumed a new mantle in the 1990s when the study of heritage came of age politically and intellectually. However, I do not suggest that archaeological or heritage scholarship lacked a political or moral compass before the 1990s; rather that the scale has been amplified and the global nature of that recognition has been consequential. Earlier signals of change in archaeology came with the sanction of South Africa scholars during apartheid and the formation of the World Archaeological Congress (Ucko 1987), an organization with a global and ethical mandate. Archaeology would be tested further by the renewed resurgence of ethnic and religious tension over the 1992 destruction of Ayodhya in India (Bernbeck and Pollock 1996). Engagement with larger international framings and ethical implications for archaeologists and connected communities in their efforts abroad provided a hint of things to come. No longer could practitioners claim to be objective and passive bystanders or their research to be immune from political processes and perspectives, whether at home or abroad.

Heritage work in the 1980s was largely motivated by concerns over heritage management (Cleere 1989; Hewison 1987) and the heritage industry of the West generally (but see Hall 1984, 1988; Trigger 1980, 1984). Yet in the early 1990s, the word "heritage" was still largely synonymous with descriptive accounts of estates, castles, and great houses from static, rather than dynamic and contested, perspectives. This constituted a largely unpeopled and uncontroversial field of study, being neither deeply archaeological nor anthropological in its methodology. Lacking reflection upon wider intellectual or political concerns, many mainstream academics in archaeology and anthropology would stand apart from this kind of heritage work as compared to the situation today. However, the work of geographer David Lowenthal (1985, 1996, 1998) is an exception in this regard. Given developments in Europe such as the fall of the Berlin Wall and end of the Cold War, attention increasingly turned in the mid 1990s to questions of heritage and nationalism, albeit largely in Europe and confined to the symbolic dimensions of the past rather than to lived realities on the ground. State-deployed imagery, cultural performance, and disciplinary histories (Atkinson, Banks, and O'Sullivan 1996; Díaz-Andreu and Champion 1996; Kohl and Fawcett 1995) perhaps provided a necessary first step. Wider explorations of our own field practices (Meskell 1998), culpabilities, and, ultimately, responsibilities to others came later.

During the same period, ethnographic accounts were already focusing on national and colonial heritage projects of nostalgia, rehabilitation, and revisionism (Herzfeld 1991; Mitchell 1988; Ranger 1989). Anthropologists worked within local communities to see how state imperatives alongside global forces shaped people's lives in the shadow of antiquity, but also traced how these groups resisted and crafted alternative narratives of the past. Other ethnographers looked at heritage through the lens of performance and popular culture, folklore, and museums to track regimes of display and consumption (Karp and Lavine 1991; Kirshenblatt-Gimblett 1998). At roughly the same time, British-trained social geographers focused on colonial legacies abroad (Gathercole and Lowenthal 1994) as well as issues of space, tourism, and economics generally (Ashworth 1995; Graham, Ashworth, and Tunbridge 2000; Hardy 1988).

The 1990s saw heritage research embedded within a "politics of the past" approach. Scholars from some settler-colonial nations like Australia readily embraced an early post-colonial critique (Byrne 1996; Langford 1983; Meehan 1995) and have become associated with critical heritage interventions (Byrne 2003; Lilley 2000; Logan 2013; Lydon 2009; Smith and Wobst 2005). Conversely, disciplinary reflexivity in the United States proved more difficult and indigenous intervention often met with a recalcitrant positivist discipline. However, new forms of engaged scholarship and collaborative field practice actively sought to ameliorate this negative history of relationships (Colwell-Chanthaphonh 2010; Colwell-Chanthaphonh and Ferguson 2004, 2007; Ferguson and Colwell-Chanthaphonh 2006; Silliman 2008; Stoffle, Zedeno, and Halmo 2001). Newly defined nations like South Africa offered contexts from which to ask whether it was possible to be post-colonial at all, or if the architecture of oppression could ever truly be erased. Numerous case studies around historic sites and landscapes exposed tensions over ethnic difference and indigeneity, the inequities of land and labor, economic freedoms versus civic rights, and the continued unfreedom of the poor (Hall 2001, 2005; Meskell 2005, 2009b, 2011; Shepherd 2002, 2003; Weiss 2007, 2014).

The intersection of ethics, archaeology, and heritage broadly emerged during the same period (Colwell-Chanthaphonh and Ferguson 2004; Green 1984; Lynott and Wylie 2000; Meskell and Pels 2005; Messenger 1999; Vitelli 1996). While not always directly co-terminal with heritage work, questions of ethics, particularly transcultural concerns, have impacted the types of topics and political projects recently undertaken. No longer would it be possible to consider research about the past as immune from the present, cloaked in scientific immunity and neatly segregated from the locales and locals that support our work. Heritage discourse, the tacit universals within its international framing, and the implications for those outside the frame also came to the fore (Smith 2004, 2006). We would later see this ethical commitment develop into a much broader, and often more fraught, set of debates about heritage and human rights, questioning whether such conjunctions were possible, desirable, or even operational given the limitations of international instruments (Disko 2010; Hodder 2010; Jokilehto 2012; Lilley 2009; Meskell 2009b, 2010; O'Keefe 2000; Schmidt 1995; Silverman and Fairchild Ruggles 2008; Weiss 2014).

Historically, while nationalism has been of sustained interest to archaeology and anthropology, recent scholarship extends beyond the narrow understandings of the 1980s and 1990s to a broader interrogation of sovereignty and internationalism. Despite the recognition of ever-expanding globalization, we are currently witnessing a hardening of state boundaries and increasing anxieties concerning migration and border crossings, alongside transnational flows of capital, labor, ideas, and cultures (Brown 2010). As a result of these tensions, some scholars have turned to considerations of cosmopolitanism as a way to reconcile the entangled politics and responsibilities that stem from today's burgeoning local, national, and international connectivities

(Appiah 2006; Breckenridge et al. 2002; Hannerz 2006; Meskell 2009; Werbner 2008). Attending to issues of scale has become a priority and it is increasingly necessary to tack between multiple levels of fieldwork and analysis to grasp the fuller understanding of the heritage landscape. Given the vast scope of these emergent international domains and complexities, heritage research cannot simply describe changes within the conservation arena, for instance, without considering collaboration or communities; nor can they deal with an issue like development without being cognizant of dislocated populations, site destruction, new infrastructures, international capital, and so on.

In tandem with the ramping up of socio-economic and political developments impacting upon the heritage sphere, our methodologies have also changed and expanded. It is more common today for researchers to draw from, and integrate, a broad swathe of methods including archival analysis, archaeological fieldwork, material culture and museum studies, economic analysis, and ethnography. Much of this also aims to be collaborative and multidisciplinary. Scholarship has, at the same time, become both more qualitative and quantitative. It is also the case that significant regions of the world have opened up for investigation that were previously little studied, such as Asia (Daly and Winter 2011; Winter 2014), while other nations emerging from post-Soviet, post-colonial, and post-conflict contexts (Giblin 2014; Plets et al. 2013; Shnirelman 2012; Winter 2007) are pursuing liberated heritage agendas. Just a decade or two ago, limited fieldwork would have been possible in countries like Russia, China, Cambodia, Myanmar, Rwanda, Albania, Armenia, and so on. Today the possibilities for heritage research have greatly expanded in both scope and complexity.

Interdisciplinary Heritage

As the foregoing suggests, the study of heritage has recently gained maturity and political awareness, following in large part from the importance and leverage now placed upon heritage places by nation states on the global stage. The impact of these transnational social, economic, and political forces is shaping the field practices, discourses, and disciplines that scholars now need to actively engage with. This volume contributes to that emergent dialogue, suggesting that it is no longer possible to capture the scope of international heritage without proper consideration of global institutions, national politics, and local developments and social movements.

Taken together, these chapters reflect the burgeoning scale of heritage scenarios today as they affect millions of people across the globe. While the issues we outline are certainly timely, and the disciplines we draw upon diverse, we are bound together by our focus on ethnographic and embedded perspectives, as well as a commitment to ethical engagement. The chapters are broadly grouped in three overlapping categories: institutions, politics, and economies. Writing together as we do provides an opportunity to embrace multiple geographies, disciplines, literatures, and case studies. Each of the chapters develops two strands of scholarly contribution to the field of heritage. The first part of each paper reviews of the most compelling recent literature for each theme, while the second describes innovative projects that chart the way forward for future heritage directions. Structuring the volume in this way is an attempt to capture the current dynamism of the field, to be as geographically inclusive as possible, and to reflect the many perspectives and writings that have been produced in various fields.

Institutions

In this section institutions might refer to formal agencies and structures such as UNESCO (United Nations Educational, Science and Cultural Organization) and its various international conventions, while it might also encompass global visions such as international conservation and rights movements. Both reflect upon the overarching settings and frameworks that have come to aspire to universal adoption and implementation. Meskell and Brumann focus specifically on UNESCO's World Heritage program as part of a growing program of intra-disciplinary scholarship emanating from anthropology, archaeology, economic, political science, and law. And, while UNESCO has a global vision and remit, their work underscores that (just as in other globalizing arenas) the creation of UNESCO and the emphasis on global patrimony has resulted in reinforcing the interests of nation-states. The desire for a universal heritage remains tightly sutured to national identification, prestige, socio-economic benefits, and the recognition of a particular modernity. Indeed the state continues to be a particularly intransigent force in all of UNESCO's operations by the very structure of the organization that has states as its members. As they describe, since UNESCO is an intergovernmental agency, the nation states, or States Parties, are in fact the most powerful decision makers in the World Heritage process, particularly those that enjoy representation on the World Heritage Committee.

Their own respective research relies on a number of integrated analyses from ethnographic fieldwork to archival and econometric analyses. Meskell looks at the dynamics of the BRICS nations (Brazil, Russia, India, China, and South Africa) to underline the pacting and political bargaining power of these emergent nations in securing their individual World Heritage site inscriptions and at the same time in staving off any potential World Heritage in Danger listings. Ethnographic observation, particularly at World Heritage Committee meetings, demonstrates how some alliances are strategic and shifting, and might, at any one time, be based on religious, regional, political, or economic linkages. Brumann emphasizes the role of other world regional leaders such as Mexico and Egypt in what he sees as the emergence of a new mode of operation in the World Heritage Committee. He suggests that we have recently witnessed a conceptual shift in the World Heritage Committee from the largely expert-driven national delegations of the 1990s, led by conservation specialists heavily steeped in national traditions and legal frameworks, to the dominance of the career diplomats sent by member states to UNESCO. This too, he suggests, reflects the growing importance of World Heritage within nationalist agendas.

Together Meskell and Brumann argue that an embedded and ethnographic approach is necessary to capture the dynamic political complexities as they unfold. Similar to other anthropologists studying UN organizations, they demonstrate that World Heritage processes have global impacts, albeit in often unexpected and unpredictable ways that are not always revealed in official texts or agendas. Relying solely on archives or online documents may in fact mislead researchers since substantive political issues are often masked as technical ones. Documentary data only gain depth and salience if researchers have the necessary insights into the processes that produced them. Coombe and Weiss make a similar claim in the sphere of human rights and neoliberalism, arguing that examining heritage requires a more anthropologically nuanced and theoretically informed understanding if scholars are to address the motivations behind heritage regulation.

Coombe and Weiss are concerned with the intersection of governmentality, neoliberalism, and rights within the heritage sphere, how it has been previously understood, and where the productive tensions remain. They argue that rights-based practices and discourses function as a means by which the limits of governmentality are expressed by those who bring their own cultural resources to bear upon the very same governmental demands that consider culture as a resource. Here neoliberalism is understood largely as a political process rather than simply an ideological or an economic program. Recent heritage work then recognizes neoliberal restructuring, not as a withdrawal of the state, but as a new distribution of governmental powers in which nations, sovereignty, territories, and rights are all reconfigured. New forms of governmentality are proliferating, they suggest, as reflected in the increasing desire to map and inventory cultural properties, conferring legibility through new forms of documentation, archiving, and access. However, Coombe and Weiss do not position communities and other stakeholders as simply the passive bystanders in such processes or, in fact, see governments and communities as oppositional. Instead they suggest that "heritage as government" operates in and through "community" as the subject of its technological address and the object of its activities, thereby activating a semi-autonomous political agent.

In respect to human rights, Coombe and Weiss argue that they should not simply be viewed as institutionally compromised obstacles to social justice. Whereas prior heritage research focused on the right to participate in cultural life narrowly construed, these authors posit a more expansive remit that interrogates how human rights vocabularies provide rhetorical resources with which to protest injustice, insist upon new forms of social justice, and assert distinctive understandings of human dignity in diverse social fields. This "social life of rights" approach traverses multiple scales across state, regional, and international regimes since rights talk is mobilized transnationally by international agencies, NGOs, aid institutions, social movements, and so on. Coombe specifically explores culturalized rights in the Latin American context as they intersect with the emergence of entrepreneurial cultural communities. Heritage and cultural rights have been mobilized in numerous Amazonian communities to secure territorial rights and responsibilities for traditional medicine, bilingual education, and archaeological sites. One salient example is the Potato Park in Peru, where six Quechua-speaking villages have constituted themselves as a community in line with national legislation thus bypassing the arduous process of securing indigenous land title. Coombe underlines how this autonomous territory is rooted in a local responsibility for potato biodiversity at the global scale. Thus the communities are employing resources from indigenous and cultural heritage regimes with other forms of neoliberal government in order to safeguard and revitalize their practices.

Weiss draws upon her fieldwork on liberation in South Africa to show how the nation's first democratic governments utilized heritage as a multicultural national platform for post-apartheid recognition and reconciliation. National heritage institutions, she states, have increasingly adopted a neoliberal program of heritage as a self-sustaining component of urban revitalization and tourist development in which socioeconomic rights are to be delivered through market-based imperatives. Specifically, she focuses upon the growing number of informal settlements in South Africa where over four million people live today. The struggle against apartheid was also a struggle against landlessness. Yet the spaces of informal communities, shack settlements, slums, and transitory encampments represent some of the most egregious exclusions of modern rights under neoliberal governmentality. Weiss examines informal communities that have self-capacitated by harnessing traditional practices as resources, in particular the shack dweller movement whose activities form the front line of urban rights struggles in South Africa. Coombe and Weiss remind us that engaging in this type of fieldwork entails new ethical concerns for heritage research by recognizing these shifting sites of empowerment and vulnerability and their paradoxical capacities as resources for emergent political agency.

Kersel and Luke take up other forms of institutional heritage and politics in their chapter on cultural diplomacy and civil society. They acknowledge the long history of world-making through heritage diplomacy and the institutional effects of such projects globally to forge international relationships, enhance mutual understanding, and assuage political tensions. However, in the twenty-first century, heritage diplomacy is presented and packaged to the public as promoting the ideals of democracy and civil society. This affords new leverage around heritage places and practices through the intercalation of cultural diplomacy, foreign relations, and soft power. Many of these projects are often laced with overt agendas that instantiate new imperialisms. The "West knows best" stance, Kersel has argued, is reflected across the heritage landscape from the level of local projects to the global guidelines promulgated by international agencies such as ICOM (International Council of Museums), ICOMOS (International Council on Monuments and Sites), and UNESCO. But they also show how new players such as Middle Eastern and Asian nations are now driving archaeological and heritage development in countries from Cambodia to Sudan. The directives, whether from international or national agencies, are often the driving mechanisms behind what is preserved, what is excavated, and what is on display as representative of a particular locality, nation, or culture.

Why is heritage now seen as such a powerful diplomatic tool worldwide? Kersel and Luke argue that foreign assistance for heritage operates as a soft power, a partnership that is considered above the coercive sphere of politics, economics, or military aspirations. Thus heritage occupies a highly strategic place in development agendas because it is through attraction, rather than force, that results are achieved. They provide the example of the US Ambassador's Fund that has supported over 750 projects in 132 countries at a cost of some US$ 40 million. Initially aimed at supporting the preservation, rehabilitation, and promotion of places of historical significance for local constituencies, the aims of grants have shifted through time to support initiatives that might combat negative perceptions of the United States worldwide following the invasion of Iraq. In the aftermath of September 11, 2001 and the 2003 invasion of Iraq, the Ambassadors Fund increased funding to predominantly Islamic nations and projects associated with Islam. Using the language of UNESCO and actively promoting the "heritage of mankind," the US effectively distanced itself as solely responsible for the destruction of cultural heritage in Iraq or Afghanistan. This developed into a special allocation solely for World Heritage sites within the Ambassadors Fund, the aim being to convey a softer side of the United States abroad, one invested in the protection of "our shared heritage."

Luke provides another very different model of international aid and diplomacy through the Turkish Cooperation and Coordination Agency, or TIKA. Established in 1992 with an overt political, religious, and cultural mandate to support Turkish heritage and ideals, she explains that TIKA is now the fourth largest agency for international aid. TIKA's model is aggressive and highly strategic, from Albania to Senegal. One of their high profile initiatives is directed towards Islamic heritage, specifically the restoration of mosques in the Balkans, the Middle East, and Africa. Like the previous US example, TIKA has strategically partnered with UNESCO, whether on Islamic projects in Albania or components of the Silk Road nomination for World

Heritage inscription. Kersel and Luke trace how all of these institutions effectively contribute to the forms of heritage understood and presented to the global public, while simultaneously reinforcing the idea that other countries care about culture. Yet, in the cases explored here, the "culture" or heritage identified and restored is extremely specific, targeted, and politically or religiously expedient to the funder.

Further exploring the ways in which World Heritage is adopted and deployed globally, Byrne and Ween address overlapping classifications of nature and culture and its subsequent effects. They consider the impacts of this classificatory regime on indigenous lifeways but also the opportunities for indigenous and non-indigenous groups to challenge and innovate around key World Heritage principles and mechanisms. Described as "boundary work," they recognize the colonial underpinnings of World Heritage, but also the issue of scale it affords and how its mechanisms might encourage new kinds of agency and resistance, echoing Coombe and Weiss's chapter. World Heritage place-making, often replete with a culture–nature dualism, is both received and struggled against by those on the margins of society and the global order. Byrne and Ween further unpack the overlapping domains of archaeology and cultural heritage practice, arguing that these domains have played a role in sustaining the culture–nature dualism.

The institutionalization of nature and culture as separate has a long history, steeped in Euro-modern culture that has no exact counterpart in non-Western traditional society, although it has assumed global significance through international instruments promulgated by UNESCO or IUCN (International Union for Conservation of Nature). Looking specifically at the premises of the Sacred Natural Sites initiative by the IUCN, Byrne imputes that the magical–supernatural aspect of local belief is translated into religious constructs that are more compatible with the conservation movement's secular–rational mentality than with the ontologies of local popular religion. Moreover, environmental protection is positioned as the endpoint of religion and therefore local communities are seen as revering a nature that remains fundamentally separate, however closely entwined they are with it. Heritage conservation and curation, whether designated as natural or cultural, is deemed paramount by these international agencies. Drawing on his extensive fieldwork in Asia, Byrne outlines how the heritage governance in Asia has long involved the "clearance" of zones identified for conservation of ancient monuments, resulting in the resettlement of local inhabitants whose lifestyle is judged incompatible with conservation objectives.

Ween draws on two case studies, Kluane in Alaska and Laponia in Sweden, to elucidate how World Heritage governance still divides culture and nature. Both are national parks populated by indigenous groups who are involved in subsistence activities. Significantly, Kluane was inscribed as a natural World Heritage site in 1979 when the concept of "wilderness" was accepted uncritically, whereas Laponia was listed as a mixed site in 1996 after the concept had come under greater scrutiny. Thus the management of Kluane continues to embody many classic features of the colonial mentality of conservation that can be seen across Africa or the Asia. A science-based natural resource management model provides the dominant foundation for governing nature: the mapping, zoning, and ordering of land; the classification of species and species populations; and the management board's governance scheme determines decision-making regarding nature. Laponia, on the other hand, provides an example of how indigenous groups are working within and against the global machinery of World Heritage to create new models of environmental management that acknowledge the co-existence of multiple life. As Byrne and Ween make explicit, these reconceptualizations might have global applicability but in no way do they imply a transcendence of the history of North–South power relations or the scalar history of relations between international institutions, nation-states, and indigenous peoples.

Each of the chapters highlights overarching heritage categories and frameworks that invite universal adoption and implementation. They also convey the consequences of these globalizing arenas, recognizing that heritage increasingly participates in world-making projects whether though diplomatic efforts, conservation movements, or indigenous forums. The protection of World Heritage, the impacts of international politics and law, human rights, and humanitarian programs all demonstrate cosmopolitan aspirations for the global good. Yet, at the same time, the resilience of the nation-state cannot be sidelined since capitalizing on culture is entwined in neoliberal and governmental projects. In some cases this also affords creative spaces for redefinition and repurposing of the past, as well as offering leverage for social justice and recognition.

Politics

The next group of chapters also examines this scalar history of relations but does so through a shared commitment to communities, while also being attendant to global politics as well as institutions. Colwell and Joy track how the everyday production and consumption of heritage impacts upon living societies, particularly indigenous groups. A new generation of scholars has increasingly turned its attention to understanding the complex intersection of people and things and how heritage work might serve the well-being of descendant communities and invested stakeholders as much as material objects and historical places. While communities were never completely out of the frame, only a few decades ago most debates centered on the competing heritage rights of nations and humanity as a whole. Considerations of local communities have emerged more recently because of multiple converging lines of argument and social critiques, in particular in North America, New Zealand, and Australia. In post-colonial settings, control over who owns, has access to, or claims rights of representation for cultural heritage can best be understood in terms of dignity and well-being. It is in this vein that Colwell and Joy consider the specific contexts surrounding heritage tensions and ethical responsibilities, whether in the American Southwest or in Mali, across international, national, and intranational scales.

In the case of Mali, Joy recounts how the World Heritage site of Djenné reflects an elite, Eurocentric vision of cultural heritage that is imposed upon a disenfranchised local community. UNESCO's international vision of the town is limited to architecture and archaeology, whereas the residents of Djenné struggle for survival amidst food insecurity, political uncertainty, and precarious livelihoods. In terms of ethics, Djenné's World Heritage status might detract from the most pressing issues facing the community, namely the radical global economic asymmetry that has led to the conditions of poverty found in Mali today. Capturing the global media in 2012, the destruction of sites around Timbuktu by the radical Islamist group Ansar Dine led to international vocal condemnation from UNESCO and many international leaders. That cultural destruction even served as a catalyst for the French military intervention in the conflict. In a post-colonial setting, money might flow into Mali in the name of cultural heritage protection, yet this still leaves unanswered the question of global economic asymmetries exacerbated by trade restrictions that are imposed by the very same countries providing financial aid for heritage. Joy asks who precisely

Angkor. A system of new regulations has impinged upon traditional land use and practices by local communities, while inhabitants near the temples of Angkor Wat and Angkor Thom were relocated. In the 1990s, after the Cambodian civil war ended, conservation work resumed under the auspices of French and Japanese agencies and experts. Further tensions arose when a new set of restrictions banned local residents from rice cultivation, collecting forest products, and grazing cattle that had long supported traditional livelihoods. These harsh restrictions have led to impoverishment and unemployment, along with most recently intimidation, violence, and curtailment of human rights. This is ironic since the restoration and tourist development of Angkor is often held up in the international community as one of the few success stories involving heritage humanitarianism and post-conflict rebuilding.

While much heritage work has historically focused on politics and nationalism, González-Ruibal and Hall address a burgeoning scholarship that deals with the fraught legacies of heritage violence, as an outgrowth of global, civil, and ethnic wars, genocides, colonialism, and dictatorship. Specifically these authors examine civil conflict along ethnic lines in Sri Lanka, violence perpetrated by the state across a range of countries in South America, and circumstances wherein the heritage of violence has an international dimension. They also consider the proliferation of engaged practice and memory work that surrounds conflictual heritage and suggest this work will continue to gain momentum and significance in the future. While this might sound positive, some troubling aspects have lately emerged. Without political, aesthetic, or other conventions that define and limit that for which heritage can be mobilized, the commodification of the past is not restricted to positive values and goods. It can also embrace pain, disease, trauma, or violence; one striking example of this cannibalization of suffering is the phenomenon of dark tourism.

González-Ruibal and Hall draw important distinctions that enable researchers to understand the processes surrounding conflict with more nuance; for example, whether a conflict is currently active or not, or whether conflicts are denied by those who control the territory (such as in the Armenian genocide), thereby produce heritage not in situ, but through diaspora. Ongoing struggles, like the Israeli–Palestinian conflict, hamper forms of memorialization and the transformation of places into heritage sites. Moreover, if a conflict has ended with the victory of a specific side or through international intervention, this too significantly effects the politics of remembrance. Other factors affecting the status of conflict and potential memorialization include the characteristics and extent of state intervention, or whether there is a shared master narrative or not. In one case study, González-Ruibal reveals the negative heritage of twentieth-century dictatorships in South America. In the aftermath of authoritarian regimes, the demand for evidence forged a broad alliance of heritage practitioners with expertise in oral and written testimony, forensic research, and archaeology. In his view this continent-wide system of violence has a distinctive heritage that is inscribed in the materiality of places, buildings, and the apparatus of terror, all of which are interwoven with personal testimony and memory.

Hall reflects on the more recent experience of conflict and violence in Sri Lanka, where between 80,000 and 100,000 people died. While defined by local religious and ethnic tension, its narrative is inseparable from wider claims to heritage rights that were intensified by UNESCO's involvement and World Heritage inscription. Inflamed by ethnic stereotyping, interpretations of the island's cultural heritage have been cast as a unilinear narrative of successive Buddhist states that withstood external aggression, on the basis of some two millennia of architecture, art, and written texts. Yet neither the documentary nor the archaeological evidence unequivocally supports the state's account. The case of Sri Lanka demonstrates how heritage can be deployed as an artefact of aggression during conflict and how international agencies, claiming to be above politics, can be co-opted by partisan positions. Hall believes that, since all claims to cultural identities and rights are based on accounts of the past and thus inseparable to the determinants of violence, it is difficult to foresee reconciliation without first resolving the nation's master narrative.

De Cesari and Herzfeld take a spatialized view on heritage violence and exclusion. They acknowledge the close association between the heritagization of places and radical shifts in their social geographies, most often evictions, that can be observed both in the past in the service of nationalist and colonial violence and today as part of the neoliberal forces that have increasingly supplanted those older formations. They detail the ways in which heritage is used to support claims to particular places and to shape these places. Paralleling arguments made by Coombe and Weiss, they note how the inhabitants of these spaces deploy heritage for rights of residence, for better livelihoods, for spaces of public debate and so on. As outlined above, materiality is a key component in all forms of heritage attachment, anchoring struggles over place, resistance movements, memory, and belonging.

Herzfeld further develops his concept of spatial cleansing, namely the social and cultural evacuation of space, that takes place typically when urban areas are monumentalized and the local population is removed either by eviction in the name of a contested "common good" or due to escalating property values and market pressures. Spatial cleansing is also related to the mobilizations of heritage by both state and non-state actors as a governmental technique that impinges upon social life in areas inhabited by people variously classified as dangerous. Neoliberal tactics might involve seemingly benign actors and concepts, such as NGOs and their rhetoric, to consolidate control over value-laden spaces such as historic centers, national heritage, and so on. These tactics co-opt the symbolism of nationalism to serve ends that clearly transcend national borders and have more to do with *capital accumulation* than with the symbolic importance of *capital cities*. Drawing on his fieldwork in Bangkok, Herzfeld draws attention to broader conflicts over the interpretations of law, history, and belonging. At the site of Pom Mahakan questions remain in a long-standing battle over who has the ultimate responsibility for curating this important heritage site.

In the Palestinian examples De Cesari describes, conflicting interpretations over heritage likewise serve the aims of disputants to a territorial conflict. Heritage discourse can fuel inter-ethnic and intranational conflict alike, as González-Ruibal and Hall's chapter also illustrates. De Cesari maps recent developments particularly in fraught contexts where heritage as place-making shifts under new forms of neoliberal governance, securitization, and dispossession. One example is the expropriation of Wadi Hilwah, also called the City of David, outside the Old City of Jerusalem. Here an exclusionary narrative of the past has been mobilized to displace Palestinians and their living heritage and urban life in favor of the new settlers. She recounts the destructive potential of archaeology where Israeli excavation encroaches upon, besieges, and sometimes destroys their homes. Since the early years of the state, archaeology has played a key function in Israeli society and state-building process. Palestinian residents must further endure violence from border police while living with the constant threat of demolition or expropriation, and are thus forced to live a subjugated and less than urban life in a heavily securitized neo-biblical landscape of ruins and fences. De Cesari reiterates that Wadi Hilwah is not an exception but reproduces a pattern critical to the workings of the Israeli nationalist–colonial project.

Such examples remind us that spatial cleansing may veer dangerously close to ethnic cleansing, and that the processes of colonization itself cannot be relegated to history.

This set of chapters draws our attention to negative aspects of heritage by examining global, civil, and ethnic wars, genocides, colonialism, and spatial cleansing. In doing so the authors remind us that heritage conflict cannot be consigned to the past but rather has decidedly material effects today. They moreover underline that organizations are not neutral, that their impacts can be devastating over the long term, and that, for many, being post-colonial is a desire rather than a reality. They propose other histories of conservation and management, indeed other ways of *doing* heritage, preserving it as a living practice. They suggest we refocus, to see something called "heritage" from a local point of view, but perhaps not always to foreground heritage above all else. Instead, heritage might be seen to offer a lens onto other more pressing issues, including global asymmetry, histories of oppression, desires for recognition and rights, and struggles for self-determination.

Economics

The constitution of global heritage increasingly relies on the multifarious flows of global capital coupled with interventions from international development programs. Labadi and Gould unpack the entwined histories of development and sustainability in their chapter and consider the connection of these two major themes to communities. Specifically they are concerned with the theoretical, practical, and ethical implications for heritage projects that are pursued under the banner of sustainable development. There are many critics of development programs, including heritage specialists, who have shown how external aid coupled with technocratic expertise has endorsed corrupt and undemocratic nation-state governments primarily at the expense of the poorest citizens, rather than enhancing people's lives and capabilities. That critique also favors moving away from purely economic metrics to broader measures of well-being so that development can also extend to enhancing the capacity of individuals to pursue their own objectives and ensuring that they have the freedom and capability to do so. And, while slow to emerge, culture and heritage are now finally being realized in several UN resolutions focusing on the importance of culture and sustainable development. The linkage between sustainable development and communities gained official recognition in UNESCO conventions from the 1990s, while the World Heritage Convention only became officially associated with the notion of sustainable development from 2002 onwards.

In recent decades economists have developed a full complement of analytical tools designed to place a monetary value on tangible and intangible aspects of culture. Labadi and Gould remind us, however, that these economic measures do not capture the full contribution of cultural and heritage resources to the lives of people. Their chapter features case studies that address issues of sustainable development from both top-down and bottom-up perspectives to address the practical economic and political challenges faced by community-based heritage. Gould's detailed work in the Parchi della Val di Cornia, Italy analyzes the development of a park system designed to include and support the local community. The park network operates through a jointly owned company and numerous sites and buildings have been restored and repurposed to serve as restaurants, meeting spaces, museums, and other park facilities. Charting its variable successes and vulnerabilities, Gould shows how the fate of the park system is susceptible to economic and political forces – local, national, and international – that can undermine community-based sustainability.

Labadi focuses on Mahabodhi Temple Complex, India to consider the wider issues of infrastructural development and the management of mass tourism that are central in sustainable approaches to heritage sites globally. Given the importance of this site, new infrastructures including an airport, hotels, visitor facilities, and foreign land acquisition have both flourished and impinged upon conservation and communities. Sustainable development as a concept is difficult to translate and implement at World Heritage pilgrimage sites like Mahabodhi, specifically in the face of numerous international, religious, economic, and social pressures. Furthermore, governments and local authorities do not routinely collect the data necessary to evaluate the success of their management efforts. Labadi and Gould reinforce the idea that bureaucratic inertia, a lack of data and metrics, external economic forces, and local political conflict can all impact outcomes, such as community disempowerment or economic failure, which are the opposites of sustainability. They argue cogently that academic training in the heritage sphere should focus not simply on the archaeological record or local communities, but also on the global and national economic and political forces that ultimately shape the future of heritage sustainability.

Lafrenz Samuels and Lilley continue this theme by highlighting the key roles played by economic development in bringing heritage to the international stage and the central actors involved in heritage internationalism. At one level, these relationships combine archaeological research and heritage management into the compliance work needed for meeting the social and environmental safeguards set by multilateral development banks and private corporations, what they term *heritage in development*. At another, cultural heritage is considered a resource to be developed for economic growth and thus defined as *heritage as development*, or simply heritage development. This work is often undertaken by the same actors as those setting safeguards, including development banks and corporations, but might also embrace transnational actors such as NGOs, global cultural resource management firms, and professional networks. Lafrenz Samuels and Lilley describe the pervasive economic incentivizing encapsulated in corporate social responsibility (CSR) as well as the fallouts from compliance archaeology projects in international settings. Consultancy culture is on the rise in the arena of archaeology and heritage, bringing with it a new swathe of ethical concerns and responsibilities.

Considering the politics of development, Lilley locates the effects of escalating transnational efforts within compliance archaeology, or heritage *in* development, particularly via public private partnerships or PPPs. He documents one attempt to formulate a global compliance regime, involving a mining company and a university partnering, to develop a resource guide for integrating cultural heritage management into communities. He believes that while advances are being made around heritage issues with and through transnational corporations, these measures have not been universally accepted within the archaeological and heritage community. There has been vocal condemnation of any such involvement with industry, especially the resource extraction sector.

The escalating capitalization of culture is further underscored by the World Bank's global dominance in developing heritage, specifically in North Africa, as described by Lafrenz Samuels. One of their first large-scale heritage projects was Fez in Morocco, initiated at the behest of the UNESCO World Heritage Centre. Fez acts as a global case study demonstrating the promise of cultural heritage for economic growth and poverty reduction. Increasingly national governments nominate sites for inscription on the World Heritage List with the aim of attracting private investment and boosting tourism revenues. And, as Kersel and Luke likewise indicate, participating in the World

Heritage process is also an avenue to international diplomacy, being perceived as supporting democracy, good governance, and transparency, and thus bringing certain nations in line with the funder's aspirations. Another salient example comes from the Arctic, where cultural heritage is being materially produced by climate change. With increasing environmental stress, the rapidly changing lifeways it creates become both a disappearing and a desirable heritage, and as such is taken up as a resource to be developed and marketed. Lafrenz Samuels argues that heritage development in the Arctic is becoming particularly visible in the cruise industry, as is investment in the cultural sector by oil and gas corporations.

Analyzing the intersection of global heritage and global tourism is the central concern of Salazar and Zhu's chapter. They show how private and public sectors, whether in tandem or not, are converting heritage resources across the globe into destinations and attractions. They estimate that one-third of all international tourism is geared towards visiting heritage sites. Yet the constitution of heritage properties into destinations is vastly complex and can be politically, economically, and socially fraught. Within tourist economies, heritage might be mobilized in many ways with different imperatives and by a variety of stakeholders. Salazar and Zhu are especially interested here in both the positive and negative effects of this mobilization in relation to local communities and the role of social imaginaries. Both cultural and nature heritage have the potential to create a foundation for tourism's growth, and that tourism can potentially generate funds that make preservation possible. However, they caution that state authorities or private individuals may retain those funds and so thus impede benefits to local communities. Far worse is the heritage violence that can erupt around sites, especially when tourism can lead to a rise in the price of land or admission fees, gentrification, and increasingly forced removals.

Salazar is interested in the expansion of the World Heritage List that largely coincides with the growth of global tourism as a major form of economic and socio-cultural development. The 1972 Convention however does not explicitly reference tourism and UNESCO has been generally slow to integrate tourism into its heritage agenda. Indeed, World Heritage status was never originally intended to promote tourism, yet it increasingly operates in that way, acting as a global brand. Many nations see tourism in terms of profit and development, which can often equate to erasing local, traditional cultural practices in the quest for new capitalizations and modernities. Zhu's work in Lijiang, China reveals how, after UNESCO inscription, the historic trade town has been transformed into a commercial heritage site. As a result Han Chinese from outside Lijiang have come to control the tourism sector rather than local people, who have been leaving their homes to tourists and entrepreneurs. This brings us back to broader ethical concerns including land ownership, impingement of lifestyle, property rights, and the interaction between social structures and expectations that can lead to conflict. Furthermore, in Lijiang local culture has become eroticized and ethnicized through tourism imaginaries jointly produced by the local government, tourism practitioners, and locals. This produces and reaffirms asymmetrical power relations between hosts, brokers, and guests that, in some contexts, can also generate social and cultural conflicts.

Salazar and Zhu underscore the significant economic, social, political, management, conservation, and interpretation differences within heritage tourism between developed and developing nations. There are many issues in developing countries that impede the sustainable development and management of heritage, including local capacity and empowerment, community participation in decision making, benefit sharing, ownership of historic places and artefacts, lack of funding and skills, and forced displacement to accommodate tourism growth. While the rhetoric and promise of sustainable heritage tourism is appealing, the reality is that low-income countries rich in heritage, such as Tanzania, Nepal, and Cambodia, receive only a fraction of global tourism revenues. They suggest that international agencies are increasingly aware of the mistakes made in the past and their lack of attention to the living practices of local inhabitants and their knowledge. However, there remains an urgent need for new ideas and concepts that reconcile tourism and preservation with the need for sustainable development.

The chapters in this section show an emergent trend in heritage internationalism, mapping new roles for archaeology and heritage on the global stage in terms of social and economic development: for practitioners and for local stakeholders alike, heritage matters in new ways. In each, there is a commitment to community benefits by probing the theoretical, practical, and ethical implications for heritage projects that are pursued with the express purpose of sustainable development. Instead of focusing solely on economic benefits, however, they also interrogate the potential of the past to enhance people's lives and capabilities, whether in the commercialization of their past for tourism or for other forms of social benefit and uplift. Recent histories of development and sustainability make clear that international agencies have been slow to integrate heritage into their agendas. Yet international agencies and their directives now have major influence, as do corporations and their compliance regimes, and of course the workings of international capital whether in the form of tourism or extractive industries. By unpacking the technics of the UN (United Nations), UNESCO, UNDP (United Nations Development Programme), and the World Bank, these chapters take us full circle back to the issue of institutions.

Heritage Futures

The three intertwined themes offered above – institutions, politics, and economics – represent only one way in which this set of papers, and the myriad issues that they cover, could be arranged. They could have equally been organized under the themes of ethics, development, governmentality, internationalism, indigeneity, or communities, such is the nature of the overlap. This complexity is characteristic of a new generation of scholarship where research traverses multiple topics and disciplines as much as it does cosmopolitan geographies and scales of analysis. Indeed, the contributions in the volume make a case for reconsidering the more familiar categories of heritage, whether the dualities of nature and culture, rethinking the operationalization of rights or compliance, or embracing new modalities such as econometric and legal analyses. Taken together these authors chart various new directions in heritage scholarship, while acknowledging and building upon some established fundamentals including perspectives from politics, ethics, and materiality studies.

As the chapters in this book illustrate, issues of scale are increasingly relevant in research examining the politics of the past and its various afterlives in contemporary society. Heritage work must then traverse and translate across multiple scales if we want to grasp the full swathe of politico-economic effects that heritage leverages out there in the world, as well as the implications these effects have on the smaller scale, at the individual and group level. Our fieldwork then needs to account for multilocality as much as it has for multivocality (Owens 2002). In recent writing there has been a much needed focus on the local, especially directed towards indigenous and minority communities, their participation in archaeological and heritage projects, and the potentials for fruitful collaboration. That same level of ethical acuity now needs to be scaled up to the international agencies, conventions, regimes, and capital flows that have determinations for national and local constituencies. While we may not always know the key players in global organizations, as we might within our host communities, ethnographic and other qualitative methodologies may prove useful in uncovering the motivations and processes at work on the international stage (see also Merry 2006; Tsing 2005). Whether addressing agencies like UNESCO or the World Bank, in practices from spatial cleansing to rights-based activism, or through the metrics of international development, diplomacy, and heritage tourism, the logics of heritage must now be followed along local, national, and global circuits to productively capture their capillary effects.

Globalizing heritage is a world-making endeavor. Whether we consider it apposite or not, the past is now progressively called upon to authenticate, reconcile, uplift, capacitate, develop, and benefit nations and persons more that at any other time in our history. Today it is part of an intense field of socio-economic, political, religious, and even military imperatives that recast once familiar geographies into new terrain. Heritage is called into being through the ongoing process of interpretation, selection, reaction, response, and responsibility that Derrida captured in his notion of the dangerous supplement to history. Human hopes and expectations for heritage then set an impossible burden upon the material remnants of past peoples and places. As the stakes around heritage are raised, so too are the consequences. And as we have seen in the recent conflict zones of the former Yugoslavia, Iraq, Mali, Syria, and returning to Iraq again, the past is more easily a target for denial and destruction than for emancipation and empowerment.

ACKNOWLEDGMENTS

Rosalie Robertson first proposed the idea of this reader during her time at Blackwell and I am very grateful for her support for this project and others over the years. Ben Thatcher and Mark Graney have kindly seen her work through to fruition. Lauren Yapp has done an extraordinary job improving and finalizing this text and made its final submission a pleasure. I am also very grateful to the other authors in the volume for their intellectual insights and generosity. This book is dedicated to three remarkable colleagues in acknowledgment of their inspiration and support during my time at Columbia and Stanford.

REFERENCES

Appiah, K. A. (2006) *Cosmopolitanism*. New York: Norton.

Ashworth, G. (1995) Heritage, Tourism and Europe: A European Future for a European Past?, in D. Herbert (ed.), *Heritage, Tourism and Society*. New York: Mansell, pp. 69–84.

Atkinson, J. A., I. Banks, and J. O'Sullivan (eds) (1996) *Nationalism and Archaeology*. Glasgow: Cruithne.

Bernbeck, R. and S. Pollock (1996) Ayodhya, archaeology, and identity. *Current Anthropology* 37: 138–142.

Breckenridge, C., H. Bhabha, S. Pollock, and D. Chakrabarty (eds) (2002) *Cosmopolitanism*. Durham, NC: Duke University Press.

Brown, W. (2010) *Walled States, Waning Sovereignty*. New York: Zone Books.

Byrne, D. (1996) Deep nation: Australia's acquisition of an indigenous past. *Aboriginal History* 20: 82–107.

Byrne, D. (2003) Nervous landscapes: race and space in Australia. *Journal of Social Archaeology* 3: 169–193.

Cleere, H. (ed.) (1989) *Archaeological Heritage Management in the Modern World*. London: Unwin Hyman.

Colwell-Chanthaphonh, C. (2010) *Living Histories: Native Americans and Southwestern Archaeology*. Lanham, MD: AltaMira.

Colwell-Chanthaphonh, C. and T. J. Ferguson (2004) Virtue ethics and the practice of history: Native Americans and archaeologists along the San Pedro Valley of Arizona. *Journal of Social Archaeology* 4: 5–27.

Colwell-Chanthaphonh, C. and T. J. Ferguson (eds) (2007) *Collaboration in Archaeological Practice: Engaging Descendant Communities*. Lanham, MD: AltaMira.

Daly, P. T. and T. Winter (eds) (2011) *Routledge Handbook of Heritage in Asia*. London: Routledge.

Derrida, J. (1976) *Of Grammatology*. Baltimore, MD: Johns Hopkins University Press.

Díaz-Andreu, M. and T. Champion (1996) *Nationalism and Archaeology in Europe*. London: University College London Press.

Disko, S. (2010) World Heritage Sites in Indigenous Peoples' Territories: Ways of Ensuring Respect for Indigenous Cultures, Values and Human Rights, in D. Offenhäußer, W. Zimmerli, and M.-T. Alberts (eds), *World Heritage and Cultural Diversity*. Cottbus: German Commission for UNESCO, pp. 167–177.

Ferguson, T. J., C. Colwell-Chanthaphonh, and R. Anyon (2004) One valley, many histories: Tohono O'odham, Hopi, Zuni, and Western Apache history in the San Pedro Valley. *Archaeology Southwest* 18: 1–16.

Ferguson, T. J. and C. Colwell-Chanthaphonh (2006) *History Is in the Land: Multivocal Tribal Traditions in Arizona's San Pedro Valley*. Tucson: University of Arizona Press.

Gathercole, P. W. and D. Lowenthal (eds) (1994) *The Politics of the Past*. London: Routledge.

Giblin, J. D. (2014) Post-conflict heritage: symbolic healing and cultural renewal. *International Journal of Heritage Studies* 20: 500–518.

Graham, B., G. J. Ashworth, and J. E. Tunbridge (2000) *A Geography of Heritage: Power, Culture and Economy*. London: Arnold.

Green, E. L. (ed.) (1984) *Ethics and Values in Archaeology*. New York: Free Press.

Hall, M. (1984) The burden of tribalism: the social context of southern African Iron Age Studies. *American Antiquity* 49: 455–467.

Hall, M. (1988) Archaeology under apartheid. *Archaeology* 41: 62–64.

Hall, M. (2001) Social archaeology and the theaters of memory. *Journal of Social Archaeology* 1: 50–61.

Hall, M. (2005) Situational Ethics and Engaged Practice: The Case of Archaeology in Africa, in L. M. Meskell and P. Pels (eds), *Embedding Ethics: Shifting the Boundaries of the Anthropological Profession*. Oxford: Berg, pp. 169–194.

Hannerz, U. (2006) Cosmopolitanism, in J. Vincent and D. Nugent (eds), *A Companion to the Anthropology of Politics*. Oxford: Blackwell, pp. 69–85.

Hardy, D. (1988) Historical geography and heritage studies. *Area* 20(4): 333–338.

Herzfeld, M. (1991) *A Place in History: Social and Monumental Time in a Cretan Town*. Princeton, NJ: Princeton University Press.

Hewison, R. (1987) *The Heritage Industry: Britain in a Climate of Decline*. London: Methuen.

Hodder, I. (2010) Cultural heritage rights: From ownership and descent to justice and well-being. *Anthropological Quarterly* 83: 861–882.

Jokilehto, J. (2012) Human rights and cultural heritage: Observations on the recognition of human rights in the international doctrine. *International Journal of Heritage Studies* 18: 226–230.

Karp, I. and S. Lavine (1991) *Exhibiting Cultures: The Poetics and Politics of Museum Display*. Washington, DC: Smithsonian Institution Press.

Kirshenblatt-Gimblett, B. (1998) *Destination Culture: Tourism, Museums, and Heritage*. Berkeley: University of California Press.

Kohl, P. L. and C. Fawcett (eds) (1995) *Nationalism, Politics and the Practice of Archaeology*. Cambridge: Cambridge University Press.

Langford, M. (1983) Our heritage – your playground. *Australian Archaeology* 16: 1–6.

Lilley, I. (ed.) (2000) *Native Title and the Transformation of Archaeology in the Postcolonial World*. Oceania Monographs, Vol. 50. Sydney: University of Sydney.

Lilley, I. (2009) Strangers and Brothers? Heritage, Human Rights, and Cosmopolitan Archaeology in Oceania, in L. M. Meskell (ed.), *Cosmopolitan Archaeologies*. Durham, NC: Duke University Press, pp. 48–67.

Logan, W. (2013) Australia, Indigenous Peoples and World Heritage from Kakadu to Cape York: State Party behaviour under the World Heritage Convention. *Journal of Social Archaeology* 13: 153–176.

Lowenthal, D. (1985) *The Past is a Foreign Country*. Cambridge: Cambridge University Press.

Lowenthal, D. (1996) *Possessed by the Past: The Heritage Crusade and the Spoils of History*. New York: Free Press.

Lowenthal, D. (1998) *The Heritage Crusade and the Spoils of History*. Cambridge: Cambridge University Press.

Lydon, J. (2009) Young and Free: The Australian Past in a Global Future, in L. M. Meskell (ed.), *Cosmopolitan Archaeologies*. Durham, NC: Duke University Press, pp. 28–47.

Lynott, M. J. and A. Wylie (eds) (2000) *Ethics in American Archaeology*. Washington, DC: Society for American Archaeology.

Meehan, B. (1995) Aboriginal Views on the Management of Rock Art Sites in Australia, in K. Helskog and B. Olsen (eds), *Perceiving Rock Art: Social and Political Perspectives*. Oslo: Institute for Comparative Research in Human Culture, pp. 295–316.

Merry, S. E. (2006) *Human Rights and Gender Violence: Translating International Law into Local Justice*. Chicago: University of Chicago Press.

Meskell, L. M. (ed.) (1998) *Archaeology under Fire: Nationalism, Politics and Heritage in the Eastern Mediterranean and Middle East*. London: Routledge.

Meskell, L. M. (2002) Negative heritage and past mastering in archaeology. *Anthropological Quarterly* 75: 557–574.

Meskell, L. M. (2005) Archaeological ethnography: Conversations around Kruger National Park. *Archaeologies: Journal of the World Archaeology Congress* 1: 83–102.

Meskell, L. M. (ed.) (2009a) *Cosmopolitan Archaeologies*. Durham, NC: Duke University Press.

Meskell, L. M. (2009b) The Nature of Culture in Kruger National Park, in L. M. Meskell (ed.) *Cosmopolitan Archaeologies*. Durham, NC: Duke University Press, pp. 89–112.

Meskell, L. M. (2010) Human rights and heritage ethics. *Anthropological Quarterly* 83: 839–860.

Meskell, L. M. (2011) *The Nature of Heritage: The New South Africa*. Oxford: Wiley Blackwell.

Meskell, L. M. and P. Pels (eds) (2005) *Embedding Ethics*. Oxford: Berg.

Messenger, P. M. (ed.) (1999) *The Ethics of Collecting Cultural Property*. Albuquerque: University of New Mexico Press.

Mitchell, T. (1988) *Colonising Egypt*. Cambridge: Cambridge University Press.

O'Keefe, P. (2000) Archaeology and human rights. *Public Archaeology* 1: 181–194.

Owens, B. M. (2002) Monumentality, identity, and the state: Local practice, world heritage, and heterotopia at Swayambhu, Nepal. *Anthropological Quarterly* 75: 269–316.

Plets, G., N. Konstantinov, V. Soenov, and E. Robinson (2013) Repatriation, doxa, and contested heritages. *Anthropology and Archeology of Eurasia* 52: 73–98.

Ranger, T. (1989) Whose heritage? The case of the Matobo National Park. *Journal of Southern African Studies* 15: 217–249.

Schmidt, P. (1995) A human right to a cultural heritage: African expressions and configurations. *East African Journal of Peace and Human Rights* 2: 41–52.

Shepherd, N. (2002) The politics of archaeology in Africa. *Annual Review of Anthropology* 31: 189–209.
Shepherd, N. (2003) State of the discipline: Science, culture and identity in South African archaeology, 1870–2003. *Journal of Southern African Studies* 29: 823–844.
Shnirelman, V. (2012) Archaeology and the National Idea in Eurasia, in C. Harlet, G. Bike Yazicioglu and A. T. Smith (eds), *The Archaeology of Power and Politics in Eurasia*. Cambridge: Cambridge University Press, pp. 15–36.
Silliman, S. (ed.) (2008) *Collaborating at the Trowel's Edge: Teaching and Learning in Indigenous Archaeology*. Tucson: University of Arizona Press and the Amerind Foundation.
Silverman, H. and D. Fairchild Ruggles (eds) (2008) *Cultural Heritage and Human Rights*. New York: Springer.
Smith, C. and M. Wobst. (eds) (2005) *Indigenous Archaeologies: Decolonizing Theory and Practice*. London: Routledge.
Smith, L.-J. (2004) *Archaeological Theory and the Politics of Cultural Heritage*. Routledge: London.
Smith, L.-J. (2006) *Uses of Heritage*. London: Routledge.
Stoffle, R. W., M. N. Zedeno, and D. B. Halmo (eds) (2001) *American Indians and the Nevada Test Site: A Model of Research and Consultation*. Washington: US Government Printing Office.
Trigger, B. G. (1980) Archaeology and the image of the American Indian. *American Antiquity* 45: 662–676.
Trigger, B. G. (1984) Alternative archaeologies: Nationalist, colonialist, imperialist. *Man* 19: 355–370.
Tsing, A. (2005) *Friction: An Ethnography of Global Connection*. Princeton, NJ: Princeton University Press.
Ucko, P. (1987) *Academic Freedom and Apartheid: The Story of the World Archaeological Congress*. London: Duckworth.
Vitelli, K. D. (ed.) (1996) *Archaeological Ethics*. Walnut Creek, CA: AltaMira Press.
Weiss, L. (2007) Heritage-making and political identity. *Journal of Social Archaeology* 7(3): 413–431.
Weiss, L. M. (2014) Informal settlements and urban heritage landscapes in South Africa. *Journal of Social Archaeology* 14: 3–25.
Werbner, P. (ed.) (2008) *Anthropology and the New Cosmopolitanism*. Oxford: Berg.
Winter, T. (2007) *Post-Conflict Heritage, Postcolonial Tourism: Tourism, Politics and Development at Angkor*. London: Routledge.
Winter, T. (2014) Beyond Eurocentrism? Heritage conservation and the politics of difference. *International Journal of Heritage Studies* 20: 123–137.

1

UNESCO and New World Orders

Lynn Meskell and Christoph Brumann

UNESCO and Cultural Heritage

It is remarkable how thoroughly an organization once set up to propagate the *new* – "since wars begin in the minds of men, it is in the minds of men that the defences of peace must be constructed," as the most quoted sentence from its constitution has it – is now publicly associated with conserving the *old*. In the most broadly defined portfolio of any UN body, the United Nations Educational, Scientific and Cultural Organization (UNESCO) with its headquarters in Paris has increasingly shifted from E to C. Education continues to be the primary commitment and to drive its programmatic vision, however, globally UNESCO has come to stand for heritage, and it is the heritage programs that attract the largest part of the extra-budgetary resources on which the cash-strapped organization so heavily depends. That heritage is so tightly linked with UNESCO and that long sections of recent scholarly overviews of the field (Harrison 2012; Smith 2006; Tauschek 2013) are dedicated to the UNESCO conventions is significant, given the small operating budgets of the UNESCO programs (Meskell 2013a). Clearly, UNESCO's symbolic weight is considerable and can be converted into power and material gains in many domains.

The rise of heritage within UNESCO is indicative of a changed orientation towards human diversity within the organization. UNESCO's early initiatives, such as its statements on race, highlighted human unity, enlisting the services of prominent anthropologists such as Claude Lévi-Strauss. The organization strove to disseminate literacy, Western agricultural models, and birth control – a unitary package of modernity – to the states of the Global South that have always been a key concern. For a progress so conceptualized, cultural diversity was an obstacle, not a virtue. During the 1960s and 1970s, however, the optimistic belief in economic development faded, and, instead, the 1972 World Heritage Convention and other activities began to highlight the outstanding achievements of particular cultures in order to make them world property, attempting to wrest them away from the national frameworks of cultural and natural conservation. A further shift has occurred in the 1990s and 2000s where the common heritage of humanity worthy of preservation expanded,

Global Heritage: A Reader, First Edition. Edited by Lynn Meskell.

from the wonders of nature and material culture to customary practices and even cultural diversity as such (Stoczkowski 2009). In UNESCO pronouncements, economic development and globalization are now a threat rather than a promise, bound to dissolve ethnic, national, and religious identities; against this specter, the celebration of cultural diversity and the variety of human accomplishments is expected to promote the mutual respect and understanding that ensures world peace and human advancement. Targeting "the right kind of culture" (Nielsen 2011) for UNESCO entails customs and practices that respect basic human rights and are tolerant of their contenders. How much of this is wishful thinking in a world divided by cultural values and alignments should be obvious. But for an organization working to be inclusive of its members – the world's national governments – such aspirational formulations sidestep uncomfortable pronouncements about desirable and undesirable values and practices.

Given these constraints, edifying and aesthetically pleasing places and practices are easier to agree upon than some cultural norms of proper female comportment, for example, and this has certainly contributed to bringing heritage as (ideally) harmless culture to center stage within UNESCO contexts. Fitting for an organization so much premised on the aftermath of war, the first step in 1954 was the Hague Convention for the Protection of Cultural Property in the Event of Armed Conflict (to which a Second Protocol was added in 1999), and the 1970 Convention on the Means of Prohibiting and Preventing the Illicit Import, Export and Transfer of Ownership of Cultural Property too especially applies to conflict and post-conflict societies. Yet with the 1972 Convention Concerning the Protection of the World Cultural and Natural Heritage, the focus shifted to all kinds of heritage sites, also those not immediately endangered by destructive or criminal human action. Some thirty years on, the 2001 Convention on the Protection of the Underwater Cultural Heritage was of a more specialized nature but the 2003 Convention for the Safeguarding of Intangible Cultural Heritage and the 2005 Convention on the Promotion and Protection of the Diversity of Cultural Expressions decidedly widened the scope established by the World Heritage Convention. The 2003 Convention in particular enjoys comparable attention because of its analogous lists of global fame with all their celebratory potential. Even so, the World Heritage Convention continues to play in a league of its own, starting with the fact that intangible heritage "cultural expressions" are often (and mistakenly) referred to as "World Heritage" whereas the reverse does not usually occur. In this chapter we concentrate on World Heritage and the 1972 UNESCO Convention that aspired to create and conserve it.

The History and Institutional Framework of World Heritage

Many modern precepts of heritage crystallized in Europe in synchrony with the origins of the nation-state. Intimately connected to the Enlightenment project, the formation of national identity relied on a coherent national heritage that could be marshaled to fend off the counter-claims of other groups and nations. In the post-Westphalian world, "sovereign nation-states no longer exclusively define the field of global political relations or monopolize many of the powers organizing that field, yet states remain significant actors as well as symbols of national identification" (Brown 2010: 24). As in many other globalizing arenas, the creation of UNESCO and the shift to global heritage ended up reinforcing the interests of the state since it is so strongly pegged to national identification, prestige, and the recognition of a particular modernity. In fact, the state continues to be a particularly intransigent force in all of UNESCO's operations by the very structure of the organization that has states as its members. Within the UN family, nation-states are impossible to bypass or dislodge whether one is talking about human rights or heritage rights and, in cases of doubt, political sovereignty often takes precedence over the protection of people or things. Underwriting all practices of protection is the tension of balancing preservation with the material needs of living communities. Indeed much recent work underscores that conservation, like corporatization, has effectively displaced both human histories and local presence (Breen 2007; Brockington and Igoe 2006; West, Igoe, and Brockington 2006).

UNESCO's commitment to peace, humanitarianism, and intercultural understanding developed out of the universalist aspirations for global governance envisaged by the League of Nations (Singh 2011; Valderrama 1995). While upholding modernist principles of progress and development, it simultaneously subscribes to the liberal principles of diplomacy, tolerance, and development. It should be noted that UNESCO's mission stemmed from a specifically European organization called the International Committee on Intellectual Co-operation (ICIC) which operated between 1936 and 1946 (Droit 2005; Hoggart 2011), rather than being a direct offshoot from the United Nations. Founded by prominent intellectuals such as Henri Bergson, Marie Curie, Albert Einstein, and Thomas Mann, the ICIC was established to create a "state of mind conducive to the peaceful settlement of international problems within the framework of the League of Nations" (Valderrama 1995: 3). Not surprisingly, its activities were focused on education, universities and libraries, and internationalism. Given this history of emphasizing recognition and reconciliation, the long-standing ethos of cultural diversity, and the protection of minority lifeways, it is not surprising that UNESCO has emerged as the most prominent structural avenue to the global governance and promotion of cultural heritage. Within the United Nations, UNESCO may not be as powerful as high-profile international peacekeeping, environmental initiatives, or development programs. Rather, it is perceived as the cultural arm, the visionary agency, and the "ideas factory" for the larger organization (Pavone 2008).

The principle that natural and cultural heritage situated across the globe requires an international mandate and authority for its management, preservation, and protection stretches back a century. From the League of Nations in 1919, to the International Institute of Intellectual Cooperation (IIIC) and its International Museums Office in 1926, to the Athens Conference of 1931 on the protection and conservation of monuments of art and history, there has been a growing international movement. In 1945, UNESCO was created with a constitution mandating "the conservation and protection of the world's inheritance of books, works of art and monuments of history and science." With modernist construction and development projects and unseen ecological damages heightening a sense of urgency, this commitment transformed into proactive international assistance: the first in a series of safeguarding missions coordinated by UNESCO was launched in 1959 for the Nubian monuments of Egypt, threatened by the construction of the Aswan Dam but then transplanted to a site out of reach of the rising waters (Allais 2013; Hassan 2007). International expert meetings such as that held in Venice in 1964 were responsible for drafting the International Charter for the Conservation and Restoration of Monuments and Sites (the Venice Charter) and for the founding of ICOMOS (see below). During the 1965 US White House Conference, the idea of a World Heritage Trust was proposed and the term "world heritage" was coined (Allais 2013: 7;

Bandarin 2007). In what outside a North American context was an innovative move, the initiative came to incorporate both cultural and natural heritage, and after some negotiation (Stott 2011), it was decided to house it at UNESCO, whose General Conference adopted The Convention Concerning the Protection of the World Cultural and Natural Heritage in 1972. The Convention created a set of obligations to protect the past for future generations, an aspiration for a shared sense of belonging, and an ideal of global solidarity (Choay 2001: 140). More recently, other heritage bodies have either replicated or been influenced by this international vision of support, whether the Islamic Educational, Scientific and Cultural Organization (ISESCO) (Bouasria 2001) or the World Monuments Fund and Global Heritage Fund based in the United States (see also Winter 2011). The Convention was part of a larger trend in international law to superimpose a "common heritage of mankind" onto the interaction between nation states that is the standard subject matter of international law (Wolfrum 2009). Other such treaties, however, concerned spaces outside state jurisdiction – Antarctica, the high seas, outer space – whereas in World Heritage, national and supranational competencies were imagined to henceforth overlap.

The 1972 Convention was adopted as a new provision for the international and collective protection of heritage with "Outstanding Universal Value" (Jokilehto and Cameron 2008; Labadi 2013; Titchen 1996).[1] The World Heritage Center (WHC) was established in 1992 to act as the secretariat and coordinator within UNESCO for all matters related to the Convention. The Center organizes the annual sessions of the World Heritage Committee and provides advice to States Parties, or signatories to the Convention, in the preparation of site nominations. The World Heritage Center along with the Advisory Bodies also administers international assistance from the World Heritage Fund and coordinates both the reporting on the condition of sites and the emergency action undertaken when a site is threatened. As the number of World Heritage sites exceeds 1,000, requests to these bodies for international assistance and field missions mount, commitments to sustainable development and enhanced capacity-building increase, and heritage conflict in countries like Mali or Syria intensifies.

The Advisory Bodies are international organizations whose experts are relied upon for monitoring missions and evaluations: the International Centre for the Study of Preservation and Restoration of Cultural Property (ICCROM) in Rome, the International Council on Monuments and Sites (ICOMOS) headquartered in Paris, and the International Union for Conservation of Nature (IUCN) headquartered in Gland, near Geneva. ICCROM was set up in 1959 as an intergovernmental organization and is only involved in "state of conservation" reporting and some monitoring missions in a limited manner, focusing on training and capacity-building instead. ICOMOS was founded in 1965 and is a non-governmental membership organization; IUCN was established in 1948 and is an "organization of organizations" with both governmental and non-governmental members. Both ICOMOS and IUCN provide technical evaluations of nominations and monitor inscribed sites; ICOMOS for the cultural sites including cultural landscapes, IUCN for the natural sites, and both for the mixed sites. ICOMOS and IUCN communicate their findings in lengthy reports and presentations at the World Heritage Committee meetings, although their technical approaches and priorities are being increasingly challenged.

In an intergovernmental agency which is part of the UN family, the States Parties are in fact the most powerful decision makers (Askew 2010), particularly those that currently have representation on the World Heritage Committee. The Committee is made up of twenty-one States Parties, elected at the biannual General Assembly, that serve a four-year term. Formally, the Committee is independent from the general UNESCO governing bodies. The Committee makes the final decisions about nominations to the List, measures for already listed sites, budget allocation, and general policies, and does so with a firm sense of independence from the Advisory Bodies and the World Heritage Center. Once a site has been inscribed, the World Heritage Committee has both the right and the duty to monitor its state of conservation, relying again on the expert services of ICOMOS, IUCN, ICCROM, and the Center. The Committee has the final say on whether a property is inscribed on the World Heritage List or on the List of World Heritage in Danger.[2] By signing the Convention, each country pledges to conserve not only World Heritage properties situated on its territory but also its broader national heritage. The Convention enjoys almost universal membership with 191 signatories. States Parties with World Heritage sites garner international and national prestige, have access to the World Heritage Fund for monetary assistance, and can tap the potential benefits of heightened public awareness, tourism, and economic development.

However, this Fund has increasingly limited means to support nominations and conservation measures. The underlying assumption and precondition for listing is that the nominating nation itself is capable of conserving the site, and, with the prestige of a World Heritage title, it is indeed often much easier to attract investors and donors. Moreover, there are real constraints within the UNESCO World Heritage arena that are often overlooked, also by scholars of heritage. For instance, there is little that the World Heritage Committee can impose upon a recalcitrant nation state, even when government promises made before inscription are not honored afterwards. While sites can be deleted from the World Heritage List, this has happened only twice in forty years.

The World Heritage List is often criticized for its Eurocentrism (Labadi 2005, 2007). Yet it is noteworthy that the first inscriptions included quite a few African sites[3] and that, until 1990, India was the overall leader in the number of World Heritage properties.[4] European and in particular Western European states, however, have been particularly conscious of the benefits of World Heritage listing and can marshal the resources for state-of-the-art nominations. Coupled with an implicit initial conceptualization of World Heritage around the typical built heritage of this part of the world (and certainly also influenced by the tendency for ICOMOS and IUCN personnel to be educated and based there), European sites have accounted for almost half the listings until the present, with China only beginning to challenge the numerical pole position of Italy and Spain in recent years. The balanced representation of natural and cultural sites that was initially envisaged has not materialized either: today some 75 percent of the List is cultural.

Attempts to impose nomination quotas or even moratoriums on nations with large numbers of sites have had only limited success. This certainly contributed to efforts to reform the World Heritage system in the 1990s that greatly expanded the conceptual boundaries. The category of Cultural Landscapes was introduced in 1992 to celebrate outstanding examples of human interaction with nature (Rössler 2003). The Global Strategy for a Representative, Balanced and Credible World Heritage List, launched in 1994 (Labadi 2013), prioritized living heritage and everyday culture "in their broad anthropological context."[5] The notion of authenticity was broadened in the Nara Document on Authenticity of the same year, in a manner belying the widespread assumption that heritage designation invariably has a "freezing" effect' (cf. Brumann 2014a). Much of the impetus for these reforms came from the regional and professional "semiperipheries" of the world system (cf. Wallerstein 1974) of heritage – Canadians, Japanese, Australians, and Norwegians, not French or Italians; anthropologists, geographers, or industrial archaeologists, rather than art historians (Gfeller 2013, personal communication). Other UNESCO programs in the 2000s, including the Convention for the Safeguarding of the Intangible Cultural Heritage (UNESCO 2003) and the Convention on the Protection and Promotion of the Diversity of Cultural Expressions (UNESCO 2005), have also emphasized geographical balance and cultural diversity.

Studying the World Heritage Arena

UNESCO's World Heritage program has recently attracted heightened attention from ethnographers, archaeologists, economists, political scientists, and legal scholars writing on a wide range of topics, including governance and bureaucracy (Bertacchini, Saccone, and Santagata 2011; Logan 2012b; Schmitt 2009, 2012), list credibility (Askew 2010; Zacharias 2010), global strategy and representation (Labadi 2005, 2007; Schmitt 2008; Willems and Comer 2011), the politics of culture and rights (Berliner 2012; De Cesari 2010a; Eriksen 2009; Logan 2012a), and cultural economics (Bertacchini, Saccone, and Santagata 2011; Frey, Pamini, and Steiner 2011; Frey and Steiner 2011; van Blarcoma and Kayahana 2011). Sociocultural anthropologists have focused much of their attention on the 2003 UNESCO Convention for the Safeguarding of Intangible Cultural Heritage because it is here where they, not art historians or others, are generally ascribed special expertise (e.g., Arantes 2007; Bortolotto 2007, 2010, 2011; Brown 2004; Eriksen 2001; Hafstein 2009; Kuutma 2007).

Studies based on the analysis of documents come from a wide range of disciplinary perspectives including economics (specifically cultural economics), legal studies, and international relations, as well as a vast outpouring of work that comes under the banner of heritage studies. Many of the political, legal, and economic analyses are based on UNESCO-produced documentation and reveal a good working knowledge of the institution, whereas many heritage studies that deal in some way with UNESCO or more specifically the World Heritage Center tend to be anecdotal and rhetorical, sometimes lacking a full understanding of the actual players, processes, and politics that currently shape the organization, for instance by routinely ascribing agency to UNESCO in its undifferentiated entirety (e.g., Di Giovine 2009). Part of this occlusion is due to the way in which documents are produced, especially at annual Committee sessions, and then "neutrally" reproduced for online consumption. Overall, the degree to which these documents are the results of endless revisions and compromises, at the cost of coherence and consistency, seems to be underestimated by many observers.

UNESCO has, of late, become a particular interest to European cultural economists, particularly those based at UNESCO's Category II Center at the University of Turin, Italy. These scholars have been working on addressing the imbalances of the World Heritage List, crafting policy mechanisms for global governance (Bertacchini, Saccone, and Santagata 2011), and examining the political economy of heritage globally (Bertacchini and Saccone 2012). One proposal is to create a World Heritage tax (Bertacchini, Saccone, and Santagata 2009; Bertacchini, Saccone, and Walter 2010) to generate new economic resources from cultural tourism and to redistribute them on a regional scale. Other scholars suggest novel schemes to effectively preserve World Heritage with a system of certificates. The international community would then decide on the level of contribution, assign certificates, and be able to trade them internationally (Frey and Pamini 2009). How to put these schemes into practice against the resistance of cost-conscious nation-states, however, is an altogether different question.

Economic research has focused on the historic imbalances of the World Heritage List, specifically the assessment of the 1994 Global Strategy (see also Labadi 2007; UNESCO 2011). Steiner and Frey (2012) argue that, in fact, the skewed distribution of sites has not decreased, but rather increased over time. Listing success is found to be correlated with a number of factors such as historical GDP and population, membership in the UN Security Council, size of the the tourist sector, and composition of the World Heritage Committee: these are economic and political factors unrelated to heritage, including rent-seeking by politicians (Bertacchini and Saccone 2012; Frey, Pamini, and Steiner 2011). Cultural geographer Schmitt (2009) also confirms that GDP and the number of World Heritage sites are strongly correlated across the treaty states. Similarly, Labadi's analysis from 1994 to 2004 supports the idea that while there was a widespread need to rectify thematic, geographical, and chronological discrepancies, these have not yet been alleviated (2005). She points to the lack of local and indigenous community involvement in the nomination, conservation, and management of sites (see also Logan 2013; Meskell 2013b).

Frey and Steiner (2011) have questioned the validity of the World Heritage List yet argue that it can make sense when national authorities do not prioritize these sites, or financial resources are inadequate for conservation. However, reliance on the market and strong national conservation is even more beneficial when the sites are already popular and listing does not contribute to detrimental tourist impact. Much of this work traverses economic and political fields and has implications for UNESCO's policy and governance. For instance, Saccone and Bertacchini (2011) have examined the relationship between heritage preservation and the economic, social, and institutional factors that characterize a nation's level of development. While heritage is increasingly seen as a driver for development and poverty reduction, they argue that there is little evidence for understanding which conditions trigger the valorization of cultural resources. They suggest that poor countries are trapped, since a lack of development restricts cultural promotion, leading to an inability to promote national heritage that in turn restricts the advancement of culture-based development strategies.

From a legal perspective, scholars are concerned with the effects of economic globalization of World Heritage properties, given the significant amount of private investment being poured into preserving and presenting sites to the public worldwide (Vadi 2013). Since direct foreign investment can have such force, with the capacity to change landscapes and erase certain pasts, is there adequate legislation to protect the wealth of nations? Vadi suggests that, while international investment law has not developed a mechanism to protect World Heritage through investment dispute resolution, a jurisprudential trend has emerged that at least considers cultural heritage.

Another legal issue, explored primarily on documentary materials, is the intersection of human rights implementation and World Heritage designation and site management. Some scholars have attempted to find a rights-based approach within the existing documents (Jokilehto 2012) whereas others have argued that greater linkages need to be made explicit within the heritage sphere (Ekern et al. 2012; Logan 2009, 2012a; Meskell 2010). For more than a decade, this has been a concern of the World Heritage Center as well as numerous indigenous groups worldwide.

However, to date this has not been reflected in the Operational Guidelines – the "code of law" – of the Convention. Disko (2010) argues that with the 2007 Declaration on the Rights of Indigenous Peoples (UNDRIP) there already exists a framework to change the implementation of the World Heritage Convention, allowing the inclusion of indigenous understandings and values into site management. One way to ensure indigenous participation would be to insist on the free, prior informed consent stipulated in UNDRIP, starting from the nomination process (Hales et al. 2012). Various case studies of such efforts have been made in Australia (Carter 2010; Logan 2012a, 2013), New Zealand (Kawharu 2009), Canada (Lemelin and Bennett 2010), and Norway (Ween 2012). In the early 2000s, the World Heritage Indigenous Peoples Council of Experts (WHIPCOE) was proposed to ensure greater indigenous participation and control over World Heritage properties. The Committee did not install it, however, due to harsh criticism from nations like France and the United States (Meskell 2013b), but, in recent sessions, pressure by the United Nations Permanent Forum on Indigenous Issues (UNPFII) has kept the issue on the agenda.

Much has been written about the key concepts of authenticity, integrity, and Outstanding Universal Value (OUV) within the World Heritage sphere. Stovel (2007) suggests that that these central tenets are distinct in terms of conservation strategies and subsequently require restructuring. Others have examined these criteria (Jokilehto 2006) and concluded that it is not easy to define what is eligible for inclusion on the List and what should remain national patrimony. Critical analyses of UNESCO's concept of OUV have been conducted and criticized by a number of authors (Alberts and Hazen 2010; Pendlebury, Short, and While 2009; Titchen 1996), most recently Labadi (2013) in a book-length treatment. Brumann (2013) shows how the new authenticity conceptions of the 1990s are part of a wider trend to prioritize immaterial aspects of heritage not just in the 2003 Convention, but also within the World Heritage system. As he points out and Rudolff (2010) also observes, there is much conceptual traffic between the two conventions, even when the experts associating themselves with each may sometimes be in conflict. These exchanges concern not only ideas but also procedural details and the piecemeal diffusion of informal session behavior, argumentation styles, and strategies.

Following the pioneering work by Turtinen (2000, 2006) and just like Brumann (2011, 2012, 2014b) and Meskell (2011, 2012, 2013a, 2014), Schmitt (2009) has used official observer status at the World Heritage Committee sessions to examine the role of the Advisory Bodies. He argues that there are markedly different understandings of concepts like OUV as well as the instruments such as the List of World Heritage in Danger, yet such pluralism need not be detrimental to global governance. Decision making within the Committee, however, has become fraught and, as Logan (2012b) details for many Asian nations, there is palpable frustration that the inspirational rhetoric of the organization does not always match with the aspirations of nation-states. He notes rising criticism of governance arrangements and limitations. As Director of the World Heritage Center, Kishore Rao (2010) contends that current developments run counter to the intent of the Convention and its emphasis on international cooperation and mutual understanding. He proposes a new paradigm to overcome present limitations, by instituting a progressive inscription process with an enhanced and proactive role for the World Heritage Committee to prioritize at an early stage those sites that merit inclusion on the List. This, he believes, would have a beneficial impact on the issue of global balance and representativity. Skepticism is allowed for, however, since whether Committee member states with all their vested interests would accept anything that impeded their desire for inscription is another matter.

In the past few decades, increasing attention has been directed towards issues of stakeholder collaboration around World Heritage properties (Aas, Ladkin, and Fletcher 2005), the inclusion of local voices and values, and more recently the connection between site designation and local development strategies (Araoz 2011; Isar 2011), the most pressing of which is poverty reduction. The world over, managing such sites has come under scrutiny (Brattli 2009; Landorf 2009; Leask and Fyall 2006; Winter 2007). Much of the fieldwork conducted by archaeologists has focused on the political dimension of UNESCO designation and its subsequent afterlife. In the Palestinian context, De Cesari (2010b) describes how UNESCO's own shift towards liberal multiculturalism might end up reinforcing cultural differences and asymmetries. Through examining UNESCO workshops in Jerusalem and Ramallah, she argues that innovative Palestinian practices of heritage conservation and the specifics of locality are effectively elided by overlaying the template of World Heritage. Despite Israeli measures, Assi (2012) argues that the Palestinian management program has been a positive step and, while this is one of the most complex settings for UNESCO, researchers on the ground argue that even during armed conflict cultural heritage remains key to identity (Scham and Yahya 2003). In the same way, Tibetan World Heritage sites have been discussed in the context of human rights and Chinese hegemony and the lasting impacts of local culture, particularly with the opening up for international tourism (Shepherd 2006; Sinding-Larsen 2012). These frictions between the universal and the local are clearly evidenced in the World Heritage arena.

The role of international expertise and its translation into local cultural practice has become increasingly visible in recent heritage ethnographies. In her study of post-tsunami Indonesia, Rico (2008, 2011) examines the intersection of cultural traditions in Banda Aceh and the vernacularization of international preservation imperatives through the global construct of "heritage at risk." The Acehnese developed distinct ways to represent history, identity, and the culture of disaster into a coherent program that does not sit easily with Western preservation philosophies. Such heritage does not wait to be legitimized by global heritage experts but has already effectively responded to local democratic structures. By assessing the successes of grounded local measures and the perceived failures of established global preservation rhetoric, she calls into question the entire notion of a risk-centered framework, as promulgated by agencies like ICOMOS and UNESCO. Similarly, Lafrenz Samuels (2009) traces the expansion of this expertise across the Middle East and North Africa region, where material heritage is mobilized by international agencies such as UNESCO and the World Bank to reduce poverty. At sites like the medina of Fez, the economic value of heritage is at the forefront, yet international expertise often results in the marginalization, exclusion, and even removal of local inhabitants.

Anthropologists doing fieldwork in World Heritage sites have usually concentrated on the experience of local populations, particularly those affected by the consequences of list inscription, surging tourism, tightened conservation regulations, and so on. Memory and nostalgia are the driving force behind heritage-making according to Berliner (2010, 2012) but the question of whose nostalgia is being protected remains. From his extensive work in Luang Prabang, Laos, he suggests that there are multiple attachments rooted in personal experience but also inflected with issues of history, expertise, development, and culture. He distinguishes the "endo-nostalgia" of those who have actually grown up in the place and whose memories of the good old days are based, however selectively, on actual experience from the "exo-nostalgia" of many tourists and technical experts for a colonial Indochina they have never seen themselves or which never existed to begin with. Just as nostalgia is performative, so too is the creation and transformation of heritage spaces by UNESCO experts and national civil servants.

Probst (2004, 2011) has been following the transformation of the sacred grove of Osun in Osogbo, Nigeria, for more than a decade. This tract of primary forest is no longer just a cult place for the protector goddess of the surrounding city of Osogbo. It became also the site of a major artistic revival where, in the post-independence period of the 1960s and 1970s, European expatriates and young local artists created a new and distinctive style of sculpture and painting. Today, the annual Osun festival continues to be a major rallying point for the transatlantic African diaspora. This site was successfully promoted to World Heritage status in 2005, as a cornerstone in President Obasanjo's cultural policies, and it provides a vivid illustration of how short the time horizons of heritage have become: what was a stronghold of African modernity and innovation just a moment ago is now under a conservation regime. The Osun grove also demonstrates that when religious, political, commercial, and curatorial demands collide, this can increase local authorities' maneuvering space: the traditional king (*oba*) can now point to the site's heritage status when promoting the festival, thus fending off any allegations of supporting what Christian and Muslim constituencies might consider pagan practices.

Prior to the current civil war, Salamandra (2004) investigated the rediscovery of the courtyard houses in the old city of Damascus which is a World Heritage property, albeit one in danger. Old families, often from the former professional and entrepreneurial elite, who previously had left for the suburbs and rented out the subdivided houses to rural migrants, were now reclaiming their homes and converting them to new purposes such as shops, galleries, and restaurants. Salamandra interprets this as an assertion of symbolic dominance over the new political leadership that lacks a long-standing connection to the city. She describes a largely private and uncoordinated movement of heritage reappropriation in which the World Heritage institutions play only a small role. Such movements may be more typical for urban than rural heritage (Brumann 2009), and parallel phenomena have been observed elsewhere in the Arab world, for instance in the medina of Fez (Istasse 2011) where the residents' very personal relationships to the houses are much more decisive for the way these are maintained then the often autocratic rulings of heritage authorities.

Exploring the conditions of urban World Heritage further, a research group led by Brumann at the Max Planck Institute for Social Anthropology in Halle, Germany, currently compares the local appropriation of the global title in Istanbul (Marquart 2014); Melaka in Malaysia (being studied by Pierpaolo De Giosa); and Xi'an in China (being studied by Leah Cheung Ah Li), whose Silk Road-related monuments, following up on the grave of the first Qin emperor with the Terracotta Army near the city, were added to the List in 2014. All three places are former hubs of empire and major destinations of cultural tourism and, in all of them, heritage recognition ranges all the way from palaces to humble town houses. Yet while specific buildings and archaeological remains are instrumental to contemporary nation-building, transmitting the greatness of past civilizations (Istanbul and Xi'an) and multicultural co-existence (Melaka), conservation often has to stand back when contemporary building projects transform urban space. Reference to the past is often required also in new developments, however, be it the wooden facades of Istanbul residential developments that gentrify run-down inner-city areas, historical-looking malls in luxury condominiums in Melaka, or the theme-park style approach of the Qujiang Corporation that is in charge of real-estate development around famous historic sites in Xi'an. This set of studies encourages us to take the commercial aspects of World Heritage seriously: increasingly, heritage is expected to pay its way, particularly in the up-and-coming states of the Global South. This presupposes the spread of lifestyle and leisure preferences in these countries to which a touch of history adds significant value.

While in Osogbo, Damascus, or Melaka, a substantial number of people are (or were) content with the economic and other opportunities afforded by World Heritage status, other anthropologists have shown how listing often goes hand in hand with the dispossession of local populations. In an edited volume, Hauser-Schäublin and colleagues (2011) have traced this in detail for Angkor in Cambodia. This vast and impressive site has been a prime beneficiary of multinational development cooperation and support, up to the level of an intergovernmental body (the International Coordinating Committee for the Safeguarding and Development of the Historic Site of Angkor, or ICC-Angkor), and archaeologists and heritage managers from across the Global North have descended upon the site to coordinate research and restoration measures. Tourism, particularly from Asian countries, has exploded in recent years and, as a symbol of reconciliation and nation-building in a post-genocidal society, Angkor is much relied upon. Yet most profits from tourism bypass the local communities, and their use of the vast expanses for raising fish, cultivating rice, or collecting forest products is now as suspect as their continued worship at, and active maintenance of, temples that are now subject to conservation regimes.

For Chichén Itzá, Breglia (2005; see also Hannigan 2006) has likewise documented how heritage-related benefits largely bypass the local Maya population. There is nonetheless widespread pride in the global fame of the site, and the descendants of those Maya who once excavated it still hang on to moderate privileges as state-employed guards and shopkeepers. They no longer live on site as they used to and their football matches in the shadow of the Great Pyramid are a remote memory now. One local family of mestizo land-owners and tourism entrepreneurs, however, retains ownership of the land on which the monuments stand. Although private ownership was previously known, it only became a point of contention when Chichén Itzá was promoted as a candidate for the New Seven Wonders of the World internet contest. In response to the outcry over private possession, a parastatal subsidiary of the federal state bought up central portions, making it communal land as befits a World Heritage site (Breglia forthcoming).

Joy (2011a, 2011b) describes the challenges that the World Heritage inscription of the picturesque mud architecture of the city of Djenné, Mali, brings to its residents. Prior to the current conflict, French colonial romanticism and a national government intent on gaining a place on the global cultural map imposed a conservation regime that, together with the weekly market and an annual music festival, help to attract foreign tourists as one of the few sources of income. Yet many citizens feel a heavy burden when the regular re-mudding of houses consumes more resources than the less "authentic" tiling of façades, especially considering that basic amenities such as a sewage system are still lacking in this poverty-stricken environment. Bruner (1996) has shown how publicly recognized and supposedly communal heritage can remain very significant in highly individual searches for roots and one's own personal heritage. He follows African American tourists through the World Heritage site of Elmina Castle in Ghana, the main entrepôt for the North American slave trade. The tourists' joint walk through the dungeons and the infamous Door of No Return is often an overwhelming emotional experience, yet all the more disconcerting are encounters with the Ghanaians outside the castle who lack a personal history of slavery. For them, the guests are *obruni* (whitemen) by virtue of their wealth, rather than long-lost brothers and sisters returning "home."

Case Studies: World Heritage Committee Mechanics

Recent work on UNESCO's World Heritage program has focused on the new geopolitical alliances and power bases that have only emerged in the past few years, in an effort to challenge the perceived hegemony of European nations within the organization. Ethnographic observation, particularly at World Heritage Committee meetings, demonstrates how alliances can be shifting and mutable and might at any one time be based on religious, regional, political, or economic linkages. Some of these short-lived coalitions revolve around specific nodal sites and issues, such as the 2012 nomination of Palestine's first site, the Church of the Nativity in Bethlehem.[6] Given the regional and political position of Palestine and the well-rehearsed standoffs between Israel and the Arab states in the World Heritage Committee, one might have expected support to come mainly from other Middle Eastern delegations, yet it was largely Christian countries like France, Russia, and South Africa that provided the strongest backing. Obviously, the site was mainly perceived in its religious dimension, not in its geographic and political ones. Expedient alliances, fluctuations in political alignments, and entrenched long-term coalitions all influence the operations of the World Heritage Committee today.

It is instructive to see which are the most active nations by the number of World Heritage nominations put forward from 2002 to 2013: China (17), Iran (14), India and Italy (12), Germany (11), Mexico and the Russian Federation (10), and France and Israel (9). While European countries remain active, the geographical axis has shifted, with specific Asian and African countries now well represented. This challenges the older critique that World Heritage is tacitly Eurocentric, and while the List is a historical product indeed filled with French, Italian, Spanish, and German sites, the geopolitical coordinates have changed significantly.

One grouping that has received a great deal of scholarly attention is BRICS, the politico-economic alliance formed between Brazil, Russia, India, China, and South Africa (Claudi 2011; Ferdinand 2012; Meskell 2011, 2013a). The acronym was coined at Goldman Sachs (O'Neill 2001) for this group of (sub-)continental leaders at a similar stage of economic development in order to highlight the shift in global economic power away from the developed G7 countries towards these ambitious nations seeking a more significant role in a multilateral world and global decision making (Ferdinand 2012). For the past six years there has been an annual BRICS summit and during the 2014 meeting the BRICS Development Bank was formalized as an alternative to the World Bank and IMF. Over the past years, all five BRICS nations have served on the World Heritage Committee and often expressed dissatisfaction with the recommendations of the Advisory Bodies (Claudi 2011: 53). BRICS presence and mutual support greatly benefitted both South Africa and Russia during discussion of their national parks potentially endangered by mining concessions within or adjacent to their borders (Esterhuysen 2009; Jørgensen and Hønneland 2006). These rising powers tend to pact in the World Heritage arena, whether in support of inscribing their own candidates and avoiding painful decisions, or assisting "client" nations with controversial nominations or conservation issues such as the recent cases of Palestine and Panama (Meskell 2013a, 2014). An overall uniformity of BRICS voting has been observed across the United Nations General Assembly, although there is notable divergence in their positions on human rights and nuclear disarmament (Ferdinand 2012).

Formalized BRICS multilateralism can be seen in the 2011 Sanya Declaration[7] whereby all five nations pledged support for "boosting global economic growth, enhancing multilateralism and promoting greater democracy in international relations." Specifically, the Declaration calls for "multilateral diplomacy with the United Nations" as well as "comprehensive reform of the UN" system. They propose to establish a BRICS-UNESCO Group at UNESCO, "aiming at developing common strategies within the mandate of the Organization." World Heritage negotiations can thus be seen as an exercise in soft power (Luke and Kersel 2012), while harnessing and building upon more expansive politico-economic forces that have greater repercussions elsewhere (Meskell 2013a, 2014). Claudi's ethnographic work traces mutual support between Brazil, Russia, India, and China within the World Heritage Committee in their efforts to have their sites inscribed on the List. BRICS members have strategic, explicitly stated objectives within the Committee, which include challenging the decisions of Advisory Bodies whom they see as biased toward "the West" and whose legitimacy and credibility they consider inherently compromised. Other stated objectives for these nations included enhanced visibility and greater diplomatic ties, since all their delegations have strict instructions from their respective governments (Claudi 2011: 45–46).

In collaboration with cultural economists Bertacchini and Saccone (Bertacchini and Saccone 2012; Bertacchini, Saccone, and Santagata 2011), archaeologists Meskell and Liuzza have examined the effects of decision making and political pacting between BRICS nations in the World Heritage Committee in the last decade (Meskell et al. 2014). From 2002 to 2012, BRICS nations nominated 45 (or 15 percent) of the 295 sites put forward for inscription. Given that BRICS represents only five nations, from 190 signatory State Parties (or 2 percent) participating in the Convention, this combined activity is noteworthy. Moreover, properties proposed by BRICS members benefitted from having the decisions of the Advisory Bodies overturned more frequently in their favor. For example, Advisory Body recommendations for Non-Inscription of sites were predominantly turned into Referrals (66.7 percent); recommendations for Deferral were pushed up to either Referral (26.7 percent) or Inscription (53.3 percent); and those recommended for Referral were consistently moved to Inscription (100 percent). (In the context of the World Heritage Committee, a "Referral" decision amounts to asking for minor amendments whereas a "Deferral" decision implies a substantial revision of the nomination, usually requiring a new inspection mission by the Advisory Bodies.) In comparison, non-BRICS nations had lower instances of these favorable changes, suggesting that their political influence may not be so robust. Advisory Body recommendation for Non-Inscription led to Deferral (42.9 percent) as often as to Referral (42.9 percent), and recommendations of Deferral (40.9 percent) or Referral (77.8 percent) were pushed up to Inscription more rarely too. Comparison of discussion time is also informative. The time taken in reaching a decision in the Committee, often entailing the overturning of ICOMOS and IUCN recommendations, was in almost every case shorter for nominations by BRICS nations than those of non-BRICS countries, suggesting a more powerful, strategic, and concerted effort by the alliance to assert their political will.

While Brumann (2014b) acknowledges the importance of BRICS, he also emphasizes the role of other world regional leaders such as Mexico and Egypt in what he sees as the emergence of a new mode of operation in the World Heritage Committee. The above-mentioned phase of conceptual reform in the 1990s was largely expert-driven, somewhat against the conservationists' ingrained habitus, since their everyday practice is heavily steeped in national traditions and legal frameworks. The procedural refinement or, depending on the viewpoint, procedural hypertrophy of the 2000s occurred when the career diplomats sent by member states to UNESCO took precedence. This too reflects the growing importance of World Heritage. While the experts remain, these diplomats now lead most of the delegations and determine the strategies. One might posit that they are more cosmopolitan than the heritage experts, but their career prospects are much more closely tied to their national responsibilities. Since the 2010 session in Brasilia, the general respect previously accorded to the Advisory Bodies and their recommendations has declined (Meskell 2013a), and the frustration and impatience among BRICS states and other regional leaders of the Global South was decisive. Incoming Committee members from the "old guard" such as Germany or Japan, however, have swiftly adapted since they are equally intent on seeing their sites achieve World Heritage status. Even when diplomats are not under orders from their home ministries, they often prioritize smooth international relations and a sense of global equity and fairness over the conservation of specific sites. As Meskell (2014) has detailed for Panamá Viejo, the historical quarter of Panama City, lobbying states and the corporations that drive them secure Committee support well before the meetings, and obviously counterfactual claims and violations of given promises may go unsanctioned. There is opposition to the new trend, with Sweden, Switzerland, and Estonia being outspoken critics in recent sessions. Yet, given that in terms of World Heritage properties per population, they lead their Committee peers by far, they may be under a correspondingly weaker domestic pressure to attain further listings at all costs, such that they can afford to refrain from the exchange of favors that is believed to expedite this objective (Brumann 2011: 37, 2014b).

In this regard, it will be interesting to see how full press access and the web-streaming of World Heritage Committee sessions begun at the 2012 session in St. Petersburg will influence their future evolution. This innovation was decided upon one year earlier by clearly inattentive delegates and surprised many when it was announced. Reformists had hoped that this change in procedure would have a positive, tempering influence on diplomatic negotiations during the sessions. Yet, while some delegations were now rumored to receive text messages from home ministries detailing and prescribing their every move (Brumann 2014b), no immediate effect on session behavior was initially apparent. A year later, however, Britta Rudolff (personal communication) saw some delegates as moving to yet another new mode of operation: conscious of increased global visibility, much of their remarks were no longer just instrumentally directed to their Committee colleagues but also intended as statements of cultural diplomacy, targeting the online observers whose number is sure to increase over the coming years. World Heritage Committee sessions therefore are also a laboratory for observing the effects of procedural changes in a prominent intergovernmental setting, and to follow these will be one of the research tasks for the future.

Along with other anthropologists researching UN organizations (Bendix 2013; Müller 2013; Wright 1998) and the complex political negotiations therein, our work traces how UNESCO processes have global impacts, albeit in often unexpected and unpredictable ways that are not always revealed in official agendas. Following Müller (2013: 10), international bureaucracies help nation states to perform their "transparency" – a word used more and more in World Heritage Committee meetings – that typically hides as much as it reveals. She asserts that when anthropologists study the actions of individuals and states within international agencies, these bodies appear at the same time more active, contradictory, and perhaps even less "rational." Yet, as we argue, if researchers rely solely on the documents, substantive political issues are often masked as technical ones. Documentary data only gain depth and salience if researchers have the necessary insights into the processes that produced them, according to Bendix (2013: 25). One has to consider the relationships and the hierarchies among those who produced the texts and the difference between fully capturing the discussions in the room and what was formalized into a record for posterity. We suggest that "being there" is essential to track the global machinations playing out today in the new world heritage order.

NOTES

1 UNESCO defines Outstanding Universal Value (OUV) as cultural and/or natural significance that is so exceptional as to transcend national boundaries and to be of common importance for present and future generations of all humanity. Statements of Outstanding Universal Value are made up of several elements: a brief description of the property, a Statement of Significance, a Statement of Authenticity, a Statement of Integrity, and a section describing how the World Heritage site is protected and managed.
2 UNESCO, *World Heritage List*. Available at: http://whc.unesco.org/en/list. Accessed December 1, 2014.
3 UNESCO, *World Heritage List Statistics*. Available at: http://whc.unesco.org/en/list/stat. Accessed December 1, 2014.
4 UNESCO, *World Heritage List*. Available at: http://whc.unesco.org/en/list. Accessed December 1, 2014.
5 See World Heritage Committee Eighteenth session, Phuket, Thailand,12-17 November 1994, Expert meeting on the "Global Strategy" and thematic studies for a representative World Heritage List. Available at: whc.unesco.org/archive/global94.htm#debut. Accessed December 1, 2014.
6 UNESCO, *World Heritage List*. Birthplace of Jesus: Church of the Nativity and the Pilgrimage Route, Bethlehem. Available at: http://whc.unesco.org/en/list/1433. Accessed December 1, 2014.
7 University of Toronto, BRICS Information Centre, Sanya Declaration, April 14, 2011. Available at: http://www.hcindia-au.org/pdf/Sanya%20Declaration.pdf. Accessed December 3, 2014.

REFERENCES

Aas, C., A. Ladkin, and J. Fletcher (2005) Stakeholder collaboration and heritage management. *Annals of Tourism Research* 32: 28–48.
Alberts, H. C. and H. D. Hazen (2010) Maintaining authenticity and integrity and Cultural World Heritage Sites. *The Geographical Review* 100: 56–73.
Allais, L. (2013) Integrities: The salvage of Abu Simbel. *Grey Room* 50: 6–45.
Arantes, A. A. (2007) Diversity, heritage and cultural politics. *Theory, Culture and Society* 24: 290–296.
Araoz, G. F. (2011) Preserving heritage places under a new paradigm. *Journal of Cultural Heritage Management and Sustainable Development* 1: 55–60.

Askew, M. (2010) The magic list of global status: UNESCO, World Heritage and the agendas of states, in S. Labadi and C. Long (eds), *Heritage and Globalisation*. London: Routledge, pp. 19–44.

Assi, E. (2012) World heritage sites, human rights and cultural heritage in Palestine. *International Journal of Heritage Studies* 18: 316–323.

Bandarin, F. (2007) *World Heritage: Challenges for the Millennium*. Paris: UNESCO.

Bendix, R. (2013) The power of perseverance: Exploring the negotiation dynamics at the World Intellectual Property Organization, in B. Müller (ed.), *The Gloss of Harmony: The Politics of Policy-Making in Multilateral Organisations*. London: Pluto Press, pp. 23–45.

Berliner, D. (2010) Perdre l'esprit du lieu: Les politiques de l'Unesco à Luang Prabang (RDP Lao). *Terrain* 2: 90–105.

Berliner, D. (2012) Multiple nostalgias: The fabric of heritage in Luang Prabang (Lao PDR). *Journal of the Royal Anthropological Institute* 18: 769–786.

Bertacchini, E. and D. Saccone (2012) Toward a political economy of World Heritage. *Journal of Cultural Economics* 36: 327–352.

Bertacchini, E., D. Saccone, and W. Santagata (2009) *Enhancing the valorisation of UNESCO World Heritage Sites: a Pigouvian Approach*. Working Paper, International Centre for Research on the Economics of Culture, Institutions, and Creativity, University of Turin.

Bertacchini, E., D. Saccone, and W. Santagata (2011) Embracing diversity, correcting inequalities: Towards a new global governance for the UNESCO World Heritage. *International Journal of Cultural Policy* 17: 278–288.

Bertacchini, E., D. Saccone, and S. Walter (2010) *Loving diversities, correcting inequalities: A proposal for a world heritage tax*. Working Paper, International Centre for Research on the Economics of Culture, Institutions, and Creativity, University of Turin.

Bortolotto, C. (2007) From objects to processes: UNESCO's intangible cultural heritage. *Journal of Museum Ethnography* 19: 21–33.

Bortolotto, C. (2010) Globalising intangible cultural heritage? Between international arenas and local appropriations, in S. Labadi and C. Long (eds), *Heritage and Globalisation*. London: Routledge, pp. 97–114.

Bortolotto, C. (ed.) (2011) *Le patrimoine culturel immatériel: Enjeux d'une nouvelle catégorie*. Paris: Maison de Sciences de l'Homme.

Bouasria, A. (2001) ISESCO and The International Knowledge Order: Pro-action, reaction or in-action. *The American Journal of Islamic Social Science* 18: 63–88.

Brattli, T. (2009) Managing the archaeological world cultural heritage: Consensus or rhetoric? *Norweigian Archaeological Review* 42: 24–39.

Breen, C. (2007) Advocacy, international development and World Heritage sites in sub-Saharan Africa. *World Archaeology* 39: 355–370.

Breglia, L. C. (2005) Keeping World Heritage in the family: A genealogy of Maya labour at Chichén Itzá. *International Journal of Heritage Studies* 11: 385–398.

Breglia, L. C. (forthcoming) The business of wonder: Public meets private at the World Heritage site of Chichén Itzá, in C. Brumann and D. Berliner (eds), *World Heritage on the Ground: Ethnographic Perspectives*.

Brockington, D. and J. Igoe (2006) Eviction for conservation: A global overview. *Conservation and Society* 4: 424–470.

Brown, M. M. (2004) The UNDP's commitment to defend cultural diversity with UNESCO. *Museum International* 56: 18–23.

Brown, W. (2010) *Walled States, Waning Sovereignty*. New York: Zone Books.

Brumann, C. (2009) Outside the glass case: The social life of urban heritage in Kyoto. *American Ethnologist* 36: 276–299.

Brumann, C. (2011) Unser aller Kulturgut: Eine ethnologische Annäherung an das UNESCO-Welterbe. *Sociologus* 61: 19–43.

Brumann, C. (2012) *Multilateral ethnography: Entering the World Heritage arena*. Max Planck Institute for Social Anthropology Working Papers, Vol. 136.

Brumann, C. (2013) Comment le patrimoine mondial de l'Unesco devient immatériel. *Gradhiva* 18: 5–29.

Brumann, C. (2014a) Heritage agnosticism: A third path for the study of cultural heritage. *Social Anthropology* 22: 73–88.

Brumann, C. (2014b) Shifting tides of world-making in the UNESCO World Heritage Convention: Cosmopolitanisms colliding. *Ethnic and Racial Studies* 37: 2176–2192.

Bruner, E. M. (1996) Tourism in Ghana: The representation of slavery and the return of the black diaspora. *American Anthropologist* 98: 290–304.

Carter, J. (2010) Displacing indigenous cultural landscapes: The naturalistic gaze at Fraser Island World Heritage area. *Geographical Research* 48: 398–410.

Choay, F. (2001) *The Invention of the Historic Monument*. Cambridge: Cambridge University Press.

Claudi, I. B. (2011) The New Kids on the Block: BRICs in the World Heritage Committee. M.A. thesis, Department of Political Science, University of Oslo, Norway.

De Cesari, C. (2010a) Creative heritage: Palestinian heritage NGOs and defiant arts of government. *American Anthropologist* 112: 625–637.

De Cesari, C. (2010b) World Heritage and mosaic universalism. *Journal of Social Archaeology* 10: 299–324.

Di Giovine, M. A. (2009) *The Heritage-Scape: UNESCO, World Heritage, and Tourism*. Lanham, MD: Lexington Books.

Disko, S. (2010) World Heritage Sites in Indigenous Peoples' Territories: Ways of Ensuring Respect for Indigenous Cultures, Values and Human Rights, in D. Offenhäußer, W. Zimmerli, and M.-T. Alberts (eds), *World Heritage and Cultural Diversity*. Cottbus: German Commission for UNESCO, pp. 167–177.

Droit, R.-P. (2005) *Humanity in the Making: Overview of the Intellectual History of UNESCO 1945–2005*. Paris: UNESCO.

Ekern, S., W. Logan, B. Sauge, and A. Sinding-Larsen (2012) Human rights and World Heritage: preserving our common dignity through rights-based approaches to site management. *International Journal of Heritage Studies* 18: 213–225.

Eriksen, T. H. (2001) Between universalism and relativism: A critique of the UNESCO concept of culture, in J. K. Cowan, M.-B. Dembour, and R. Wilson (eds), *Culture and Rights: Anthropological Perspectives*. Cambridge: Cambridge University Press, pp. 127–148.

Eriksen, T. H. (2009) Between universalism and relativism: A critique of the UNESCO concept of culture, in M. Goodale (ed.), *Human Rights: An Anthropological Reader*. Oxford: Wiley Blackwell, pp. 356–371.

Esterhuysen, A. (2009) Undermining heritage. *South African Archaeological Bulletin* 64: 1–3.

Ferdinand, P. (2012) Rising powers at the UN: An analysis of the voting behaviour of BRICSAM states in the General Assembly, 1974–2008. Paper presented at 'Rising Powers and the Future of Global Governance,' 16–17 May 2012, University of Sussex, UK.

Frey, B. S. and P. Pamini (2009) Making world heritage truly global: The Culture Certificate Scheme. *Oxonomics* 4: 1–9.

Frey, B. S., P. Pamini, and L. Steiner (2011) *What determines the World Heritage List? An econometric analysis*. University of Zurich Department of Economics, Working Paper No. 1.

Frey, B. S. and L. Steiner (2011) World Heritage List: Does it make sense? *International Journal of Cultural Policy* 17: 555–573.

Gfeller, A. E. (2013) Negotiating the meaning of global heritage: "Cultural landscapes" in the UNESCO World Heritage Convention, 1972–1992. *Journal of Global History* 8: 483–503.

Hafstein, V. T. (2009) Intangible heritage as a list: From masterpieces to representation, in L. Smith and N. Akagawa (eds), *Intangible Heritage*. London: Routledge, pp. 93–111.

Hales, R. J., J. Rynne, C. Howlett, J. Devine, and V. Hauser (2012) Indigenous free prior informed consent: A case for self determination in World Heritage nomination processes. *International Journal of Heritage Studies* 19(3): 1–18.

Hannigan, J. (2006) *Environmental Sociology*. London: Routledge.
Harrison, R. (2012) *Heritage: Critical Approaches*. London: Routledge.
Hassan, F. (2007) The Aswan High Dam and the International Rescue Nubia Campaign. *African Archaeological Review* 24: 73–94.
Hauser-Schäublin, B. (2011) Preah Vihear: From Object of Colonial Desire to a Contested World Heritage Site, in B. Hauser-Schäublin (ed.), *World Heritage, Angkor and Beyond: Circumstances and Implications of UNESCO Listings in Cambodia*. Göttingen Studies in Cultural Property 2. Göttingen: Universitätsverlag Göttingen, pp. 33–56.
Hoggart, R. (2011) *An Idea and Its Servants: UNESCO from Within*. Piscataway, NJ: Transaction.
Isar, Y. R. (2011) UNESCO and Heritage: Global Doctrine and Global Practice, in H. K. Anheier and Y. R. Isar (eds), *Cultures and Globalization: Heritage, Memory and Identity*. London: Sage, pp. 39–52.
Istasse, M. (2011) Unesco World Heritage and Tourist Development in Fez, Morocco, in L. Bourdeau and S. Chassé (eds), *Actes du colloque sites du patrimoine et tourisme, 2–4 juin 2010, Québec, Canada*. Quebec: Presses de l'Université Laval, pp. 645–656.
Jokilehto, J. (2006) World Heritage: Defining the outstanding universal value. *City and Time* 2: 1–10.
Jokilehto, J. (2012) Human rights and cultural heritage. Observations on the recognition of human rights in the international doctrine. *International Journal of Heritage Studies* 18: 226–230.
Jokilehto, J. and C. Cameron (2008) *The World Heritage List: What Is OUV?: Defining the Outstanding Universal Value of Cultural World Heritage Properties*. Berlin: Bässler.
Jørgensen, J. H. and G. Hønneland (2006) Implementing global nature protection agreements in Russia. *Journal of International Wildlife Law and Policy* 9: 33–53.
Joy, C. (2011a) Negotiating material identities: Young men and modernity in Djenné. *Journal of Material Culture* 16: 389–400.
Joy, C. (2011b) *The Politics of Heritage Management in Mali: From UNESCO to Djenné*. Walnut Creek, CA: Left Coast Press.
Kawharu, M. (2009) Ancestral landscapes and world heritage from a Maori viewpoint. *Journal of the Polynesian Society* 118: 317–338.
Kuutma, K. (2007) The Politics of Contested Representation: UNESCO and the Masterpieces of Intangible Cultural Heritage, in D. Hemme, M. Tauschek, and R. Bendix (eds), *Prädikat "Heritage": Wertschöpfungen aus kulturellen Ressourcen*. Studien zur Kulturanthropologie/Europäischen Ethnologie. Berlin: Lit, pp. 177–196.
Labadi, S. (2005) A review of the Global Strategy for a balanced, representative and credible World Heritage List 1994–2004. *Conservation and Management of Archaeological Sites* 7: 89–102.
Labadi, S. (2007) Representations of the nation and cultural diversity in discourses on World Heritage. *Journal of Social Archaeology* 7: 147–170.
Labadi, S. (2013) *UNESCO, Cultural Heritage and Outstanding Universal Value*. Walnut Creek, CA: AltaMira Press.
Lafrenz Samuels, K. (2009) Trajectories of development: International heritage management of archaeology in the Middle East and North Africa. *Archaeologies* 5: 68–91.
Landorf, C. (2009) Managing for sustainable tourism: A review of six cultural World Heritage Sites. *Journal of Sustainable Tourism* 17: 53–70.
Leask, A. and A. Fyall (2006) *Managing World Heritage Sites*. London: Routledge.
Lemelin, R. H. and N. Bennett (2010) The proposed Pimachiowin Aki World Heritage Site project: Management and protection of Indigenous World Heritage sites in a Canadian context. *Leisure/Loisir* 34: 169–187.
Logan, W. (2009) Playing the devil's advocate: Protecting intangible cultural heritage and the infringement of human rights. *Historic Environment* 22: 14–18.
Logan, W. (2012a) Cultural diversity, cultural heritage and human rights: Towards heritage management as human rights-based cultural practice. *International Journal of Heritage Studies* 18: 231–244.

Logan, W. (2012b) States, governance and the politics of culture: World heritage in Asia, in P. Daly and T. Winter (eds), *Handbook of Heritage in Asia*. London: Routledge, pp. 113–128.

Logan, W. (2013) Australia, indigenous peoples and World Heritage from Kakadu to Cape York: State Party behaviour under the World Heritage Convention. *Journal of Social Archaeology* 13(2): 153–176.

Luke, C. and M. M. Kersel (2012) *Soft Power, Hard Heritage: U.S. Cultural Diplomacy and Archaeology*. London: Routledge.

Marquart, V. (2014), Insurmountable tension? On the relation of World Heritage and rapid urban transformation in Istanbul. *European Journal of Turkish Studies* 19. Available online at http://ejts.revues.org/5044.

Meskell, L. M. (2010) Human rights and heritage ethics. *Anthropological Quarterly* 83: 839–860.

Meskell, L. M. (2011) From Paris to Pontdrift: UNESCO meetings, Mapungubwe and mining. *South African Archaeological Bulletin* 66: 149–156.

Meskell, L. M. (2012) The rush to inscribe: Reflections on the 35th Session of the World Heritage Committee, UNESCO Paris, 2011. *Journal of Field Archaeology* 37: 145–151.

Meskell, L. (2013a) UNESCO's World Heritage Convention at 40: Challenging the economic and political order of international heritage conservation. *Current Anthropology* 54: 483–494.

Meskell, L. M. (2013b) UNESCO and the fate of the World Heritage Indigenous Peoples Council of Experts (WHIPCOE). *International Journal of Cultural Property* 20: 155–174.

Meskell, L. (2014) States of conservation: Protection, politics, and pacting within UNESCO's World Heritage Committee. *Anthropological Quarterly* 87: 217–244.

Meskell, L. M., C. Liuzza, E. Bertacchini, and D. Saccone (2014) Multilateralism and UNESCO World Heritage: Decision making, states parties and political processes. *International Journal of Heritage Studies* 21(3).

Müller, B. (2013) Lifting the Veil of Harmony: Anthropologists Approach International Organizations, in B. Müller (ed.), *The Gloss of Harmony: The Politics of Policy-Making in Multilateral Organisations*. London: Pluto Press, pp. 1–20.

Nielsen, B. (2011) UNESCO and the 'right' kind of culture: Bureaucratic production and articulation. *Critique of Anthropology* 31: 273–292.

O'Neill, J. (2001) *Building Better Global Economic BRICs*. New York: The Goldman Sachs Group.

Pavone, V. (2008) *From the Labyrinth of the World to the Paradise of the Heart: Science and Humanism in UNESCO's Approach to Globalization*. New York: Lexington.

Pendlebury, J., M. Short, and A. While (2009) Urban World Heritage Sites and the problem of authenticity. *Cities* 26: 349–358.

Probst, P. (2004) Keeping the goddess alive: Performing culture and remembering the past in Osogbo, Nigeria. *Social Analysis* 48: 33–54.

Probst, P. (2011) *Osogbo and the Art of Heritage: Monuments, Deities, and Money. African Expressive Cultures*. Bloomington: Indiana University Press.

Rao, K. (2010) A new paradigm for the identification, nomination and inscription of properties on the World Heritage List. *International Journal of Heritage Studies* 16: 161–172.

Rico, T. (2008) Negative heritage: The place of conflict in world heritage. *Conservation and Management of Archaeological Sites* 10: 344–352.

Rico, T. (2011) The Heritage of Aftermath: Making "Heritage at Risk" in Post-Tsnumai Banda Aceh. Ph.D. dissertation, Department of Anthropology, Stanford University, California.

Rössler, M. (2003) Linking Nature and Culture: World Heritage Cultural Landscapes, in *Cultural Landscapes: the Challenges of Conservation*. World Heritage Papers 7. Paris: UNESCO, pp. 10–15.

Rudolff, B. (2010) *"Intangible" and "Tangible" Heritage. A Topology of Culture in Contexts of Faith*. Bonn: Scientia Bonnensis.

Saccone, D. and E. Bertacchini (2011) *Culture, heritage and economic development – empowering developing countries*. Working Paper, International Centre for Research on the Economics of Culture, Institutions, and Creativity, University of Turin.

Salamandra, C. (2004) *A New Old Damascus: Authenticity and Distinction in Urban Syria*. Indiana series in Middle East studies. Bloomington: Indiana University Press.

Scham, S. and A. Yahya (2003) Heritage and reconciliation. *Journal of Social Archaeology* 3: 399–416.

Schmitt, T. M. (2008) The UNESCO concept of safeguarding intangible cultural heritage: Its background and Marrakchi roots. *International Journal of Heritage Studies* 14: 95–111.

Schmitt, T. M. (2009) Global cultural governance: Decision-making concerning world heritage between politics and science. *Erdkunde* 63: 103–121.

Schmitt, T. M. (2012) *Cultural Governance: Zur Kulturgeographie Des UNESCO-Welterberegimes*. Wiesbaden: Franz Steiner.

Shepherd, R. (2006) UNESCO and the politics of cultural heritage in Tibet. *Journal of Contemporary Asia* 36: 243–257.

Sinding-Larsen, A. (2012) Lhasa community, world heritage and human rights. *International Journal of Heritage Studies* 18: 297–306.

Singh, J. P. (2011) *United Nations Educational, Scientific and Cultural Organization (UNESCO): Creating Norms for a Complex World*. London: Routledge.

Smith, L. (2006) *Uses of Heritage*. New York: Routledge.

Steiner, L. and B. S. Frey (2012) Correcting the imbalance of the world heritage list: Did the UNESCO strategy work. *Journal of International Organizations Studies* 3: 25–40.

Stoczkowski, W. (2009) UNESCO's doctrine of human diversity: A secular soteriology? *Anthropology Today* 25: 7–11.

Stott, P. H. (2011) The World Heritage Convention and the National Park Service, 1962–1972. *The George White Forum* 28: 279–290.

Stovel, H. (2007) Effective use of authenticity and integrity as world heritage qualifying conditions. *City and Time* 2: 21–36.

Tauschek, M. (2013) *Kulturerbe: Eine Einführung*. Berlin: Reimer.

Titchen, S. M. (1996) On the construction of "outstanding universal value": Some comments on the implementation of the 1972 UNESCO World Heritage Convention. *Conservation and Management of Archaeological Sites* 1: 235–242.

Turtinen, J. (2000) *Globalising Heritage: On UNESCO and the Transnational Construction of a World Heritage*. Stockholm: Stockholm Center for Organizational Research.

Turtinen, J. (2006) Väldsarvets villkor: Intressen, förhandlinger och bruk i internationell politik. Ph.D. dissertation, University of Stockholm, Sweden.

UNESCO (2003) *Convention for the Safeguarding of the Intangible Cultural Heritage*. Document No. MISC/2003/CLT/CH/14. Paris: UNESCO.

UNESCO (2005) *Convention on the Protection and Promotion of the Diversity of Cultural Expressions*.

UNESCO (2011) *Evaluation of the Global Strategy and the PACT Initiative*. WHC-11/35. COM/9A. 27 May 2011. Paris: UNESCO.

Vadi, V. S. (2013) When cultures collide: Foreign direct investment, natural resources, and indigenous heritage in international investment law. *Columbia Human Rights Law Review* 28: 123–143.

Valderrama, F. (1995) *A History of UNESCO*. Paris: UNESCO.

van Blarcoma, B. L. and C. Kayahana (2011) Assessing the economic impact of a UNESCO World Heritage designation. *Journal of Heritage Tourism* 6: 143–164.

Wallerstein, I. R. (1974) *The Modern World-System: Capitalist Agriculture and the Origins of the European World-Economy in the Sixteenth Century*. New York: Academic Press.

Ween, G. B. (2012) World Heritage and Indigenous rights: Norwegian examples. *International Journal of Heritage Studies* 18: 257–270.

West, P., J. Igoe, and D. Brockington (2006) Parks and people: The social impacts of protected areas. *Annual Review of Anthropology* 35: 251–277.
Willems, W. and D. Comer (2011) Africa, archaeology, and World Heritage. *Conservation and Management of Archaeological Sites* 13: 160–173.
Winter, T. (2007) *Post-Conflict Heritage, Postcolonial Tourism: Tourism, Politics and Development at Angkor*. London: Routledge.
Winter, T. (2011) The Political Economies of Heritage, in H. K. Anheier and Y. R. Isar (eds), *Cultures and Globalization: Heritage, Memory and Identity*. London: Sage, pp. 70–138.
Wolfrum, R. (2009) Common Heritage of Mankind, in R. Wolfrum (ed.), *Max Planck Encyclopedia of Public International Law*. Oxford: Oxford University Press.
Wright, S. (1998) The politicization of "culture." *Anthropology Today* 14: 7–15.
Zacharias, D. (2010) The UNESCO Regime for the Protection of World Heritage as Prototype of an Autonomy-Gaining International Institution, in A. von Bogdandy (ed.), *The Exercise of Public Authority by International Institutions*. Berlin: Springer, pp. 301–336.

2

Neoliberalism, Heritage Regimes, and Cultural Rights

Rosemary J. Coombe and Lindsay M. Weiss

Introduction

The critical study of cultural heritage faces crucial challenges if it is to fully attend to fundamental shifts in the global political economy and global approaches to heritage protection. Heritage studies needs a more anthropologically nuanced and theoretically informed understanding of neoliberalism, governmentality, and human rights to address the changing conditions of heritage regulation and to understand the political struggles in which new "heritagized" claims are now imbricated. Although we find the dominant modes of critique characteristic of heritage studies to be too narrow to address the configurations of these contemporary arenas of governance, we highlight critical scholarship that is advancing these insights in an incremental fashion.

Under conditions of neoliberalism, we are witnessing shifts from liberal state-based regimes of protection of patrimony (understood as state property) to multiscalar and multisectoral assemblages of governmental regulation. The enactment of government policy relies increasingly upon the self-empowerment of capacitated citizens and self-organized communities in marketized relationships which position cultural heritage as a resource. Both "government through freedom" (Rose 1999: xxiii) and the "double-movement of commodification" (Polanyi 2001 [1944]), provoke rights-based discourses and practices in new forms of culturalized "politics" that exceed and may even be illegible to the state, but appeal to a wider variety of publics.

First, we move beyond the narrow understanding of neoliberalism characteristic of heritage studies to delineate dimensions of the critical study of neoliberalism particularly relevant to understanding heritage governance under conditions in which culture is a resource for new forms of capital accumulation. Rights-based practices and discourses function as a means by which the limits of governmentality are expressed by peoples who bring their own cultural resources to bear upon governmental demands that they employ culture as a resource. Such social articulations serve to enlarge rights-based discourse and practice in fields of heritage politics. Heritage scholars can

Global Heritage: A Reader, First Edition. Edited by Lynn Meskell.

only recognize such struggles to the extent that they move beyond a formalist and institutionally based understanding of human rights, adopting and adapting the perspectives of legal and cultural anthropologists who have fundamentally transformed social science understandings of human rights since the turn of the century.

Neoliberalism in Heritage Studies and Anthropology

The concept of neoliberalism is so ubiquitous that some scholars complain that it has lost all meaning. Others insist upon abandoning it as a noun and decry its use as an all-encompassing negative epithet. In heritage studies, neoliberalism is used as a generic adjective for states, policies, and economic practices, a process of economizing heritage goods and/or promoting socio-economic development in competitive global economies. It is often conflated with economic globalization and the instrumental expansion of international tourism.

Many heritage scholars characterize neoliberalism as an ideology privileging economic rationality that has contributed to a profit-driven conception of heritage; others describe it as "an ideological approach to the state"s role in economy and society" (Gattinger and Saint-Pierre 2010: 280). Herzfeld defines it as "an ideology based upon the centrality of rights to individual choice" that encourages competitive relations and "engenders a 'dominant model' of the past and thereby 'reifies experience'" (2009: 114, 120). We disagree with the reduction of neoliberalism to ideology, and will argue, instead, that if heritage studies were to engage in more sustained conversation with the anthropology of neoliberalism, it could make some unique contributions.

Reconfiguring the state

Only recently have heritage scholars begun to engage in dialogue with the theoretical debates and ethnographic research on neoliberalism in the wider fields of anthropology and political geography. In these larger debates, neoliberalism is not understood primarily as an ideology or an economic system, but as an inescapably *political* program best understood through "its realisation in the form of variously reconfigured, re-engineered, restructured and redeployed states, in contrast with the generative (and still pervasive) myths of state withdrawal" (Peck and Theodore 2012: 181). Critical heritage scholarship is focusing new attention upon the state (e.g., Bendix et al. 2012), and, in so doing, challenging this same simplification. Today the market is the state's organizing principle and effective governance "is measured with reference to asset management, to the attraction of enterprise, to the facilitation of the entrepreneurial activities of the citizen as *homo economicus*, and to the capacity to foster accumulation" (Comaroff 2011: 145).

Generally, theorists of neoliberalism have addressed it as field of contemporary regulatory transformation (Brenner, Peck, and Theodore 2010) that is not predominantly ideological, but rather a project of imposing market disciplinary regulatory forms in restructured territories. Anthropology has made significant contributions to this field, contesting totalizing visions of the overreach and underspecification of political economy and contributing to an understanding of neoliberalism as a variegated process facilitating "marketization and commodification while simultaneously *intensifying* the uneven development of regulatory forms across places, territories, and scales" (Brenner, Peck, and Theodore 2010: 184).

Anthropological work developing the Foucaultian concept of governmentality has been particularly influential in its focus upon rationalities of government, technologies of government, and subjects of government; "that is, the diverse types of selves, persons, actors, agents, or identities that emerge from and inform governmental activity" (Inda 2005: 10). When exploring rationalities of government, states are not treated as unified autonomous actors, ruling domestically and pursuing interests upon the world stage, but rather as a specific (modern liberal) way of dividing a "political" from other non-political spheres in which certain technologies of government are given institutional durability (Rose and Miller 2010: 275). The state, however, is only one means of accomplishing this.

Recent work on heritage similarly recognizes neoliberal restructuring, not as a withdrawal of the state, but as a new distribution of governmental powers in which nations, sovereignty, territories, and rights are reconfigured. Instead of any simple abandonment of heritage management to local authorities, for instance, we witness a devolution of authority to new agencies and coalitions of agencies, joint partnerships, public–private alliances, and multiscalar assemblages of NGOs, international authorities, and transnational agencies (Coombe 2012: 378). A proliferation of relevant fields of authority, influence, and decision making in heritage policy work increasingly make simple state–society dichotomies difficult to maintain when heritage governance is constituted synergistically through international policy, national legislation, local rules, and market demands.

An interpenetration of civil society, state, and market forces may increasingly be the norm. In China it appears that World Heritage site nomination criteria assembles both public and private entities in new cohesions, while legitimating a larger scope of municipal autonomy than would otherwise be permitted under the authoritarian state (Wang 2011). Exploring heritage governance in the Caribbean, Scher (2010, 2011) shows how the reconfigured neoliberal state is manifest in increasingly dispersed cultural interventions including transnational and decentralized institutional oversight backed by new legal protections for diversifying cultural markets. Kockel (2012) suggests that "the state" can refer to any of a number of levels of governance, or a combination thereof, represented by the coordinated activity of agents from different sectors supported by various NGOs. A governmental approach to neoliberal heritage must therefore explore discursive and non-discursive practices in "sites situated in liminal zones of standard institutionalist cartographies" (Brenner, Peck, and Theodore 2010: 199).

Technologies

If anthropological approaches to neoliberalism approach the state differently, they do so with an awareness that government operates via technologies (Ong 2007) – mundane programs, calculations, apparatuses, techniques, forms of examination, and processes of assessment, through which "governing at a distance" is accomplished. These are understood as "technologies of subjectification" (Hilgers 2010: 359), which seek to make locales and persons "capable of bearing a kind of regulated freedom" (Rose and Miller 2010: 272). Rather than constraining people, the cultivation of personal autonomy is one means through which such technology does its social work. Ethnographically grounded illustrations are needed to "track the haphazard migration of governmental techniques and programming technologies, their deployment in diverse sociopolitical settings, and their eclectic translation and operationalization" (Brenner, Peck, and Theodore 2010: 199). Heritage management is clearly accomplished through increasingly specialized technologies of inventory, notation, digital preservation, site monitoring, and inscription, all of which shape subjective agencies, suggesting that heritage scholars have a great deal to contribute to these larger conversations.

Scholars critical of heritage regimes have long been concerned with the social consequences of activities that quantify, audit, and represent cultural goods and practices in ways that may be alien to or misrepresent local communities. From a governmentality perspective, however, "the "representation" of that which is to be governed is itself an active, technical process" (Rose and Miller 2010: 283) that dynamically intervenes in rather than passively represents or misrepresents social realities. In short, it is a central means through which reality is made stable, subject to evaluation, calculation, and intervention. The design and use of inventories, cultural mappings, traditional knowledge registers, and 3-D renderings are but a few means by which cultural resources are rendered legible as forms of governmental power. To enjoin others "to write things down and count them" is to exercise a form of government "without encroaching upon their 'freedom' or 'autonomy'" and "often precisely by offering to maximize it" (Rose and Miller 2010: 285). This would seem to be especially the case when people are asked to count, map, and inscribe those sites, artifacts, practices, and landscapes they believe (or are led to believe) best distinguish, define, and identify them, as they are when their cultural heritage is under valuation (Buchli 2013).

In global heritage politics, we see enhanced priority given to practices of mapping and inventorying cultural properties, qualities, and attributes of significance while making these legible through new forms of documentation, archiving, and publication (Bennett 2007; Hafstein 2009; Tauschek 2012). Multilateral institutions and transnational corporations increasingly configure cultural diversity and heritage resources as a form of currency subject to international surveillance and scientific control. States and local authorities are encouraged to treat these as forms of capital to be developed and marketed, and seek international partnerships with holders of the necessary expertise to effectively accomplish this. Communities may also shape these demands to new ends.

Heritage governmentality prompts extended surveys and inventories of cultural sites and practices, as well as new regulations pertaining to authenticity and who constitutes a legitimate "stakeholder," "tradition bearer," or local expert (Collins 2012; Coombe 2012; Ellis 2012; Scher 2011; Smith 2007; Vrasti 2013). Becoming a heritage subject entails being subjected to the political technologies of the state and the managerialist gaze of transnational governmental actors and is a means of making visible and tangible what was previously intangible and taken for granted (De Cesari 2012: 409) for purposes of intervention (Arantes 2007; Meskell and Brumann in this volume; Waterton and Smith 2010). As De Cesari summarizes, heritage governmentality encompasses diverse "ways of shaping people's behavior by applying specialized bodies of knowledge" recognized as expertise (2012: 401).

Communities of experts emerge in parallel with neoliberal techniques for "constituting persons as owing allegiance to a particular locus of identity and authority, assembling subjects, and inculcating skills and solidarities" (Rose and Miller 2010: 276). Heritage resource management in particular mobilizes new fields of expertise in its practices of subject formation. For example, in the Azores archipelago, the protected area of Sete Cidades is home to a community increasingly subject to both environmental regulatory measures and government-sponsored conservation models (da Silva 2014). Enduring restrictive land tenure contracts and oversight by biologists, environmental engineers, and NGO agents working within the protected landscape, all of whom profess superior expertise, local residents assert their "culturally specific collective identity" (da Silva 2014: 9) as the source of an alternative expertise grounded in traditional ecological knowledge and practices of resource management. They challenge new impositions of "eco-governmentality" by affirmatively embracing the subject position of stewardship historically taken up by indigenous peoples under global biodiversity norms; in so doing, however, they may subject themselves to unanticipated demands. Lafrenz-Samuels nicely describes neoliberal heritage institutions as building local capacity by fostering "internal modes of self-monitoring and self-discipline" in areas in which "the hegemony of expert knowledge is masked by a discourse of cosmopolitanism which privileges a localized diversity that must be managed by inculcating the correct habituations of local subjects in the ostensible objective of alleviating poverty" (2010: 205–206).

Subjectification

Neoliberalism is marked by new modes of subjectification that shape social agents to enable competitive relations in markets by "capacitating" people to bear a kind of regulated freedom as "responsibilized" individuals or communities (Brenner, Peck, and Theodore 2010). The molding of new subjectivities is crucial to harnessing cultural goods and practices as heritage resources, optimizing agents to maximize advantages as "autonomized" entities in extended markets, a process that requires social agents be invested with possessive attitudes and vested with proprietary rights so as to engage in market relations.

Many generic observations support this. Archaeologists, as contracted specialists, strategically balance the requirements of impact assessment reports with site-based needs for commercial funding, while grappling with professional techniques for incorporating local community expertise (Hollowell and Nicholas 2009). Entrepreneurial state heritage administrators facilitate rapid permit granting for commercial development of tourist heritage zones and solicit private contracts via corporate social initiatives for heritage development, while navigating policies advocating best practices in heritage management. Volunteer groups and tourists are enrolled in the assumption of responsibilities for local heritage development – channeled through allegedly "non-governmental" organizations (Vrasti 2013). Mining companies on resource frontiers practice corporate social responsibility, funding local heritage projects that facilitate community capacitation to meet global industry standards and displacing public authorities to further entrench private regulation (Coombe and Baird in press; Meskell 2011, 2012; Paterson and Telesetsky 2012), sometimes even organizing and funding heritage governance by way of providing "cultural heritage offsets" (Seagle 2013).

Neoliberalism is supported by globalizing processes driven by information technologies, in which, as heritage scholars are slowly recognizing, culture is not only drawn into relations of economic exchange but becomes a force of production in its own right (Long and Labadi 2010). We see an accelerated imposition of new forms of ownership to encourage tourism, foster foreign direct investment, promote product differentiation, and otherwise capitalize upon cultural resources for sustainable development. Given the relationship between informational technologies and informational capital, topics of property, personhood, and propriety are renewed subjects of anthropological interest, not least because of the expansion of intellectual property to new subject matter and new regions, a proliferation of new forms of cultural property, and an extension of branding activity (Ahmed, Coombe, and Schnoor 2007; Aronczyck 2013; Aylwin and Coombe 2014; Comaroff and Comaroff 2009; Coombe 2009; Manning 2010). The lack of engagement between heritage and property scholarship in anthropology is unfortunate, but we must also resist the presumption that all heritage rights are proprietary ones or that all cultural rights are essentially rooted in property principles. Heritage scholars will increasingly encounter new struggles over property and propriety, given the multiplicity of legal and policy regimes in which cultural goods and resources are targeted for developmental intervention in newly recognized communities.

Neoliberal Governmentality and Community

A new form of governmental rationality is emerging under neoliberal conditions as a constitutive form of cultural policy focused on "the organization of self-regulating and self-managing communities" (Bennett 1998, 2000: 142). "Community" recognition responds to the politics of human rights movements but it is also tied to the neoliberal policies of trade agreements and the aid programs of multilateral organizations. In diverse fields of international law and policy "communities" are privileged as autonomized collectives enrolled in practices of cultural governance through transnational networks of activism (Coombe 2011). This is a process that will accelerate as the UNESCO regime for intangible cultural heritage management is "rolled out" and its demands for community participation and engagement are interpreted, implemented, and locally articulated (Fawcett 2010; Lixinski 2011; for discussions of the UNESCO Convention on the Safeguarding of the Intangible Cultural Heritage see Smith and Akagawa 2009). Operational guidelines are now in place to secure community participation and enhance capacity building at a more local level, although state hostility and resistance to these norms ensures that they are likely to be contested. They may also evoke instrumental behaviors, to the extent that communities may have no objective boundaries or legal existence.

Human rights principles that require greater participation by minorities and indigenous peoples are also being incorporated into heritage planning. Such norms appear to be widely operative; a "strong participatory rhetoric emphasizing the necessity to involve local communities and a poorly defined 'grassroots' in heritage decision-making" is "the cornerstone of recent UNESCO policies" (De Cesari 2012: 401). The inclusion of communities is understood to represent a new acknowledgement of social collectivities as well as attention to grassroots interests, a shift in which both indigenous rights movements and anthropological, practice-based understandings of culture were influential (Coombe and Turcotte 2012: 291). UNESCO Operational Guidelines for World Heritage sites now ideally envision governance structures involving multiple stakeholders that combine community resource management systems and privilege traditional knowledge and customary law while supporting community employment (Ekern et al. 2012; Hill et al. 2011; Meskell and Brumann in this volume; Munjeri 2004; Rössler 2006; West, Igoe, and Brockington 2006).

Critical heritage studies tends to excoriate the notion of community in heritage governance. Community is a seen as a concept that is rhetorically deployed, reified, naturalized, unreflexive, nostalgic, romantic, mystifying, and Orientalist, assuming homogeneity and cohesion, misrepresenting local social dynamics, obscuring differences in interest and internal relations of power, and ultimately a concept imposed upon people by outsiders that is more likely to undermine than safeguard the customary means by which heritage is produced (Aragon and Leach 2008; Chanock 2009; Forsyth 2012; Noyes 2006; Smith and Waterton 2012; Tauschek 2012). For anthropologists of governmentality, however, issues of misrepresentation are of less importance than the ways in which such programs reconfigure cultural agency and thereby reconstruct social fields of power (if not necessarily in accordance with the values they purport to uphold) (Li 2007a). The governmentality emphasis "demands that we go beyond asking whether neoliberal rationality adequately represents society, to consider how it operates as a politics of truth that produces new forms of knowledge and expertise that structure domains of regulation and intervention" (Coombe 2007: 286).

Heritage resource management legitimates new relations of power and knowledge while creating new subject positions for social groups. It accomplishes this by fostering the articulation of culturalized collective subjectivities in processes which may involve practices of interpellation and tutelage in the name of empowerment and participatory management. Communities are enrolled in government through practices of encouragement, motivation, incitement, and inducement. Intangible cultural heritage, for example, intervenes in subjects' relationships to traditionalized practices of cultural transmission that they are now invited to objectify through protective safeguarding (Hafstein 2007, 2014). Heritage management thus provides an obvious opportunity to use the insights of legal anthropology to explore political economies of community construction (Coombe 2011). Unlike Kurin, we do not see the traditionalized community as "a rising, alternative holder and centre of power to the state" (2007: 15) but neither are we content to dismiss it as an antiquated stereotype or a mere product of subjection. Rather, we take this to be a governmental subject position of particular provenance and potential consequence for constraining and enabling local agency.

We need to consider the conditions under which community might prove to be a dynamic resource for innovative social transformations, the directions and impact of which we cannot adequately explore using the logic of correspondence and representation. Heritage scholars, De Cesari (2012) suggests, have been too focused upon the centralization, homogenization, and cultural imperialism of heritage regimes, and insufficiently attentive to the new capacities that decentralized coalitions of parties may affect. We need to stop dichotomizing government and community as actors with and without power (Kuutma 2012) and consider, instead, that heritage as government operates *in* and *through* "community" as the subject of its technological address, the object of its activities, and, thereby, activates a semi-autonomous political agent (Li 2007b).

Contingencies of community autonomy

If we consider communities as forged in multisited networks of power and subjects of diverse policy government, then we should address the trajectories and engagements through which they are recognized, the conditions under which their particularities are rendered as cultural resources, and how such processes are taken up locally. We agree with Kuutma's suggestion that heritage scholars move beyond their normative identification with the grassroots in opposition to government (perceived of as an external imposition of unwanted powers) "to define and investigate moments of empowerment, instances of emergent agency, and situations where local actors partake in grassroots policy-making" (2012: 33).

The democratic participation and local involvement that UNESCO's current norms emphasize may afford political resources for local actors who may deploy these to insist upon new forms of influence as legitimate "stakeholders" (De Cesari 2012: 408). Sánchez-Carretero (2012) shows how the nomination and inclusion of the Camino de Santiago as a World Heritage site cultural itinerary for purposes of supporting economic development influenced Galician norms of community identity. No particular significance to local residents was actually required by the nomination, since the sites had cultural significance to Christian pilgrims and others who traversed the routes they joined. Nonetheless, municipal authorities, impressed with UNESCO's recent emphasis on community values, insisted that residents participate in the maintenance of "their heritage" and people were "made" to feel a possessive attachment to the site. Ironically, this new demand for grassroots participation became the subject of grassroots opposition. Encouraged to adopt a possessive attitude to the site, local activists sought to have the inscription changed to World Heritage in Danger to condemn the failure of authorities to protect the route from harmful forms of development or to protect resources necessary for local sustainable livelihoods. In short, the newly activated community found within the UNESCO regime effective public means to shame state authorities for their failure to protect the object of UNESCO valuation or to respect the values of those subject to the negative effects of its governance *as* heritage (Coombe 2012: 381). UNESCO bodies convene international publics that community constituencies may lobby alongside state authorities for enhanced governance, control over mining concessions, and environmental protection (e.g., Logan 2007; Lydon 2012).

Community relations to heritage governance are not, however, limited to UNESCO auspices; it is more appropriate to think "in terms of multiple overlapping and intersecting heritage regimes, related to different scales and the actors that nurture and champion them" (De Cesari 2012: 403), or "assemblages of different patrimonial paradigms ... creative contact zones between different heritage logics that compete against one another or that are combined in synergistic ways" (Tauschek 2012: 196), involving "eloquent dialogues that are in danger of remaining concealed behind apparent conformity" (da Silva 2012: 76). Thus heritage scholars are uniquely positioned to take up Stephen Collier's challenge to pursue an ethnographic investigation of neoliberalism linked to policy programs focusing on distributed networks of policy expertise and "hybrid governmental formations" (2012: 194). Heritage ethnographies almost invariably consider how experts are empowered as well as the intersection of inherited institutional landscapes and neoliberal forms of regulatory restructuring.

The newly "responsibilized" community that stewards local cultural resources is a global subject position with a diverse policy provenance; communities are intervened in through a number of regulatory regimes. From global environmental norms of preserving and maintaining traditional knowledge, emerging international intellectual property policies for the protection of traditional cultural expressions, and NGO policies promoting cultural industries to further sustainable development, people located in communities are faced with overlapping demands to value, register, map, and create inventories of heritage goods as resources (Forsyth 2012: 1). Heritage scholars need to become more cognizant of the full range of regulatory initiatives at work in sequestering heritage resources, their institutional provenance, norms, and agencies of interpretation.

Governmental power manages communities *by* empowering them (De Cesari 2012: 409), specifically through eliciting the "continued participation, sacrifice and self-monitoring" of involved community participants (Meskell 2009: 97). The particular forms that such "empowerment" assumes in historically shaped contexts should be the subject of analysis. If in some areas, norms of community autonomy may be linked with new agencies of self-determination, recognition as a "stakeholder" in safeguarding cultural resources may also invest communities in the economies of their abandonment. The mapping of community cultural resources in twenty-first-century Japan, for example, enrolls residents in participatory projects of cataloguing significant local attributes (Love 2013). A governmental project "activates" rural residents in "treasure hunts" through which they come to see the areas in which they live as places rich in unique resources. Designed to spur local sustainability in the face of economic decline, these projects of community mapping emphasize "self-propelled" stewardship in which residents are collectively motivated to preserve territories holding resources of cultural value. Treasure hunts are responses to processes of neoliberal decentralization in recessionary Japan, which include the withdrawal of tax subsidies from a depopulating countryside. This devolution of responsibility "organizes rural inhabitants to participate in acts of self-recognition – to generate a distinctive and reaffirming notion of their collective identity" (Love 2013: 114) based in the localities they steward. Experts tutor them in locating and inscribing things "important to an area"s way of life" (116), encouraging them in enterprises such as renewed marketing of rural heritage foods and revival of ancestral industries through which community competition will "diminish needs for central government supports" (120). Under such circumstances, communities are easily blamed for their own failure to sustain themselves (see also Lafrenz-Samuels 2010).

Contingencies of assemblage

We cannot, however, simply presume that the reification and government of responsible communities will lead to their abjection and dispossession. The governmental embrace of community in neoliberal heritage management provides opportunities as well as constraints. As Kuutma (2012) asserts, heritage scholars cannot limit critique to dismissing heritage regimes as elitist impositions of social engineering, but must also explore local political agencies in these projects. We agree; it is an important, if remarkably overlooked premise of governmentality theory that:

> agents within governmental networks are not faithful relays, mere creatures of a controller ... They utilize and deploy whatever resources they have for their own purposes ... Each actor, each locale, is the point of intersection between forces, and hence a point of particular resistance to any one way of thinking and acting, or a point of ... promulgation of a different or oppositional programme. Entities may defect from a network, may refuse to be enrolled, or may bend its operations at certain points beyond all recognition.
>
> (Rose and Miller 2010: 287–288)

Government, in short, "is a congenitally failing operation" (Rose and Miller 2010: 288); unanticipated outcomes emerge from the intersection of diverse technologies, the conjunction of new techniques and old conditions may enable things to work in new and different ways. This seems especially probable in heritage projects where culture, understood in terms of group identity, essence, and value, is approached as a resource through a lens that emphasizes social propriety (local norms and values) as well as proprietary relations.

If neoliberal governmentality has shaped "cultural realms in the production and affirmation of diversity through the commodification of difference" (Perreault and Martin 2005: 193), its effects are uneven (Kingfisher and Maskovsky 2008) and its mandates are reworked by enterprising subjects, who may subvert the opportunities it affords for new purposes (Bondi and Laurie 2005). Moreover, they may use other dimensions of their perceived heritage to do so. Even neoliberal policies are anchored in bodies, representations, and practices which have been inscribed by successive regimes of power and policy which continue to provide resources for interpreting new structures (Hilgers 2012: 91). Forces of commodification tend to provoke alternative articulations:

> As Polanyi long ago recognized, double movements against the excesses of commodification or marketization may take a variety of politically mediated forms; both in principle and in (emergent) practice, there is scope for politically progressive and "more social" responses to the failures of neoliberal programming.
>
> (Peck and Theodore 2012: 182–183)

Despite institutional mandates, policy dictates, disciplinary pressures, and expert direction, the fact that neoliberalism can only exist in socially embedded form (Cahill 2012) "means that transformative dynamics can never be *exclusively* assigned to neoliberalism. The hybrid (re)combinations within which neoliberalism dwells are themselves generative; it is not that neoliberalisation is active, while its socio-institutional "hosts" are merely inert, residual" (Peck and Theodore 2012: 183). Thus peoples' social goods, their histories of struggle, social norms and historical values, are all resources that may be revitalized precisely under such conditions.

Far from a "uniform global condition," neoliberalism takes place in specific "assemblages" that migrate "from site to site" through a promiscuous entanglement of global and local logics (Ong 2006: 14, 2007: 4). As an analytic category neoliberalism may be approached as an assemblage of technologies, techniques, and practices that are selectively appropriated and come into uncomfortable encounters with local politics and cultural understandings. Assemblage, as a constellation of articulations, *assembles*, "forming and sustaining associations between diverse constituents," as "orders emerge and endure across differences" in which the constituent factors and forces retain dynamic and autonomous capacities (Anderson et al. 2012: 174, 176).

Emerging Articulations of Heritage and Rights

Rights constitute dynamic and emergent constituents in heritage assemblages. To explore this, however, heritage scholars need to approach human rights in a more anthropological fashion. Reviews of international human rights conventions, policy declarations, drafting histories, and professional bylaws are rife in heritage scholarship. This legal formalism is often linked to an institutional instrumentalism in which human rights are approached as purely juridical tools, governed entirely by litigation and administrative determination. To the extent that rights are addressed primarily as textual, they are negatively evaluated for lacking enforceability (Hodder 2010; Logan 2007, 2008, 2012), which usually assumes that their primary social arena is institutional and their primary addressee is the state.

Given the emphasis with which UNESCO continually revisits and elaborates human rights as one of its programs' primary normative contexts (see Meskell and

Brumann in this volume), it is entirely consonant with heritage scholars' dominant institutional focus to reiterate these founding principles. Certainly this is preferable to denunciations of cultural rights which simply ignore their legal articulation and interpretation, their historical evolution, and the scholarship in the field (e.g., Kapchan 2014). Some heritage scholars see the primary right relevant to heritage as the right to participate in community cultural life (e.g., Silberman 2012), a right historically understood as both ambitious and ambiguous. The rights that may be asserted *through* heritage, however, are far less narrow.

Heritage rights remain an uncertain domain of the already "soft" category of cultural rights within human rights regimes (Stamatopolou 2012: 1171). While early declarations of heritage protection were rooted within clearly delineated state patrimonial contexts of preserving historic sites, buildings, and monuments, later charters and conventions have addressed more fluid and intangible dimensions of cultural lifeworlds (Beazley and Deacon 2007). This shift in emphasis reflects an expanded recognition of minority, indigenous, refugee, and diasporic rights and a recognition that heritage provides political resources for social movement struggles (De Cesari 2012: 310–311; Labadi 2011; Langfield, Logan, and Craith 2012; Logan 2007, 2008; Silverman 2014; Waterton and Smith 2010). Unfortunately, this insight has not fundamentally changed the ways in which heritage scholars approach human rights.

Rights dynamics

The emphasis in heritage studies on the formal content and procedural enactment of cultural rights doctrine not only ignores the tensions and shifting sands upon which such policies are instantiated and interpreted (Lydon 2009; Meskell 2010, 2012, 2013), it is fundamentally at odds with an anthropological understanding of rights. Anthropologists approach law as an authoritative cultural discourse that provides legitimating political resources in social struggles – contingent, socially constitutive, politically interpreted, and the subject of ongoing contestation. As perhaps the only authoritative normative discourse available to counter the excesses of neoliberalism, human rights afford a powerful set of rhetorical resources through which understandings of power and injustice may be expressed. Rather than seeing human rights as institutionally compromised obstacles to social justice, then, heritage scholars might explore the ways in which human rights vocabularies provide rhetorical resources with which to protest injustice, insist upon new forms of social justice, and assert distinctive understandings of human dignity in diverse social fields, or, in short, attend to "the social life of rights" (Wilson 1997: 13, cited in Lydon 2009: 32). Recognizing only the weighted symbolism of rights in heritage institutional policy fails to attend to the broader social genealogy of human rights in our areas of fieldwork or the broader publics to whom rights-based political claims are made.

Rights are enunciated in performative iterations at multiple scales in which their normative content is continually reinterpreted to express injury, grievance, aspiration, dispossession, and entitlement. Human rights discourses have state, regional, and transnational as well as international provenance. They may be called upon in movements of self-determination that seek greater autonomy from the modern state; they may also subject the state itself to scrutiny, judgment, and discipline. Rights vocabularies are spread transnationally by NGOs, development banks, aid institutions, and social movements in networks that enable coalitions to be forged and norms to be articulated, as internationally validated vocabularies of legitimacy are woven into local expressions of enduring significance.

Asking if the right to cultural heritage is a human right unduly narrows the heritage scholar's field of inquiry by putting too great a priority upon possessive claims, and too little upon the much wider range of practical entitlements that might flow from a broader emphasis upon culture as a political and social resource (Robbins and Stamatopolou 2004). For example, the UN Independent Expert in the Field of Cultural Rights affirms that the "right of access to and enjoyment of cultural heritage forms part of international human rights law, finding its legal basis, in particular, in the right to take part in cultural life, the right of members of minorities to enjoy their own culture, and the right of indigenous peoples to self-determination and to maintain, control, protect and develop cultural heritage" (Shaheed 2011). At the very least this means acknowledging a wider range of rights (such as those protecting indigenous peoples, traditional knowledge, and traditional cultural expression) as interrelated in heritage governmentality (Coombe 2008, 2009).

Cultural heritage is not merely a fossilized inheritance but "a dialogic medium for promoting discussions about social justice and cultural creativity in the present" (Silberman 2012: 7). So too are human rights part of an intercultural dialogue. Silberman acknowledges that a considerable body of theoretical work on the interrelationship between human rights and cultural heritage has yet to be integrated into either the practice or the scholarship of heritage management. To do so, we agree, will not only require attention to a broader range of human rights principles but to the various activities through which heritage is publically communicated and interpreted, precisely because both "rights" and "culture" have performative as well as referential functions (Silberman 2012: 2–3).

To some degree, cultural heritage practices inevitably emphasize how people identify themselves, what they value, and how they define practices of significance, all of which may encourage normative reflexivity. Global legal instruments, however inadequate as grounds for institutional action, are also taken up dynamically and in diverse modes that afford an increasingly broad repertoire of activity. Instead of asking whether heritage claims are rights claims in an abstract sense or assuming that all evocations of heritage tend to violate other more fundamental rights (Kapchan 2014; Klein 2014), we might ask how and when heritage as a field of governmentality provokes rights-based practices and consider their social consequence.

Heritage as dialogic rights media

Despite the facility with which heritage scholars discuss local deployments of heritage regimes using metaphors of translation and domestication (Bortolotto 2012; da Silva 2012), they rarely do so with respect to human rights. Legal anthropologists, however, explore rights in different registers, recognizing the social life of human rights in rights discourses and rights practices and in multiple social fields that vernacularize rights (Merry 2006, 2009; Preis 2009). Indeed, in efforts to counter neoliberalism and articulate decolonial alternatives in the Americas, rights are appropriated in new ways which encapsulate locally relevant histories and refuse the allegedly universal meanings they have in Western liberal political discourse to give voice to new ethical imaginaries (Goldstein 2012: 304). Such universalist forms are appropriated, tactically received, and transformed in vocabularies and practices that travel transnationally, "scaling up" to recursively transform fields of power.

In her study of Mali's preparations for the 2005 nomination of transhumance festivals for UNESCO"s Masterpieces of the Oral and Intangible Heritage of Humanity, for example, Leblon (2012) suggests that the attention, energy, and investment that UNESCO processes bring to the "cultural" practices of those with land-based livelihoods might still be diverted to support local movements for rights to territory, resources, and new forms of self-determination. The Malian National Directorate of Cultural Heritage seemed prepared only to encompass a very narrow range of heritage as falling within UNESCO's masterpiece candidacy dossier criteria. Most of this had little to do with the increasingly threatened practices of raising and herding livestock and served primarily to ratify the expertise of already privileged elites. Fulbe pastoralists, however, seized upon the nomination of the *yaaral* and *degal* as well as new UNESCO emphases on community participation as opportunities to assert rights to land tenure, food security, political participation, and health. The ideological legacies of prior regimes of heritage governmentality appear to have blocked local practitioners in this instance but the inscription of the *yaaral* and *degal* cultural spaces coincided with a new "safeguarding action plan" that permanently established subregional cultural heritage offices and participatory local networks endowed with new capacities for interrupting and transforming prior regimes.

Ethnographic work considering governmentality's *limits* is necessary because the relations and processes with which government is concerned involve "histories, solidarities and attachments that cannot be reconfigured according to plan" (Li 2007a: 17). The study of particular regimes of governmental power must involve "a diachronic understanding of the emergence of new forms of knowledge, technics and subjects as well as their encounter with habitual forms of practice and historical identification which may restrict [the latter's] realms of encompassment" (Coombe 2007: 285). Neoliberal heritage regimes deploy various technologies to bring a new level of scrutiny upon local understandings of identity, prompting new identifications, connecting these with social as well as economic valuation while engaging enterprising subjects to exploit such values to diverse ends.

Heritage as a resource is mobilized through the energies of states and corporations, NGOs and regional associations, UN bodies and civil society movements, all of which have particular interests in empowering communities as entrepreneurs, owners, stewards, custodians, or guardians of scarce and endangered forms of knowledge, difference, and distinction. While governmental practices may attempt to identify and attach groups to the kinds of heritage most easily managed as commodifiable resources, they do not necessarily succeed. It is "important to look not just at the forms of collective and individual identity promoted by practices of government, but also at how particular agents negotiate these forms – at how they embrace, adapt, or refuse them" (Inda 2005: 11). Heritage scholars are well positioned to explore governmentality's limits as well as the "forms of political possibility" that neoliberalism's freedoms and autonomies may afford (Ferguson 2010: 183). The "congenitally failing" quality of neoliberal government also marks the point of entry for imaginative assertions of human rights framed in terms of community values, ideals of well-being, *buen viver* (good life), or *Sumak Kawsay* (well living).

To the extent that actually existing neoliberalism is encountered in governmental assemblages, it is dialogically articulated with rights-based practice and struggle (Coombe 2007, 2011). All forms of government are engaged with rights discourses and practices that express some of "the few moral injunctions the legitimacy of which is still acknowledged internationally" (Hristov 2005: 89) to justify practices of negotiation, terms of accommodation, and, in some cases, resistance and refusal. Rights practices target state governments, international economic institutions, and transnational corporations (and to a lesser degree NGOs and communities themselves) as subjects bearing obligations that must be continually reinterpreted and reiterated. The "friction" (Tsing 2005) produced when the intensifications of governmentality come up against and potentially ignite rights-based struggles and politics offers great promise as a field of critical heritage inquiry.

Vernacular resources such as understandings of tradition, moral economies of customary practice, and beliefs about the nature of human dignity and human obligation are all cultural means through which situated senses of injustice may be articulated, alternative forms of aspiration expressed, and hope given voice. When culture (practices, abilities, and relational capacities) is a resource (sometimes coded as social capital) "incentivized" via technologies through which communities are made responsible for heritage as that with which they identify, reflexivity about identity, history, memory, and value is encouraged. Thus "possessive" rights to cultural heritage may be used to insist upon particular proprieties as well as properties, and to express aspirations for specific futures based upon particular pasts.

Even the predictable forms of visible "difference" that tourist economies cultivate may be used to voice particular forms of dissent. Cultural heritage management in Havana attracted international co-financing and NGO participation, the energies of local officials and elites, and new venture capital (Pichler 2012). Nonetheless, Pichler suggests that the means through which cultural distinction was made legible, and publicly "staged" for calculable forms of consumption, were appropriated by actors with alternative agendas. The Cuban government was clearly influenced by UNESCO interest in intangible heritage when it allowed long-suppressed Afro-Cuban religious groups to adopt their traditional dress as an instance of visible cultural diversity to serve tourist industry needs. By adopting the distinctive white dress of initiates into Afro-Cuban religions, however, female relatives and supporters of jailed dissidents used the markers of these formerly suppressed religious groups to mark and remark upon the state's heritage of oppressing political dissent and denying freedom of expression. Thus they put the cultural resources of heritage government to work as human rights resources for wider consumption.

Actually Existing Heritage: A Resource for Cultural Rights Practice

Assertions of rights are increasingly culturalized; the concept of heritage is doing political work well outside of official heritage regimes. Heritage is a new language of political currency for seeking investment, but it has also assumed enhanced value in advancing the political agendas of grassroots, minority, and indigenous actors (e.g., Albro 2010; Castañeda 2009; De Cesari 2012: 403; Schofield 2014). The reduction of culturalized rights claims to a politics of recognition, however, misrecognizes the materiality of the struggles in which they figure (Robbins and Stamatopolou 2004). Under neoliberal conditions in which class-based identities have lost political resonance and peoples struggle to have colonial and modern state-based dispossession redressed, the cultural frame may provide the only means through which a "right to have rights" may be articulated (Jung 2003, 2008). Although such struggles might not be recognized as political within a modern liberal imaginary, there is no reason why heritage scholars should so limit their own gaze.

An idealized modern constitution (Latour 1993) tends to render certain politics illegible by freezing a particular "rights imaginary" in which "culture" is either conceived as national state patrimony or the basis for minority "recognition" and limited forms of "inclusion" commensurable with liberal state norms. Nonetheless, the modern category of the cultural also remains an amorphous "placeholder," an immanent contextual remainder (or dangerous supplement) within the human rights framework, historically available for imaginative political investments and articulations of aspiration by the governed (Appadurai 2013; Rajagopal 2003). For example, peoples whose "religions" are not characterized by individuated interiorized belief but by intergenerational and cross-species spiritual socialities, must choose environmental or cultural grounds (or hybridize these) to stake claims.

Indeed, to the extent that meaningful challenges to neoliberalism are emerging, they tend to be articulated in a new hybrid rhetoric linking human rights to social change, first adopted during the post-apartheid transition in South Africa (Goodale and Postero 2013), but finding unique expression in social movements for cultural, environmental, and collective rights which "agitate for fundamental ruptures with the symbolic organization of colonial modernity" in the inscribed surfaces of neoliberal decline (Natera 2013: 254). From the perspective of those for whom the modern is predominantly an experience of the colonial power matrix, the category of the "cultural" may figure as a place of political potentiality "beyond" the modern, articulated through the rhetoric of rights to legitimately express injury, loss, grievance, and the need for support, or to insist upon distinctive responsibilities so as to assert new autonomies. Neoliberal governmental attention to culture as a resource ironically enables the articulation of new hybridized cultural rights which exceed market-based concerns. Heritage studies might contribute to the anthropological study of "actually existing neoliberalism" by "mapping the middle" (Merry 2006), tracing the networks between international institutions and norms, national legislation, and vernacular understandings and practices manifest in the "rights-based practices" (Goodale 2007, 2009; Pitarch, Speed, and Solano 2008; Speed 2008) through which cultural heritage is invoked. In the wake of rapid restructuring and the increasing precarity of labor markets, contemporary assertions of cultural rights may deploy culturalized rhetoric to make claims to dignity that involve access to electricity, sanitation, or assert responsibilities for the resilience of biocultural territories (to name just two of our own ethnographic findings). In so doing they may knit and root cultural rights into struggles to overcome historical forms of dispossession that express decolonized, "amodern" (Latour 1993) futures within the spaces of neoliberal governmentality itself.

In the wake of state restructuring and neoliberal governmentality, it has become ever more urgent to assert rights in new ways to new publics. If rights generally are interpreted and understood in the vernacular, this process is accelerated when liberal procedural apparatuses are increasingly unavailable and the state is no longer the sole or primary body from whom recognition is sought, or to whom grievances must be addressed. To reiterate, there are now numerous international and transnational regimes that animate and provide incentives for cultural collectivities to assemble and constitute themselves as political constituencies. Culturalized claims and assertions figure in unexpected topographies of insurgent political agencies that constitute new social movements which transform modern legal categories as they occupy them against the grain. Mapping this shifting terrain will be the major challenge facing scholars exploring cultural heritage rights in the (not quite) neoliberal future.

Rights, responsibilities, and heritage resources in Latin America

If, for the modern liberal state, sovereignty was the only field in which properly political activities were legible as such, indigenous peoples have always represented a generative source of alterity (Shaw 2008). To the extent that neoliberal regimes of governmentality inculcate possessive relations to goods from which indigenous peoples were historically dispossessed by modern states, such as public goods, common heritage, or public domain (lands, subsistence resources, cultural properties, religious ceremonies, customs, and languages), new forms of governmentality may assist indigenous peoples seeking to establish new territories for self-determination.

In neoliberal Andean and Amazonian Latin America cultural rights have proliferated alongside newly capacitated entrepreneurial culturalized communities. Cultural heritage has been to a large degree liberated from state monopoly, turning "the customary law of cultural property into an available frame of mutual recognition for the cross-sector work of political coalition building" (Albro 2010: 161). The "empowerments" of governmentality and its regulatory assemblages have often been diverted and deployed in the service of rights-based movements for political autonomy, natural resources, territorial rights, and distinctive forms of citizenship. Such movements were based upon the assertion of indigenous (and sometimes African American) cultural differences performed as a subject position of unique, globally significant but locally exercised environmental responsibilities and obligations (e.g., Escobar 2008; Hvalkof 2006; Radcliffe and Anthias 2013; Ulloa 2006).

Achieving title to territory and cultural recognition from the state, however, may not serve peoples' needs to develop futures of their own choosing in the absence of sustainable forms of production and transnational networks of support (Hale 2011). Amazonian communities have astutely used cultural rights and the concept of heritage to forge territorial autonomies in which environmental responsibilities are linked to supports for traditional medicine, bilingual education, and control over archaeological sites that provide meaningful and sustainable opportunities for stewardship (e.g., Cepek 2012; Greene 2010; Hutchins and Wilson 2010). There is Andean work of articulation along similar lines (Shepherd 2010). Throughout Latin America, indigenous collective territories mediate market, society, and state relations in unique ways that give rise to "not-quite neoliberal spaces" (Radcliffe and Anthias 2013: 2).

The elucidation of the concept of biocultural heritage resources (Swiderska 2009), the establishment of biocultural heritage territories (Graddy 2013), and the articulation of the principle of biocultural design for sustainable development in rural communities (Davidson-Hunt et al. 2012) are further examples of creative hybridizations of modern rights categories by indigenous peoples under conditions of informational capital. In a Potato Park near Pisaq, Peru, six Quechua-speaking villages constituted themselves as a community and their growing areas as a park pursuant to national legislation, thereby bypassing the notoriously slow process of indigenous land titling in Peru. They created an autonomous territory justified by their local responsibility for global potato biodiversity, through stewardship over potato varieties that were repatriated from an international seed bank as their cultural patrimony. In the process, they revitalized customary law and forged new livelihood enterprises around the articulation of traditional Andean *ayllu* values. They did so by skillfully drawing upon the subjectifications afforded by neoliberal government and the technologies and discursive resources offered by global biodiversity, food and agriculture, intellectual property, and indigenous rights regimes (Coombe and Griebel n.d.). Opportunities afforded by neoliberal governmentality provoked a local reconsideration of history, identity, and tradition in the creation of a sustainable enterprise which now offers a model for indigenous self-determination. This work of articulation affords glimpses of an ontologically different politics and less standardized politics of possibility (de la Cadena 2010).

"Cultural politics at the limits of liberal legibility" in Guatemala

If neoliberal governmentalities have encouraged indigenous peoples in Latin America to further articulate the unique cosmovisions that define them, the ensuing cosmopolitics challenge both the rights categories of modern liberal states (de la Cadena 2008) and the capitalist imperatives of neoliberal governance. Neoliberal multiculturalism has been criticized as too narrowly focused upon seeking cultural recognition from the modern nation-state (Hale 2002, 2006; Hale and Millamán 2004) but Latin American cosmopolitics, suggest, instead, that the publics to which such politics appeal transcend and crosscut the state as an arbiter of indigeneity. Moreover, recognition is an inadequate concept to encompass the solidarities that culturalized claims may assert or the responsibilities assumed. To illustrate, we draw an example from Central America.

The Q'eqchi' Maya community Setzuul, in Guatemala, struggled to reclaim sacred lands in 2008, as Megan Ybarra (2012) recounts with great insight. The area in question encompassed the Candeleria caves, which figured not only in their cosmologies but in their historical constitution as a community seeking safety from guerrilla armies and government counterinsurgency campaigns that enforced "self-defense" patrols. They were dispossessed of these caves by a French entrepreneur with military backing who sought to privately develop them as a tourist attraction. Failing in that enterprise, he convinced the Ministry of Culture to declare the zone a national park housing significant cultural patrimony on the basis of reports of ancient Mayan artifacts. The existence of a living Mayan community in the region, Ybarra explains, was illegible to the cash-strapped national government in the late 1990s; hence an educated, well-resourced foreigner with a conveniently located hotel was deemed the more desirable caretaker for national cultural patrimony ripe for "archaeo-ecotourism" development.

At the turn of this century, however, Setzuul had access to a wider range of international interlocutors, as well as a wider range of neoliberal governmental and rights-based resources with which to make the historical significance of their relationship to the land manifest. With US Peace Corps volunteers, urban indigenist activists, and a European environmental NGO, they took advantage of new mapping technologies, community-based natural resource management norms, and the environmental subjectivities internationally offered to indigenous collectivities as guardians of biocultural diversity, to finally obtain legal title. For these Q'eqchi' peoples, this positioning as stewards better reflected their understanding that the Candelaria caves were not properly theirs to own, because the only legitimate land-owners were the spirits (*tzuultaq'as*) who provided support to people through secret rituals of spiritual renewal (*mayejak*) during the long civil war. The evocation of the sacred, despite the alien nature of that category to local understandings, enabled a distinctive claim to be voiced. Significantly, the Guatemalan state had never granted territorial rights to a Mayan collectivity as such, making this legal acknowledgement of cultural significance "an opportunity to link the politics of recognition with the politics of distribution" (Ybarra 2012: 594).

Mayan activists refused the liberal rights categories through which their place-based practices might be made legible, either to the modern state or to the transnational fields of governmentality in which they clearly find resources for agency. If culture is a term they learned to use, they clearly distinguish it from the Ladino folklorized "custom" with which the modern state had sequestered their difference, so as to insist upon the irrevocable fusion of the spiritual, political, territorial, and agricultural practices that sustain them as a people. If Quechua communities in Peru hybridized resources from indigenous and cultural heritage regimes with other forms of neoliberal government in order to safeguard and revitalize such practices, the history of modern state heritage regimes in Guatemala foreclosed such options. Nonetheless, within the broader field of cultural rights articulations, the Q'eqchi' Setzuul community, like the Quechua Potato Park collective, engaged in a significant struggle for self-determination, although both may be illegible as rights politics within a modern liberal imaginary.

Heritage within South African social movements

Rights practices in most parts of the world are rooted in much longer histories of struggle. Anti-colonial struggle in South Africa drew upon liberation theology, pan-Africanism, and socialism. It was only in the shadow of protests against the Sharpeville massacre that anti-colonialism and international human rights came to cohere under the banner of the human rights norm of self-determination, locally expressed through the trope of secular liberation (Moyn 2010). These were not conceived of in the postcolonial national context as purely civil and political rights, but also as socioeconomic rights based upon a cultural and communitarian concept of collective national development. Indeed, an independent state that protected the socioeconomic rights of all citizens was the cornerstone of the anti-apartheid struggle, expressed in the Freedom Charter and enshrined in the country's groundbreaking constitution. From the outset, however, a collectivist vision of redistribution was overtaken by projects of neoliberal statecraft which prioritized governmental projects of empowerment, delivered via public–private partnerships between the state and civil society organizations, international NGOs, and private (corporate) consultants (Weiss 2007, 2014a, 2014b).

If, for South Africa's first democratic governments, heritage was emphasized as a multicultural national platform for post-apartheid recognition and reconciliation, national heritage institutions have steadily pivoted towards a neoliberal vision of heritage as a self-sustaining component of urban revitalization and tourist development in which socioeconomic rights are to be delivered through market-based vehicles (Meskell 2009, 2012). If "liberation" still structures the heritage imaginary, the freedoms it connotes are increasingly viewed through a liberal procedural lens (Robins 2008: 3) that discounts urgent contemporary economic security and material needs. South Africa has proposed a liberation heritage route connecting key sites of anti-apartheid struggle as a potential World Heritage site. The proposed anchor sites for South Africa's liberation heritage route include Robben Island, the Nelson Mandela house in Soweto, the site of the Sharpeville protest, and Walter Sisulu Square (where the ANC's founding Freedom Charter was tabled). Arguably, however, these sites of anti-apartheid struggle are romantically rendered assertions of civil and political rights heroically achieved and wholly divorced from current forces of social and economic dispossession – a typical dynamic of revolutionary liberation heritage repurposed towards economic revitalization (Shepherd 2012; Tappe 2011).

With one of the highest income inequality coefficients in the world, South Africa has made heritage a vehicle for community capacitation only insofar as it can "pay for itself" (Meskell 2012: 16). The conditions for heritage as a capacity-building and responsibilization project are increasingly relevant in the context of growing informal settlements. The percentage of South African households living in shacks has approximately doubled between 1995 and 2006 (Hunter and Posel 2012: 290) and today over four million South Africans live in shack communities, many of them skirting large municipalities. The struggle against apartheid was also a struggle against landlessness and colonial segregation in which the urban informal sector contributed critical skills and resources, but residents of today's informal settlements have been been largely ignored in processes of identifying and developing historically significant sites for South Africa's liberation heritage route (Weiss 2014a).

The spaces of informal communities, shack settlements, slums, and transitory encampments represent some of the constitutive exclusions of modern rights under neoliberal governmentality. The normative parameters for political recognition, cultural consultation, or urban transformation cannot generally be met in the face of transitory occupancy, failing material conditions, and formal unemployment. Within this context, however, some informal communities have built collective capacities by harnessing traditional practices as political resources. For example, the *Abahlali baseMjondolo* shack dweller movement's activities on behalf of informal dwellers has become internationally recognized in human rights circles as being on the front lines of urban rights struggles in South Africa. Consisting of 25 informal settlements in KwaZulu Natal, and 35 across South Africa, with 12,000 members and up to 30,000 supporters, it won repeal of the province's slum clearance act in the Constitutional Court in 2009. Arguably, however, its political work is more legible to transnational justice publics (Niezen 2010) than it is to a national government beholden to neoliberal imperatives.

When *Abahlali baseMjondolo* mobilize for all people's "Right to the City" they understand themselves to be continuing a history of struggle absolutely core to a living heritage of liberation. Indeed, *Abahlali* represents the pre-eminent continuation of this culture of struggle, employing the same modes of peaceful protest, collectivist meeting structures, and methods for producing urban disruption and ungovernability that were established by the youth movements and labor unions during the battles against apartheid. The shack-dweller movements' claim to South Africa's liberation heritage links their work to the mantle of the "living legend of Mandela" while refusing pre-emptive exclusion from a national liberation narrative that would dehistoricize their social life and separate it from the national story. *Abahlali* thus marks the continuation of a collectivist spirit and communitarian assertion of collective rights far more characteristic of South Africa's history than the privatized delivery of services.

Excluded from the official liberation heritage nomination, such organizations nonetheless collectively assert alternative and autonomous modes of honoring heritage. *Abahali* settlements celebrated heritage days in 2011 and 2012, memorializing the legacy of coordinated strikes, court battles, protests, and raids as central to shack-dweller "culture" – or *abhlalism,* which translates as "living communism." Recently, "unfreedom day" events were held in settlements on the country's "freedom day" – providing community dwellers a forum to question the limitations and narrative closure on freedom suggested by the ANC's official heritage story (Beresford 2012; Weiss 2014a, 2014b). Their demand for the full inclusion of South Africa's most impoverished in city decision making pushes against the way that heritage governance tends to conceive of historic urban landscapes. It also remarks upon constitutive forms of blindness in the grid of urban revitalization, while speaking pointedly to UNESCO's renewed charge to accommodate the "dynamic nature of living cities" (Weiss 2014a). Indeed, *Abahlali* had its origins in failed municipal consultation processes with respect to waste, water, and health services in Durban and their self-capacitation as an essentially collective policy constituent was born of this experience.

If requirements for community consultation in heritage planning are notoriously ambiguous given South Africa's histories of mass displacement of migrant labor, the potential for settlers engaged in populist practices of urban citizenship to differentially occupy and thus transform the places afforded by neoliberal community stakeholder engagement should not be discounted. The living urban heritage *they* recognize as the 'culture' with which they identify should provoke us to understand rights-based practices as marking the limits of neoliberal heritage governmentality as well as the prospects for its transformation. Like the autonomous Quechua Potato Park, the *Abahlali* collectives constitute a counterpublic that has successfully sought to make the means and tools of its alternative modalities of governance legible to wider publics. More globally, such movements mark an inclusive horizon for civic activism and urban heritage planning, yoking the affordances of neoliberal governmentality with historical practices of struggle to assert the heritage significance of more politicized urban landscapes (e.g., Ellis 2012). For example, Nakamura describes how the "encroachment" practices of Mumbaikar informal urban settlers reveal "a radical history of struggle that predates, and in substantial ways, makes possible, the genesis of the formal city" (Nakamura 2014: 4). Again, we see the living urban heritage of collective and autonomous capacitation asserted on the dynamic frontiers of neoliberal development.

Conclusion

Neoliberal governmentalities position heritage scholars within increasingly distributed and dispersed legal and policy frameworks and institutional circuits of power, knowledge, and normative discourse in which the sites from which and the stakes in which cultural claims are made have proliferated and intensified. Such culturalized rights-based practices may be illegible to modern states and appeal to broader publics, challenging the modern state as the sole arbiter of the political while asserting stakes and claims well beyond those of recognition. Politicized assertions of cultural heritage may employ similar claims to expertise and/or use vocabularies, instruments and technologies drawn from neoliberal governmental assemblages, while expressing distinctive understandings of history, identity and value. At the very least, heritage scholars must grapple with a new field of ethical considerations entailed by shifting sites of empowerment and vulnerability while considering the paradoxical capacities of neoliberal technologies to serve as resources for emergent political agency.

REFERENCES

Ahmed, M., R. J. Coombe, and S. Schnoor (2007) Bearing cultural distinction: Informational capital and new expectations for intellectual property. *University of California Davis Law Review* 40(3): 891–917.

Albro, R. (2010) Neoliberal Cultural Heritage and Bolivia's New Indigenous Public, in C. J. Greenhouse (ed.), *Ethnographies of Neoliberalism*. Philadelphia: University of Pennsylvania Press, pp. 146–161.

Anderson, B. et al. (2012) On assemblages and geography. *Dialogues in Human Geography* 2: 171–189.

Appadurai, A. (2013) *The Future as Cultural Fact: Essays on the Global Condition*. London: Verso.

Aragon, L. and J. Leach (2008) Arts and owners: Intellectual property law and the politics of scale in Indonesian arts. *American Ethnologist* 35(4): 607–631.

Arantes, A. A. (2007) Diversity, heritage and cultural politics. *Theory, Culture and Society* 24(7–8): 290–296.

Aronczyk, M. (2013) *Branding the Nation: The Global Business of National Identity*. New York: Oxford University Press.

Aylwin, N. and R. J. Coombe (2014) Marks indicating conditions of origin in rights-based sustainable development. *University of California-Davis Law Review* 47: 753–786.

Beazley, O. and H. Deacon (2007) Safeguarding Intangible Heritage Values under the World Heritage Convention: Auschwitz, Hiroshima and Robben Island, in J. Blake (ed.), *Safeguarding Intangible Heritage: Challenges and Approaches*. Builth Wells: Institute of Art and Law, pp. 93–107.

Bendix, R. et al. (eds) (2012) *Heritage Regimes and the State*. Gottingen: Universitatsverlag Gottingen.

Bennett, T. (1998) *Culture: A Reformer's Science*. London: Sage.

Bennett, T. (2000) Acting on the social: Art, culture and government. *American Behavioral Scientist* 43(9): 1412–1428.

Bennett, T. (2007) The work of culture. *Cultural Sociology* 1(1): 31–47.

Beresford, A. (2012) The politics of regenerative nationalism in South Africa. *Journal of Southern African Studies* 38(4): 863–884.

Bondi, L. and N. Laurie (eds) (2005) *Working the Spaces of Neoliberalism: Activism, Professionalisation and Incorporation*. New York: Blackwell.

Bortolotto, C. (2012) The French Inventory of Intangible Cultural Heritage: Domesticating a Global Paradigm into French Heritage Regime, in R. Bendix et al. (eds), *Heritage Regimes and the State*. Gottingen: Universitatsverlag Gottingen, pp. 265–282.

Brenner, N., J. Peck, and N. Theodore (2010) Variegated neoliberalization: Geographies, modalities, pathways. *Global Networks* 10(2): 182–222.

Buchli, V. (2013) *An Anthropology of Architecture*. New York: Bloomsbury Academic.

Cahill, D. (2012) The Embedded Neoliberal Economy, in D. Cahill, L. Edwards, and F. Stillwell (eds), *Neoliberalism: Beyond the Free Market*. Cheltenham: Edward Elgar, pp. 110–127.

Castañeda, Q. E. (2009) Heritage and Indigeneity: Transformations in the Politics of Tourism, in M. Baud and A. Ypeji (eds), *Cultural Tourism in Latin America: The Politics of Space and Imagery*. Boston, MA: Brill, pp. 263–296.

Cepek, M. (2012) *A Future for Amazonia*. Austin: University of Texas Press.

Chanock, M. (2009) Branding Identity and Copyrighting Culture: Orientations towards the Customary in Traditional Knowledge Discourse, in C. Antons (ed.), *Traditional Knowledge, Traditional Cultural Expressions and Intellectual Property Law in the Asia-Pacific Region*. Dordrecht: Kluwer Law International, pp. 177–193.

Collier, S. J. (2006) Global assemblages. *Theory, Culture and Society* 23(2–3): 399–401.

Collins, J. (2012) Reconstructing the "Cradle of Brazil": The detachability of morality and the nature of cultural labor in Salvador, Bahia's Pelourinho World Heritage site. *International Journal of Cultural Property* 19(Special Issue 03): 423–452.

Comaroff, J. (2011) The end of neoliberalism? What is left of the Left. *The Annals of the American Academy of Political and Social Science* 637(1): 141–147.

Comaroff, J. L. and J. Comaroff (2009) *Ethnicity, Inc.* Chicago, IL: University of Chicago Press.

Coombe, R. J. (2005) Legal claims to culture in and against the market: Neoliberalism and the global proliferation of meaningful difference. *Law, Culture and Humanities* 1(1): 32–55.

Coombe, R. J. (2007) The work of rights at governmentality's limit. *Anthropologica* 49(2): 284–299.

Coombe, R. J. (2008) First Nations' Intangible Cultural Heritage Concerns: Prospects for Protection of Traditional Knowledge and Traditional Cultural Expressions in International Law, in C. Bell and R. Paterson (eds), *First Nations' Cultural Heritage: Rights and Reconciliation*. Vancouver: University of British Columbia Press, pp. 313–362.

Coombe, R. J. (2009) The expanding purview of cultural properties and their politics. *The Annual Review of Law and Social Sciences* 5: 393–412.

Coombe, R. J. (2011) "Possessing Culture": Political Economies of Community Subjects and Their Properties, in V. Strang and M. Busse (eds), *Ownership and Appropriation*. New York: Berghan, pp. 105–127.

Coombe, R. J. (2012) Managing Cultural Heritage as Neoliberal Governmentality, in R. Bendix et al. (eds), *Heritage Regimes and the State*. Gottingen: Universitatsverlag Gottingen, pp. 375–387.

Coombe, R. J. and M. Baird (in press) The Limits of Heritage: Corporate Interests and Cultural Rights on Resource Frontiers, in W. Logan, U. Kockel, and M. N. Craith (eds), *Companion Guide to the New Heritage Studies*. Oxford: Wiley Blackwell.

Coombe, R. J. and M. Griebel (n.d.) Biocultural heritage: Working potatoes and properties in an era of informational capital. Unpublished manuscript on file with author.

Coombe, R. J. and J. F. Turcotte (2012) Indigenous Cultural Heritage in Development and Trade: Perspectives from the Dynamics of Cultural Heritage Law and Policy, in C. Graber et al. (eds), *International Trade in Indigenous Cultural Heritage*. Cheltenham: Edward Elgar, pp. 272–305.

da Silva, L. (2014) Foucault in the landscape: Questioning governmentality in the Azores. *Landscape Research*.

da Silva, M. C. (2012) Castles Abroad: Nations, Culture and Cosmopolitanisms in African Heritage Sites of Portuguese Origin, in R. Bendix et al. (eds), *Heritage Regimes and the State*. Gottingen: Universiitatsverlag Gottingen, pp. 61–78.

Davidson-Hunt, I. J. et al. (2012) Biocultural design: A new conceptual framework for sustainable development in rural indigenous and local communities. *SAPIENS. Surveys and Perspectives Integrating Environment and Society* 5(2): 33–45.

De Cesari, C. (2012) Thinking Through Heritage Regimes, in R. Bendix et al. (eds), *Heritage Regimes and the State*. Gottingen: Universitatsverlag Gottingen, pp. 399–413.

de la Cadena, M. (2008) Alternative indigeneties: Conceptual proposals. *Latin American and Caribbean Ethnic Studies* 3(3): 341–349.

de la Cadena, M. (2010) Indigenous cosmopolitics in the Andes: Conceptual reflections beyond "politics." *Cultural Anthropology* 25(2): 334–370.

Ekern, S. et al. (2012) Human rights and World Heritage: preserving our common dignity through rights-based approaches to site management. *International Journal of Heritage Studies* 18(3): 213–225.

Ellis, R. (2012) "A world class city of your own!": Civic governmentality in Chennai, India. *Antipode* 44(4): 1143–1160.

Escobar, A. (2008) *Territories of Difference: Place, Movements, Life, Redes*. Durham, NC: Duke University Press.

Fawcett, M. (2010) The Market for Ethics: Culture and the Neoliberal Turn at UNESCO. Ph.D. dissertation, New York University, ProQuest, UMI Dissertations Publishing, 3380290.

Ferguson, J. (2010) The uses of neoliberalism. *Antipode* 41(s1): 166–184.

Forsyth, M. (2012) Lifting the lid on "the community": Who has the right to control access to traditional knowledge and expressions of culture? *International Journal of Cultural Property* 19: 1–31.

Gattinger, M. and D. Saint-Pierre (2010) The "neoliberal turn" in provincial cultural policy and administration in Québec and Ontario: The emergence of "quasi-neoliberal" approaches. *Canadian Journal of Communication* 35(2): 279–302.

Goldstein, D. (2012) Decolonizing "actually existing neoliberalism." *Social Anthropology* 20(3): 304–309.

Goodale, M. (2007) Locating Rights, Envisioning Law between the Global and the Local, in M. Goodale and S. Merry (eds), *The Practice of Human Rights: Tracking Law between the Global and the Local.* Cambridge: Cambridge University Press, pp. 1–38.

Goodale, M. (2009) Introduction: Human Rights and Anthropology, in M. Goodale (ed.), *Human Rights: An Anthropological Reader.* Oxford: Wiley Blackwell, pp. 1–20.

Goodale, M. and N. Postero (2013) Revolution and Retrenchment: Illuminating the Present in Latin America, in M. Goodale and N. Postero (eds), *Neoliberalism Interrupted: Social Change and Contested Governance in Contemporary Latin America.* Stanford, CA: Stanford University Press, pp. 1–22.

Graddy, T. G. (2013) Regarding biocultural heritage: In situ political ecology in the Peruvian Andes. *Agriculture and Human Values* 30: 587–604.

Greene, S. (2010) *Customising Indigeneity.* Stanford, CA: Stanford University Press.

Hafstein, V. (2007) Claiming Culture: Intangible Heritage Inc., Folklore@, Traditional Knowledge™, in D. Hemme, M. Tauschek, and R. Bendix (eds), *Pradikat HERITAGE: Wertschopfungen aus kulturellen Ressourcen.* Berlin: Lit, pp. 75–100

Hafstein, V. (2009) Intangible Heritage as List: From Masterpieces to Representation, in L. Smith and N. Akagawa (eds), *Intangible Heritage: Key Issues in Cultural Heritage.* New York: Routledge, pp. 93–111.

Hafstein, V. (2014) Protection as Dispossession: Government in the Vernacular, in D. Kapchan (ed.), *Cultural Heritage In Transit: Intangible Rights as Cultural Rights.* Philadelphia: University of Pennsylvania Press, pp. 25–57.

Hale, C. (2002) Does multiculturalism menace? Governance, cultural rights and the politics of identity in Guatemala. *Journal of Latin American Studies* 34: 485–524.

Hale, C. (2006) *Mas que un Indio (More than an Indian): Racial Ambivalence and Neoliberal Multiculturalism in Guatemala.* Santa Fe, NM: School of American Research Press.

Hale, C. (2011) Resistance, pur qui? Territory, autonomy and neoliberal entanglements in the empty spaces of Central America. *Economy and Society* 40(2): 184–210.

Hale, C. and Millamán, R. (2004) Rethinking indigenous politics in the era of the "indio permitido.". *NACLA Report on the Americas* 38 (2): 16–21.

Herzfeld, M. (2009) Rhythm, tempo, and historical time: Experiencing temporality in the neoliberal age. *Public Archaeology* 8(2–3): 108–123.

Hilgers, M. (2010) The three anthropological approaches to neoliberalism. *International Social Science Journal* 61(202): 351–364.

Hilgers, M. (2012) The historicity of the neoliberal state. *Social Anthropology* 20(1): 80–94.

Hill, R. et al. (2011) Empowering indigenous peoples' biocultural diversity through World Heritage cultural landscapes. *International Journal of Heritage Studies* 17(6): 571–591.

Hodder, I. (2010) Cultural heritage rights: From ownership and descent to justice and well-being. *Anthropological Quarterly* 83: 861–882.

Hollowell, J. and G. P. Nicholas (2009) Using ethnographic methods to articulate community-based conceptions of cultural heritage management. *Public Archaeology: Archaeological Ethnographies* 8(2–3): 141–160.

Hristov, J. (2005) Indigenous struggles for land and culture in Cauca, Colombia. *The Journal of Peasant Studies* 32: 88–117.

Hunter, M. and D. Posel (2012) Here to work: The socioeconomic characteristics of informal dwellers in post-apartheid South Africa. *Environment and Urbanization* 24(1): 285–304.

Hutchins, F. and P. C. Wilson (eds) (2010) *Editing Eden: A Reconsideration of Identity, Politics, and Place in Amazonia*. Lincoln, NE: University of Nebraska Press.

Hvalkof, S. (2006) Progress of the Victims: Political Ecology in the Peruvian Amazon, in A. Biersack and J. B. Greenberg (eds), *Reimagining Political Ecology*. Durham, NC: Duke University Press, pp. 195–232.

Inda, J. X. (2005) Analytics of the Modern: An Introduction, in J. X. Inda (ed.), *Anthropologies of Modernity: Foucault, Governmentality, and Life Politics*. Malden, MA: Blackwell, pp. 1–20.

Jung, C. (2003) The politics of indigenous identity: Neoliberalism, cultural rights and the Mexican Zapatistas. *Social Research* 70: 433–462.

Jung, C. (2008) *The Moral Force of Indigenous Politics: Critical Liberalism and the Zapatistas*. Cambridge: Cambridge University Press.

Kapchan, D. (2014) Intangible Rights: Cultural Heritage in Transit, in D. Kapchan (ed.), *Cultural Heritage in Transit: Intangible Rights as Human Rights*. Philadelphia: University of Pennsylvania Press, pp. 1–22.

Kingfisher, C. and J. Maskovsky (2008) Introduction: The limits of neoliberalism. *Critique of Anthropology* 28(2): 115–126.

Klein, B. (2014) Cultural Heritage, Human Rights, and Reform Ideologies: The Case of Swedish Folklife Research, in D. Kapchan (ed.), *Cultural Heritage in Transit: Intangible Rights as Human Rights*. Philadelphia: University of Pennsylvania Press, pp.113–124.

Kockel, U. (2012) Borders, European Integration and UNESCO World Heritage: A Case Study of the Curonian Spit, in R. Bendix et al. (eds), *Heritage Regimes and the State*. Gottingen: Universitatsverlag Gottingen, pp. 227–248.

Kurin, R. (2007) Safeguarding intangible cultural heritage: Key factors in implementing the 2003 Convention. *International Journal of Intangible Heritage* 1: 10–20.

Kuutma, K. (2012) Between Arbitration and Engineering: Concepts and Contingencies in the Shaping of Heritage Regimes, in R. Bendix et al. (eds), *Heritage Regimes and the State*. Gottingen: Universitatsverlag Gottingen, pp. 21–36.

Labadi, S. (2011) Intangible heritage and sustainable development – realistic outcome or wishful thinking? *Heritage and Society* 4(1): 115–118.

Lafrenz-Samuels, K. (2010) Material Heritage and Poverty Reduction, in S. Labadi and C. Long (eds), *Heritage and Globalization*. London: Routledge, pp. 202–217.

Langfield, M., W. Logan, and M. N. Craith (eds) (2012) *Cultural Diversity, Heritage and Human Rights: Intersections in Theory and Practice*. New York: Taylor Francis.

Latour, B. (1993) *We Have Never Been Modern*. Trans. C, Porter. Cambridge, MA: Harvard University Press.

Leblon, A. (2012) A Policy of Intangible Cultural Heritage between Local Constraints and International Standards: "The Cultural Space of the *yaaral* and the *degal*," in R. Bendix et al. (eds), *Heritage Regimes and the State*. Gottingen: Universiitatsverlag Gottingen, pp. 97–120.

Li, T. M. (2007a) Governmentality. *Anthropologica* 49(2): 275–281.

Li, T. M. (2007b) *The Will to Improve: Governmentality, Development, and the Practice of Politics*. Durham, NC: Duke University Press.

Lixinski, L. (2011) Selecting heritage: Intersections of art, politics and identity. *European Journal of International Law* 22: 81–100.

Logan, W. S. (2007) Closing Pandora's Box: Human Rights Conundrums in Cultural Heritage Protection, in H. Silverman and D. Fairchild Ruggles (eds), *Cultural Heritage and Human Rights*. New York: Springer, pp. 33–52.

Logan, W. S. (2008) Cultural Heritage and Human Rights, in B. J. Graham and P. Howard (eds), *Ashgate Research Companion to Heritage and Identity*. Farnham: Ashgate, pp. 439–454.

Logan, W. S. (2012) Cultural diversity, cultural heritage and human rights: Towards heritage management as human rights-based cultural practice. *International Journal of Heritage Studies* 18: 231–244.

Long, C. and S. Labadi (2010) Introduction, in S. Labadi and C. Long (eds), *Heritage and Globalization*. London: Routledge, pp. 1–16.

Love, B. (2013) Treasure hunts in rural Japan: Place making at the limits of sustainability. *American Anthropologist* 115: 112–124.

Lydon, J. (2009) Young and Free: The Australian Past in a Global Future, in L. Meskell (ed.), *Cosmopolitan Archaeologies*. Durham, NC: Duke University Press, pp. 28–47.

Manning, P. (2010) The semiotics of brand. *Annual Review of Anthropology* 39: 33–49.

Merry, S. E. (2006) Transnational human rights and local activism: Mapping the middle. *American Anthropologist* 108(1): 38–51.

Merry, S. E. (2009) Legal Transplants and Cultural Translation: Making Human Rights in the Vernacular, in M. Goodale (ed.), *Human Rights: An Anthropological Reader*. Oxford: Wiley Blackwell, pp. 265–302.

Meskell, L. (2009) The Nature of Culture in Kruger National Park, in L. Meskell (ed.), *Cosmopolitan Archaeologies*. Durham, NC: Duke University Press, pp. 89–112.

Meskell, L. (2010) Human rights and heritage ethics. *Anthropological Quarterly* 83(4): 839–859.

Meskell, L. (2011) From Paris to Pontdrift: UNESCO meetings, Mapungubwe and mining. *South African Archaeological Bulletin* 66(194): 149–156.

Meskell, L. (2012) *The Nature of Heritage in the New South Africa*. Oxford: Wiley Blackwell.

Meskell, L. (2013) UNESCO and the fate of the World Heritage Indigenous Peoples Council of Experts (WHIPCOE). *International Journal of Cultural Property* 20(3): 155–174.

Moyn, S. (2010) *The Last Utopia: Human Rights in History*. Cambridge, MA: Harvard University Press.

Munjeri, D. (2004) Anchoring African cultural and natural heritage: The significance of local community awareness in the context of capacity-building, in E. de Merode et al. (eds), *Linking Universal and Local Values*. Paris: UNESCO World Heritage Center, pp. 75–80.

Nakamura, C. (2014) Mumbai's quiet histories: Critical intersections of the urban poor, historical struggles, and heritage spaces. *Journal of Social Archaeology* 14(3): 271–295.

Natera, M. A. C. (2013) Postscript: Insurgent Imaginaries and Postneoliberalism in Latin America, in M. Goodale and N. Postero (eds), *Neoliberalism Interrupted: Social Change and Contested Governance in Contemporary Latin America*. Stanford, CA: Stanford University Press, pp. 249–268.

Niezen, R. (2010) *Public Justice and the Anthropology of Law*. Cambridge: Cambridge University Press.

Noyes, D. (2006) The judgment of Solomon: Global protections for tradition and problem of community ownership. *Cultural Analysis* 5: 27–56.

Ong, A. (2006) *Neoliberalism as Exception: Mutations of Citizenship and Sovereignty*. Durham, NC: Duke University Press.

Ong, A. (2007) Neoliberalism as a mobile technology. *Transactions of the Institute of British Geographers* 32(1): 3–8.

Patterson, R. and H. Telesetsky (2012) Heritage Inc.: A mini symposium on heritage protection and private actors. *International Journal of Cultural Property* 19(4): 549–571.

Peck, J. and N. Theodore (2012) Reanimating neoliberalism: Process geographies of neoliberalisation. *Social Anthropology* 20(2): 177–185.

Perreault, T. and P. Martin (2005) Geographies of neoliberalism in Latin America. *Environment and Planning* 37(2): 191–201.

Pichler, A. (2012) The Dynamics of Heritage Choice and Heritage Regimes in the "Making of Old Havana," in R. Bendix et al. (eds), *Heritage Regimes and the State*. Gottingen: Universitatsverlag Gottingen, pp. 39–60.

Pitarch, P., S. Speed, and X. L. Solano (eds) (2008) *Human Rights in the Mayan Region: Global Politics, Cultural Contentions and Moral Engagements*. Durham, NC: Duke University Press.

Polanyi, K. (2001 [1944]) *The Great Transformation: The Political and Economic Origins of Our Time*. Boston, MA: Beacon Press.

Preis, A. (2009) Human Rights as Cultural Practice: An Anthropological Critique, in M. Goodale (ed.), *Human Rights: An Anthropological Reader*. Oxford: Wiley Blackwell, pp. 332–355.

Radcliffe, S. and P. Anthias (2013) The ethno-environmental fix and its limits: The production of not-quite-neoliberal natures in Bolivia. *Geoforum*,

Rajagopal, B. (2003) *International Law from Below: Development, Social Movements and Third World Resistance*. Cambridge: Cambridge University Press.

Robbins, B. and E. Stamatopolou (2004) Reflections on culture and cultural rights. *South Atlantic Quarterly* 103: 419–434.

Robins, S. L. (2008) *From Revolution to Rights in South Africa: Social Movements, NGOs and Popular Politics after Apartheid*. Scottsville: University of Kwazulu-Natal Press.

Rose, N. (1999) *Powers of Freedom: Reframing Political Thought*. Cambridge: Cambridge University Press.

Rose, N. and P. Miller (2010) Political power beyond the state: Problematics of government. *The British Journal of Sociology* 61(1): 271–303.

Rössler, M. (2006) World Heritage cultural landscapes: A UNESCO flagship programme. *Landscape Research* 31(4): 333–353.

Sánchez-Carretero, C. (2012) Heritage Regimes and the *Camino de Santiago*: Gaps and Logics, in R. Bendix et al. (eds), *Heritage Regimes and the State*. Gottingen: Universitatsverlag Gottingen, pp. 141–156.

Scher, P. (2010) UNESCO conventions and culture as a resource. *Journal of Folklore Research* 47(1–2): 197–202.

Scher, P. (2011) Heritage tourism in the Caribbean: The politics of culture after neoliberalism. *Bulletin of Latin American Research* 30(1): 7–20.

Schofield, J. (2014) *Who Needs Experts?: Counter-Mapping Cultural Heritage*. Farnham: Ashgate Publishing.

Seagle, C. (2013) Discourse, Development and Legitimacy: Nature/Culture Dualism of Mining Engagements in Biodiversity Offsetting and Conservation in Madagascar, in S. Evers et al. (eds), *Contest for Land in Madagascar: Environment, Ancestors and Development*. Boston: Brill, pp. 187–220.

Shaheed, F. (2011) *Report of the Independent Expert in the Field of Cultural Rights*. United Nations General Assembly, Human Rights Council, Seventeenth Session. Doc A/HRC/17/38, 2011.

Shaw, K. (2008) *Indigeneity and Political Theory: Sovereignty and the Limits of the Political*. New York: Routledge.

Shepherd, C. J. (2010) Mobilizing local knowledge and asserting culture. *Current Anthropology* 51(5): 629–654.

Shepherd, R. (2012) *Faith in Heritage: Displacement, Development, and Religious Tourism in Contemporary China*. Walnut Creek, CA: Left Coast Press.

Silberman, N. A. (2012) Heritage interpretation and human rights: Documenting diversity, expressing identity, or establishing universal principles? *International Journal of Heritage Studies* 18: 245–256.

Silverman, C. (2014) Balkan Romani Heritage, Human Rights and the State: Whose Heritage? In D. Kapchan (ed.), *Cultural Heritage in Transit: Intangible Rights as Human Rights*. Philadelphia: University of Pennsylvania Press, pp. 125–147.

Smith, L. (2007) Empty Gestures? Heritage and the Politics of Recognition, in H. Silverman and D. Fairchild Ruggles (eds), *Cultural Heritage and Human Rights*. New York: Springer, pp. 159–172.

Smith, L. and N. Akagawa (2009) *Intangible Heritage*. London: Routledge.

Smith, L. and E. Waterton (2012) Constrained by Commonsense: The Authorised Heritage Discourse in Contemporary Debates, in J. Carman, R. Skeates, and C. McDavid (eds), *The Oxford Handbook of Public Archaeology*. Oxford: Oxford University Press, pp. 153–171.

Speed, S. (2008) *Rights in Rebellion: Indigenous Struggle and Human Rights in Chiapas*. Stanford, CA: Stanford University Press.

Stamatopolou, E. (2012) Monitoring cultural human rights: The claims of culture on human rights and the response of cultural rights. *Human Rights Quarterly* 34(4): 1170–1192.

Swiderska, K. (2009) Protecting Traditional Knowledge: A Holistic Approach based on Customary Laws and Bio-cultural Heritage, in K. Ninan (ed.), *Conserving and Valuing Ecosystem Services and Biodiversity*. London: Earthscan, pp. 331–344.

Tappe, O. (2011) From revolutionary heroism to cultural heritage: Museums, memory and representation in Laos. *Nations and Nationalism* 17(3): 604–626.

Tauschek, M. (2012) The Bureaucratic Texture of National Patrimonial Policies, in R. Bendix et al. (eds), *Heritage Regimes and the State*. Gottingen: Universitatsverlag Gottingen, pp. 195–212.

Tsing, A. (2005) *Friction: An Ethnography of Global Connection*. Princeton, NJ: Princeton University Press.

Ulloa, A. (2005) *The Ecological Native: Indigenous Peoples' Movements and Eco-Governmentality in Colombia*. New York: Routledge.

Vrasti, W. (2013) *Volunteer Tourism in the Global South: Giving Back in Neoliberal Times*. New York: Routledge.

Wang, D. (2011) China's Longmen Grottoes and the regulation and marketization of heritage. Paper presented at the workshop on "Heritage Regimes and the State", Gottingen University, July 17–19, 2011.

Waterton, E. and L. Smith (2010) The recognition and misrecognition of community heritage. *International Journal of Heritage Studies* 16(1-2): 4–15.

Weiss, L. M. (2007) Heritage-making and political identity. *Journal of Social Archaeology* 7(3): 413–431.

Weiss, L. M. (2014a) Informal settlements and urban heritage landscapes in South Africa. *Journal of Social Archaeology* 14(1): 3–25.

Weiss, L. M. (2014b) The historical narration of rights in South Africa: Past, present and future tense. *Heritage and Society* 7(2): 121–138.

West, P., J. Igoe, and D. Brockington (2006) Parks and people: The social impacts of protected areas. *Annual Review of Anthropology* 35: 251–277.

Wilson, R. (1997) *Human Rights, Culture and Context: An Introduction*. London: Pluto Press.

Ybarra, M. (2012) You cannot measure a tzuultaq'qa: Cultural politics at the limit of liberal legibility. *Antipode* 45(3): 584–601.

3

Civil Societies? Heritage Diplomacy and Neo-Imperialism

Morag M. Kersel and Christina Luke

Introduction

The use of heritage to cultivate relationships between foreign partners, to encourage mutual understanding, to mend fences, and to build bridges on the international stage is not a new occurrence. For years people and objects have acted as unofficial agents of diplomacy, traveling the globe and representing the places from which they came. Only recently has this notion of archaeology and artifacts as part of the larger sphere of cultural diplomacy and foreign relations come to the forefront of discussion in the realm of heritage studies. Here we review some of the emergent issues associated with heritage diplomacy and archaeology within the wider discussion of neo-imperialism and development, the primary points of departure for understanding the currents of cultural diplomacy and policy. At the core of our argument is the ethical implication(s) of such legacies and relationships as they defined (and continue to define) the field of archaeology, and how (if) we can move beyond this dialectic. Our research points to a very close relationship between principles of twenty-first century diplomacy as they are presented and packaged to the public through the ideals of democracy and civil society. These programs, however, are laced with overt agendas that reify neo-imperialistic legacies. At times, the consequences of such engagements are often unclear, at times uncertain, and they may not always be in the best interests of both parties; but the best-case scenario is that through open and honest dialogue, productive and lasting relationships emerge. In this way, successful heritage diplomacy can illuminate existing and emergent contact zones, *sensu* Pratt (1991) and Clifford (1997).

What Is Heritage?

"Invented tradition" introduced by Hobsbawm and Ranger (1983: 1) continues to have a significant impact on how the academic community conceptualizes heritage:

Global Heritage: A Reader, First Edition. Edited by Lynn Meskell.

> a set of practices, normally governed by overtly or tacitly accepted rules and of a ritual or symbolic nature, which seek to inculcate certain values and norms of behavior by repetition, which automatically implies continuity with the past. In fact, where possible, they normally attempt to establish continuity with a suitable historic past.

Heritage encompasses a broad and overarching term: "it" is something that someone or a collective considers to be worthy of being valued, preserved, catalogued, exhibited, restored, admired. Heritage is both intensely personal and intensely political. Harrison (2013) reminds us that heritage is everywhere; Herzfeld (2010: 259) acknowledges that heritage is grounded in culturally specific ideologies of kinship, residence, and property; and Luke (2013) argues that heritage projects reflect targeted geographies of power.

Winter (2013a) suggests that heritage itself is a Western construct based on a series of historical events and practices – the birth of the museum, the first archaeological excavations, early declarations of individual and collective cultural property rights. This historical legacy has resulted in heritage praxis (regardless of where it occurs) that is de facto measured against Western ideals; the "result" most often produces conflict and exclusion of the local (see Armakolas 2012 for Mostar, Bosnia and Herzegovina; Byrne 2013 for Bali, Indonesia; Herzfeld 2009 for Rome, Italy; Luke 2013 for Izmir, Turkey; Silverman 2013 for Cuzco, Peru). This privileging of the West in conceptualizing heritage results in policies that dictate and embolden hegemonic and diplomatic overtures. In most cases these actions have been subtle, even considered "natural," so that members of the US Congress or European governments have considerable difficulty in conceptualizing the inherent bias in heritage practice. The "West knows best" reflects the heritage landscape from the local to the guidelines set forth by international agencies such as ICOM, ICOMOS, and UNESCO; these organizations reinforce the dichotomous relationships between theory and practice embedded in the Orientalist legacy and the inability to move beyond the nation state to embrace fluid and flexible categories and boundaries.

Precisely because of its plasticity, heritage has the potential to define a group ethos, increasing solidarity and fomenting relationships, but it also can be a double-edged sword: heritage can be isolating and exclusionary to those on the fringes of the dominant, national culture. Numerous case studies and assessments from Africa (Agyei-Mensah 2006; Meskell 2012a; Mowatt and Chancellor 2011), Asia (Akagawa 2014; Chapman 2013; Guha-Thakurta 2004; Pai 2013; Thussu 2013), Europe (Armakolas 2012; Dietler 1994; Hamilakis 2007; Luke 2013), Latin America (Castañeda 2005; Silverman 2013), and the Middle East (Abdi 2001; Abu El-Haj 2001; Bernhardsson 2005; Colla 2007; Elkasrawy and El Kasrawy 2012; Shaw 2003; Silberman and Small 1997) tease out how heritage is used as a tool in legitimizing governments or dominant groups, reinforcing perceptions of local and/or national identities. With disparate definitions and the legacy of colonialism and impending neo-imperialistic advances how, then, can heritage be an effective part of cultural diplomacy?

What Is Diplomacy?

Diplomacy is generally viewed as the means by which a sovereign nation communicates with publics in other countries. This interaction is aimed at informing and influencing overseas audiences for the purpose of promoting the national interest and advancing its foreign policy goals. The aim of diplomacy is predominantly positive in nature, with real and imagined benefits for both states. Management, negotiation, and interaction are all common themes in any definition of diplomacy. In his recent consideration of diplomacy Cornago (2013, drawing from Böhmelt 2010) defines three tracks: (1) official statecraft involving high-level political and military leaders concentrating on outcomes such as peace, ceasefires, and treaties; (2) unofficial dialogue emphasizing problem-solving activities aimed at building relationships and encouraging new ways of thinking, typically involving senior academics, non-governmental organizations, and often religious leaders (neutral non-governmental parties); and (3) people-to-people interaction focusing on programs at the grassroots level, characteristically in the form of conferences, meetings, advocacy, and the inclusion of local publics in the actions (see Lane 2013 for examples of French cultural diplomacy). In order for the third track of diplomacy to be successful, Cornago (2013: 19) infers that resources (i.e., money) must be made available. Financial resources are, in many cases, supplied by agencies in fiscally secure states and thus there is often much influence on the part of non-local actors. Heritage slots nicely into each track of diplomacy and is used by many nations in augmenting foreign relationships as well as in structuring strategic agendas. Examples of successful diplomacy that involved financial resources can be found in Lane (2013) and in the recent award by the Japanese government of US$ 6.7 million for the construction of a museum, which will showcase historical and archaeological artifacts discovered in the Petra region of Jordan, and raise the local community's awareness on protecting both the tangible and intangible heritage of Petra (Jordan Times 2014).

Diplomacy is conventionally circumscribed to specific professions and communities such as official state envoys, often ignoring the practical knowledge developed or acquired by unofficial diplomats, a concept explored by Berman and Johnson (1997). Unofficial cultural ambassadors include archaeologists (professionals and students), conservators, museum practitioners, and preservationists. In her examination of particular desired pasts and the appropriation of the results of archaeological investigations in Israel and Palestine, Scham (2009: 163) notes the significance of these "desires" and how they can and do affect, both positively and negatively, cultural diplomatic relations. The importance of the unofficial diplomat should not be underestimated in realizing the goals of heritage diplomacy (see Lane 2013; Luke 2012; Luke and Kersel 2013a), but nor should the fundamental political and diplomatic strings attached to the financial resources offered by one country to another, under the pretext of a common notion about the past, go unacknowledged. Neo-imperialist agendas associated with international, national, and state agencies are often the driving mechanisms behind what is preserved, what is excavated, and what is on display as representative of a particular locality, nation, or culture.

Formal centers supporting archaeology in various nations are often referred to as schools, centers, or institutes – terms that neutralize their historical diplomatic position. The United States (Council of American Overseas Research Centers, CAORC), Germany (the German Archaeological Institute, Deutsches Archäologisches Institut, DAI), the United Kingdom (the Council for British Research in the Levant), and France (Le Centre national de la recherche scientifique and the Institut français du Proche-Orient), among others, provide assistance to researchers and scientists. In so doing, they provide a physical venue for the exchange of knowledge (see Lane 2013; Luke and Kersel 2013a). In addition to formal "centers," countries also promote initiatives through their ministries of foreign affairs. Japan is among the most active.

Small stickers representing the flag of Japan are subtle reminders of the support. One finds these on the laboratory and archival equipment, as well as the chairs and tables, even bookcases, in the National Museum of El Salvador, the libraries in Cetinje, Montenegro, and the state of the art complex at Kaman Kalehöyük, Turkey. In addition to these projects, Japan has also provided sustained support to Peru, a country that has colonial ties to Japan. In the last three decades Japan has provided more than US$ 16 million for cultural programs (museums, archaeological research, conservation and more) to Peru. Through formal or informal efforts to promote culture countries are exerting their diplomatic influence whether or not it is acknowledged as such.

Heritage and Diplomacy

Recent studies (Bertacchini, Saccone, and Santagata 2011; Lane 2013; Luke and Kersel 2013a; Scham 2009; Thussu 2013; Winter 2013a, 2013b, 2014a, 2014b) have acknowledged that diplomacy and international governance often represent the forces behind programs of preservation, exploration, and presentation. In 2010 the French Ministry of Foreign and European Affairs supported some 150 conservation, excavation, and restoration projects abroad, including six new site investigations in Cambodia, Ecuador, Egypt, Iraq, and Spain (Lane 2013). The motivating criteria of scientific excellence, the training of heritage professionals, and a perceived contribution to the understanding of the history of the areas concerned, are augmented by the understated goal of the strengthening of cultural cooperation (Lane 2013). Yet, the political landscape of heritage support is no longer just the usual suspects. In an unprecedented move reported in various newspaper outlets in April 2014, the State of Qatar allocated US$ 135 million for archaeological projects (multination, including UK and US projects) in Sudan (AFP 2014). This is part of its billion-dollar package to support development worldwide. Whether financially backed by France or Qatar, the practice of archaeology and policies of heritage practice are pursued with increasing visibility to ameliorate diplomatic rifts, and to enhance mutual understanding of our collective cultural past.

Historically, recognition of the importance of heritage in foreign relations was the domain of the West and often closely tied to global colonial endeavors (see Goode 2007; Hamilakis 2007; Reid 2002; Shaw 2003). Winter and Daly (2012) outline the case for the link between science and Orientalism as manifest in the colonial constructions of culture and history: a *shared* heritage of humankind. Advancement of imperial powers was the goal behind archaeology, conservation, museums, and heritage sites (Winter 2013b) in places such as Cambodia (Edwards 2007), Egypt (Colla 2007; Meskell 2004; Mitchell 2002; Reid 2002), India (Guha-Thakurta 2004), Honduras (Luke 2006), Iraq (Bernhardsson 2005), Peru (Silverman 2013), and Turkey (Atakuman 2010; Given 2004; Shaw 2003; Tanyeri-Erdemir 2006).

The place of the emerging, large-scale national economies of the BRICS (Brazil, Russia, India, China, and South Africa) has occasioned increased attention to cultural heritage by these nations (Akagawa 2014; Guha-Thakurta 2004; Pai 2013; Winter 2013b; Winter and Daly 2012). The MIST (Mexico, Indonesia, South Korea, and Turkey) group, too, shows intensifying interest in cultural diplomacy as part of their self-presentation. Recent economic growth in the BRICs and MIST nations, in tandem with a greater understanding of the strategic importance of culture, has generated greater commitments abroad (Akagawa 2014; Jordan Times 2014;

Luke 2013; Pai 2013). A successful cultural heritage, tourism, and economic package includes world heritage nominations, new museums, and increased tourism numbers. The World Tourism and Travel Council (WTTC) lists China and Turkey as top "new" destinations, both having opened more museums than any other countries in the world within the last two years, and both having among the most robust tentative lists for future nominations to World Heritage status. The packages from these two nations offer a good litmus test for other countries, such as Peru – listed twenty-first for future development by the WTTC, with its robust in-country museum development policy, its appointment as a board member of the UNESCO World Heritage Committee, and its key role in the six-nation World Heritage joint nomination for the Andean Road.

While Lane (2013) traces French cultural diplomacy back to the sixteenth century, it was the post-World War II era that unleashed a flurry of diplomatic activity associated with culture and heritage. Simultaneously the emergence of the United Nations Educational, Scientific and Culture Organization (UNESCO) and its mission to promote "collaboration among the nations through education, science and culture" resulted in an awareness of culture on a global scale. Envisioned as apolitical, and concerned with mutual respect and understanding, along with international imprimatur, cultural diplomacy became a focus of countries like Germany and Japan, who battled negative images in the aftermath of World War II. As Kennedy (2007) notes in his history of the United Nations, such organizations were established at a time when it was widely believed that little or no social and cultural progress could be achieved in the absence of a robust economic environment (Winter 2013b: 538). This proved true for the United States and some European nations with the capital to finance projects like the Aswan Dam in Egypt (Gissen 2009; Hassan 2007). However, programs emanating out of this era and with a mantra of a united notion of a common heritage were, and still are, often viewed as suspect: they were and remain programs with ulterior political motives and with strings attached.

Among the primary challenges in adopting archaeology as a platform for cultural diplomacy is the immense divide between top-down and bottom-up efforts. The practice of archaeology becomes mired in a morass of diplomacy for two primary reasons: archaeological resources and the associated heritage tends to be a public good, controlled by the respective governmental entity, generally a ministry of culture and their respective municipal branches; and it is likely to be tied to the (strategic) interests of the nation state (see Goode 2007; Luke and Kersel 2013a). Nation-states are critical to cultural heritage oversight both within their constructed boundaries and within the international arena as more independent entities recognize the importance of fostering relationships through heritage – yet they also represent a liability precisely because heritage is woven into the fabric of diaspora discourses, traumascapes, and, more generally, geographies of power embedded in gentrification and rehabilitation projects (see Herzfeld 2010).

Development agendas (local, national, and international) supporting heritage in "high-risk" countries, defined by the US Congress as those in the bottom two-thirds of the UN Human Development Index, are most often tied to unhinging and altering current political climates. In recognizing this uneasy dichotomy, transparency in both the funding motives and the mission (winning hearts and minds, showing the kinder side of a country, or a genuine interest in cultural heritage) must become an integral element of heritage diplomacy. Here we agree with Phillips (2005: 106–107) and her assertion that the locus of innovation is the new collaborative and multivocal model of research with community partners with vested, ongoing participation whatever the funding and political motives. The key to effective heritage diplomacy is true collaboration.

Diplomatic Tracks and Power

Approaches that are able to influence the behaviors of others in order to achieve a desired outcome form the backbone of successful diplomacy, and have been become part of "soft power" strategies (see Nye 2004). The self-evident nature of economic and military might is borne out by the various programs implemented by aid agencies, and studies demonstrate that much of the aid invested during the early nineteenth century and the post-World War II "Decade of Development" (the 1960s) has had a long-term net benefit for US-affiliated companies, such as those working in Egypt (see Mitchell 2002), Vietnam (Mekong Delta, Biggs 2006), and Central America (banana republics and development, Luke 2006). Rigorous analysis of the long-term legacies of US financial assistance, furnished under the ruse of protecting and preserving the collective past of humanity, is slowly becoming part of the academic research agenda (see papers in Davis 2013). While the message of a communal past may be firmly embedded in the global, the concept of the importance of heritage may not be shared at the local level, especially five decades on.

Heritage takes on the pretext of collaboration and conversation. The reality, however, is less often about facts on the ground. Rather, what is far more common is that an outside entity supports a project to preserve a particular monument because it (the project) fulfills a neo-imperialistic objective, which may or may not coincide with local desires or interests. The perception of the importance of supporting places of heritage to politicians and their constituencies, however, has become a collective cultural and historical past. Foreign assistance for heritage presents a "softer side" of a nation's image, one that, it is believed, falls outside of political clout, military posturing, and economic agendas. And, in this way, heritage occupies a highly strategic place in development because it is through attraction, rather than force, that results are achieved. Albro (2012) has questioned why any nation-state would employ coercive actions over less intimidating, softer choices. He suggests that because they are softer, heritage initiatives often have much more successful diplomatic outcomes.

Heritage, indeed, has a proven record as an excellent soft power option (see Akagawa 2014; Luke and Kersel 2013a; Schneider 2010; Winter 2014b). But, precisely because heritage plays a crucial role in defining community values, it is also fraught with peril. In some cases, heritage can be part of very positive outcomes, such as a renewed sense of pride in a place or a restored monument, or increased attempts at inclusivity in public spaces, especially when returning to ancestral spaces and places (see Agyei-Mensah 2006 for a discussion of the positive aspects of colonial heritage in Cape Coast, Ghana). On the other hand, notions of heritage can erupt in uncomfortable displays of power, such as looted archaeological sites, plundered places of worship, and vandalized archives. Prohibitively strict cultural heritage regulations often preclude local engagement and in so doing foster distrust and resentment (see Winter 2014a). Uninformed diplomats often unintentionally step into a morass of bureaucracy laden with local political tensions, such as supporting museum retentionist policies that reject the repatriation of items, or military interventions and installations that wreak havoc in heritage zones (particularly during initial occupation). Edited volumes by Stone and Farchakh Bajjaly (2008) and Rothfield (2008) highlight some of the existing tensions regarding heritage in the aftermath of the 2003 coalition forces' invasion of Iraq. In other situations, objects become pawns, employed by ministries of culture to broker repatriations and loans for exhibitions. High-profile repatriations of artifacts to Italy by the J. Paul Getty Museum including a 2,400-year-old statue of a woman believed to be Aphrodite (Frammolino 2011) resulted in a recent exhibition of never before seen artifacts from Sicily in 2013. The second part of the exhibit (at the Cleveland Museum of Art) was cancelled by Sicilian cultural authorities, which claimed that the artifacts had been away from home for too long, damaging tourism at a time of economic difficulty. Yet one might wonder whether the recent denials of repatriation requests by the Cleveland Museum of Art might also have played a factor in the cancellation of the exhibit.

The landmark repatriation case involving artifacts from Machu Picchu housed at Yale University for over a century gives us pause. In 2011 the material was repatriated to Peru under the guise of "cooperation" and news reports and press releases described Yale's tone as moving from one of resistance to one of cooperation. A formal memorandum of understanding was promoted between Yale and the University of San Antonio Abad del Cusco. The official story highlighted a joint center in Cuzco that would oversee the collection (conservation, exhibition, and research). Local and national newspapers covered the story, and it continues to grace the pages of the *New York Times*, including the essay by Rachel Donadio in the Sunday edition on April 17, 2014 (Donadio 2014). The press coverage is superficial at best and, to understand this case fully, one needs to visit Lima as well as the museum in Cuzco where the material is currently on display – one needs to talk with people.

Upon repatriation, the collection was housed at the presidential palace in Lima. And, it was during this initial period that further negotiations with Yale ensued concerning where the material would be displayed and how it would be curated. At that time a rehabilitation project at the Casa Concha in Cuzco was underway (funded by the Peruvians); this is the current home of the repatriated material. In conversations with Peruvian heritage professionals one learns that Yale directed not only the exhibition text, but also the design of the displays, down to the color of the walls, the lighting, and the titles of the exhibition rooms. Even though the artifacts have been sent back to Peru, Yale is still exercising a heavy hand in the public display and interpretation of the material. In these ways, the underbelly of diplomacy reveals not only colonial legacies, but also the decentralized place of "culture" in the diplomatic toolkit. The position of the US Embassy on this particular exhibition and the local negativity associated with the contested repatriation is unclear. This is somewhat unusual, especially given the Memorandum of Understanding between the US and Peru under the Cultural Property Implementation Act (see Luke and Kersel 2013a). Archaeologists and museum practitioners describe the United States as behind a fortress in Lima, a fortress from which they emerge only for press conferences. Indeed, during a two-day symposium in February 2014 held on the floor of Peruvian Congress that focused on cultural property, the US Embassy was not represented. To claim ignorance of the event, too, is disingenuous given the Memorandum of Understanding focused specifically on this event, not to mention the posters that advertised it on public buses and the primetime broadcast of the sessions.

Thus, the series of messages sent from the colonial encounters are mixed at best: do we support local interests or are we subject to contemporary trends that serve immediate, and often political and commercial, purposes? Examined extensively by Gonzalez (2014) this notion of "heritage as a commons" is that the "common possession" (heritage) shared by communities (local, national, and international) is becoming a valuable asset within the global hierarchy of value where the primitive, the local, the traditional, and the exotic are cherished (Hardt and Negri 2009). Gonzalez (2014) contends that the esteem for heritage results in a commodification by governments, academics, and funding institutions; and the long-term result is one that alienates local communities from their heritage. Can there truly be altruistic motives behind the common goal of a protected past? And what is the utility of diplomacy in realizing this goal?

Heritage Diplomacy Apparatuses

Zerilli (2010) suggests that the adjective "soft" denotes, at least metaphorically, flexible or informal legal practices. Within the sphere of heritage, "soft law" is embodied within non-binding legal instruments such as codes of conduct, conventions, declarations, guidelines, opinions, recommendations, and resolutions. The various documents of UNESCO are the soft law principles by which heritage diplomacy is governed and implemented on a global level. Despite its international, transnational, or global range, soft law is always the product of concrete social and historical arrangements and institutional practices in specific locales and temporalities (Zerilli 2010: 10): UNESCO's conventions and recommendations form the common thread for global discussions, yet most are linked to additional implementing in-country legislation (hard law). These various instruments tend to be reactive, rather than proactive – those conventions and agreements (see Table 3.1) most often used to build diplomatic networks and to invoke policy changes were all promulgated in response to world events, notably the post-World War II era or other cases of the unbridled destruction of cultural sites and monuments during conflicts (see Di Giovine 2008; Meskell 2012b, 2013, 2014; and Meskell and Brumann in this volume for further discussion of UNESCO).

The operating assumption is that these conventions and guidelines equalize the playing field: they provide diplomatic avenues for economically disadvantaged states to pursue policy standards in-country to which their economically advantaged counterparts will provide assistance. The juxtaposition of legal instruments and policies

Table 3.1 UNESCO Conventions and Regulations related to Heritage

UNESCO Conventions and Regulations related to Heritage
The Convention on the Protections and Promotion of the Diversity of Cultural Expression (2005)
The Convention for the Safeguarding for the Intangible Cultural Heritage (2003)
The Convention on the Protection of the Underwater Cultural Heritage (2001)
The Convention Concerning the Protection of the World Cultural and Natural Heritage (1972)
The Convention on the Means of Prohibiting and Preventing the Illicit Import, Export and Transfer of Cultural Property (1970)
The Convention for the Protection in the Event of Armed Conflict with Regulations for the Execution of the Convention (1954): First Protocol (1954), Second Protocol (1999),
The Agreement on the Importation of Educational, Scientific and Cultural Materials, with Annexes to E (1950)

are vital to this discussion. Considerations of heritage often begin with an invocation of "the law" – literally understood as well as broadly perceived (see Appiah 2007; Cuno 2008; Forrest 2010; Labadi 2013; Lenzerini and Borelli 2012; Miller 2002; Stamatoudi 2011; Vrdoljak 2006). Yet it was largely in response to the plundering of archaeological sites and museums by economically advantaged colonial entities that nascent states implement(ed) national ownership laws (hard law). Scholars have examined the phenomenon of implementing hard law to protect cultural heritage in Benin (Kiwara-Wilson 2013), Cambodia (Davis 2011), Egypt (Colla 2007; Reid 2002), Greece (Athanassopoulos 2002; Hamilakis 2007), Honduras (Luke 2006), India (Guha-Thakurta 2004), Iran (Abdi 2001), Iraq (Bernhardsson 2005; Goode 2007), Palestine (Kersel 2008, 2010), and Turkey (Shaw 2003). These same national ownership laws are also tied to a heightened awareness of nationalistic paradigms emphasizing the adoption of heritage for purposes of state identity. The universal efforts are aimed at leveling the playing field in terms of prestige and policy on the international stage, notably the World Heritage Convention (1972) and the strong linkage to development funding (see Labadi 2013; Luke and Kersel 2013a; Rodwell 2012). Access to places of heritage is regulated through in-country hard law and through softer law at the international stage. Both purport to implement heritage protocols and shared perceptions of the relative value of heritage on a global scale.

Theoretically policies and programs associated with the enactment of hard law are intended to complement the soft law of international bodies like UNESCO, although Miller (2002) challenges the efficacy of such policies – both national and international efforts – that are proscriptive and universal in their intent. He suggests that such initiatives overlook the local and, if they are to be at all successful, the underlying objective has to be clear and inclusive – heritage policy that neglects the local has a high likelihood of failure, as the aforementioned Yale–Cuzco case illustrates. Without engagement with in-country colleagues and meaningful, sustained partnerships, the specific landscapes, sites, objects, and traditions are merely pawns in a diplomatic dance (see Akagawa 2014; Albro 2012; Luke 2013; Luke and Kersel 2013a; Winter 2014b; Winter and Daly 2012). Nowhere is this more evident than in the increasingly pervasive language in the many conventions, with an emphasis on "local" perspectives. There is passing reference to the local (UNESCO's fifth "C," community), but the process of engaging in dialogue with various stakeholders often presents a very uncomfortable and extremely difficult road to negotiate (Meskell 2013: 492). As scholars begin to unpack these relationships, they find themselves confronting clear patterns of Eurocentrism woven into UNESCO's policies, procedures, and programs (De Cesari 2010; Isar 2011; Labadi 2007; Winter 2014a). Commitment to community is merely a veneer, a lip service.

The UNESCO paradigm of "a common heritage for humankind" is entrenched and reinforced at regional and local levels with policies in place to protect heritage in almost every nation-state. Seeking World Heritage status (a much sought-after crowning jewel made possible by the 1972 World Heritage Convention) for particular sites is of paramount importance for states; receiving the imprimatur of the pre-eminent international cultural heritage organization translates into increased tourism revenue, perceptions of a grand historical ancestry, and historical continuity (see Bertacchini, Saccone, and Santagata 2011; Cleere 2011; Di Giovine 2008; Elkasrawy and El Kasrawy 2012; Elliot and Schmutz 2012; Ryan and Silvanto 2009; Salazar 2012; Salazar and Zhu in this volume). UNESCO seeks to codify the sentiments of a shared past into moral standards and edicts of best practice. But can this communal sense of heritage be categorized to suit all parties? Or do these efforts merely reinforce imperialist traditions of thought and practice that conceive of heritage as global endeavor to "protect humanity's achievements" (Bernbeck and Pollock 2004: 337)? Gonzalez (2014: 367) suggests that this universalist understanding of common heritage implies a Western rationality that often eclipses local needs and desires. Effective management of heritage is reliant on a collective (local, national, and international) caring about the past, its presentation and interpretation. These points all lead to questions: how and where does management of the past become meaningful – and is it possible? Here laws are invoked, but are they enforced? How do they correspond to contemporary policies regarding land use and conservation efforts? Such power is vested in financial independence. And, over the last century, these resources have most often come from agencies and patrons outside national boundaries and with little or no community participation – yet with clear strategic and lucrative reasons for foreign entities to contribute resources. Is there a viable model for greater collaboration?

Heritage Diplomacy as Contact Zone

In order for heritage diplomacy to be successful there must be contact between those wishing to influence hearts and minds and those being influenced. Utilizing the Diplomatic Tracks 2 and 3 (see above), heritage diplomacy stems from the premise that there is a common notion of heritage. Anthony Appiah's (2007) argument in *Cosmopolitanism* provides a general framework: a set of principles dependent on a nexus of common morals within humanity, beyond real and imagined boundaries. Appiah's challenge to archaeologists is to recognize their obligations to a wider public and to participate in a much more diverse set of conversations, rather than merely "science" or "preservation" (see Meskell 2009 and Cuno 2008 for further discussion). Meskell (2009) situates cosmopolitanism within the sphere of cultural difference, recognizing the broad role of multiple histories and multiple voices that contribute to how the past is launched into present communities, particularly communities that have been underrepresented within the traditional heritage paradigm. Other practitioners (see Bennett 1998; Boast 2011; Klimaszewski, Bader, and Nyce 2012) have echoed these sentiments, calling for inclusive collaboration and local input. Success does not, however, derive from mere pretense. There has to be sustained, long-term commitment and engagement through contact – people-to-people programs – for heritage diplomacy to be successful.

Across the globe there are excellent examples of people-to-people engagement involving cultural heritage, including the Sustainable Preservation Initiative[1] supporting projects in South America; the Palestinian Association for Cultural Exchange (Yahya 2004); the Temple of the Winged Lions Cultural Resource Management Initiative (Tuttle 2013) and Umm el-Jimal (de Vries 2013) in Jordan; various projects on Cyprus (see below and Counts et al. 2013); and in Southeast Asia, including Burma, Cambodia, Laos, Malaysia, Thailand (Chapman 2013), and Indonesia (Scott 2012). Many of these examples draw on colonial legacies, yet they offer a new perspective, one that recognizes the past and moves towards new initiatives. The 2003–2006 Netherlands-Indonesia Shared Cultural Heritage Project in Indonesia (Scott 2012) focused on research about the objects that involved not only the history of museum practice in both countries, but also the continued exchange of students.

If heritage has particular potency to contemporary communities, then our challenge becomes how to understand contact zones and moments for dialogue, following Pratt (1991) and Clifford (1997). In 1991 Pratt defined a contact zone as the social space where cultures meet, clash, and grapple with each other, often in contexts of asymmetrical relations of power, as the legacies of colonial and slavery attest (Pratt 1991: 34). Though Pratt envisions these zones as unequal places, Clifford (1997) imagines these zones as consultative space(s) within the paradigm of the new museum, urging practitioners to move beyond background, institutional, and economic imbalances. Clifford (1997) argues that in order to be relevant to the contemporary public, museums and curators can no longer work with material culture in isolation; they must collaborate with the host communities. Collaboration reaches beyond "consultation and sensitivity" in the museum setting, such that the realized products are achieved only through "active collaboration and a sharing of authority" (Clifford 1997: 210). Analysis of the relationship between archaeology, development, and diplomacy as a nested group within spheres of cultural policy reveals that there are varying degrees of collaboration embedded within power structures. The legacies of neo-imperialism manifest in past and current foreign policies and attached funding demonstrate the need to study-up (echoing Nader 1972). Archaeology in the twenty-first century is still recovering from the break between the museum and the research institution, corresponding with the abandonment of *partage*, and the fundamental purpose of archaeological fieldwork in-country.

While the lens of the contact zone is useful for an examination of the complexities surrounding heritage diplomacy, it is not without its problems and detractors. Some (Klimaszewski, Bader, and Nyce 2012) suggest the contact zone is a clinical collaboration that is designed from the outset to appropriate the resources necessary for those utilizing heritage in the diplomatic sphere. The relationship is orchestrated with well-defined, expected outcomes directed by one partner in the relationship – typically the entity providing the funds. As the case studies below demonstrate, the heritage diplomacy contact zone is a lopsided space where the periphery comes to win some small monetary and strategic advantage, but where the center ultimately gains, both in power and influence.

Researchers involved in cultural heritage preservation need to adopt an inclusive research methodology that pays closer attention to how power, class, and status shape communities and, in turn, how decisions surrounding funding impact those same communities. In his critique of museums as neocolonial contact zones Boast (2011: 56) suggests that while "dialogue and collaboration are the name of the game these days and there are few museums with anthropological or even archaeological collections that would consider an exhibition that did not include some form of consultation," there is a dark underbelly to the museum as contact zone. And, under current policies, heritage diplomacy does not typically take place at the local level. There is little or no interaction between the financial donors and the communities "benefitting" from the funds.

There is a wild disparity in what constitutes collaboration and consultation. As Boast (2011: 58) writes, it is not enough to "talk to a native": host communities should be fundamental to heritage diplomacy and future planning. In November 1989, the *Into the Heart of Africa* exhibition opened at the Royal Ontario Museum (ROM) in Toronto and just about everything that could go wrong with an exhibition did (Schildkrout 1991). The guest curator Jeanne Cannizzo set out to denounce colonialism and to criticize white Canada's attitudes to Africa. In using irony, a large number of text panels, and unexplained images of missionaries and Africans to convey her intent, Cannizzo angered many black and white Toronto residents, who staged protests. For them the museum became a symbol of uncaring, unrepentant white power and was nicknamed the Racist Ontario Museum (Butler 2007). One of the main criticisms of Cannizzo and the ROM museum process was the lack of local engagement, input, and collaboration on the original vision for the exhibit (Butler 2007; Schildkrout 1991). There were no local focus groups and no consultations with descendant communities, black or white.

An intriguing example of true cooperation where the impetus, direction, and outcomes have come from the local, albeit with Western funding, is the Oriental Institute-National Museum of Afghanistan Partnership and Cultural Heritage Protection Work (Stein 2013). The Museum director and staff, along with a team of archaeologists and conservators from the University of Chicago's Oriental Institute (OI), are collaborating on a three-year project (funded by the US government) to register every object in the National Museum of Afghanistan collections and to create a bilingual digital record. Rather than the traditional model of the foreign specialists flying in imparting their knowledge and then leaving, members of the OI team are based in Kabul for the duration of the project, working daily with the Afghani professionals to complete the inventory and conservation of the irreplaceable collections (Nordland 2014). This mutually beneficial museum partnership illustrates the marriage of heritage and diplomacy at the local level, but under the specter of neo-imperialism – there are clear diplomatic advantages for the US support of museums and culture in Afghanistan.

Extending influence over foreign nations through the lens of diplomacy invariably involves inferences for heritage. The nexus of neo-imperialism and heritage diplomacy and the ethical implications of certain neo-imperialist heritage initiatives have resulted in aid packages, which while they support heritage, have and continue to reinforce the asymmetries of power between the haves and have-nots. Financial resources influence which archaeological sites are excavated, protected, and interpreted, which objects are exhibited and loaned, and which histories are presented to the public. Less-developed nations are reliant on wealthier entities to provide support (logistical, intellectual, and financial) in order to protect the past. But at what cost? Bernbeck and Pollock (2004) suggest foreign archaeologists, in contrast with those who hold national, in-country citizenship, generally work within imperialist traditions: archaeology is a global endeavor.

A leader in current neo-imperialistic heritage diplomacy, the United States deploys targeted giving through the United States Agency for International Development (USAID) and the Ambassadors Fund for Cultural Preservation (AFCP); these and other programs influence how heritage is protected, promoted, and presented throughout the world. But the US is not the only country participating in heritage diplomacy. The granting of funds and the activities of research institutes abroad are under the joint authority of the French Ministry of Foreign Affairs and of the Centre National de la Recherche Scientifique (CNRS) (Lane 2013: 70). Under the mantra of safeguarding cultural heritage for the benefits of the host country, France is contributing to the long-term development of the local economy and heritage. Winter (2014b) suggests it is the dissatisfaction with Western approaches to conservation and heritage management that has resulted in investment and heritage diplomacy carried out by other countries like China (Wang 2012), India (Thussu 2013), Japan (Akagawa 2014; Pai 2013), and Turkey (Luke 2013). And, if one wonders about the potential scale and impact of such projects, one need only look to the Saadiyat Cultural District in Abu Dhabi, United Arab Emirates. The Tourism Development and Investment Company (TDIC) presents a feast of culture for the visitor as well as the citizen, constructing historical narratives and framing future paradigms. Collaboration has been the name of the game, yet it is hard to disentangle from the jaws of marketing and branding: the multimillion dollar annual contracts to the Louvre for use of the name and consultation with curators to build the collections speaks to the current style of French cultural diplomacy, which is not without a colonial flare (Luke and Kersel 2013b).

Case 1: Re-Establishing the Contact Zone – Ambassadors and Heritage Diplomacy

Embassies abroad and their representative staff are often the first point of contact in issues of cultural diplomacy. Recognizing European/global emphases on and interest in cultural heritage, the United States accepted that it was missing a key element in its diplomatic arsenal (see Lane 2013; Winter 2014b). In response to a need for positive visibility the Ambassadors Fund for Cultural Preservation was born. Established by the US Department of State at the request of the US Congress (Public Law 106-553), over the last twelve years the Ambassadors Fund has focused on a variety of cultural heritage initiatives, funding more than 750 projects in 132 countries, totaling almost US$ 40 million (the latest statistics available from the US Department of State, December 2013).

In the original configuration of the Ambassadors Fund, the concept of the heritage as a contact zone was integral to the success of projects. In-country staff and even the US Ambassador nominate worthy projects, often with guidance from local heritage NGOs and ministries of culture. The only clearly stated criterion for eligibility was that countries fall within the bottom two-thirds of the United Nations Human Development Index (US Department of State 2004). In the early days of the Ambassadors Fund, grants were typically between US$ 10,000 and US$ 40,000, and were focused on funding local initiatives with very little foreign interaction and input. It was this aspect of the Ambassadors Fund – supporting the local in-country aims and objectives, funding non-traditional initiatives rather than the big ticket iconic sites "branded" as heritage (see Holtorf 2007; Meskell 2012b; Ryan and Silvanto 2009 for further discussion) – that set it apart from other initiatives such as the Global Heritage Fund, the World Monuments Fund, and UNESCO. These grants instead targeted the preservation, rehabilitation, and/or celebration of cultural traditions and places of historical significance to local constituencies. They were not intended to support Western perceptions of local importance by funding World Heritage sites – most being legacies of colonial agendas. Rather, the initial aim of Ambassadors Fund grants was to support proposals written, managed, and carried out by locals with little or no input from foreign entities or experts (Luke 2012, 2013; Luke and Kersel 2013a; Schneider 2010). In the third cycle of the call for Ambassadors Fund proposals, directives changed and became mired in the more overt goals of a neo-imperialist machine that was instituted to combat negative perceptions of the United States in the global arena in the post-9/11 and Iraq invasion era (Kennedy 2003; Luke and Kersel 2013a; Rothfield 2008; Schneider 2010; and Stone and Farchakh Bajjaly 2008).

September 11, 2001 profoundly changed US approaches to the role of government in foreign affairs and perceptions of the United States in the global sphere. In this period of self-assessment, policy analysts broadened their attempts to put together programs that would convey not only a positive message about the United States, but also one that promoted the United States as a nation accepting of many cultures, religions, and people. These positions from the hallways of Congress and the offices of the Department of State advocated for a greater role for culture in the war on terrorism (Kennedy 2003; Rothfield 2008; Schneider 2010; Stone and Farchakh Bajjaly 2008). Collaboration with various in-country actors or interlocutors outside of the official governmental representatives was deemed necessary – the contact zone became a critical area for support. Heritage diplomacy found firm footing: winning hearts and minds and building trust through long-term programs and policies aimed at protecting, preserving, and promoting a shared global heritage and a common interest in the past.

In the aftermath of September 11, 2001 and the 2003 invasion of Iraq by coalition forces, the Ambassadors Fund increased funding to projects associated with Islam or from predominantly Islamic nations (those with a Muslim population over 50 percent) – there was a Muslim Imperative. The US Senate Report (108-144) recommended increased funding for the Ambassadors Fund from US$1 million to US$ 1.75 million, but with the stipulation that a specified amount (US$ 700,000) should be used solely for projects from the Middle East. The 2004 Senate Report read, "[t]he Committee acknowledges the critical role that public diplomacy plays in both addressing the root causes of terrorism and in US foreign relations generally." Heritage diplomacy was part of the official toolkit in the fight against terrorism (see Laos 2011; Luke and Kersel 2013a; Scham 2008; Schneider 2010).

Ambassadors Fund Islamic projects include the restoration, preservation, and conservation of mosques and religious institutions in places such as Afghanistan, Benin, China, and Montenegro; the preservation and conservation of Islamic manuscripts in Mali, Mauritania, and Turkmenistan; and the encouragement of traditional crafts and architectures in Egypt and Thailand, among other projects. Current funding ranges from US$ 7,000 to US$ 750,000. Over the last 12 years nearly US$ 5 million has been allocated to some 66 projects with an Islamic focus. Just over a quarter of the US$ 40 million of Ambassadors Fund money has been apportioned to over 250 projects in countries with a predominantly Muslim population, with awards ranging from US$ 7,000 to US$ 850,000 USD.

Scham (2008: 166–167) suggests that during the 2001 War on Terror and the post-2003 invasion of Iraq by Coalition Forces, the United States appropriated (quietly and quickly) the heritage of the Middle East as a neo-imperalistic overture. When referring to Iraq as holding the archaeological heritage of the cradle of civilization, the US, and by extension the Ambassadors Fund, adopted UNESCO vocabulary; in so doing, they stepped from the local to the global. By focusing the conversation around the "heritage of mankind," Scham (2008) asserts that the United States no longer had to take sole responsibility for the situation in Afghanistan, nor their failure to protect the cultural institutions in Iraq. To ameliorate any misconceptions that it was in fact responsible for any destruction of the cultural heritage of mankind, the United States, through the Ambassadors Fund, made a strategic decision to support the preservation of this heritage to foster and further diplomatic relations.

By 2010 it was clear that the Ambassadors Fund (then in its tenth year) was continuing to shift from an emphasis on the local contact zone to an implementation of the ideals of "outstanding universal value" set forth by UNESCO and other Western heritage organizations. That year the Ambassadors Fund awarded 12 grants to well-known World Heritage sites (US Department of State 2010), totaling more than $US 700,000. In a departure from the earlier guiding principles of the Ambassadors Fund, money was granted to sites that were believed to have merit by the nominating committees of the respective countries, an international adjudicating panel, and the UNESCO Committee on World Heritage. Traditionally very little local input is sought on World Heritage site nominations, reinforcing Meskell's (2002, 2012b) assertion that World Heritage sites are an assortment of places that governments believe best represent the importance of their national identity (see also Askew 2010; Cleere 2011; Elliot and Schmutz 2012; Frey and Steiner 2011). The decision to acknowledge the tenth anniversary of the Ambassadors Fund by moving from the initial objective of supporting locally nominated and supported projects that would "make the most amount of difference with a small amount of money" coincides with US foreign relation objectives on the global rather than in the local sphere.

The special Ambassadors Fund allocation for World Heritage sites, in the eyes of the US Congress and the State Department, conveyed to the world a subtle, softer side of the United States, one invested in the preservation and protection of "our shared heritage." Yet US respect for the heritage of other countries is sometimes problematic precisely because places and monuments of heritage often represent the single most contested spheres within a nation state. The preservation and restoration of specific objects, monuments, and practices may promote social cohesion, yet it may also fracture and/or meddle with contested cultural spheres at local, national, and international levels – this is especially true in areas such as Cyprus or Palestine, or in the delicate space of heritage that is tied to religious or diaspora communities.

Yet, initiatives like the Ambassadors Fund can and do produce excellent examples of Track 3 types of diplomatic efforts – the people-to-people interaction aimed at the grassroots and the local. At the archaeological site of Umm el-Jimal in Jordan, combined funding from the Ambassadors Fund, United Nations Women, and UNESCO lead to a project to assist women in managing site for tourists (Shaw 2014). In Bolivia Ambassadors Fund monies for the restoration of chapels in the Santiago de Curahuara de Carangas Parish have resulted in greater community cohesion, providing places of worship and much-needed spaces where locals can gather for other purposes (US Embassy 2013). An advantage of the original concept for this US government funding rests with the assumption that there is a process of local collaboration and agreement on the meaning of heritage and the rationale for its preservation, documentation, and presentation. Returning to the original intent of the Ambassadors Fund that "there are unique opportunities for the American embassies to develop stronger relationship with local communities" will set in motion a shift from the top-down approach of the current priorities and programs to the conceptualization of heritage diplomacy as a contact zone that will ensure participation at the local level, dispelling associated neo-imperialist connotations.

Case 2: Mediterranean Diplomacy and Development

The explicit "apolitical" message attached to US government heritage-specific funding discredits the purpose and the outcomes of the associated projects. An alternative model is that of the Turkish Cooperation and Coordination Agency, known as TIKA (see Luke 2013), an agency that does attempt to hide its political, religious, and/or cultural motivations in its support of heritage and the fostering of Turkish ideals. Established in 1992, TIKA has grown slowly into a powerhouse of international aid, currently ranked forth in the world. TIKA funding supports education and infrastructure (for instance, water), as well as agricultural development from Africa to Guatemala. Among the targeted initiatives is a program focused on Islamic Heritage. The emphasis of this work is on mosques, as explained on the website: TIKA "continues to maintain the protection of our cultural heritage by restoring ancestral relic mosques in a number of countries, starting with the Balkans and the Middle Eastern and African countries. The efforts of TIKA respond to the ongoing need for the protection of cultural heritage of the Turkish Islam Civilization."[2] In addition, TIKA has partnered with UNESCO on projects in Albania, as well as the wider Silk Road initiative.[3] TIKA's model is aggressive and highly strategic. Turkey's diplomatic corps take great pride in the work that that they do, from water to roads. These are the "important" components, the heart of the development engine. Support for Islamic heritage initiatives, in contrast, has been described to Luke as a resurrection of Turkish philanthropy. The increased support for Islamic projects from private individuals and foundations for community-based projects is among the most successful in Turkey; and it transcends borders through its offshoot, the Pious Foundation. Thus, on one hand we find a new face of Ottoman-legacy support for public, historic spaces, yet on the other we find TIKA balancing development models with long-term foci on the political economy in much the same way as USAID. Among the most interesting locales for USAID-supported work is in Cyprus – in both the south (Greek) and the north (Turkish).

The US-backed work in Cyprus represents a particularly poignant example of targeted cultural diplomacy and funding in a highly contested zone. As reported by Remsen and Şevketoğlu (2008: 1):

> The United States Agency for International Development (USAID) [supported] economic growth in the Turkish Cypriot Community (TCC) to foster a durable settlement in Cyprus. In 2005 [the] International Resources Group (IRG) won the $10.1 million USD contract to establish the SAVE (Supporting Activities that Value the Environment) Program. In addition to Cultural Heritage Conservation, major SAVE activities [included] environment and natural resources management and capacity building and geographical information systems (GIS) for improved land use planning.

In the preface to their 2009 report (Bağışkan 2009), SAVE acknowledges the potential for cultural heritage to foster collaboration, to build bridges. This is among the first programs (and publications) to consider heritage on the entire island of Cyprus – that is, bridging the contested landscapes of Greek–Turkish claims to sovereignty that have tarnished cultural relations since December 1963. In 1974, integrated cross-border connections, especially for sites tied to ethnicity and identity such as Islamic or Christian spaces, became impossible. The global community recognizes the southern half of the island as a state; the north as an independent state remains acknowledged only by Turkey. The Green Zone, between North and South Cyprus, presents a fascinating time capsule: a plane sits on the runway, gear in place; restaurants and other public spaces have been untouched, jackets and dishes in place. Time, in many ways, stands still – yet the eventual deterioration of goods and of fabrics marks the march of years in this contested space.

The United States is unable to provide direct funding for programs that take place in disputed (occupied) territories not officially recognized by the United Nations. Most recently, this policy has resulted in political calamity for US participation in UNESCO, ensuring financial hardship for that organization (see Kersel and Luke 2012).

In order to circumvent political restrictions there are diplomats who negotiate this slippery contact zone successfully, finding opportunities to dedicate money to heritage programs through local and international agencies. In northern Cyprus, USAID is able to channel money to specific projects through UNDP – Action for Cooperation and Trust (UNDP-ACT[4]); funding has resulted in the fostering of relations between northern Cyprus and the Republic, and heritage is often the common denominator.

Initiated in 2010, the Potamia Bi-Communal Village is described as "one of the last mixed villages on the island and the two communities there live in relative harmony."[5] Located in the Green Zone, the town, once dominated by Turkish Cypriots, is an excellent example of co-existence between Greek and Turkish Cypriots. While many of the Potamia programs are very familiar (conservation, documentation, presentation), Phase II (2012–2013) stresses a new element: "participatory democracy." There is an attempt to balance the dispersal of funds to different heritage legacies, akin to the unofficial, yet clearly discernible pattern of policy in the Balkans under the Ambassadors Fund for Cultural Preservation (Luke 2013; Luke and Kersel 2013a). In northern Cyprus, support has included the Apostolos Andreas Monastery – a joint program with the Turkish Pious Foundation branch in Turkish Cyprus and the Church of Cyprus (UNDP 2013). This work complements UNDP-ACT support for Armenian heritage in north Nicosia (UNDP-USAID 2013). These and other projects are part of building civil society, as expressed on the website: "In addition to the beauty of the cultural and historical places visited, both Turkish Cypriot and Greek Cypriot participants gathered to walk together, talk together and share together, becoming good friends along the way. I think that in order to attain peace we need to understand each other better and I am very happy to have been a part of such an effort by joining in this activity" (UNDP-USAID 2013). Various philanthropic and non-governmental organizations, including the Severis Foundation and EU support to the UN Technical Committee on Cultural Heritage, Rehabilitation & Infrastructure keep these programs shuffling along.

Moments when we see "results" are often subtle, with little indication of the major international sectors behind the scenes. Such was the case in April 2014. The headlines of *ABC NEWS* read, "Religion Builds Bridges in Ethnically Split Cyprus" and described the event as "faith-based" diplomacy (Hadjicostis 2014). On 18 April, 2014, the *Greek Reporter* ran the story, "Thousands of Orthodox Worshippers Flock to Famagusta," and described the event as follows: "The service, the first since 1957 at the church in the medieval town, *should* send a message of hope and reunification, said leaders of both major parties AKEL and DISY on their way to the thronged church and its courtyard" (emphasis added, Nikolouli 2014). The *Turkish Hürriyet Daily News* (2014) read, "Historic mass in Turkish northern Cyprus 'like a miracle,'" and the article suggested that serious efforts aimed at reconciliation are currently under negotiation. Yet, local papers in Greek Cyprus reported churches in Turkish Cyprus in need of immediate repair, and claimed that restoration dollars are put towards Islamic mosques, rather than Christian churches. No mention was made in the news reports of the EU-UNDP Partnership for the Future programs, the 2009–2010 inventory of cultural heritage sites and subsequent reports funded by USAID and UNDP, or the Turkish Pious Foundation Islamic initiatives and many others. Cypriot Christian Greeks wish to see greater efforts aimed at preservation initiatives of churches in northern Cyprus. At the same time, Turkish citizens with ancestral connections to Crete or Kosovo lament the deterioration of the Islamic heritage: it is crumbling before their eyes. To this end, TIKA has taken center stage, pouring in millions of dollars (over US$

60 million dedicated only to Islamic heritage in Albania) for such efforts; in so doing, TIKA has carved out a strategic position on the heritage stage, perhaps ensuring future influence in various spheres.

Regardless of assertions to the contrary, support of cultural heritage initiatives is political and strategic, at times reifying and augmenting neo-imperialist agendas, while, at others, standing as excellent examples of collaborative, locally focused, sustained engagements. It is naive not to acknowledge the role that cultural heritage plays in fostering relationships related to diplomacy; and we would be remiss to consider heritage independent from the tourism economy.

Conclusion: Ethical Dimensions of Heritage Diplomacy

Heritage diplomacy was, ostensibly, formulated in order to support the objectives of standard diplomacy and a shared notion of protecting aspects of culture. But this common belief in the importance of the past and its use as an element of diplomacy is laden with ethical dimensions. What gets preserved depends to a significant degree on who has the power to define the past that matters and, by implication, which pasts do not (Bernbeck and Pollock 2004). Heritage diplomacy as contact zones could be sources of knowledge and catalysts for new relationships – both within and between communities if funding agencies were more collaborative in their approach – as was the original intent of the Ambassadors Fund for Cultural Preservation. Often programs such as heritage diplomacy use the subterfuge of collaboration and consultation, while the institution (in this case the funding body) controls the resource. One of the biggest changes in social science theory has been the acceptance of the idea that societies and groups cannot always be characterized by shared beliefs but by different understandings and definitions of those shared beliefs. Implicit in this understanding is not just the acknowledgement that a variety of cultural beliefs exist, but also that beliefs themselves undergo constant modification. Therefore, understanding heritage means taking into account how individuals believe they got to their current situation, and learning what they would like to see happen to them in the present and in the future. While the direction of any preservation project must be determined by empirical, theoretically informed research, we can and must assume that there will always be a variety of stakeholders in any community with complementary, competing, and sometimes colliding desires. This leads to a number of authenticities (authentic histories) based on which elements people chose to inform their understanding of the past and present. Funding from different resources (AFCP, EU, TIKA, UNESCO, USAID) all contribute to the types of heritage understood and presented to the public, while at the same time reinforcing the idea that other countries care about culture.

NOTES

1 http://sustainablepreservation.org/.
2 http://www.tika.gov.tr/en/.
3 http://www.unesco.org/new/en/culture/themes/dialogue/routes-of-dialogue/silk-road/.
4 http://www.undp-act.org/.
5 http://potamiaheritage.com/.

REFERENCES

Abdi, K. (2001) Nationalism, politics, and the development of archaeology in Iran. *American Journal of Archaeology* 105(1): 51–76.

Abu El-Haj, N. (2001) *Facts on the Ground. Archaeological Practice and Territorial Self-Fashioning in Israeli Society*. Chicago, IL: University of Chicago Press.

AFP (2014) Qatar invests unprecedented $135 million in largest funding for Sudan archaeology project. *Agence France-Presse,* March 23, 2014. Available at: http://www.rawstory.com/rs/2014/03/23/qatar-invests-unprecedented-135-million-in-largest-funding-for-sudan-archaeology-project/. Accessed November 18, 2014.

Agyei-Mensah, S. (2006) Marketing its colonial heritage: A new lease of life for Cape Coast, Ghana? *International Journal of Urban and Regional Research* 30(3): 705–716.

Akagawa, N. (2014) *Heritage Conservation and Japan's Cultural Diplomacy: Heritage, National Identity, and National Interest*. London: Routledge.

Albro, R. (2012) Cultural Diplomacy's Representational Conceit. December 3, 2012. Available at: http://uscpublicdiplomacy.org/blog/cultural_diplomacys_representational_conceit. Accessed November 18, 2014.

Appiah, K. A. (2007) *Cosmopolitanism: Ethics in a World of Strangers*. New York: Norton.

Armakolas, I. (2012) MOSTAR: Heritage Reconstruction in a Divided City. Cultural Heritage and the Reconstruction of Identities after Conflict (CRIC) Research Project. Available at: http://www.youtube.com/watch?v=T1Cz6UzwDrg. Accessed November 18, 2014.

Askew, M. (2010) The Magic List of Global Status: UNESCO, World Heritage and the Agendas of States, in S. Labadi and C. Long (eds), *Heritage and Globalization*. London: Routledge, pp. 19–44.

Atakuman, Ç. (2010) Value of heritage in Turkey: History and politics of Turkey's World Heritage nominations. *Journal of Mediterranean Archaeology* 23(1): 107–132.

Athanassopoulos, E. F. (2002) An "ancient" landscape: European ideals, archaeology, and nation building in early modern Greece. *Journal of Modern Greek Studies* 20: 273–305.

Bağışkan, T. (2009) *Ottoman, Islamic and Islamised Monuments in Cyprus*. Trans. T. A. Sinclair. Nicosia: Cyprus Turkish Education Foundation.

Bennett, T. (1998) *Culture: A Reformer's Science*. London: Sage.

Berman, M. and J. E. Johnson (eds) (1977) *Unofficial Diplomats*. New York: Columbia University Press.

Bernbeck, R. and S. Pollock (2004) The Political Economy of Archaeological Practice and the Production of Heritage in the Middle East, in L. Meskell and R. W. Preucel (eds), *A Companion to Social Archaeology*. Oxford: Blackwell, pp. 335–352.

Bernhardsson, M. T. (2005) *Reclaiming a Plundered Past. Archaeology and Nation Building in Modern Iraq*. Austin: University of Texas Press.

Bertacchini, E., D. Saccone, and W. Santagata (2011) Embracing diversity, correcting inequalities: Towards a new global governance for the UNESCO World Heritage. *International Journal of Cultural Policy* 17(3): 278–288.

Biggs, D. (2006) Reclamation nations: The U.S. Bureau of Reclamation's role in water management and nation building in the Mekong Valley, 1945–1975. *Comparative Technology Transfer and Society* 4(3): 225–246.

Boast, R. (2011) Neocolonial collaboration. *Museum Anthropology* 34(1): 56–70.

Böhmelt, T. (2010) The effectiveness of tracks of diplomacy strategies in third-party interventions. *Journal of Peace Research* 47(2): 167–178.

Butler, S. R. (2007) *Contested Representations: Revisiting "Into the Heart of Africa."* Toronto: University of Toronto Press.

Byrne, D. (2013) Gateway and Garden: A Kind of Tourism in Bali, in R. Staiff, R. Bushell, and S. Watson (eds), *Heritage Tourism: Place, Encounter, Engagement*. London: Routledge, pp. 26–44.

Castañeda, Q. E. (2005) The Carnegie mission and vision of science: Institutional contexts of Maya archaeology and espionage. *Histories of Anthropology Annual Volume* 1: 27–60.

Chapman, W. (2013) *A Heritage of Ruins: The Ancient Sites of Southeast Asia and Their Conservation*. Honolulu: University of Hawai'i Press.

Cleere, H. (2011) The 1972 UNESCO World Heritage Convention. *Heritage and Society* 14: 173–186.

Clifford, J. (1997) *Routes: Travel and Translation in the Late Twentieth Century*. Cambridge, MA: Harvard University Press.

Colla, E. (2007) *Conflicted Antiquities: Egyptology, Egyptomania, Egyptian Modernity*. Durham, NC: Duke University Press.

Cornago, N. (2013) *Plural Diplomacies: Normative Predicaments and Functional Imperatives*. Leiden: Brill.

Counts, D., E. Cova, P. N. Kardulias, and M. K. Toumazou (2013) Fitting in: Community in Athienou, Cyprus. *Near Eastern Archaeology* 76(3): 166–177.

Cuno, J. (2008) *Who Owns Antiquity?: Museums and the Battle over Our Ancient Heritage*. Princeton, NJ: Princeton University Press.

Davis, J. (2013) Philhellenism, philanthropy, or political convenience? American archaeology in Greece. *Hesperia (Special Issue on Philhellenism)* 82(1): 1–14.

Davis, T. (2011) Supply and demand: Exposing the illicit trade in Cambodian antiquities through a study of Sotheby's auction house. *Crime Law and Social Change* 56: 155–174.

De Cesari, C. (2010) Creative heritage: Palestinian heritage NGOs and defiant arts of government. *American Anthropologist* 112(4): 625–637.

De Vries, B. (2013) Archaeology and community in Jordan and Greater Syria: Traditional patterns and new directions. *Near Eastern Archaeology* 76(3): 132–141.

Di Giovine, M. (2008) *The Heritage-Scape: UNESCO, World Heritage, and Tourism*. Lanham, MD: Lexington Books.

Dietler, M. (1994) Our ancestors the Gauls: Archaeology, ethnic nationalism, and the manipulation of Celtic identity in modern Europe. *American Anthropologist* 96(3): 584–605.

Donadio, R. (2014) Vision of home. Repatriated works back in their countries of origin. *New York Times,* April 17, 2014. Available at: http://www.nytimes.com/2014/04/20/arts/design/repatriated-works-back-in-their-countries-of-origin.html. Accessed November 18, 2014.

Edwards, P. (2007) *Cambridge: the Cultivation of a Nation*. Honolulu: University of Hawai'i Press.

Elkasrawy, S. F. and S. F. El Kasrawy (2012) Evaluating the status of UNESCO World Heritage sites in Egypt. *International Journal of Management Cases* 14(1): 25–41.

Elliot, M. A. and V. Schmutz (2012) World Heritage: Constructing a universal cultural order. *Poetics* 40(3): 256–277.

Forrest, C. (2010) *International Law and the Protection of Cultural Heritage*. New York: Routledge.

Frammolino, R. (2011) The goddess goes home. *Smithsonian Magazine*, November. Available at: http://www.smithsonianmag.com/history/the-goddess-goes-home-107810041/?no-ist. Accessed November 18, 2014.

Frey, B. and L. Steiner (2011) World Heritage List: Does it make sense? *International Journal of Cultural Policy* 17(5): 555–573.

Gissen, D. (2009) The architectural production of nature, Dendur/New York. *Grey Room* 34: 58–79.

Given, M. (2004) *The Archaeology of the Colonized*. London: Routledge.

Gonzalez, P. A. (2014) From a given to a construct: Heritage as a commons. *Cultural Studies* 28(3): 359–390.

Goode, J. F. (2007) *Negotiating for the Past: Archaeology, Nationalism, and Diplomacy in the Middle East, 1919–1941*. Austin: University of Texas Press.

Guha-Thakurta, T. (2004) *Monuments, Objects, Histories: Institutions of Art in Colonial and Postcolonial India*. New York: Columbia University Press.

Hadjicostis, M. (2014) Religion builds bridges in ethnically split Cyprus. *ABC News,* April 19, 2014. Available at: http://bigstory.ap.org/article/religion-builds-bridges-ethnically-split-cyprus. Accessed April 19, 2014.

Hamilakis, Y. (2007) *The Nation and Its Ruins*. Oxford: Oxford University Press.

Hardt, M. and A. Negri (2009) *Commonwealth*. Cambridge, MA: Harvard University Press.

Harrison, R. (2013) *Heritage: Critical Approaches*. London: Routledge.

Hassan, F. A. (2007) The Aswan High Dam and the International Rescue Nubia Campaign. *African Archaeological Review* 24: 73–94.

Herzfeld, M. (2009) *Evicted from Eternity: The Restructuring of Modern Rome*. Chicago, IL: University of Chicago Press.

Herzfeld, M. (2010) Engagement, gentrification, and the neoliberal hijacking of history. *Current Anthropology* 51(S2): S59–S67.

Hobsbawm, E. and T. Ranger (eds) (1983) *The Invention of Tradition*. Cambridge: Cambridge University Press.

Holtorf, C. (2007) *Archaeology Is a Brand: The Meaning of Archaeology in Contemporary Popular Culture*. Walnut Creek, CA: Left Coast Press.

Hürriyet Daily News (2014) Historic mass in Turkish Northern Cyprus "like a miracle." *Hürriyet Daily News,* April 19, 2014. Available at: http://www.hurriyetdailynews.com/historic-mass-in-turkish-northern-cyprus-like-a-miracle.aspx?pageID=517&nID=65274&NewsCatID=351. Accessed November 19, 2014.

Isar, Y. R. (2011) UNESCO and Heritage: Global Doctrine, Global Practice, in D. Viejo-Rose, H. K. Anheier, and Y. R. Isar (eds), *Heritage, Memory & Identity*. The Cultures and Globalization Series. Los Angeles, CA: Sage, pp. 39–52.

Jordan Times (2014) Japan grants Jordan JD4.76m to build Petra museum. *Jordan Times,* March 1, 2014. Available at: http://jordantimes.com/japan-grants-jordan-jd476m-to-build-petra-museum. Accessed November 18, 2014.

Kennedy, L. (2003) Remember September 11: Photography as cultural diplomacy. *International Affairs* 79(2): 315–26.

Kennedy, P. (2007) *The Parliament of Man: The Past, Present, and Future of the United Nations*. New York: Vintage.

Kersel, M. M. (2008) The trade in Palestinian antiquities. *Jerusalem Quarterly* (Winter) 33: 21–38.

Kersel, M. M. (2010) The Changing Legal Landscape for Middle Eastern Archaeology in the Colonial Era, 1800–1930, in G. Emberling (ed.), *Pioneers to the Past: American Archaeologists in the Middle East, 1919–1920*. Oriental Institute Museum Publications 30. Chicago, IL: Oriental Institute, pp. 85–90.

Kersel, M. M. and C. Luke (2012) Editorial introduction: A crack in the diplomatic armor: The United States and the Palestinian Authority's bid for UNESCO recognition. *Journal of Field Archaeology* 36(2): 255–256.

Kiwara-Wilson, S. (2013) Restituting colonial plunder: The case for the Benin bronzes and ivories. *Journal of Art, Technology and Intellectual Property Law* 23(2): 375–425.

Klimaszewski, C., G. E. Bader, and J. M. Nyce (2012) Studying up (and down) the cultural heritage preservation agenda: Observations from Romania. *European Journal of Cultural Studies* 15(4): 479–495.

Labadi, S. (2007) Representations of the nation and cultural diversity in discourses on world heritage. *Journal of Social Archaeology* 7(2): 147–170.

Labadi, S. (2013) *UNESCO, Heritage and Outstanding Universal Value*. Walnut Creek, CA: Altamira Press.

Lane, P. (2013) *French Scientific and Cultural Diplomacy*. Liverpool: Liverpool University Press.

Laos, N. (2011) *Foundations of Cultural Diplomacy. Politics among Cultures and the Moral Autonomy of Man*. New York: Algora.

Lenzerini F. and S. Borelli (eds) (2012) *Cultural Heritage, Cultural Rights, Cultural Diversity: New Developments in International Law*. Leiden: Martinus Nijhoff.

Luke, C. (2006) Diplomats, banana cowboys, and archaeologists in western Honduras: A history of the trade in pre-Columbian materials. *International Journal of Cultural Property* 13(1): 25–57.

Luke, C. (2012) The science behind US smart power in Honduras: Archaeological heritage diplomacy. *Diplomacy and Statecraft* 23(1): 110–139.

Luke, C. (2013) Cultural sovereignty in the Balkans and Turkey: The politics of preservation and rehabilitation. *Journal of Social Archaeology* 13(3): 350–370.

Luke, C. and M. M. Kersel (2013a) *US Cultural Diplomacy ad Archaeology: Soft Power, Hard Heritage*. London: Routledge.

Luke, C. and M. M. Kersel (2013b) Global conversations: Museums, diplomacy, and provenance. *Journal of Field Archaeology* 38(4): 362–363.

Meskell, L. M. (2002) Negative heritage and past mastering in archaeology. *Anthropological Quarterly* 75(3): 557–574.

Meskell, L. M. (2004) *Object Worlds in Ancient Egypt: Material Biographies Past and Present*. New York: Berg.

Meskell, L. M. (ed.) (2009) *Cosmopolitan Archaeologies*. Durham, NC: Duke University Press.

Meskell, L. M. (2012a) *The Nature of Culture: The New South Africa*. Oxford: Wiley Blackwell.

Meskell, L. M. (2012b) The rush to inscribe: Reflections on the 35th session of the World Heritage Committee, UNESCO, Paris 2011. *Journal of Field Archaeology* 37(2): 145–151.

Meskell, L. M. (2013) UNESCO's World Heritage Convention at 40. *Current Anthropology* 54(4): 483–494.

Meskell, L. M. (2014) States of conservation: Protection, politics, and pacting within UNESCO's World Heritage Committee. *Anthropological Quarterly* 87(1): 217–244.

Miller, H. (2002) *Post Modern Public Policy*. Albany: State University of New York Press.

Mitchell, T. (2002) *Rule of Experts. Egypt, Techno-Politics, Modernity*. Berkeley: University of California Press.

Mowatt, R. A. and C. H. Chancellor (2011) Visiting death and life: Dark tourism and slave castles. *Annals of Tourism Research* 38(4): 1410–1434.

Nader, L. (1972) Up the Anthropologist: Perspectives Gained from Studying Up, in D. Hynes (ed.), *Reinventing Anthropology*. New York: Pantheon Books, pp. 285–311.

Nikolouli, S. (2014) Thousands of Orthodox worshippers flock to Famagusta. *Greek Reporter*, April 18, 2014. Available at: http://greece.greekreporter.com/2014/04/18/%CF%84housands-of-orthodox-worshippers-flock-to-famagusta/. Accessed November 18, 2014.

Nordland, R. (2014) Saving relics, the Afghans defy the Taliban. *New York Times*, January 13, 2014, A1.

Nye, L. (2004) *Soft Power: The Means to Success in World Politics*, 5th edn. New York: Public Affairs.

Pai, H. I. (2013) *Heritage Management in Korea and Japan: The Politics of Antiquity and Identity*. Seattle: University of Washington Press.

Phillips, R. (2005) Re-placing objects: Historical practices for the second museum age. *Canadian Historical Review* 86(1): 83–110.

Pratt, M. L. (1991) Arts of the contact zone. *Profession:* 33–40.

Reid, D. M. (2002) *Whose Pharaohs? Archaeology, Museums, and Egyptian National Identity from Napoleon to World War I*. Berkeley: University of California Press.

Remsen W. and M. Şevketoğlu (2008) The SAVE Program: USAID-funded cultural heritage conservation in Cyprus. Paper presented at 11th US/ICOMOS International Symposium: Developing a comprehensive approach to US participation in the global heritage community. Available at: http://www.archive.usicomos.org/Symposium/SYMP08/Abstracts/Remsen.pdf. Accessed November 18, 2014.

Rodwell, D. (2012) The UNESCO World Heritage Convention, 1972–2012: Reflections and directions. *Historic Environment: Policy and Practice* 3(1): 64–85.

Rothfield, L. (ed.) (2008) *Antiquities under Siege: Cultural Heritage Protection after the Iraq War*. Lanham, MD: Rowman and Littlefield.

Ryan, J. and S. Silvanto (2009) The World Heritage Site List: The making and management of a brand. *Place Branding and Public Diplomacy* 5(4): 290–300.

Salazar, N. B. (2012) Shifting Values and Meanings of Heritage: From Cultural Appropriation to Tourism Interpretation and Back, in S. M. Lyon and C. E. Wells (eds), *Global Tourism: Cultural Heritage and Economic Encounters*. Lanham, MD: Altamira, pp. 21–41.

Scham, S. (2008) Disinheriting Heritage: Explorations in the Contentious History in the Middle East, in M. Liebmann and U. Z. Rizvi (eds), *Archaeology and the Postcolonial Critique*. Walnut Creek, CA: Altamira, pp. 165–176.

Scham, S. (2009) Diplomacy and desired pasts. *Journal of Social Archaeology* 9(2): 163–199.

Schildkrout, E. (1991) Ambiguous messages and ironic twists: Into the Heart of Africa and the other museum. *Museum Anthropology* 15(2): 16–23.

Schneider, C. (2010) The unrealized potential of cultural diplomacy: "Best practices" and what could be, if only… *Journal of Arts Management, Law, and Society* 39(4): 260–279.

Scott, C. (2012) Sharing the divisions of the colonial past: An assessment of the Netherlands-Indonesia Shared Cultural Heritage Project, 2003–2006. *International Journal of Heritage Studies* 20(2): 181–195.

Shaw, G. (2014) Jordan women in archaeology management plan. *The Art Newspaper*, March 4, 2014. Available at: http://www.theartnewspaper.com/articles/Jordan-women-in-archaeology-management-plan/32020. Accessed November 18, 2014.

Shaw, W. M. K. (2003) *Possessors and Possessed. Museums, Archaeology, and the Visualization of History in the Late Ottoman Empire*. Berkeley: University of California Press.

Silberman, N. A. and D. B. Small (1997) Introduction, in N. A. Silberman and D. B. Small (eds), *The Archaeology of Israel: Constructing the Past, Interpreting the Present*. Sheffield: Sheffield University Press, pp. 17–31.

Silverman, H. (2013) Cuzcotopia: Imagining and Performing the Incas, in R. Staiff, R. Bushell, and S. Watson (eds), *Heritage: Place, Encounter, Engagement*. London: Routledge, pp. 128–151.

Stamatoudi A. I. (2011) *Cultural Property Law and Restitution: A Commentary to International Conventions and European Union Law*. London: Edward Elgar.

Stein, G. (2013) Oriental Institute-National Museum of Afghanistan Partnership and Cultural Heritage Protection Work, in *The Annual Report of the Oriental Institute of the University of Chicago*. Chicago, IL: University of Chicago, pp. 89–97.

Stone, P. and J. Farchakh Bajjaly (eds) (2008) *The Destruction of Cultural Heritage in Iraq*. Woodbridge: Boydell Press.

Tanyeri-Erdemir, T. (2006) Archaeology as a source of national pride in the early years of the Turkish Republic. *Journal of Field Archaeology* 31(4): 381–393.

Thussu, D. K. (2013) *Communicating India's Soft Power: Buddha to Bollywood*. Basingstoke: Palgrave Macmillan.

Tuttle, C. (2013) Preserving Petra sustainably (one step at a time): The Temple of the Winged Lions Cultural Resource Management Initiative as a step forward. *Journal of Eastern Mediterranean Archaeology and Heritage Studies* 1(1): 1–24.

UNDP-USAID (2013) FAST FACTS: UNDP action for cooperation and trust in Cyprus, Future Together in Potamia. United Nations Diplomacy Programme-United States Agency for International Development. Available at: http://www.cy.undp.org/content/dam/cyprus/docs/ACT%20Publications/Factsheet-Potamia%20doc.pdf. Accessed December 2, 2014.

UNDP (2013) Apostolos Andreas Monastery: UNDP signs project document and contribution agreements. United Nations Diplomacy Programme: Partnership for the Future. Press Release UNDP-PFF 222/13.

US Department of State (2004) *Ambassadors Fund for Cultural Preservation Annual Report, 2003–2004*. Available at: http://eca.state.gov/files/bureau/2003-4afcpannual.pdf. Accessed November 18, 2014.

US Department of State (2010) Ambassadors Fund for Cultural Preservation awards grants for the Ishtar Gate and other landmarks at ancient Babylon. US Department of State Media Note. Electronic document. Available at: http://m.state.gov/md151888.htm. Accessed December 2, 2014.

US Embassy (2013) Bolivia: Chapels bring communities closer together, November 19, 2013. Available at: http://iipdigital.usembassy.gov/st/english/publication/2013/09/20130930283770.html#ixzz2vYi5AFSF. Accessed November 18, 2014.

US Senate Report (2004) *Departments of Commerce, Justice, and State, the Judiciary, and Related Agencies Appropriations Act, 2004*. Senate Report 108-144, 108th Congress.

Vrdoljak A. F. (2006) *International Law, Museums and the Return of Cultural Objects*. Cambridge: Cambridge University Press.

Wang, Z. (2012) *Never Forget National Humiliation: Historical Memory in Chinese Politics and Foreign Relations*. New York: Columbia University Press.

Winter, T. (2013a) Heritage studies and the privileging of theory. *International Journal of Heritage Studies* 20(5): 556–572.

Winter, T. (2013b) Clarifying the critical in critical heritage studies. *International Journal of Heritage Studies* 19(6): 532–545.

Winter, T. (2014a) Beyond Eurocentrism? Heritage conservation and the politics of difference. *International Journal of Heritage Studies* 20(2): 123–137.

Winter, T. (2014b) Heritage conservation futures in an age of shifting global power. *Journal of Social Archaeology* 14(3): 319–339.

Winter, T. and P. Daly (2012) Heritage in Asia: Converging Forces, Conflicting Values, in P. Daly and T. Winter (eds), *Routledge Handbook of Heritage in Asia*. London: Routledge, pp. 1–35.

Yahya, A. (2004) A Palestinian organization works to preserve sites in the West Bank in the midst of war. *Near Eastern Archaeology* 65(4): 279–291.

Zerilli, F. M. (2010) The rule of soft law: An introduction. *Focaal-Journal of Global and Historical Anthropology* 56: 3–18.

4

Bridging Cultural and Natural Heritage

Denis Byrne and Gro Birgit Ween

Introduction

One of the hallmarks of Western modernity has been its dualistic, or binary, view of the world as consisting of distinct realms of culture and nature. Nature is held to be categorically distinct from humanity and to exist as a resource for humanity, an object for contemplation, or an endangered entity calling for conservation by humans. Critical commentary on culture–nature dualism is on the tip of the tongue these days in the humanities, the social sciences, and elements within the biological sciences. The damage that this dualistic mentality has done over the past three or four centuries is laid out before us in denuded landscapes and depressing statistics on species loss. The ontological separation of humanity from all other species maps onto the earth's surface as, on the one hand, vast tracts of urban-industrial-agricultural landscape and seascape where other species can only exist as resources, pets and ornamental plantings, and, on the other hand, "protected areas" (such as national parks) where non-human species are more-or-less shielded from human harm.

This chapter addresses two theatres of practice in which culture–nature dualism is both a constraining influence and a focus of resistance and attack. First, we explore ways World Heritage listing has simultaneously impacted indigenous lifeways and offered opportunities for indigenous groups and non-indigenous scholars and activists to challenge key World Heritage principles and innovate within its mechanisms. This boundary work arises from the colonial foundations of World Heritage, but also out of the inherent scalability that World Heritage implies. It challenges the foundational mechanism of culture–nature dualism and its position within Western modernist ontology. The dualism is bridged, transgressed, or rewritten from the position of post-coloniality, posthumanism, science and technology studies, environmental philosophy, postdevelopment theory, and from the perspective of indigenous ontologies. This boundary work facilitates new kinds of agency and highlights the ways culture–nature dualism is received and struggled against by those on the margins of society and the global order. The cases we present display how World Heritage intervenes in the lives of people and their landscapes, but also how these spaces and peoples offer resistance.

Global Heritage: A Reader, First Edition. Edited by Lynn Meskell.

The second theatre of practice we address is that consisting of the overlapping domains of archaeology and cultural heritage practice. These domains have played a role in sustaining culture–nature dualism, and while in some respects they continue to do so, in others they challenge it and devise ways out of it. As an example of the work of critique in this theatre we question some of the premises of the Sacred Natural Sites initiative of the International Union for Conservation of Nature (IUCN), a program by conservation biologists aimed at bridging the gap between Western science and religious ontologies globally, specifically in regard to sacred forests and other "sacred natural sites."

The Anthropocene

So dramatic and far-reaching has been human influence on the Earth in recent millennia that some commentators propose it constitutes a new geological epoch, the anthropocene (Crutzen and Stoermer 2000). Indicators of the existence of the anthropocene include human-precipitated climate change, large-scale species extinction, and widespread anthropogenic soil modification. Its archaeological identifiers include vastly extensive layers of "artificial ground" (Edgeworth 2010) and of "anthropocene rock" consisting of concrete, bitumen, and other artifactual strata (Zalasiewicz et al. 2010). For Dibley (2012), the particular folding of the human into the Earth's systems that constitutes the anthropocene means "Nature has ended, Man is dead" – neither category can now be entertained as meaningfully discrete.

And yet it is precisely the habit of thinking of Nature and Man as categorically discrete that has, over the last four hundred years or so, brought the anthropocene to fruition as a global catastrophe. So while it is important to examine the influence of culture–nature dualism on heritage practice and nature conservation it is also worth taking stock of what might be called the heritage of culture–nature dualism, a project that would see much of the cultural heritage record of the last four centuries as testimony to the anthropocene's unfolding. Anthropocene heritage, as a field of practice, might for example take as its object the preservation and exhibition of such items as big game hunting camps and associated weaponry as evidence of how the world arrived at its current situation.

This field might also undertake a reinterpretation of indigenous heritage, seeing it as testimony to the alternatives to Earth domination that have existed (Lane 2011). A nuanced reading of the history of human land use is required; one that is able, for instance, to distinguish on the grounds of sustainability between different forms of land modification undertaken by humans. A useful comparison might, for example, be made between the kind of large-scale agrarian landscape modification documented in India by Kathleen Morrison (2013) that has endured and been reworked over long periods of time while remaining essentially sustainable, and the blatantly unsustainable systems of land use enacted under the category of modern industrial agriculture (Buttel 2006).

Culture–Nature Dualism

Culture–nature dualism is intrinsic to what Latour (1993) terms the "modern constitution," which he particularly links to the emergence of European natural science in the Renaissance and its enthusiasm for classifying the phenomena of the world into ontologically distinct categories. This endeavor coalesced into a meta-categorization of cultural and natural phenomena that in the seventeenth century gained strength from the Cartesian dichotomy of mind and matter. The anthropologist Philippe Descola (2013: 31–32) proposes that culture–nature dualism "as an epistemological device" be dated only to the last third of the nineteenth century, since, while the idea of nature has existed much earlier in Europe, it was only at this time that its counterpart, "culture," crystallized as an autonomous ontological domain and field of enquiry.

Latour (1993) famously argues that we have really never been modern; that, despite our commitment to the modern constitution, we have in practice never managed to maintain our separation from or control over non-human actors. What is important in the context of this chapter, however, is that fields of scholarship and professional practice have framed themselves in terms of such a separation, such that now, for instance, we have specialized fields of archaeology and heritage practice devoted to cultural heritage conservation, and we have particular branches of biology and ecology devoted to nature conservation (Harmon 2007; Nadasdy 1999). These divisions endure despite efforts by those like Berkes (2009) and Ross et al. (2011) to bridge the gap.

Culture–nature dualism developed out of Euro-modern culture. It seems to have no exact counterpart in non-Western traditional society, although it has assumed a global distribution via the West's modern era colonial-imperial extension. Arturo Escobar (1998) shows, for instance, how biodiversity, as a category, was imposed on the Global South in the context of Marshall Plan geopolitics during the Cold War, becoming embedded there in the institutions and practices of state environmental management. We can see that culture–nature dualism need not have been "natural" to the Global South in order for it to have powerfully framed modern environmental policy and programs there, any more than classic "authorized" heritage discourse (Byrne 1991; Smith 2004) needed to have roots in the cultures of the South in order to embed itself in modern heritage systems and to take on an aura of naturalness there.

The role some experts have had in disseminating culture–nature dualism has not, however, precluded other experts working to undo it. Contemporary critique of the ontology has been a shared project of scholars and activists in the South as well as the North. Parallel to this has been an increased assertion by indigenous people globally of their own ontologies. Key elements of these countermovements are reviewed in the following pages.

Postcolonial Ecologies and Ontologies

Indigenous people live in places that non-indigenous people generally think of as nature. The world can only be "nature" for a people who do not inhabit it (Ingold 2000: 40). This is Latour's (2004: 232) point when he states that "[t]raditional societies do not live in harmony with nature; they are unacquainted with it." Rather than claiming these societies have no relationship with nature, Latour is saying their relationship is non-hierarchical and non-instrumental. Morrison's (2013) archaeological research in India reminds us of the long-term temporality of such relations in contexts where agrarian groups inhabit terrain where the remains of millennia-old agricultural infrastructure are present and often incorporated into contemporary agriculture. We might say that that such people are unacquainted with a landscape that is not always already cultural or with an agricultural setting ontologically separate from "nature."

In the anthropology of Aboriginal Australia, what might be called indigenous "naturecultures" have been reported and discussed since the 1970s by Merlan (1998), Munn (1986), Myers (1986), Morphy (1991), Povinelli (1994), and Rose (1996, 2000). Deborah Rose (2000) developed a critique of culture–nature dualism from her ethnographic work with Aboriginal groups in northern Australia, people whose relationship with nature she finds to be the antithesis of dualism, one embodying a connectivity and mutual responsibility that equates with an ontology in which humans and other species are kin (Rose 2000).

Australian archaeology and heritage practice have by no means been insulated from these shifts. They are manifest, for example, in the archaeological investigation of pre-colonial midden deposits in Cape York, Queensland, where a human–dugong relational ontology is revealed in which hunting magic is central to cross-species communication (McNiven 2013). In heritage practice it is exhibited in new intensely collaborative landscape management approaches in Australia (e.g., Byrne 1991; Greer 2010; Greer, Harrison, and McIntyre-Tamwoy 2002; Guilfoyle et al. 2009; Moreton and Ross 2011; Ross, Ulm, and Tobane 2013) and similarly in Southeast Asia (Brockwell, O'Connor, and Byrne 2013). It is evident also in projects, such as Greer's (2010), which show how pre-colonial archaeological sites and artifacts can become "catalysts" for the reproduction in contemporary indigenous society of the knowledge systems they represent.

World Heritage Practice

In order to bring into view the nature that emerges in World Heritage practice, we turn to the construction of the notion of World Heritage itself. The background to the 1972 *Convention Concerning the Protection of World Cultural and Natural Heritage* lay in the experience of devastation produced by the two world wars of the twentieth century, along with the sense of optimism that followed successful international cooperation to safeguard such sites as the temples of Abu Simbel in Egypt, Venice in Italy, Moenjodaro in Pakistan, and Borobudur in Indonesia.

The post-World War II era was one in which nature protection also gained new meaning as the fallout of late industrialization led to questioning of the doctrine of progress. Alarm caused by environmental crises, such as oil spills and the phenomenon of acid rain, combined with a new and widespread perception that nature was rapidly disappearing (Asdal 2003; Blaser 2010). In the West, an emergent managerial approach to the "environment" (Blaser 2010: 87) was reflected in the 1965 White House conference which called for a World Heritage Trust to be formed in order to stimulate international cooperation to protect "the world's superb natural and scenic areas and historic sites for the present and the future of the entire world citizenry" (Turtinen 2000: 7). Although nature and culture were to be protected together, the way they were defined set them apart. While in the World Heritage Convention cultural heritage celebrated the capacities of mankind, nature was defined as a realm without humans (see Articles 1 and 2 in the World Heritage Convention as discussed by Turtinen 2000: 8).

Although many states sought to keep nature and culture categorically separate by the mechanism of forcibly removing people from areas designated "natural" (for instance at Yellowstone, Dukuduku, and the Matobo Hills) this strategy failed to retain legitimacy in the face of trends in the field of natural resource management. The introduction of the 1971 Man and the Biosphere model represented a significant change, seeking as it did to secure the co-existence of protected nature and the people who lived in it. While the Man and the Biosphere model could be described as an early postcolonial move, it is a model based upon an instrumental understanding of nature as a place where human and non-human species can be ordered and moved according to scientifically derived understandings of the needs of particular places and species. The model rests on the belief that there exist *out there* natures with objective needs for protection, and that such needs can be located, registered, compared, and evaluated from a panoptical point of view. Within such a positivist frame there is little room for reflexive perspectives, such as that which holds plant rarity to be an outcome of the limitations of where scientists go looking for plants (Kohler 2006; Ween and Risan 2015).

Since the 1970s, widespread recognition of a Western bias in the World Heritage Convention has prompted a series of revisions. The imbalance in favor of inscriptions of cultural properties over natural properties was first noted in 1979, resulting in a search for criteria to assess natural outstanding value (Turtinen 2000: 15–16). There was an awareness that the majority of listed natural sites were in Australia, Brazil, and the African continent, while Europe predominantly had cultural sites (Meskell 2012: 26). The 1994 "Global Strategy" sought to provide better balance by introducing thematic categories for listing, such as "human co-existence with the land," and "human beings in society" (Turtinen 2000: 16; see Labadi 2013 for a critical appraisal of the Global Strategy from a cultural heritage perspective).

In a parallel development, efforts were made to reinstate and re-empower indigenous peoples as a living part of World Heritage landscapes. This was associated with the larger indigenous rights movement and the enactment of indigenous rights legislation in countries like Australia and Canada. It was a major theme of the Rio Conference in 1992 and of several International Union for the Conservation of Nature (IUCN) programs. In the early 1990s, the move towards indigenous co-management of protected areas began to gain ground.

With such initiatives, boundaries between nature and culture have become increasingly blurred. One way of putting this is that objects have crossed divides and become subjects (Blaser 2010: 92). With the Rio Declaration and the UN's Agenda 21, sustainable development and the management of risk became the mantra of environmental agencies. Numerous international reports served to confirm the existence of indigenous and minority peoples in "natural landscapes" and to confirm their right to subsist in them. In line with these developments, at the beginning of the 1990s UNESCO became more focused on the joint conservation of culture and nature, a move spearheaded by the Cultural Landscape program (Rössler 2000; Rössler in Meskell 2012: 14).

From 1992, recognition of the extent to which humans have shaped "natural environments" led to the cultural landscape category being introduced into the World Heritage arena (Lennon 2012). In 1993 Mount Tongariro in New Zealand became the first property to be inscribed on the World Heritage List under this category. The mountain has cultural and religious significance for the Maori people, embodying their spiritual links with the environment (Baird 2013).[1]

Many discussions were held on how to recognize the associative value of landscapes and landscape features for indigenous people and on the importance of protecting biological diversity *together* with cultural diversity in cultural landscapes (Rössler 2000: 29). Meskell (2012: 21), however, argues that the acknowledgment of people in nature, and what Ingold described as the co-shaping of people and landscapes, has not greatly benefitted minority groups and indigenous peoples. According to Meskell (2012: 21), residents of such cultural landscapes are often evicted or persecuted, their continued use of "endangered sites" is questioned, they are frequently characterized as interlopers in the country of the "original" peoples, and they are sometimes seen as an impediment to tourism and the revenue it generates for protected area conservation.

The Sacred Natural Sites Initiative

In the 1990s the IUCN's World Commission for Protected Areas (WCPA) established the Cultural and Spiritual Values of Protected Areas theme in acknowledgment of the role religious beliefs and practices play in protecting "natural" landscapes. It formulated a series of actions to integrate nature conservation programs and strategies with these beliefs and practices, believing this would be of dual benefit to local religious practice and biodiversity conservation.[2] As the term "sacred natural sites" gained currency, a number of edited volumes appeared promoting the synergy between the values of conservation biology and those of local religion (Mallarach 2008; Verschuuren 2007; Verschuuren and Wild 2010; Wild and McLeod 2008). They contained papers reporting on projects where conservationists have collaborated with local people to manage and protect "sacred natural" areas. Reading through this literature, a certain evasion is evident wherein the magical-supernatural aspect of local belief is translated into religious constructs that are more compatible with the conservation movement's secular-rational mentality than with the ontologies of local popular religion (Byrne 2013).

For example, most of the case study chapters in *The Importance of Sacred Natural Sites for Biodiversity Conservation* (UNESCO 2003) begin with a fairly cursory description of the religious significance of areas (mostly forests) determined to have high biodiversity value, then move on to describe the biodiversity conservation measures implemented there. There is very little detailed discussion of just how religious belief and practice has acted to conserve biodiversity. Environmental protection seems to be regarded as an inherent function and endpoint of religion, and local religious believers are seen as revering a nature that remains ontologically separate, however closely entwined locals are with it. Missing here is the mutually constitutive people–environment relationality that Anna Tsing (1993) describes in the case of forest people such as the Meratus Dayaks of Borneo, that Zerner (2003) describes in the case of Mandar fishermen in the Makassar Strait, or that Roseman (2003) describes in the case of the Temiars of Peninsular Malaysia. In sacred natural sites discourse there is a failure to grasp the way such people apprehend more-than-human actors (e.g., plants, animals, rocks, the sea) as at once natural and supernatural, and the way they engage with these actors partly via practices of magic.

The secular-rational character of the nature conservation movement has its antecedents in the sixteenth-century Protestant Reformation and its rejection of the miraculous sacramental landscape of medieval Christianity (in which divine force was everywhere manifest). The Reformation held that religion was a matter between one's soul and a God who dwelt in heaven (Eire 1986), a God relegated to the sidelines of earthly life and removed from nature as a miraculous, causal force. The Reformation opened nature up to understanding via learned inquiry rather than religious doctrine. A new "buffered" European self (Taylor 2007: 300), fortified by Cartesian dualism, stood at a sufficiently critical distance from "nature" to construct it as the proper subject of human agency.

Yet in large parts of southern Europe the magical-supernatural continues to be integral to popular Christianity (Carroll 1992; Schama 1996: 436–443; Stewart 1991), just as it is in Chinese popular religion (Chau 2006; Dean 2003; Feuchtwang 2001) and popular Buddhism in Thailand (Jackson 1999; Tambiah 1970; Wijeyewardene 1986). In modern-era Asia, the magical supernatural has been seen by reformist elites and the nation-state as inimical to scientific economic and social development. Glossed as superstition, it became the target of proscriptive state campaigns in modern China (Goossaert and Palmer 2011), Thailand (Jackson 1999), Vietnam (Taylor 2004), and other Asian countries (see Byrne 2013, 2014 for an overview of these campaigns and their significance for heritage practice in Asia).

Conservation biology's uneasiness with the idea of the supernatural has deep roots both in European and Asian modernity. Until the implications of this history are properly acknowledged, the nature conservation field will be hobbled in its efforts to engage with local cultures in the Global South. This history stands in the way of efforts to dispense with culture–nature dualism in favor of the concept of a "pluriverse" (Blaser 2010) of natureculture categories. The foundational premise still stands: nature is "out there," an external entity that can be inspected, compared, and categorized according to scientific procedures and standards (Blaser 2010: 150).

While the sacred natural sites movement represents a laudatory effort by conservation biologists to accommodate the "life in nature" of people living in the environments it wishes to conserve, it remains framed substantially within the old nature–culture dualism. It would be facile to identify the movement directly with the anti-superstition campaigns of Asia described above, but it does share with them a foundation in the secular-rationalism of modernity's disenchanted ontology, effecting a critical separation between the human and non-human realm.

Culture and Nature in the Vortex of Asian Modernity

The era of modernity in Asia has taken a huge toll on non-human species and their habitats but also, in a related manner, on the archaeological heritage record. Under conditions of colonial modernity large swathes of existing agricultural landscapes in British India, British Burma and Malaya, French Indochina, and the Dutch East Indies were "rationalized" for the production of export crops such as cotton and rice. Mono-cropping and the expansion of agriculture into forest and wetland terrain had similar ecological impacts to the carving out of rubber plantations in Malaya and Vietnam and to colonial-commercial timber extraction in India, Burma, and quasi-colonial Siam (Beinart and Hughes 2007; Dunlap 1999; Grove 1995; Grove, Damodaran, and Sangwan 1998; Kathirithamby-Wells 2005). While the ecological and social impact of colonial economies has attracted great attention from environmental historians and anthropologists since the 1970s, there has been no equivalent study of their impact on the archaeological record, although one might guess this was on a scale similar to that of the advent of agriculture in Southeast Asia 5,000 years ago (Higham 1989).

In Asia in the second half of the twentieth century a new wave of agricultural intensification, associated with the Green Revolution, together with fast-tracked industrialization and rapid urban expansion have acted to degrade the environment and heritage record. In the post-World War II decades in the capitalist nations of Asia – including Japan, Korea, Thailand, and Indonesia – this was underwritten by Truman doctrine developmentalism which classified the Global South as underdeveloped

(Escobar 1995). In communist China it was driven by the Maoist vision of taking a shortcut to advanced industrial society, a shortcut that necessitated a "war against nature" (Shapiro 2001).

In Henri Lefebvre's (1991) account, modern government seeks to project its authority evenly over the entire space of the state via spatial regimes of leveling that have been immensely destructive of local spatial orders (see also Scott 1998). These regimes have frequently cut across the attachments of local people to sites of social and ritual significance. In Siam, from the mid-nineteenth century the modernizing state acted to discourage unorthodox, magical elements of folk Buddhism that included the worship of local spirits and deities, at the same time as it began compiling a central inventory of ancient monuments deemed worthy of protection, a list which excluded the shrines and natural landscape sites of local cult worship. These latter sites and the "disorderliness of the supernatural realm" to which they belonged lacked the "unifying potential" needed for the project of national identity building (Jackson 1989: 59). As ancient Buddhist monuments and outlier sanctuaries of the Angkorean Empire were pulled into the national grid of "authorized" heritage (Smith 2004) the local veneration of these sites for their miraculous powers was denied official recognition and excluded from the new public sphere (Byrne 2014). Turning to China, Mayfair Yang's (2004) study of the Wenzhou area in the post-1949 era provides a casebook example of the erosion of place-based local cultures by a highly centralized state.

During the 1930s, Japanese architects and urban planners, inspired by Le Corbusier, designed utopian settlements for Japanese-occupied Manchuria. Their modernist tabula rasa approach treated the landscape as a cultural blank over which a new modern order could be built from scratch (Koolhaas and Obrist 2011: 29, 31). Jini Kim Watson (2011) points to how a tabula rasa mentality has more broadly informed the development of the "new Asian city"; she points to the historical antecedents of this in the way the Japanese "fundamentally reorganised" Seoul and Taipei in the early twentieth century and in the way the British "effectively erased any trace of the Malay-inhabited island that preceded Singapore" (Watson 2011: 94).

The clean slate ideal has also been common to much of modernity's program of landscape development in Asia and has informed programs of nature conservation and cultural heritage conservation. The harvesting of "natural resources" in Asia by the British, French, and Dutch, as elsewhere in the Global South, resulted in incidents of environmental degradation or collapse that by the second half of the nineteenth century led colonial authorities to be seriously alarmed (Adams 2003: 29–33; Grove 1995). Their responses ranged from regulation to conservation but a key strategy was to create protected areas of various kinds, in the process of which the inhabitants in target areas were either excluded or subjected to novel forms of regulation designed to drive a wedge between them and the plants and animals of their lands (Adams 2003: 39).

The new postcolonial nation-states in Southeast Asia adopted the "wiring" of colonial governmentality, most notably in the colonial institutions of census, mapping, and museology (Anderson 2006: 160). In "crypto-colonial" (Herzfeld 2002) China and Siam from the late nineteenth century, governments acquired these same technologies, chiefly by employing Western advisors and sending young men to be educated in the West. The colonial-postcolonial technology of topographic mapping has been particularly significant in the way it has denied visibility to the cultural topographies of shifting agriculturists and hunter-gatherers in forested terrain, setting the scene for the appropriation of this terrain for "natural resource" extraction or for nature conservation (e.g., Roseman 2003; Tsing 1993). Meskell (2005, 2013a) documents equivalent processes in Kruger National Park in South Africa. Via such processes, indigenous people are separated not merely from the plants and animals that sustain them but from ritual sites and storied places, including those we would term heritage. Byrne (2008) has reviewed "countermapping" strategies where environmental anthropologists have worked with local people to map the social topography of their habitat as a basis for negotiating with government and developers.

Heritage governance in Asia has itself often involved "clearance" of zones identified for conservation of ancient monuments, entailing the resettlement of local inhabitants whose lifestyle is deemed incompatible with conservation objectives. In Thailand, this occurred when the Fourth National Economic and Social Development Plan (1977–1981) identified nine monumental heritage complexes for development as "historical parks" (Peleggi 2007: 177–178).

In the course of these and similar projects – at Angkor, for instance (Edwards 2007; Winter 2007) – frequently the recent social history of local space is blanked out in order to produce it as a realm of heritage. Recent work by Denes (2013: 244) describes how, following a government restoration project at the Khmer sanctuary of Phanom Rung, in northeast Thailand, local villagers were prevented from using candles, incense, and gold leaf at the site on the grounds that these had a deleterious effect on the monument's stone fabric. At Phanom Rung, state ritual was substituted for local ritual: the long-established annual pilgrimage to the site was reworked by the authorities as a tourist pageant that locals had to pay to participate in (Denes 2013: 236–237). This effacement of contemporary social life at monumental heritage sites is partly intended to facilitate a touristic illusion of stepping back into the past, just as the removal of shifting agriculturalists to locations outside a new national park fosters the visitor's sense of stepping into a realm of pure nature.

Co-Management in the Global North: "Kluane" World Heritage Site

We turn now to look at ways indigenous people, working in the context of a system of World Heritage governance still embedded in culture–nature dualism, have striven to achieve recognition for their own ontologies of culture–nature symmetry, which implicitly recognize multiple kinds of agency. Kluane/Wrangell-St Elias/Tatshenshini-Alsek World Heritage site in Alaska (hereafter Kluane World Heritage site) and the Laponia World Heritage site in Sweden are both national parks where indigenous groups live on the land and continue to engage in subsistence activities. That these parks were established at two very different points in time is key to understanding their different contexts in World Heritage. The Kluane site was listed in 1979 when the concept of wilderness still had broad uncritical acceptance, whereas Laponia was listed after wilderness had been problematized (Blaser 2010; Ween 2009).

Three Yukon aboriginal groups have their traditional territories in the greater Saint Elias region: the Kluane, the White River, and the Champagne and Aishihik First Nations. The parks were ordered according to the Man and the Biosphere model, with four general land classes recognized in the park. "Subsistence harvest" was originally permitted in some of each of the four land classes while a pre-existing game sanctuary in the Saint Elias foothills remained closed to aboriginal use (Cruikshank 2001: 251; Danby and Slocombe 2005: 254–255).

But Kluane National Park was not set apart from culture for long: with the Champagne and Aishihik First Nation Final Agreement and the Kluane First Nation Final Agreement introduced in the 1990s, a new era of management was initiated. In 1994, Tatshenshini-Alsek Provincial Wilderness Park was added to the existing World Heritage site but this time on the grounds of cultural criteria.[3]

Since then, following agreements with the Canadian federation, First Nations representatives have been granted the majority of votes on the Kluane National Park Management Board, the game sanctuary was revoked and subsistence activities were accorded priority over recreational activities in the park. Acknowledging the importance of allowing local knowledge to inform contemporary land management (De Walt 1993; Gadgil, Berkes, and Folke 1993; Huntington 2000; Johannes 1993), the traditional knowledge of the Kluane First Nations was accorded an equal role to scientific research in guiding management decisions (Nadasdy 1999). In addition, funds were allocated to help First Nations to facilitate reintroduction of subsistence activities on the land in the game sanctuary where formerly they had been prohibited.[4]

However, looking more closely at the Kluane National Park, and in particular at the 2010 Reserve Management Plan, it becomes clear that First Nations engagement is mostly confined to cultural activities. First Nations are enabled to educate tourists in cultural awareness and they are provided with opportunities within the tourist economy. To be fair, the plan does show dedication to the recording of history and local knowledge, and there are activities designed to realize the ambition of integrating science and local knowledge. These latter include the staging of science camps and joint species monitoring programs (Danby et al. 2003). Still, in the Park Management Plan these activities and the pages that describe them are physically as well as administratively set apart from natural resource management. Reading through the 2010 Kluane Management Plan it becomes clear that that First Nations initiatives are still, ten years after the Final Agreement was in place, ordered *alongside* rather than integrated with actual nature management (Danby et al. 2003; Ween and Colombi 2013). Science-based natural resource management stands firm in its position as the foundation for governing nature and the infrastructure of nature conservation decision making remains the same: the mapping, zoning, and ordering of land, the classification of species and species populations, and the management board's governance model remain the basis on which decisions regarding nature are made (Nadasdy 1999; Ween and Risan 2014).

World Heritage as Sites of Indigenous People-Politics

The management of World Heritage properties, such as the Kluane park, that were among the earliest listed for their natural values, tends to embody many classic features of the colonial mentality. Indigenous peoples are constrained to make claims within systems that are largely incompatible with their custodial responsibilities, knowledge practices and customary laws (Baird 2013: 337). There are similarities with the treatment of Native Americans when Yellowstone National Park was established in the late nineteenth century and, more recently, with the situation at the Matobo Hills property in Zimbabwe, which was emptied of African residents in the lead-up to World Heritage listing in 2003 (Ranger 1999), and at Dukuduku National Park and the St Lucia Wetlands in South Africa, which were nominated for World Heritage listing in order stop local people using the area for subsistence purposes (Nustad 2011).

To some extent, what might be termed "postcolonial" developments in the World Heritage Convention, its institutions, and its policies and practices have supported indigenous peoples and minority groups, for instance by the suggestion in 2000 that a World Heritage Indigenous Peoples Council of Experts (WHIPCOE) be established (Logan 2013), although this idea was put to rest within a year (Meskell 2013b). Many nations have little ambition to cater to indigenous cultural practices (Ween 2012), and there is little the World Heritage Committee can do to enforce "best practice" among its member countries (Hazen 2008: 254). Even if countries have signed indigenous rights conventions such as ILO 169, there is still often a lack of awareness of these conventions among lower level bureaucrats, with the result that these obligations do not so easily "trickle down" into bureaucratic practice (Ween 2009).

Embracing Ontological Difference

Authors such as Cruikshank (2001), Fienup-Riordan (2005), Nadasdy (1999, 2005), Ingold (2000), and Wishart (2004) have described how world-making in Alaska and Canada includes an understanding that game will present itself to good hunters. As long as hunters and their families, as far as possible, show respect to animals both in life and in death, the animals will continue to make themselves available to people. To live well entails living morally correct lives, killing in appropriate ways, avoiding waste, and sharing that with which people are provided. Here, nature needs to be used in order to remain plentiful. In a larger perspective, the question of whether nature is healthy or not entails the question of how people behave towards each other and towards the land. If there is hostility, unrest, self-destruction, and moral decline then this will be reflected in nature and within and between animal populations. Such a situation speaks to Cruikshank's concern regarding "historical and cultural crevasses separating narratives so deep that they rarely intersect" (Cruikshank 2001: 387). On the basis of studies of such crevasses, anthropologist Paul Nadasdy (1999) concluded that information obtained through ontologies that are as different as those of indigenous peoples and the peoples of the Global North cannot be integrated, and that attempts to do so would actually work against aboriginal empowerment.

The Alaskan/Canadian First Nations discussed here have life projects with regard to what we call nature that are not dissimilar to those of the Sámi people in northern Scandinavia. Here too nature consists of a number of non-human actors with which one must try to cooperate. In such situations, relations between humans and animals, as Ingold (2000) has described, are based upon trust: trust that animals will return or that new prey will be secured. It is a trust based upon ongoing sharing with animals (Ingold 2000: 69). Kuokkannen (2006) elaborates on this, using the Sami term *láhi* as a starting point (Guttorm 2011). *Láhi* is about what we receive from nature and our ability to share what we receive. This contrasts with the accountable and controllable nature enacted through natural resource management. Kuokkanen (2006), and later Guttorm (2011), have emphasized that in Sami world-making nature is not entirely predictable. An often-repeated Sami saying is that "one year is not the brother of the next," meaning humans cannot control nature. We can facilitate, do what is good and necessary, but there is no guarantee of an outcome.

Laponia: An Experiment in Co-Management

Laponia was inscribed as a "mixed" World Heritage site in 1996. It was nominated as an outstanding landscape, as Europe's largest area of almost untouched nature, as a unique example of a cultural practice, and as one of the last areas in the world where an ancestral way of life based on the seasonal movement of livestock is extant. Anthropologists Dahlström (2003) and Green (2009) both describe how the Sami in Laponia felt that reindeer herding had been forced into a position where it was valued more for museum and tourism purposes than as the basis of Sami livelihood (Ween 2012; Ween and Risan 2014). Sami reindeer herders despaired at the prospect of their lands being classified as "wilderness" and rewritten as a cultural void (Green 2009: 123). Deeply suspicious of natural resource management and its understanding of how nature could be controlled (Green 2009: 123), they sought majority representation on the Park Management Board.

The non-profit organization Laponiatjuottjudus was established in August 2011 to take over management of the Laponia World Heritage site. Reindeer herder representatives are a majority on the board. Laponiatjuottjudus aspires to a holistic management approach based on equity between Sami culture, the reindeer herding industry, and conservation of the heritage of past lives in the park. A "learning management" policy was adopted, employing Sami philosopher Mikkel Nils Sara's (2004) term *searvelatnja*, meaning "a site of learning." An example of such a site is the reindeer corral where young and old people, men and women, friends and family participate in the separation of reindeer and learn from each other. *Searvelatnja* embodies a conviction that differences cannot be resolved hierarchically (Länsstyrelsen Norrbotten 2009). Decision making involves *rádedibme* (open meetings) where locals and other interest groups convene out on the land in order to gain first-hand awareness of land management issues. The intention is to build "new local knowledge", a term positioned in relation to the frequently used "traditional ecological knowledge," to offer a hybrid concept stemming from a belief that local knowledge is neither "traditional" nor static (Nadasdy 1999).

Conclusions

The achievement of a sustainable relationship between humans and non-humans is humanity's most critical global challenge in this century and perhaps in this millennium. It is foremost on the agenda of the environmental sciences, environmental anthropology, the environmental conservation movement, and the ecological humanities. We believe it is also of key importance for the fields of archaeology, heritage studies, and heritage practice. In these fields there is a burgeoning impatience with the lingering culture–nature binary and the fiction it promotes that "cultural sites" are discontinuous with environmental phenomena.

There is by now, for instance, a well-established appreciation among archaeologists that human material culture arises from and endures in a "collective" of human and non-human phenomena that expresses the "distributed" and symmetrical agency of humans, their artifacts, and their environments (e.g., Meskell 2004; Olsen 2003, 2010; Whitmore 2007). The rejection of Cartesian dualism implied here cannot be confined to the human–object binary; it inevitably spills over into a rejection of the dualism that dichotomizes culture and nature. Countering this dualism, terms like "natureculture" (Haraway 1997; Latour 1993) and "socionature" (Swyngedouw 1999) help us towards a non-binary conception of the entanglement and "dance" of human and non-human agency (Pickering 2010) in which we exist as natural-cultural beings.

These reconceptualizations clearly have global applicability but in no way do they imply a transcendence of the history of North–South power relations or the history of relations between nation-states and indigenous peoples. In embracing the idea of human–object and culture–nature continuity and symmetry we thus bear in mind the history of global *asymmetry*, and the various forms of enslavement, inequity, exploitation, and manipulation which made up that history. Over the last century, asymmetry has been evident in the hegemonic global extension of Western discourses and models of practice in the fields of heritage conservation and nature conservation. But in the early twenty-first century we witness a counter-trend, manifest in a plurality of heritage practices and a plurality of "heritages" (i.e., alternative conceptions of heritage), which accompanies the growing assertiveness of countries in Asia, Latin America, and Africa, and of indigenous peoples globally. The situation of Laponia provides an example of how indigenous groups are working within and against the global machinery of World Heritage to create new models of environmental management framed in terms of a pluriverse, acknowledging the co-existence of multiple lifeworlds and different, co-existing, attributions of subjectivity and agency.

The plurality spoken of here emerges partly from the waning of global models and their power to suppress or deny visibility to indigenous and Southern ontologies. But it also emerges from the reworking of conservation ideas and practices that indigenous and Southern societies have borrowed from the North. The North may have taken a certain gratuitous satisfaction in contemplating what appeared to be the irresistibility of its civilizational model and its impact on the fragile and "endangered authenticities" of the South (Clifford 1988: 5). However, the truth is that cultural contact was never that simple. The North's colonial-imperial extension led not to "a duality between two cultural heritages," in Trinh T. Minh-ha's (1991: 195) terms, but to "a certain freedom to modify, appropriate, and reappropriate without being trapped in imitation" (1991: 161). Indigenous and Southern societies saw through the dualism encapsulated in the expression "the West and the rest." Culture–nature dualism represents a similarly flawed ontology, one whose persuasiveness is exhausted.

NOTES

1 http://whc.unesco.org/en/list/421.
2 http://www.iucn.org/about/work/programmes/gpap_home/gpap_people/gpap_tilcepa/gpap_spiritual/.
3 http://whc.unesco.org/archive/1994/whc-94-conf003-16e.pdf.
4 'Healing Broken Connections' (2004–2009).

REFERENCES

Adams, W. M. (2003) Nature and the Colonial Mind, in W. Adams and M. Mulligan (eds), *Decolonizing Nature: Strategies for Conservation in a Post-Colonial Era*. London: Earthscan, pp. 1–15.

Anderson, B. (2006) *Imagined Communities*, revised edn. London: Verso.

Asdal, K. (2003) Politikkens teknologier. Produksjon av regjerlig natur [Technologies of Politics. Production of governable nature]. Ph.D. dissertation, Department of History, University of Oslo, Norway.

Baird, M. (2013) The breadth of the mountain is my heart: Indigenous cultural landscapes and the politics of heritage. *International Journal of Heritage Studies*, 19: 327–340.
Beinart, W. and L. Hughes (2007) *Environment and Empire*. Oxford: Oxford University Press.
Berkes, F. (2009) Evolution of co-management: Role of knowledge generation, bridging organizations and social learning. *Journal of Environmental Management* 90: 1692–1702.
Blaser, M. (2010) *Storytelling Globalization from Chaco and Beyond*. Durham, NC: Duke University Press.
Brockwell, S., O'Connor, and D. Byrne (eds) (2013) *Transcending the Culture-Nature Divide in Cultural Heritage: Views from the Asia-Pacific Region*. Terra Australia 36. Canberra: ANU E Press
Buttel, F. H. (2006) Sustaining the Unsustainable: Agro-Food Systems and Environment in the Modern World, in P. Cloke, T. Marsden, and P. Mooney (eds), *Handbook of Rural Studies*. London: Sage, pp. 213–229.
Byrne, D. (1991) Western hegemony in archaeological heritage practice. *History and Anthropology* 5: 269–276.
Byrne, D. (2008) Counter-Mapping in the Archaeological Landscape, in B. David and J. Thomas (eds), *Handbook of Landscape Archaeology*. Walnut Creek, CA: Left Coast Press, pp. 609–616.
Byrne, D. (2013) The WCPA's Natural Sacred Sites Taskforce: A Critique of Conservation Biology's View of Popular Religion, in S. Brockwell, S. O'Connor, and D. Byrne (eds), *Transcending the Culture-Nature Divide in Cultural Heritage: Views from the Asia-Pacific Region*. Terra Australia 36. Canberra: ANU E Press, pp. 157–169.
Byrne, D. (2014) *Counterheritage: Critical Perspectives on Heritage Conservation in Asia*. New York and London: Routledge.
Carroll, M. P. (1992) *Madonnas that Maim: Popular Catholicism in Italy since the Fifteenth Century*. Baltimore, MD: Johns Hopkins University Press.
Chau, A. Y. (2006) *Miraculous Response: Doing Popular Religion in Contemporary China*. Stanford, CA: Stanford University Press.
Clifford, J. (1988) *The Predicament of Culture*. Cambridge, MA: Harvard University Press.
Cruikshank, J. (2001) Glaciers and climate change: Perspectives from oral tradition. *Arctic* 54: 377–393.
Crutzen, P. J. and E. F. Stoermer (2000) The "anthropocene." *Global Change Newsletter* 41: 17–18.
Dahlström, Å. N. (2003) *Negotiating Wilderness in a Cultural Landscape. Predators and Sámi Reindeer Herding in the Laponian World Heritage Area*. Uppsala Studies in Cultural Anthropology no. 32. Uppsala.
Danby, R. K., D. S. Hik, D. S. Slocombe, and A. Williams (2003) Science and the St. Elias: An evolving framework for sustainability in North America's highest mountains. *The Geographical Journal* 169: 191–204.
Danby, R. K. and D. S. Slocombe (2005) Regional ecology, ecosystem geography and transboundary protected areas in the St. Elias Mountains. *Ecological Applications* 15: 405–422.
Dean, K. (2003) Local Communal Religion in Contemporary South-East China, in D. Overmyer (ed.), *Religion in China Today*, The China Quarterly Special Issues, New Series 3. Cambridge: Cambridge University Press, pp. 32–52.
Denes, A. (2013) Mapping Living Heritage at the Phanom Rung Historical Park: Identifying and Safeguarding the Local Meanings of a National Heritage Site, in C. Baker (ed.), *Protecting Siam's Heritage*. Chiang Mai: Silkworm Books, pp. 225–256.
Descola, P. (2013) *The Ecology of Others*. Chicago, IL: Prickly Paradigm.
De Walt, B. (1993) Using indigenous knowledge to improve agriculture and natural resource management. *Human Organization* 53: 123–131.
Dibley, B. (2012) "The shape of things to come": Seven theses on the anthropocene and attachment. *Australian Humanities Review* 52. Available at: http://www.australianhumanitiesreview.org/archive/Issue-May-2012/dibley.html. Accessed November 18, 2014.

Dunlap, T. R. (1999) *Nature and the English Diaspora*. Cambridge: Cambridge University Press.

Edgeworth, M. (2010) Archaeologists should grapple with the anthropocene too... Archeolog blog. Available at: http://traumwerk.stanford.edu/archaeolog/2010/06/archaeologists_should_grapple.html. Accessed November 18, 2014.

Edwards, P. (2007) *Cambodge: The Cultivation of a Nation, 1860–1945*. Honolulu: University of Hawai'i Press.

Eire, C. M. (1986) *War against the Idols*. Cambridge: Cambridge University Press.

Escobar, A. (1995) *Encountering Development: The Making and Unmaking of the Third World*. Princeton, NJ: Princeton University Press.

Escobar, A. (1998) Whose knowledge, whose nature? *Biodiversity, conservation, and the political ecology of social movements, Journal of Political Ecology* 5: 53–82.

Feuchtwang, S. (2001) *Popular Religion in China: The Imperial Metaphor*. London and New York: Routledge.

Fienup-Riordan, A. (2005) *Wise Words of the Yupik: We Talk Because We Love You*. Omaha: University of Nebraska Press.

Gadgil, M., F. Berkes, and C. Folke (1993) Indigenous knowledge for biodiversity conservation. *Ambio* 22: 151–156.

Goossaert, V. and D. A. Palmer (2011) *The Religious Question in Modern China*. Chicago, IL: University of Chicago Press.

Green, C. (2009) Managing Laponia. A World Heritage as Arena for Sami Ethno-Politics in Sweden. Ph.D. dissertation, University of Uppsala, Sweden.

Greer, S. (2010) Heritage and empowerment: Community-based indigenous cultural heritage in Northern Australia. *International Journal of Heritage Studies* 16: 45–58.

Greer, S. R., R. Harrison, and S. McIntyre-Tamwoy (2002) Community-based archaeology in Australia. *World Archaeology* 34: 265–287.

Grove, R. (1995) *Green Imperialism: Colonial Expansion, Tropical Island Edens and the Origins of Environmentalism*. Cambridge: Cambridge University Press.

Grove, R., V. Damodaran, and S. Sangwan (eds) (1998) *Nature and the Orient: the Environmental History of South and Southeast Asia*. New Delhi: Oxford University Press.

Guilfoyle, D., B. Bennell, W. Webb, V. Gilles, and J. Strickland (2009) Integrating natural resource management and Indigenous cultural heritage: A model and case study from south-western Australia. *Heritage Management* 2: 149–176.

Guttorm, G. (2011) Arbediehtu (Sami traditional knowledge) – as a concept and in practice. *Diedut* 1: 59-73.

Haraway, D. (1997) *Modest_Witness@Second_Millennium.FemaleMan_Meets OncoMouse: Feminism and Technoscience*. New York: Routledge.

Harmon, D. (2007) A bridge over the chasm: Finding ways to achieve integrated natural and cultural heritage conservation. *International Journal of Heritage Studies* 13: 380–392.

Hazen, H. (2008) "Of outstanding universal value": The challenge of scale in applying the World Heritage Convention at national parks in the US. *Geoforum* 39: 252–264.

Herzfeld, M. (2002) The absent presence: Discourses of crypto-colonialism, *South Atlantic Quarterly* 101: 899–926.

Higham, C. (1998) *The Archaeology of Mainland Southeast Asia*. Cambridge: Cambridge University Press.

Huntington, H. P. (2000) Using TEK in science: Methods and applications. *Ecological Applications* 10: 1270–1274.

Ingold, T. (2000) *The Perception of the Environment*. London: Routledge.

Jackson, P. (1989) *Buddhism, Legitimation, and Conflict: The Political Functions of Urban Thai Buddhism*. Singapore: Institute of Southeast Asian Studies.

Jackson, P. (1999) The enchanted spirit of Thai capitalism: The cult of Luang Phor Khoon and the post-modernization of Thai Buddhism. *South East Asian Research* 7: 5–60.

Johannes, R. E. (1993) Integrating TEK and Management with Environmental Impact Assessment, in J. T. Inglis (ed.), *TEK: Concepts and Cases*. Ottawa: Canadian Museum of Nature, pp. 33–39.

Kathirithamby-Wells, J. (2005) *Nature and Nation: Forests and Development in Peninsular Malaysia*. Copenhagen: NIAS Press.

Kohler, R. E. (2006) *All Creatures: Naturalists, Collectors, and Biodiversity, 1850–1950*. Princeton, NJ: Princeton University Press.

Koolhaas, R. and H. U. Obrist (2011) *Project Japan: Metabolist Talks*. Cologne: Tashen.

Kuokkanen, R. (2006) The Logic of the Gift – Reclaiming Indigenous Peoples' Philosophies. Re-Ethnicizing the Mind?, in T. Botz-Bornstein (ed.), *Cultural Revival in Contemporary Thought*. Amsterdam and New York: Rodopi, pp. 251–271.

Labadi, S. (2013) *UNESCO, Cultural Heritage, and Outstanding Universal Value: Values-Based Analyses of the World Heritage and Intangible Cultural Heritage Conventions*. Lanham, MD: AltaMira.

Lane, P. (2011) Possibilities for a postcolonial archaeology in Sub-Saharan Africa. Indigenous and usable pasts. *World Archaeology* 431: 7–25.

Latour, B. (1993) *We Have Never Been Modern*. Cambridge, MA: Harvard University Press.

Latour, B. (2004) *Politics of Nature*. Trans. C. Porter. Cambridge, MA: Harvard University Press.

Lefebvre, H. (1991) *The Production of Space*. Trans. D. Nicholson-Smith. Oxford: Blackwell.

Lennon, J. (2012) Cultural Landscape Management: International Influences, in K. Taylor and J. Lennon (eds), *Managing Cultural Landscapes*. London and New York: Routledge, pp. 45–69.

Logan, W. (2013) Australia, indigenous peoples and World Heritage from Kakadu to Cape York: State Party behaviour under the World Heritage Convention. *International Journal of Heritage Studies* 13: 153–176.

Länsstyrelsen Norrbotten (2009) Stadgar för föreningen Laponiatjuottjudus. Available at: http://laponia.nu/wp-content/uploads/2014/08/Stadgar-Laponiatjuottjudus.pdf. Accessed November 29, 2014

McNiven, I. (2013) Between the Living and the Dead: Relational Ontologies and the Ritual Dimensions of Dugong Hunting across Torres Strait, in C. Watts (ed.), *Relational Archaeologies: Humans, Animals, Things*. London: Routledge, pp. 97–116.

Mallarach, J.-M. (ed.) (2008) *Protected Landscapes and Cultural and Spiritual Values*. Heidelberg: World Commission for Protected Areas.

Merlan, F. (1998) *Caging the Rainbow: Places, Politics, and Aborigines in a North Australian Town*. Honolulu: University of Hawai'i Press.

Meskell, L. (2004) *Object Worlds in Ancient Egypt*. Oxford: Berg.

Meskell, L (2005). Archaeological ethnography: Conversations around Kruger National Park. *Archaeologies* 1(1): 81–100.

Meskell, L. (2012) *The Nature of Heritage: The New South Africa*. Oxford: Blackwell.

Meskell, L. (2013a) A Thoroughly Modern Park: Mapungubwe, UNESCO and Indigenous Heritage, in A. Gonzalez-Ruibal (ed.), *Reclaiming Archaeology: Beyond the Tropes of Modernity*. London and New York: Routledge, pp. 244–227.

Meskell, L. (2013b) UNESCO and the fate of the World Heritage Indigenous Peoples Council of Experts (WHIPCOE). *International Journal of Cultural Property* 20: 155–174.

Minh-ha T. T., (1991) *When the Moon Waxes Red*. New York: Routledge.

Moreton, D. and A. Ross (2011) Gorenpul Knowledge of Moreton Bay, in P. Davie (ed.), *Wild Guide to Moreton Bay*. Brisbane: Queensland Museum, pp. 58–67.

Morphy, H. (1991) *Ancestral Connections: Art and an Aboriginal System of Knowledge*. Chicago, IL: University of Chicago Press.

Morrison, K. D. (2013) *The Human Face of the Land: Why the Past Matters for India's Environmental Future*. Nehru Memorial Museum and Library Occasional Paper 27.

Munn, N. (1986) *Walbiri Iconography: Graphic Representation and Cultural Symbolism in a Central Australian Society*. Chicago, IL: University of Chicago Press.

Myers, F. (1986) *Pintupi Country, Pintupi Self: Sentiment, Place, and Politics among Western Desert Aborigines*. Washington, DC: Smithsonian Institution Press.

Nadasdy, P. (1999) *Hunters and Bureaucrats. Power, Knowledge and Aboriginal State Relations in the Southwest Yukon*. Vancouver: UBC Press.

Nadasdy, P. (2005) The Anti-Politics of TEK: The Institutionalization of Co-Management Discourse and Practice. *Anthropologica*, 47(2):215-232.

Nustad, K. G. (2013) The nature of the land: The Dukuduku forest and the Mfolozi flats, KwaZulu-Natal. *Journal of Modern African Studies* 51: 487–506.

Olsen, B. (2003) Material culture after text: Re-membering things. *Norwegian Archaeological Review* 36: 87–104.

Olsen, B. (2010) *In Defense of Things: Archaeology and the Ontology of Objects*. Lanham, MD: AltaMira.

Palmer, L. (2007) Interpreting "nature": The politics of engaging with Kakadu as an Aboriginal place. *Cultural Geographies* 14: 255–273.

Peleggi, M. (2007). *Thailand: The Worldly Kingdom*. London: Reaktion.

Pickering, A. (2010) Material culture and the dance of agency, in D. Hicks and M. C. Beaudry (eds), *Material Culture Studies*. Oxford: Oxford University Press, pp. 191–208.

Povinelli, E. (1994) *Labor's Lot: The Power, History and Culture of Aboriginal Action*. Chicago, IL: University of Chicago Press.

Ranger, T. (1999) *Voices from the Rocks: Nature, Culture, and History in the Matopos Hills of Zimbabwe*. Urbana: Indiana University Press.

Rose, D. B. (1996) *Nourishing Terrains: Australian Aboriginal Views of Landscape and Wilderness*. Canberra: Australian Heritage Commission.

Rose, D. B. (2000) *Dingo Makes Us Human: Life and Land in an Australian Aboriginal Culture*. Cambridge: Cambridge University Press.

Roseman, M. (2003) Singers of the Landscape: Song, History, and Property Rights in the Malaysian Rainforest, in C. Zerner (ed.), *Culture and the Question of Rights*. Durham, NC: Duke University Press, pp. 111–141.

Ross, A., K. P. Sherman, J. G. Snodgrass, H. D. Delcore, and R. Sherman (2011) *Indigenous Peoples and the Collaborative Stewardship of Nature: Knowledge Binds and Institutional Conflicts*. Walnut Creek, CA: Left Coast Press.

Ross A., S. Ulm, and B. Tobane (2013) Gummingurru: A community archaeology knowledge journey. *Australian Archaeology* 76: 62–68.

Rössler, M. (2000) World Heritage cultural landscapes. *The George Wright Forum* 17: 27–34.

Sara, M. N. (2004) Tradisjonell samisk kunnskap i grunnskolen [Traditional Sami Knowledge in Primary School], in V. Hirvonen (ed.), *Samisk skole i plan og praksis*. Kautokeino: Samisk Høgskole.

Schama, S. (1996) *Landscapes and Memory*. London: Fontana.

Scott, J. C. (1998) *Seeing Like a State*. New Haven, CT: Yale University Press.

Shapiro, J. (2001) *Mao's War against Nature: Politics and the Environment in Revolutionary China*. Cambridge: Cambridge University Press.

Smith, L. (2004) *Archaeological Theory and the Politics of Cultural Heritage*. London: Routledge.

Stewart, C. (1991) *Demons and the Devil: Moral Imagination in Modern Greek Culture*. Princeton, NJ: Princeton University Press.

Swyngedouw, E. (1999) Modernity and hybridity: Nature, regenerationism and the production of the Spanish waterscape, 1890–1930. *Annals of the Association of American Geographers* 89: 443–445.

Tambiah, S. J. (1970) *Buddhism and the Spirit Cults in North-east Thailand*. Cambridge: Cambridge University Press.

Taylor, C. (2007) *A Secular Age*. Cambridge, MA: Harvard University Press.

Taylor, P. (2004) *Goddess on the Rise: Pilgrimage and Popular Religion in Vietnam*. Honolulu: University of Hawai'i Press.

Tsing, A. L. (1993) *In the Realm of the Diamond Queen*. Princeton, NJ: Princeton University Press.

Turtinen, J. (2000) *Globalising Heritage: On UNESCO and the Transnational Construction of World Heritage*. Stockholm: Stockholm Center for Organizational Research.

UNESCO (2003) The Importance of Sacred Natural Sites for Biodiversity Conservation, *Proceedings of the International Workshop held in Kunming and Xishuangbanna Biosphere Reserve, People's Republic of China, 17–20 February 2002*. Paris: UNESCO.

Verschuuren, B. (2007) *Believing Is Seeing: Integrating Cultural and Spiritual Values in Conservation Management*. Gland: Foundation for Sustainable Development and IUCN.

Verschuuren, B. and R. Wild (eds) (2010) *Earth: Nature, Culture and the Sacred*. London: Earthscan.

Watson, J. K. (2011) *The New Asian City: Three-Dimensional Fictions of Space and Urban Form*. Minneapolis: University of Minnesota Press.

Ween, G .B. (2009) Blåfjella-Skjækerfjella. Om forvaltning og utøving av sted/natur [Blåfjella-Skjækerfjella. About enactment of place/nature in nature management]. *Norsk Antropologisk Tidsskrift* 1(2): 95–108.

Ween, G. B. (2012) World heritage and indigenous rights: Norwegian examples. *International Journal of Heritage Studies* 18: 257–270.

Ween, G. B. and B. Colombi (2013) Two rivers: The politics of wild salmon, indigenous rights and natural resource management. *Sustainability*, 5: 478–495.

Ween, G. B. and L. Risan. (2014) Exploring heritage lives, indigenous peoples in World Heritage sites. *Primitive tider*, 2: 55-67

Whitmore, C. L. (2007) Symmetrical archaeology: Excerpts of a manifesto. *World Archaeology* 39: 546–562.

Wijeyewardene, G. (1986) *Place and Emotion in Northern Thai Ritual Behaviour*. Bangkok: Pandora.

Wild, R. and C. McLeod (eds) (2008) *Sacred Natural Sites: Guidelines for Protected Area Managers*. Gland: Task Force on the Cultural and Spiritual Values of Protected Areas, IUCN.

Winter, T. (2007) *Post-Conflict Heritage, Postcolonial Tourism*. Abingdon: Routledge.

Wishart, R. P. (2004) A Story about a Muskox: Some Implications of Tetlit Gwich in Human-Animal Relationships, in D. Anderson and M. Nuttall (eds), *Cultivating Arctic Landscapes: Knowing and Managing Animals in the Circumpolar North*. Oxford: Berghan, pp. 79–92.

Yang, M. (2004) Spatial struggles: Postcolonial complex, state disenchantment, and popular reappropriation of space in rural south-east China. *Journal of Asian Studies* 63: 719–755.

Zalasiewicz, J., M. Williams, W. Stefen, and P. Crutzen (2010) The new world of the anthropocene. *Environmental Science and Technology* 44: 2228–2231.

Zerner, C. (ed.) (2003) *Culture and the Question of Rights: Forests, Coasts, and Seas in Southeast Asia*. Durham, NC and London: Duke University Press.

5

Communities and Ethics in the Heritage Debates

Chip Colwell and Charlotte Joy

Introduction

In recent years a key contribution to research on heritage is the infusion of dialogues concerning ethics. In these works ethics are broadly conceived as the body of moral principles that should or actually do guide different kinds of heritage work. At base, this research vein is deeply concerned with how heritage operates not in the abstract, but how its everyday production and consumption impacts living societies. This research is often committed to understanding the complex intersection of people and things – how the care of heritage serves the well-being of descendant communities and invested stakeholders as much as material objects and historical places (e.g., Burström, Elfström, and Johansen 2004; Diaz-Andreu 2013; Haber 2007; Meskell 2010; Nicholas and Hollowell 2007; Smith and Jackson 2008; Wylie 2005; Zimmerman 1998).

An important frame of reference to emerge in this scholarship is the category of local and descendant communities. Although the notion of communities was never entirely disregarded in early scholarship, by the mid-twentieth century most debates concerning heritage centered on competing rights of nations and humanity as a whole (Merryman 1986, 2005, 2009). Considerations of local communities have emerged in these discussions only in the last several decades because of multiple converging lines of argument and social critiques, in particular in North America, New Zealand, and Australia (Brown 2003; Lilley 2005; Nicholas and Andrews 1997; Sully 2007). Legal attempts to protect peoples' heritage and identity through a copyright model (Brown 1998) have given way to a more discursive model, where different claims can co-exist and the ethical work is one of making space for multiple readings of the world (Habu, Fawcett, and Matsunaga 2008).

In the postcolonial landscape of much of Europe and, by implication, Europe's former colonies, there is a strong assertion of a universal (often termed "cosmopolitan") vision of heritage that includes the cultural heritage found in European museums, sites identified by UNESCO, and archaeology considered under the jurisdiction of heritage experts (Ackerly 2008; Cuno 2009; Curtis 2006; Fiskesjö 2010).

Global Heritage: A Reader, First Edition. Edited by Lynn Meskell.

On the other hand, there is the desire for self-determination on a national, local, or individual scale (Plets et al. 2013; Pwiti and Chirikure 2008; Vrdoljak 2008). In this postcolonial scenario, the control over who owns, has access to, or claims rights of representation over cultural heritage can best be understood as a conversation about dignity, as Olaniyan (2003) conceptualizes it: the desire for a return to sanity through self-determination.

Debates about heritage ethics therefore link, in a complex chain of entanglements, an individual's well-being (Hodder 2010), and his or her perception of what it means to exist in the world in a dignified way, with a national or global identity project. At a national or international level, heritage ethics become most closely identified with a cosmopolitan project of universal human rights. However, this universalism is immediately brought into conversation with different forms of relativism (Eriksen 2009) that portray the universalism as a form of Western enlightenment imperialism (Meskell 2009a). It can therefore be argued that we do not yet have a successful model within which to frame the relationship between heritage and ethics. A case-by-case consideration seems to be the best working model so far.

Ethics and the State

Nationalist projects seek to use a version of the past and associated culture products for the exclusive benefit of the state. One form of analysis is historical, with a focus on how heritage and archaeology have been subverted to construct histories that justify nationalist propaganda. Bettina Arnold's (1990; Arnold and Hassmann 1995) research on the Nazis' use of archaeology was seminal in this regard, but numerous studies show how nations around the world have employed the past for a nation's political ends (Atkinson, Banks, and O'Sullivan 1996; Diaz-Andreu and Champion 1996; Dietler 1994; Goode 2007; Jones 1994; Kaarsholm 1989; Kohl 1998; Kohl and Fawcett 1995; Krekovič 2007; Mazariegos 1998; Meskell 1998; Pai 1999; Wynn 2008). Supplementing such studies are in-depth ethnographic projects that dissect how heritage works on the ground to create national narratives, often to bolster the privileges, economies, or identities of one group (Abu el-Haj 2001; Castañeda 1996; Fontein 2006; Handler 1988).

Complementing this critique of the nationalist value of heritage has been an equally penetrating critique of how internationalist values, while physically protecting sites and objects, often come at the price of excluding local communities. Many have pointed out how UNESCO's World Heritage Centre – the most emblematic of institutions for the internationalist view – has long been Eurocentric and overly focused on the kinds of tangible and monumental heritages that epitomize Western elite notions of heritage (e.g., Jenkins 2008: 248; Labadi 2012: 15; Meskell 2013; Millar 2006: 42). Indeed, such critiques have been taken to heart by UNESCO itself, which has led to significant changes, such as concerted efforts to nominate World Heritage sites in Africa and Asia, and also to develop the 2003 Convention for the Safeguarding of the Intangible Cultural Heritage – to recalibrate what is considered to be cultural heritage by moving strictly from the material world to the embodied social relationships enabled by the material (Ahmad 2006; Nas 2002).

A recent example of this kind of analysis is Chiara De Cesari's (2010) study that explores how the UNESCO World Heritage program works in Palestine and Israel. She argues that the critique of UNESCO's Eurocentric tendencies has lead to a reformulated approach of liberal multiculturalism, which has its own limitations of how

UNESCO officials see cultural difference and still often reinforces power asymmetries. UNESCO, De Cesari argues, largely empowers the nation-state's ideals of stewardship while ignoring local and vernacular methods of heritage conservation. Other ethnographers have similarly drawn attention to the challenges and conflicts that arise when internationalist values (and power structures) are imposed on small (and frequently disempowered) local communities (Collins 2008; Jackson and Ramírez 2009; Owens 2002; Peutz 2011). Others have begun to consider (and critique) how internationalist values of heritage might still be salvaged and reconciled with local values, by thinking of local cultural heritage as a universal human right (Langfield, Logan, and Niccraith 2010; Lilley 2009; Meskell 2010; Silverman and Ruggles 2007).

Such work pays close attention to who actually benefits from heritage. Some scholars have taken this further by examining the destruction of sites and objects – a long-time concern with the heritage industry, and particularly international legal regimes. One important line of research uses ethnography to examine why people loot archaeological sites, a way of rethinking heritage destruction in terms of the values, interests, and needs of the people who live around heritage (Colwell-Chanthaphonh 2004; Hollowell-Zimmer 2003; Matsuda 1998). Another line of research focuses on moments of iconoclasm and terrorism to unpack the political motivations and ideological benefits from attacking heritage sites (Bernbeck and Pollock 1996; Colwell-Chanthaphonh 2003; Meskell 2002, 2005). Still another line of research addresses the economies of heritage, particularly as they are built around global tourism (Breglia 2006; Dearborn and Stallmeyer 2010; Magnoni, Arden, and Hutson 2007; Mortensen 2001; Silverman 2009).

In essence, between the categories of international and national values of heritage, a third category has been established in these dialogues: that of the *intra*nationalist, which is defined as indigenous peoples and ethnic enclaves *within* nations (Watkins 2005). In recent decades, these intranationalist groups have been ever less willing to allow outsiders to define heritage for them. They have been particularly strident in defining, preserving, and using heritage on their own terms – a process often labeled as decolonization (Atalay 2006; Bruchac, Hart, and Wobst 2010; Lilley 2006; Smith 1999; Smith and Wobst 2005; Wilson and Yellow Bird 2005). A core problem identified by intranationalist communities has been the removal of human remains from graves and the appropriation of sacred and communally owned objects (Bray 2001; Bray and Killion 1994; Cove 1995; Fine-Dare 2002; Mihesuah 2000). However, decolonization has been approached in a number of arenas, including museums, archaeological practice, and conservation (Hirofumi 2009; Hoobler 2006; Sully 2007).

Seeking the participation of intranationalist groups in heritage work is not merely a form of multiculturalism, in which equality is expanded to include all social groups (Meskell 2009b: 4). While such processes of inclusiveness are not obviously negative, they can ultimately hide cultural difference, marginalizing political minorities like Native American tribes. Rather, this is a shift towards cosmopolitanism – the recognition of the Other, and the imparting of equal dignity and worth of all people even amid great cultural difference (Ivison 2002). This kind of "emergent cosmopolitanism" seeks to embrace universal ideals (like justice) while enacting them through specific, local processes (Ivison 2006). Similarly, others have advocated for a "rooted cosmopolitanism" where consideration of humanity's condition is negotiated with local identities, politics, and well-being (Appiah 2005; Nussbaum 2002; Sen 2002). These approaches to cosmopolitanism thus bridge the local and global, while challenging the power of the state to be the exclusive guardian of the interests within its territory.

The lessons learnt from "live" cases of intranationalist conflict are starting to be appropriated by groups whose ethical claims to self-determination are geographically or temporally more distant. This includes repatriation claims (Greenfield 1989) as well as critical examinations by scholars of institutions' biographies. In Price's (2007) *Paris Primitive*, the link between politicians, collecting practices in former colonies, and nationalistic ambition is highlighted to ask important ethical questions about the legacy of colonialism. The controversial materialized legacy (in the form of the Musée du Quai Branly) can be directly related to the contemporary political relationship between the French state, its former colonies, and disenfranchised French youth of African descent, most controversially embodied by Nicholas Sarkozy's 2007 speech in Senegal in which he claimed that Africa had yet to enter into history.

Because of the quandaries and problems identified by these studies, a new crop of research has taken on what is basically an applied anthropology approach to heritage. For example, Sandra Scham has directly confronted archaeology's implications in nationalism, and has sought to use heritage as a form of social reconciliation (Scham 1998; Scham and Yahya 2003). Many practitioners particularly see so-called "difficult heritage" (or dark heritage) – prison camps, massacre sites – as key points on the landscape for healing and actively confronting the past's difficult entanglements in the present (Logan and Reeves 2009; Macdonald 2009). However, constructing sites of memory is rife with conflict; for example, the National September 11 Memorial and Museum's treatment of unidentified human remains has served to reinforce rather than alleviate the suffering of victims (Colwell-Chanthaphonh 2011). Still other practitioners are finding ways to work directly with local communities to protect heritage sites and use them for civic engagement (Fletcher et al. 2008; Little and Shackel 2007). While some laws, like repatriation laws in the United States, have essentially forced heritage managers to work with descendant communities, some projects are now actively seeking collaboration, establishing new modes of control and access to heritage, and working to invert old power structures (Atalay 2012; Srinivasan et al. 2010).

What links these diverse studies is a critical analysis of the role of diverse communities in the formation of heritage and the questions of ethics that emerge from the confrontation between different claims over the past. This line of research does not ask *what* heritage is preserved so much as for *whom* it is preserved; it is focused on things only insofar as they teach us about social relations. Thus, these studies address what happens when "universal" heritage contradicts local values, or when descendant communities seek to gain social, economic, or ideological benefits from a place declared as belonging to all of humanity. These studies pay close attention to the flows of power that surround heritage sites, and so are attuned to how ethics should be "grounded," meaning that theories are discovered through the analysis of data.

In clear-cut cases, we can find broad agreement on the ethics of heritage stewardship. For example, if a site is deemed to be locally important, relevant to the national identity, and also to have "outstanding universal value" (in the UNESCO sense of value for all of humanity), then parties that might otherwise have differing interests can consent to preserve, protect, and promote it. However, difficulties quickly arise when an intranationalist group values a site that does not receive international recognition; or when the destruction of one group's heritage actually promotes a competing group's heritage; or when the promotion (or lack thereof) of a particular kind of cultural heritage infringes on a people's sense of their human rights.

In these more complex scenarios our sense of responsibility to material culture (sites and objects) confronts our sense of responsibility to people (their dignity, self-determination, religious freedom). Who decides what kind of heritage is important for whom? Should local communities be empowered to define their own heritage, or should outside experts like curators, archaeologists, and architects be empowered? And how, in theory and in practice, should differing conceptualizations of heritage be negotiated between these groups?

Mali, Heritage, and the Ethics of Self-Determination

The city of Djenné, in the landlocked West African country of Mali, has been a UNESCO World Heritage site since 1988. The Old Towns of Djenné, consisting of approximately 1,850 mud brick houses (Bedaux et al. 2000) and its mud mosque, together with a 4-kilometer radius of surrounding archaeological sites (McIntosh 2005) were judged as meeting two criteria necessary for inscription on the World Heritage List: criteria iii, to bear a unique or at least exceptional testimony to a cultural tradition or to a civilization which is living or has disappeared; and criteria iv, to be an outstanding example of a type of building, architectural, or technological ensemble or landscape which illustrates (a) significant stage(s) in human history.

The declaration of Djenné as a World Heritage site was not a surprise. In fact it marked the continuation of a long fascination the West has had with the vernacular architecture of the region (Bedaux, Diaby, and Maas 2003; Maas and Mommersteeg 1992; Monteil 1903). The interest in this vernacular architecture grew from the time of the arrival in France of early photographs and postcards of Djenné (Morton 2000). These photographic glimpses gave the impression of Djenné as a distant urban complex with winding streets and compact architecture. Djenné, together with its sister city Timbuktu (also a UNESCO World Heritage site), captured the popular imagination in Europe as romantic desert outposts of the French colonies. In 1931, L'Exposition Coloniale Internationale held in Vincennes on the outskirts of Paris featured amongst its prized exhibits a "Rue de Djenné," built as a controlled re-creation of West African vernacular architecture, although altered in scale and color.

Despite an intuitive feeling that the housing in Djenné, being made from local materials and built by local masons, is cheap and sustainable, the reality is that the costs of the upkeep of houses in Djenné is spiraling beyond the means of many of the town's inhabitants today. The houses need to be re-mudded every few years in order to remain structurally stable, due to the heavy toll of the annual rainy season and the Harmattan wind. Changes to the water level of the river, agricultural practices, and kinship arrangements are a few of the many factors causing the inflation in building costs. As a response, local people have turned to the use of fired clay tiles (traditionally used for flooring), fixed on the outside of their homes with cement to try to cut down on the annual financial burden. Despite the Djenné masons' wide disapproval of this practice, as mud and cement are not compatible materials, most are forced to work with tiles when asked by home owners, since it is their lifelong duty (and then the duty of their descendants) to maintain the houses they build (Marchand 2009). Heritage experts condemn the use of the tiles both on aesthetic grounds and due to the fact that a crack in the tile can allow moisture to seep in and destabilize the structure of the house.

In order to retain its World Heritage status, the whole of the town must continue to be built entirely in mud; no other materials should be used for domestic housing construction. The use of the tiles is therefore an infringement of local building regulations and a cause of great concern to the Djenné Cultural Mission, a body established by the Malian state in 1994. The remit of the Mission is to ensure the material integrity of the town, to protect the archaeological sites surrounding the town from looters, and to raise the profile of cultural heritage for the local population.

A first glimpse of the situation in Djenné would seem to show a clear example of an elite, Eurocentric vision of cultural heritage being imposed on a disenfranchised local community, with the question of ethics being most appropriately investigated at a local level of entanglement. The residents of Djenné's daily realities are that of a struggle for survival with temperamental harvests, political uncertainty, and precarious economic lives, whilst UNESCO's vision of the town limits itself to its architecture and archaeology. An ethnography of people's lives in Djenné reveals a population coping with lives of poverty, unsanitary living conditions, high levels of preventable disease such as malaria and typhoid, and low levels of access to education and employment opportunities (Joy 2012).

The most troubling ethical dimension within the debate about the protection of Djenné's cultural heritage is that a concentration on the town's archaeology and architecture may distract from the real issue at hand: that of the radical global economic asymmetry that has led to the conditions of poverty found there today. UNESCO's World Heritage map is intended as a one-dimensional canvas where all sites are deemed equal. Within UNESCO, the economic asymmetry of the World Heritage map is understood yet constantly forgotten in an approach that results in the invisibility of people's lives. UNESCO's concern is located in the detail of the material preservation of the town on behalf of the whole of humanity. For this logic to hold, international heritage bodies such as UNESCO have to adopt a Durkheimian (1915) model of a common humanity, worshipping itself through its concern with specific "sacred" sites identified throughout the world. A clear recent articulation of this logic occurred in Timbuktu in the summer of 2012. The destruction by the radical Islamist group Ansar Dine of the Cheick Sidi Mahmud Tomb led to international vocal condemnation both within UNESCO and by many international leaders such as Barack Obama and François Hollande. It was a catalyst for the French military intervention in the conflict in Mali. As a retort to the destruction, the Director General of UNESCO, Irina Bokova, opened a daylong meeting convened by UNESCO in Paris on the subject of the rehabilitation of Mali's cultural heritage with the words: "When a World Heritage site is destroyed, because of stupidity and violence, the whole of humanity feels it has been deprived of part of itself; that it has been injured" (UNESCO 2013).

The language used to refer to the sites under UNESCO's jurisdiction therefore indexes far more than the materiality of the site. The destruction of the material becomes the destruction of humanity, or at least of those values that the international community holds to be central to a common concept of humanity. The performative violence of the act of destruction betrays the "stupidity" of the perpetrator who does not share in a transcendental vision of a common identity.

As well as acts of destruction played out through global media, UNESCO also responds to the gradual deterioration of sites through regular inspection, as this deterioration marks a move away from an internalized bureaucratic ideal of the "stable" measure of "outstanding universal value" that first legitimated the inclusion of the site on the World Heritage list (Jokilehto 2008). For example, in a report in

May 2012 on the state of conservation in Djenné, UNESCO delegates declared that the demolition of an old courthouse was illegitimate as it was an important example of traditional architecture in the town and had been restored by a Dutch housing restoration project. The report went on to find that the courthouse had most likely been destroyed for financial reasons, as the plot of land was valuable, and that the suggested replacement building was "an uncomfortable intrusion into the urban landscape" (UNESCO 2012: 98). The new building is a "Maison des Artisans," a space long promised to artisans in Djenné (jewelers, leatherworkers, embroiderers, potters, mud-cloth producers, etc.). UNESCO's vision for the cultural heritage in Djenné is therefore one of a de-temporalized, de-economized sacred space, that inevitably comes into conflict with a pragmatic approach to the use of space.

The culture heritage found in Djenné that is *not* of note to UNESCO is abundant; a few examples among thousands would be fishing nets (from handmade rope to plastic), the work of artisans such as the melting down of antique silver bracelets by jewelers to create new models, the changes in culinary traditions, or the use of mopeds instead of bicycles. These material changes go without note by heritage officials in the town. Similarly the consumption of Chinese goods, satellite TV, the use of mobile phones, imported fashions, and so on are of no concern. So the "medieval town" of UNESCO's imagination is only present in architecture and in the continuation of the work and knowledge transmission of the masons who build the houses and their guild association, the *Barey-Ton*.

The protected archaeological sites that surround Djenné are similarly ethically entangled in debates that include a disenfranchised local population, the Djenné heritage elite (Cultural Mission, Iman, the *Chef du Village*, and the *Préfet*), the Malian national political elite, the international academic elite, and UNESCO. The archaeological sites (most notably Djenné-Djeno) have attracted global fame due to the excavations by an American team of researchers in the 1970s (McIntosh 1998). The excavations' findings were put to rhetorical use by the ex-president of Mali, Alpha Oumar Konaré (president from 1992 until 2002), who was trained as an archaeologist by the McIntoshes and was a consultant at UNESCO from 1981 to 1992. He argued that the excavations' results were evidence of a "heterarchical" past for Mali and therefore pointed to a democratic future (McIntosh 2005: 12). Excavations at the sites also suggest a uniquely African urban settlement, lacking the elements of material culture from North Africa that had previously caused scholars to suggest an Islamic diffusionist model for early city-states in West Africa.

These entanglements mean that it is only through a symmetrical analysis of the heritage logics found both in Djenné and in the corridors of UNESCO in Paris that a clear picture can be drawn of the ethics at stake in an encounter between a bureaucratic elite and a specific community that inhabits a site that has come under UNESCO's jurisdiction. Whilst UNESCO maintains that it only ever acts indirectly through the proxy of the relevant State Party, in reality, all State Parties do not enjoy the same political presence within UNESCO (see Meskell and Brumann in this volume).

Whilst UNESCO cannot be blamed for the economic deprivation found in places such as Djenné, and has tried to evolve to include a broader conceptualization of what cultural heritage is and does, its current largely materialist approaches to cultural heritage do not easily accommodate the different ways in which people make visible the meaning they ascribe to their lives. A UNESCO archival approach to cultural heritage, even when it seeks to include intangible cultural heritage, can therefore only ever be a simplifying frame for a much wider complexity. In Djenné, for example, there is the uncomfortable question of what the celebration of a particular form of cultural heritage hides by presenting a de-temporalized, unpopulated version of a town's authenticity (however UNESCO would argue that the promotion of the masons' practices negates this critique). Money can therefore flow into Djenné in the name of the protection of its cultural heritage whilst the far more pertinent question of global economic asymmetries (in some cases caused by the trade restrictions imposed by the same countries providing financial help for the protection of cultural heritage) remains silenced. A more straightforward way of protecting Djenné's unique cultural heritage would be to ensure that people in the town had economically viable lives.

In Djenné, the question of for whom cultural heritage is being preserved is a fraught one, as the recent model of economic development through cultural tourism has collapsed due to the ongoing conflict in the country. It must therefore be asked on what basis are we sacrificing the present for the future through the protection of things? And what time frame, looking into the past and into our hopes for the future, should be imposed on our conceptualization of culture heritage?

The American Southwest, Communities, and Collaboration

The American Southwest provides an important case study to consider how ethics have become infused with heritage management, particularly in the context of descendant and Indigenous communities seeking to exert greater control over historical objects and places. The ethical relationship between Native communities and heritage workers is not a new one, but has been evolving for well more than a century (Colwell-Chanthaphonh 2010). The general trend has been a shift from a nationalist development of Native American heritage in the early 1900s to a postcolonial intranationalist approach in the early 2000s that emphasizes the interests of multiple publics in heritage, particularly descendant communities.

When archaeologists first entered the Southwest in the late 1800s, they did so most often as colonial agents, seeking to record and collect Native American cultures to build national prestige (Fowler 2000). Within a generation, archaeological explorations – which would become the foundation for the region's heritage – rapidly became more standardized to create a more systematic science of understanding the past (Fowler 2005). Also, some scholars began to more seriously resist the appropriation of the Southwest's heritage for nationalist purposes, emphasizing the economic and identity functions of heritage for local communities (Snead 2001).

The first discussions of heritage ethics in the Southwest came as scientists secured the legal roles of gatekeeper of archaeological sites, which were increasingly protected as national monuments and parks, through the Antiquities Act of 1906 and other legislation (Harmon, McManamon, and Pitcaithley 2006). Through these legal regimes, archaeologists became the primary caretaker of the Southwest's ancient heritage, excluding even the living Native communities which claimed their descent from these places (Colwell-Chanthaphonh 2005). The first discussions of ethics in the Southwest were tied to a broader national dialogue about the responsibility of archaeologists to preserve sites from looters and any other kind of damage that was not scientifically controlled. In 1935 numerous leading Southwestern archaeologists enthusiastically joined the newly formed Society for American Archaeology (SAA), whose membership required a commitment to a public, non-commercial stewardship of the past (Colwell-Chanthaphonh, Hollowell, and McGill 2008: 6). This is largely what "ethics" meant eighty years ago.

In 1961 the SAA articulated its first formal statement of ethics, expanding its reach to include four key areas: accountability to other professionals, scientific methods, data sharing, and the need for specialized training (Champe et al. 1961). However, within just a decade this notion of ethics would be challenged, and expanded further, as the cultural resource management industry exploded due to new national and state laws. Suddenly, archaeology was done not merely for science but for the public (McGimsey 1972). With more archaeological research being done to satisfy federal law and being funded with public dollars, new dilemmas of professional standards, methods, and accountability arose (Green 1984). While many archaeologists became increasingly concerned about their responsibilities to make heritage accessible to different publics, the most serious questions about the discipline were posed by Native American communities. In the Southwest are nearly fifty tribal reservations, on whose leaders increasingly joined a larger national movement to challenge the authority of non-Indian archaeologists to nearly exclusively manage American Indian heritage resources (Dongoske, Aldenderfer, and Doehner 2000; Swidler et al. 1997).

A major shift in dialogue – as much as power – occurred in the 1970s, when the Pueblo of Zuni and the Navajo Nation opened their own cultural resource management programs; over the next several decades more than a dozen tribes created similar programs (Anyon, Ferguson, and Welch 2000). These tribal-run programs had multiple impacts – economic, political, and cultural – that allowed Native communities to dictate the terms of how heritage would be studied and managed. Although in many ways, this presented a new power structure around heritage, in fact, arguably, this change was a return to centuries-old traditions of Native land stewardship (Two Bears 2006). Many Native American archaeology programs were further empowered and expanded in 1992, when changes to federal law allowed for the creation of Tribal Historic Preservation Officers, giving tribes authority to regulate heritage management on their own reservations (Stapp and Burney 2002). As part of the same legal amendments to the National Historic Preservation Act, traditional cultural properties were explicitly made eligible for the National Register of Historic Places. Ever since, most Southwestern tribes have become deeply involved in evaluating and mitigating the adverse impacts of development projects (e.g., Ferguson 2003; Martinez 2006; Othole and Anyon 1993; Stoffle, Halmo, and Austin 1997).

Although much heritage in the Southwest continues to be managed under the rubric of nationalist law, and occasionally even international law (in the case of several major sites that are on UNESCO's World Heritage List), numerous projects have argued for a community-based approach that shifts the control over and interpretation of heritage to local actors. Several projects have started with the training of students, to reframe how the next generation can view heritage through the lens of ethics, while providing them new tools to work directly with communities (Mills et al. 2008; Two Bears 2008). Other research projects have used multivocal methodologies to incorporate the viewpoints of multiple stakeholders into the past (Adler and Bruning 2008; Duff et al. 2008; Ferguson and Colwell-Chanthaphonh 2006), and have sought out explicit collaborative relationships (Kuwanwisiwma 2002, 2008). What is clear is that heritage managers can no longer deny or ignore Native American cultural affinities and political rights to their past (Begay 2004; Lopez

2007; Martinez and Suina 2005; Naranjo 2008; Swentzell 2004; Thompson 2002). Although some see such assertions as a threat to science-based heritage management (e.g., Schneider and Bonnichsen 2005), a more realistic evaluation understands how collaboration improves the quality of research (Ferguson 2009) and can make heritage relevant to communities (Gumerman et al. 2012).

An equally major shift has occurred in Southwestern museums. Increasingly, Native communities have established their own museums and used them as a tool to preserve, promote, and perpetuate traditional cultures (Fuller 1992; Isaac 2007; Welch et al. 2009). The repatriation debates, which took hold in the Southwest in the 1980s, have enabled new conversations and projects that seek to overcome the colonialist histories of museums as sites of power over heritage (Anderson 2010; Bernstein 1991), and museums now regularly seek out the participation of descendant communities (Hays-Gilpin and Lomatewama 2013; McChesney and Charley 2011). Through the frame of the ethics – questions about who has control over heritage, whose voices are heard, and who benefits from heritage – these new approaches have radically altered how many communities are connecting to heritage.

The San Pedro Ethnohistory Project is one example of an effort to incorporate these methods and theories into practice (Ferguson and Colwell-Chanthaphonh 2006). This collaborative project involved inviting four Native American communities – the Apache, Hopi, Tohono O'odham, and Zuni – to provide their perspectives on the archaeological history of a valley in southeastern Arizona. By paying particular attention to the ethical responsibilities to including Native voices about their own heritage, the project highlighted the kinds of novel historical and cultural insights that can be revealed (Colwell-Chanthaphonh and Ferguson 2004, 2006).

This collaboration illustrated how the history and heritage of the San Pedro Valley is part of an ongoing cultural dynamic, a field of meanings that allows descendent communities to understand their past and who they are today. At the same time, the project sought out the intersections of scientific archaeology and living tradition. We found it in multiple areas, from new hypotheses about the complexities of ancient migrations, to oral traditions about the rise and fall of societies that mirrors the archaeological record, to interpretations for symbols in pottery and rock art. As significantly, the project aimed to inject a sense of humanity into Southwestern history. For example, Hopi oral traditions detailing the human dramas of migration breathed life into archaeological analyses that can only track ancient movements through columns of data listing ceramic types and architectural features.

Many Native Americans value archaeological sites not as a source of data but as historical monuments that bear witness to the lives of their ancestors (Kuwanwisiwma and Ferguson 2004; Lopez 2007; Naranjo 2006). Ancient villages, arrowheads, and even scatters of artifacts are seen as integral parts of a larger landscape that unites the physical and spiritual, past and present. Places, as the Apache elders reminded us, were often named by ancestors to memorialize events or trace their presence on the land (Basso 1996). When these place names are spoken today, they reconnect people to ancient landscapes, to their ancestors and their spirits. Even at spots where names are no longer recalled, tribal advisors explained how these places evoke emotion. Thus archaeological sites are living shrines that honor those in the past and inspire those in the present.

The different perspectives assembled in this project often complemented one another, adding new stories on old ones, or sometimes co-existing as two versions of one past. Where they did conflict, the project partners saw an approach of critical multivocality – compared to a simple celebratory multivocality – as a means to evaluate different knowledge claims (Atalay 2008; Nicholas and Hollowell 2007). In this mode of collaboration, disagreement is an invitation to dialogue – a chance to explore difference – rather than a closing door (Trigger 2008: 190; Wylie 2008; Zimmerman 2008a, 2008b). Finally, this project raised important questions about heritage stewardship: who has the right to speak for the valley's 12,000-year history? By inviting these four descendant communities to share their viewpoints on heritage, the project sought a kind of "complex stewardship" (Colwell-Chanthaphonh 2009), in which a shared, universal value for the objects and places of the past is sought and negotiated, but rooted in the cultural practices and values of local communities.

Conclusion

The literature on ethics and heritage is strong on case studies but still weak on fundamental philosophical grounding. This in part comes from an ambiguity about the starting point of the discussion. As Geschiere (2009) has shown on his book on autochthony, claims to identity linked to land play out differently across the world with a great diversity of ethical consequences. Similarly, claims to belonging through genetic identity have multiple entangled consequences (Cattelino 2008). After land and blood, if the criterion is to be common ritual use of space, or the belief in the agency of devotional objects, then it is hard to provide a rationale for the exclusion of the voices of people whom the media often malign, such as Druids (Bender 1998), Goddess groups (Meskell 1995), or New Agers (Finn 1997).

If the discussion begins, as it so often does, within a Western enlightenment paradigm, it could be argued that there exists a human universal to create a sense of belonging in the world through the assemblage of a narrative involving place, artifacts, stories, genealogies, language, and so on. As things stand, the experts in this enlightenment model (the historians, scientists, anthropologists, archaeologists, geneticists, linguists, etc.) often only pay lip service to the cultural practitioners themselves. While this is beginning to change, narratives are still judged by these experts as more or less plausible and sometimes roundly debunked (Hobsbawm and Ranger 1983; Meskell 2013; Wright 2009). The wider political realities also have the effect of leaving the cultural practitioners either applauded and protected – as in the case of Native American Graves Protection and Repatriation Act (NAGPRA) legislation, UNESCO recognition, land right legislation – or denigrated and disenfranchised, as with the Romani community in Europe (Stewart 2013).

One of many paradoxes in the debate seems to be the lack of agreement about whether heritage professionals are talking about the present, past, or future. If the concern is for the present, then a different political/ethical perspective emerges which is principally concerned with well-being and dignity. Agreement need not be reached about the nature of the past or our entanglement with it beyond people's individual testimonies. This at times means putting aside the documentation proffered by archaeologists, historians, and scientists in favor of engaging with people's beliefs about the world. In practice, multiple compromises take place on all sides when considering the stewardship of cultural heritage. It is encouraging that it is in the spaces carved out during these negotiations that a lot of the ethical work happens.

REFERENCES

Abu El-Haj, N. (2001) *Facts on the Ground: Archaeological Practice and Territorial Self-Fashioning in Israeli Society*. Chicago, IL: University of Chicago Press.

Ackerly, B. A. (2008) *Universal Human Rights in a World of Difference*. Cambridge: Cambridge University Press.

Adler, M. A. and S. B. Bruning (2008) Navigating the Fluidity of Social Identity: Collaborative Research into Cultural Affiliation in the American Southwest, in C. Colwell-Chanthaphonh and T. J. Ferguson (eds), *Collaboration in Archaeological Practice: Engaging Descendant Communities*. Lanham, MD: AltaMira Press, pp. 35–54.

Ahmad, Y. (2006) The scope and definitions of heritage: From tangible to intangible. *International Journal of Heritage Studies* 12: 292–300.

Anderson, D. (2010) Collaborations with Native Peoples in the American Southwest and Midwest: 1967–2007, in L. Van Broekhoven, C. Buijs, and P. Hovens (eds), *Sharing Knowledge and Cultural Heritage: First Nations of the Americas*. Leiden: Sidestone, pp. 91–104.

Anyon, R., T. J. Ferguson, and J. R. Welch (2000) Heritage Management by American Indian Tribes in the Southwestern United States, in F. P. McManamon and A. Hatton (eds), *Cultural Resource Management in Contemporary Society: Perspectives on Managing and Presenting the Past*. London: Routledge, pp. 120–141.

Appiah, K. A. (2005) *The Ethics of Identity*. Princeton, NJ: Princeton University Press.

Arnold, B. (1990) The past as propaganda: Totalitarian archaeology in Nazi Germany. *Antiquity* 64: 464–478.

Arnold, B. and H. Hassmann (1995) Archaeology in Nazi Germany: The Legacy of the Faustian Bargain, in P. L. Kohl, and C. Fawcett (eds), *Nationalism, Politics and the Practice of Archaeology*. Cambridge: Cambridge University Press, pp. 70–81.

Atalay, S. (2006) Indigenous archaeology as decolonizing practice. *American Indian Quarterly* 30: 280–310.

Atalay, S. (2008) Multivocality and Indigenous Archaeologies, in J. Habu, C. Fawcett, and J. M. Matsunaga (eds), *Evaluating Multiple Narratives: Beyond Nationalist, Colonialist, and Imperialist Archaeologies*. New York: Springer, pp. 29–44.

Atalay, S. (2012) *Community-Based Archaeology: Research with, by, and for Indigenous and Local Communities*. Berkeley: University of California Press.

Atkinson, J. A., I. Banks, and J. O'Sullivan (eds) (1996) *Nationalism and Archaeology*. Glasgow: Cruithne Press.

Basso, K. H. (1996) *Wisdom Sits in Places: Landscape and Language among the Western Apache*. Albuquerque: University of New Mexico Press.

Bedaux, R., P. Diaby, P. Maas, and S. Sidibé (2000) The Restoration of Jenné, Mali: African Aesthetics and Western Paradigms, *Terra 2000: 8th International Conference on the Study of Earthen Architecture, Torbay, Devon, UK*. London: James and James, pp. 201–207.

Bedaux, R. M. A., B. Diaby, and P. Maas (eds) (2003) *L'architecture de Djenné, Mali: La Pérennité d'un Patrimoine Mondial*. Leiden: Rijksmuseum voor Volkenkunde.

Begay, R. M. (2004) Tsé Bíyah 'Anii'áhí: Chaco Canyon and Its Place in Navajo History, in D. G. Noble (ed.), *In Search of Chaco: New Approaches to an Archaeological Enigma*. Santa Fe, NM: School of American Research Press, pp. 55–60.

Bender, B. (1998) *Stonehenge: Making Space*. Oxford: Berg.

Bernbeck, R. and S. Pollock (1996) Ayodhya, archaeology, and identity. *Current Anthropology* 37: 138–142.

Bernstein, B. (1991) Repatriation and collaboration: The Museum of New Mexico. *Museum Anthropology* 15: 19–21.

Bray, T. L. (ed.) (2001) *The Future of the Past: Archaeologists, Native Americans, and Repatriation*. New York: Garland.

Bray, T. L. and T. W. Killion (eds) (1994) *Reckoning with the Dead: The Larsen Bay Repatriation and the Smithsonian Institute*. Washington, DC: Smithsonian Institute Press.

Breglia, L. C. (2006) *Monumental Ambivalence: The Politics of Heritage*. Austin: University of Texas Press.

Brown, M. F. (1998) Can culture be copyrighted? *Current Anthropology* 39: 193–222.

Brown, M. F. (2003) *Who Owns Native Culture?* Cambridge, MA: Harvard University Press.

Bruchac, M. M., S. M. Hart, and H. M. Wobst (eds) (2010) *Indigenous Archaeologies: A Reader on Decolonization*. Walnut Creek, CA: Left Coast Press.

Burström, M., B. Elfström, and B. Johansen (2004) Serving the Public: Ethics in Heritage Management, in H. Karlsson (ed.), *Swedish Archaeologists on Ethics*. Lindome: Bricoleur, pp. 135–147.

Castañeda, Q. E. (1996) *In the Museum of Maya Culture*. Minneapolis: University of Minnesota Press.

Cattelino, J. (2008) *High Stakes: Florida Seminole Gaming and Sovereignty*. Durham, NC: Duke University Press.

Champe, J. L., D. S. Byers, C. Evans, A. K. Guthe, H. W. Hamilton, E. B. Jelks, C. W. Meighan, S. Olafson, G. I. Quimby, W. Smith, and F. Wendorf (1961) Four statements for archaeology. *American Antiquity* 27: 137–138.

Collins, J. (2008) "But what if i should need to defecate in your neighborhood, madame?": Empire, redemption, and the "tradition of the oppressed" in a Brazilian World Heritage site. *Cultural Anthropology* 23: 279–328.

Colwell-Chanthaphonh, C. (2003) Dismembering / Disremembering the Buddhas: Renderings on the internet during the Afghan purge of the past. *Journal of Social Archaeology* 3: 75–98.

Colwell-Chanthaphonh, C. (2004) Those obscure objects of desire: Collecting cultures and the archaeological landscape in the San Pedro Valley of Arizona. *Journal of Contemporary Ethnography* 33: 571–601.

Colwell-Chanthaphonh, C. (2005) The incorporation of the Native American past: Cultural extermination, archaeological protection, and the Antiquities Act of 1906. *International Journal of Cultural Property* 12: 375–391.

Colwell-Chanthaphonh, C. (2009) The Archaeologist as a World Citizen: On the Morals of Heritage Preservation and Destruction, in L. Meskell (ed.), *Cosmopolitan Archaeologies*. Durham, NC: Duke University Press, pp. 140–165.

Colwell-Chanthaphonh, C. (2010) *Living Histories: Native Americans and Southwestern Archaeology*. Lanham, MD: AltaMira Press.

Colwell-Chanthaphonh, C. (2011) The Disappeared: Power over the dead in the aftermath of 9/11. *Anthropology Today* 27: 5–11.

Colwell-Chanthaphonh, C. and T. J. Ferguson (2004) Virtue ethics and the practice of history: Native Americans and archaeologists along the San Pedro Valley of Arizona. *Journal of Social Archaeology* 4: 5–27.

Colwell-Chanthaphonh, C. and T. J. Ferguson (2006) Memory pieces and footprints: Multivocality and the meanings of ancient times and ancestral places among the Zuni and Hopi. *American Anthropologist* 108: 148–162.

Colwell-Chanthaphonh, C., J. Hollowell, and D. McGill (2008) *Ethics in Action: Case Studies in Archaeological Dilemmas*. Washington, DC: SAA.

Cove, J. J. (1995) *What the Bones Say: Tasmanian Aborigines, Science and Domination*. Ottawa: Carleton University Press.

Cuno, J. (ed.) (2009) *Whose Culture? The Promise of Museums and the Debate over Antiquities*. Princeton, NJ: Princeton University Press.

Curtis, N. G. W. (2006) Universal museums, museum objects and repatriation: The tangled stories of things. *Museum Management and Curatorship* 21: 117–127.

De Cesari, C. (2010) World heritage and mosaic universalism: A view from Palestine. *Journal of Social Archaeology* 10: 299–324.

Dearborn, L. M. and J. C. Stallmeyer (2010) *Inconvenient Heritage: Erasure and Global Tourism in Luang Prabang*. Walnut Creek, CA: Left Coast Press.

Diaz-Andreu (2013) Ethics and archaeological tourism in Latin America. *International Journal of Historical Archaeology* 17: 225–244.

Diaz-Andreu, M. and T. Champion (eds) (1996) *Nationalism and Archaeology in Europe*. London: University College London Press.

Dietler, M. (1994) "Our ancestors the Gauls": Archaeology, ethnic nationalism, and the manipulation of Celtic identity in modern Europe. *American Anthropologist* 96: 584–605.

Dongoske, K. E., M. Aldenderfer, and K. Doehner (eds) (2000) *Working Together: Native Americans and Archaeologists*. Washington, DC: Society for American Archaeology.

Duff, A. I., T. J. Ferguson, S. B. Bruning, and P. Whiteley (2008) Collaborative research in a living landscape: Pueblo land, culture, and history in west-central New Mexico. *Archaeology Southwest* 22: 1–23.

Durkheim, É. (1915) *The Elementary Forms of the Religious Life*. New York: Macmillan.

Eriksen, T. H. (2009) Between Universalism and Relativism: A Critique of the UNESCO Concept of Culture, in J. K. Cowan, M.-B. Dembour, and R. A. Wilso (eds), *Culture and Rights: Anthropological Perspectives*. Cambridge: Cambridge University Press, pp. 127–148.

Ferguson, T. J. (2003) Anthropological Archaeology Conducted by Tribes: Traditional Cultural Properties and Cultural Affiliation, in S. D. Gillespie and D. L. Nichols (eds), *Archaeology is Anthropology*. Washington, DC: American Anthropological Association, pp. 137–144.

Ferguson, T. J. (2009) Improving the Quality of Archaeology in the United States through Consultation and Collaboration with Native Americans and Descendant Communities, in L. Sebastian and W. D. Lipe (eds), *Archaeology and Cultural Resource Management: Visions for the Future*. Santa Fe, NM: School for Advanced Research Press, pp. 169–193.

Ferguson, T. J. and C. Colwell-Chanthaphonh (2006) *History Is in the Land: Multivocal Tribal Traditions in Arizona's San Pedro Valley*. Tucson: University of Arizona Press.

Fine-Dare, K. S. (2002) *Grave Injustice: The American Indian Repatriation Movement and NAGPRA*. Lincoln: University of Nebraska Press.

Finn, C. (1997) "Leaving more than footprints": Modern votive offerings at Chaco Canyon prehistoric site. *Antiquity* 71: 169–178.

Fiskesjö, M. (2010) Global repatriation and "universal" museums. *Anthropology News* 51: 10, 12.

Fletcher, R., I. Johnson, E. Bruce, and K. Khun-Neay (2008) Living with heritage: Site monitoring and heritage values in Greater Angkor and the Angkor World Heritage site, Cambodia. *World Archaeology* 39: 385–405.

Fontein, J. (2006) *The Silence of Great Zimbabwe: Contested Landscapes and the Power of Heritage*. Walnut Creek, CA: Left Coast Press.

Fowler, D. D. (2000) *A Laboratory for Anthropology: Science and Romanticism in the American Southwest, 1846–1930*. Albuquerque: University of New Mexico Press.

Fowler, D. D. (2005) The Formative Years: Southwest Archaeology, 1890–1920, in L. S. Cordell and D. D. Fowler (eds), *Southwest Archaeology in the Twentieth Century*. Salt Lake City: University of Utah Press, pp. 16–26.

Fuller, N. (1992) The Museum as a Vehicle for Community Empowerment: The Ak-Chin Indian Community Ecotourism Project, in I. Karp, C. M. Kreamer, and S. D. Levine (eds), *Museums and Communities: The Politics of Public Culture*. Washington, DC: Smithsonian Institution Press, pp. 327–366.

Geschiere, P. (2009) *The Perils of Belonging: Autochthony, Citizenship, and Exclusion in Africa and Europe*. Chicago, IL: University of Chicago Press.

Goode, J. F. (2007) *Negotiating for the Past: Archaeology, Nationalism, and Diplomacy in the Middle East, 1919–1941*. Austin: University of Texas Press.

Green, E. L. (ed.) (1984) *Ethics and Values in Archaeology*. New York: Free Press.

Greenfield, J. (1989) *The Return of Cultural Treasures*. Cambridge: Cambridge University Press.

Gumerman, G., J. Clark, E. J. Satala, and R. Chimerica (2012) Footprints of the ancestors reengaging Hopi youth with their culture. *Museums and Social Issues* 2: 149–166.

Haber, A. F. (2007) We were sitting around the table... *Archaeologies* 3: 422–428.

Habu, J., C. Fawcett, and J. M. Matsunaga (eds) (2008) *Evaluating Multiple Narratives: Beyond Nationalist, Colonialist, and Imperialist Archaeologies*. New York: Springer.

Handler, R. (1988) *Nationalism and the Politics of Culture in Quebec*. Madison: University of Wisconsin Press.

Harmon, D., F. P. Mcmanamon, and D. T. Pitcaithley (eds) (2006) *The Antiquities Act: A Century of American Archaeology, Historic Preservation, and Nature Conservation*. Tucson: University of Arizona Press.

Hays-Gilpin, K. and R. Lomatewama (2013) Curating Communities at the Museum of Northern Arizona, in R. Harrison, S. Byrne, and A. Clarke (eds), *Reassembling the Collection: Ethnographic Museums and Indigenous Agency*. Santa Fe, NM: School for Advanced Research Press, pp. 259–184.

Hirofumi, K. (2009) Whose archaeology? Decolonizing archaeological perspectives in Hokkaido Island. *Journal of the Graduate School of Letters* 4: 47–55.

Hobsbawm, E. and T. Ranger (eds) (1983) *The Invention of Tradition*. Cambridge: Cambridge University Press.

Hodder, I. (2010) Cultural heritage rights: From ownership and descent to justice and well-being. *Anthropological Quarterly* 83: 861–882.

Hollowell-Zimmer, J. (2003) Digging in the Dirt: Ethics and "Low-End Looting," in L. J. Zimmerman, K. D. Vitelli, and J. Hollowell-Zimmer (eds), *Ethical Issues in Archaeology*. Walnut Creek, CA: AltaMira Press Press, pp. 45–56.

Hoobler, E. (2006) "To take their heritage in their hands": Indigenous self-representation and decolonization in the community museums of Oaxaca, Mexico. *American Indian Quarterly* 30: 441–460.

Isaac, G. (2007) *Mediating Knowledges: Origins of a Zuni Tribal Museum*. Tucson: University of Arizona Press.

Ivison, D. (2002) *Postcolonial Liberalism*. Cambridge: Cambridge University Press.

Ivison, D. (2006) Emergent Cosmopolitanism: Indigenous Peoples and International Law, in R. Tinnevelt and G. Verschraegen (eds), *Between Cosmopolitan Ideals and State Sovereignty*. New York: Palgrave, pp. 120–147.

Jackson, J. E. and M. C. Ramírez (2009) Traditional, transnational, and cosmopolitan: The Colombian Yanacona look to the past and to the future. *American Ethnologist* 36: 521–544.

Jenkins, G. (2008) *Contested Space: Cultural Heritage and Identity Reconstructions*. Zurich: LIT.

Jokilehto, J. (2008) *What Is OUV? Defining the Outstanding Universal Value of Cultural World Heritage Properties*. Paris: ICOMOS.

Jones, S. (1994) Nationalism, archeology, and the interpretation of ethnicity: Israel and beyond. *Anthropology Today* 10: 19–21.

Joy, C. (2012) *The Politics of Heritage Management in Mali: From Unesco to Djenné*. Walnut Creek, CA: Left Coast Press.

Kaarsholm, P. (1989) The past as battlefield in Rhodesia and Zimbabwe: The struggle of competing nationalisms over history from colonization to independence. *Culture and History* 6: 85–106.

Kohl, P. L. (1998) Nationalism and archaeology: On the constructions of nations and the reconstructions of the remote past. *Annual Review of Anthropology* 27: 223–246.

Kohl, P. L. and C. Fawcett (eds) (1995) *Nationalism, Politics and the Practice of Archaeology*. Cambridge: Cambridge University Press.

Krekovič, E. (2007) Who was first? Nationalism in Slovak and Hungarian archaeology and history. *Archaeologies* 3: 59–67.

Kuwanwisiwma, L. (2002) Hopi Understanding of the Past: A Collaborative Approach, in B. J. Little (ed.), *Public Benefits of Archaeology*. Gainesville: University Press of Florida, pp. 46–50.

Kuwanwisiwma, L. J. (2008) Collaboration Means Equality, Respect, and Reciprocity: A Conversation about Archaeology and the Hopi Tribe, in C. Colwell-Chanthaphonh and T. J. Ferguson (eds), *Collaboration in Archaeological Practice: Engaging Descendant Communities*. Lanham, MD: AltaMira Press, pp. 151–169.

Kuwanwisiwma, L. J. and T. J. Ferguson (2004) Ang Kuktota: Hopi ancestral sites and cultural landscapes. *Expedition* 46: 25–29.

Labadi, S. (2012) *UNESCO, Cultural Heritage, and Outstanding Universal Value: Value-Based Analyses of the World Heritage and Intangible Cultural Heritage Conventions*. Lanham, MD: AltaMira Press.

Langfield, M., W. Logan, and M. Niccraith (eds) (2010) *Cultural Diversity, Heritage, and Human Rights*. London: Routledge.

Lilley, I. (2005) Archaeology and the Politics of Change in a Decolonizing Australia, in J. Lydon and T. Ireland (eds), *Object Lessons*. Melbourne: Australian Scholarly Publishing, pp. 89–100.

Lilley, I. (2006) Archaeology, diaspora, and decolonization. *Journal of Social Archaeology* 6: 28–47.

Lilley, I. (2009) Strangers and Brothers? Heritage, Human Rights, and Cosmopolitan Archaeology in Oceania, in L. Meskell (ed.), *Cosmopolitan Archaeologies*. Durham, NC: Duke University Press, pp. 48–67.

Little, B. J. and P. A. Shackel (eds) (2007) *Archaeology as a Tool of Civic Engagement*. Lanham, MD: AltaMira Press.

Logan, W. and K. Reeves (eds) (2009) *Places of Pain and Shame: Dealing with "Difficult Heritage."* London: Routledge.

Lopez, D. (2007) Huhugam, in S. K. Fish and P. R. Fish (eds), *The Hohokam Millennium*. Santa Fe, NM: School for Advanced Research Press, pp. 117–121.

Maas, P. and G. Mommersteeg (1992) *Djenné: Chef-d'oeuvre architectural*. Bamako and Amsterdam: Institut des Sciences Humaines and Institut Royal des Tropiques.

Macdonald, S. (2009) *Difficult Heritage: Negotiating the Nazi Past in Nuremberg and Beyond*. London: Routledge.

Magnoni, A., T. Arden, and S. Hutson (2007) Tourism in the Mundo Maya: Inventions and (mis)representations of Maya identities and heritage. *Archaeologies* 3: 353–383.

Marchand, T. (2009) *The Masons of Djenné*. Bloomington: Indiana University Press.

Martinez, D. R. (2006) Overcoming hindrances to our enduring responsibility to the ancestors: Protecting traditional cultural places. *American Indian Quarterly* 30: 486–503.

Martinez, J. and J. H. Suina (2005) Two Pueblo Perspectives on the Pajarito Plateau, in R. P. Powers (ed.), *The Peopling of Bandelier: New Insights from the Archaeology of the Pajarito Plateau*. Santa Fe, NM: School of American Research Press, pp. 129–133.

Matsuda, D. (1998) The ethics of archaeology, subsistence digging, and artifact looting in Latin America: Point, muted counterpoint. *International Journal of Cultural Property* 7: 87–97.

Mazariegos, O. C. (1998) Archaeology and nationalism in Guatemala at the time of independence. *Antiquity* 72: 376–386.

McChesney, L. S. and K. K. Charley (2011) Body talk: New language for Hopi pottery through cultural heritage collaboration. *Practicing Anthropology* 33: 21–27.

McGimsey, C. R. (1972) *Public Archaeology*. New York: Seminar Press.

McIntosh, R. J. (1998) *The Peoples of the Middle Niger: The Island of Gold*. Oxford: Blackwell.

McIntosh, R. J. (2005) *Ancient Middle Niger: Urbanism and the Self-organizing Landscape*. Cambridge: Cambridge University Press.

Merryman, J. H. (1986) Two ways of thinking about cultural property. *American Journal of International Law* 80: 831–853.

Merryman, J. H. (2005) Cultural property internationalism. *International Journal of Cultural Property* 12: 11–39.

Merryman, J. H. (2009) The Nation and the Object, in J. Cuno (ed.), *Whose Culture? The Promise of Museums and the Debate over Antiquities*. Princeton, NJ: Princeton University Press, pp. 183–203.

Meskell, L. (1995) Goddess, Gimbutas and "New Age" archaeology. *Antiquity*: 74–86.
Meskell, L. (ed.) (1998) *Archaeology under Fire: Nationalism, Politics, and Heritage in the Eastern Mediterranean and Middle East*. London: Routledge Press.
Meskell, L. (2002) Negative heritage and past mastering in archaeology. *Anthropological Quarterly* 75: 557–574.
Meskell, L. (2005) Sites of violence: Terrorism, tourism, and heritage in the archaeological present, in L. Meskell and P. Pels (eds), *Embedding Ethics: Shifting Boundaries of the Anthropological Profession*. Oxford: Berg, pp. 123–146.
Meskell, L. (ed.) (2009a) *Cosmopolitan Archaeologies*. Durham, NC: Duke University Press.
Meskell, L. (2009b) Introduction: Cosmopolitan Heritage Ethics, in L. Meskell (ed.), *Cosmopolitan Archaeologies*. Durham, NC: Duke University Press, pp. 1–27.
Meskell, L. (2010) Human rights and heritage ethics. *Anthropological Quarterly* 83: 839–860.
Meskell, L. (2013) Unesco's World Heritage Convention at 40: Challenging the economic and political order of international heritage conservation. *Current Anthropology* 54: 483–494.
Mihesuah, D. A. (ed.) (2000) *Repatriation Reader: Who Owns American Indian Remains?* Lincoln: University of Nebraska Press.
Millar, S. (2006) Stakeholder and Community Participation, in A. Leask and A. Fyall (eds), *Managing World Heritage Sites*. Oxford: Elsevier, pp. 37–54.
Mills, B. J., M. Altaha, J. R. Welch, and T. J. Ferguson (2008) Field Schools without Trowels: Teaching Archaeological Ethics and Heritage Preservation in a Collaborative Context, in S. W. Silliman (ed.), *Collaborating at the Trowel's Edge: Teaching and Learning in Indigenous Archaeology*. Tucson: University of Arizona Press, pp. 25–49.
Monteil, C. (1903) *Soudan Français: Monographie de Djenné, Cercle et Ville*. Tulle: Jean Mazeyrie.
Mortensen, L. (2001) The local dynamics of global heritage: Archaeotourism at Copán, Honduras. *Mesoamerica* 42: 104–134.
Morton, P. (2000) *Hybrid Modernities: Architecture and Representation at the 1931 Colonial Exposition, Paris*. Cambridge, MA: MIT Press.
Naranjo, T. (2006) "We Came from the South, We Came from the North": Some Tewa Origin Stories, in D. F. Noble (ed.), *The Mesa Verde World: Explorations in Ancestral Puebloan Archaeology*. Santa Fe, NM: School of American Research, pp. 49–57.
Naranjo, T. (2008) Life as Movement: A Tewa View of Community and Identity, in M. D. Varien and J. M. Potter (eds), *The Social Construction of Communities: Agency, Structure, and Identity in the Prehispanic Southwest*. Lanham, MD: AltaMira Press, pp. 251–262.
Nas, P. J. M. (2002) Masterpieces of oral and intangible culture: Reflections on the UNESCO World Heritage List. *Current Anthropology* 43: 139–148.
Nicholas, G. P. and T. D. Andrews (eds) (1997) *At a Crossroads: Archaeology and First Peoples in Canada*. Burnaby: Archaeology Press.
Nicholas, G. P. and J. Hollowell (2007) Ethical Challenges to a Postcolonial Archaeology: The Legacy of Scientific Colonialism, in Y. Hamilakis and P. Duke (eds), *Archaeology and Capitalism: From Ethics to Politics*. Walnut Creek, CA: Left Coast Press, pp. 59–82.
Nussbaum, M. C. (2002) Patriotism and Cosmopolitanism, in J. Cohen (ed.), *For Love of Country?* Boston, MA: Beacon, pp. 3–17.
Olaniyan, T. (2003) What is "Cultural Patrimony"?, in N. Afolabi (ed.), *Marvels of the African World: African Cultural Patrimony, New World Connections and Identities*. Trenton, NJ and Eritrea: Africa World Press, pp. 23–35.
Othole, A. L. and R. Anyon (1993) A tribal perspective on traditional cultural property consultation. *CRM* 16: 42–45.
Owens, B. M. (2002) Monumentality, identity, and the state: Local practice, world heritage, and heterotopia at Swayambhu, Nepal. *Anthropological Quarterly* 75: 269–316.
Pai, H. I. (1999) Nationalism and preserving Korea's buried past: The Office of Cultural Properties and Archaeological Heritage Management in South Korea. *Antiquity* 73: 619–625.

Peutz, N. (2011) Bedouin "abjection": World heritage, worldliness, and worthiness at the margins of Arabia. *American Ethnologist* 38: 338–360.

Plets, G., N. Konstantinov, V. Soenov and E. Robinson (2013) Repatriation, doxa, and contested heritages: The return of the Altai Princess in an international perspective. *Anthropology and Archaeology of Eurasia* 52: 73–100.

Price, S. (2007) *Paris Primitive: Jacques Chirac's Museum on the Quai Branly*. Chicago, IL: University of Chicago Press.

Pwiti, G. and S. Chirikure (2008) Community involvement in archaeology and cultural heritage management: An assessment from case studies in Southern Africa and elsewhere. *Current Anthropology* 49: 467–485.

Scham, S. A. (1998) Mediating nationalism and archaeology: A matter of trust? *American Anthropologist* 100: 301–308.

Scham, S. A. and A. Yahya (2003) Heritage and reconciliation. *Journal of Social Archaeology* 3: 399–416.

Schneider, A. L. and R. Bonnichsen (2005) Where Are We Going? Public Policy and Science, in R. Bonnichsen, B. T. Lepper, D. Stanford, and M. R. Waters (eds), *Paleoamerican Origins: Beyond Clovis*. College Station, TX: Center for the Study of the First Americans, pp. 297–312.

Sen, A. (2002) Humanity and Citizenship, in J. Cohen (ed.), *For Love of Country?* Boston, MA: Beacon Press, pp. 111–118.

Silverman, H. (2009) Embodied Heritage, Identity Politics, and Tourism, in L. Mortensen and J. Hollowell (eds), *Ethnographies and Archaeologies: Iterations of the Past*. Gainesville: University Press of Florida, pp. 89–105.

Silverman, H. and D. F. Ruggles (eds) (2007) *Cultural Heritage and Human Rights*. New York: Springer.

Smith, C. and G. Jackson (2008) The Ethics of Collaboration: Whose Culture? Whose Intellectual Property? Who Benefits?, in C. Colwell-Chanthaphonh and T. J. Ferguson (eds), *Collaboration in Archaeological Practice: Engaging Descendant Communities*. Lanham, MD: AltaMira Press, pp. 171–199.

Smith, C. and H. M. Wobst (eds) (2005) *Indigenous Archaeologies: Decolonizing Theory and Practice*. London: Routledge.

Smith, L. T. (1999) *Decolonizing Methodologies: Research and Indigenous Peoples*. London: Zed Books.

Snead, J. E. (2001) *Ruins and Rivals: The Making of Southwest Archaeology*. Tucson: University of Arizona Press.

Srinivasan, R., K. Becvar, R. Boast, and J. Enote (2010) Diverse knowledges and contact zones within the digital museum. *Science, Technology, and Human Values* 35: 735–768.

Stapp, D. C. and M. S. Burney (2002) *Tribal Cultural Resource Management: The Full Circle to Stewardship*. Walnut Creek, CA: AltaMira Press.

Stewart, M. (2013) Roma and Gypsy "ethnicity" as a subject of anthropological inquiry. *Annual Review of Anthropology* 42: 415–432.

Stoffle, R. W., D. B. Halmo, and D. E. Austin (1997) Cultural landscapes and traditional cultural properties: A Southern Paiute view of the Grand Canyon and Colorado River. *American Indian Quarterly* 21: 1–22.

Sully, D. (ed.) (2007) *Decolonising Conservation: Caring for Maori Meeting Houses outside New Zealand*. Walnut Creek, CA: Left Coast Press.

Swentzell, R. (2004) A Pueblo Woman's Perspective on Chaco Canyon, in D. G. Noble (ed.), *In Search of Chaco: New Approaches to an Archaeological Enigma*. Santa Fe, NM: School of American Research Press, pp. 49–53.

Swidler, N., K. E. Dongoske, R. Anyon and A. S. Downer (eds) (1997) *Native Americans and Archaeologists: Stepping Stones to Common Ground*. Walnut Creek, CA: AltaMira Press.

Thompson, I. (2002) Native American Perspectives on Sand Canyon Pueblo and Other Ancestral Sites, in M. D. Varien and R. H. Wilshusen (eds), *Seeking the Center Place: Archaeology and Ancient Communities in the Mesa Verde Region*. Salt Lake City: University of Utah Press, pp. 257–262.

Trigger, B. G. (2008) "Alternative Archaeologists" in Historical Perspective, in J. Habu, C. Fawcett, and J. M. Matsunaga (eds), *Evaluating Multiple Narratives: Beyond Nationalist, Colonialist, and Imperialist Archaeologies*. New York: Springer, pp. 187–195.

Two Bears, D. (2006) Navajo archaeologist is not an oxymoron: A tribal archaeologist's experience. *American Indian Quarterly* 30: 381–387.

Two Bears, D. (2008) 'Ihoosh'aah, Learning by Doing: The Navajo Nation Archaeology Department Student Training Program, in S. W. Silliman (ed.), *Collaborating at the Trowel's Edge: Teaching and Learning in Indigenous Archaeology*. Tucson: University of Arizona Press, pp. 188–207.

UNESCO (2012) Old Towns of Djenné (Mali), in *State of Conservation of World Heritage Properties Inscribed on the World Heritage List*. World Heritage Committee, Document 116716. Available at: http://whc.unesco.org/en/documents/116716. Accessed November 19, 2014.

UNESCO (2013) An action plan for the rehabilitation of cultural heritage and the safeguarding of ancient manuscripts in Mali was adopted at an international experts' meeting organized by UNESCO and France at the organization's headquarters on Monday. February 19. Available at: http://whc.unesco.org/en/news/987. Accessed November 19, 2014.

Vrdoljak, A. F. (2008) Self-Determination and Cultural Rights, in F. Francioni and M. Scheinin (eds), *Cultural Human Rights*. Leiden: Martinus Nijhoff, pp. 41–78.

Watkins, J. (2005) Cultural nationalists, internationalists, and "intra-nationalists": Who's right and whose right? *International Journal of Cultural Property* 12: 78–94.

Welch, J. R., M. K. Altaha, K. A. Hoerig, and R. Riley (2009) Best cultural heritage stewardship practices by and for the White Mountain Apache Tribe. *Conservation and Management of Archaeological Sites* 11: 148–160.

Wilson, W. A. and M. Yellow Bird (eds) (2005) *For Indigenous Eyes Only: A Decolonization Handbook*. Santa Fe, NM: School for American Research.

Wright, P. (2009) *On Living in an Old Country: The National Past in Contemporary Britain*. Oxford: University of Oxford Press.

Wylie, A. (2005) The Promise and Perils of an Ethic of Stewardship, in L. Meskell and P. Pels (eds), *Embedding Ethics: Shifting Boundaries of the Anthropological Profession*. Oxford: Berg, pp. 47–68.

Wylie, A. (2008) The Integrity of Narratives: Deliberative Practice, Pluralism, and Multivocality, in J. Habu, C. Fawcett, and J. M. Matsunaga (eds), *Evaluating Multiple Narratives: Beyond Nationalist, Colonialist, and Imperialist Archaeologies*. New York: Springer, pp. 201–212.

Wynn, L. L. (2008) Shape shifting lizard people, Israelite slaves, and other theories of pyramid building: Notes on labor, nationalism, and archaeology in Egypt. *Journal of Social Archaeology* 8: 272–295.

Zimmerman, L. J. (1998) When data become people: Archaeological ethics, reburial, and the past as public heritage. *International Journal of Cultural Property* 7: 69–86.

Zimmerman, L. J. (2008a) Multivocality, Descendant Communities, and Some Epistemological Shifts Forced by Repatriation, in T. W. Killion (ed.), *Opening Archaeology: Repatriation's Impact on Contemporary Research and Practice*. Santa Fe: SAR Press, pp. 91–107.

Zimmerman, L. J. (2008b) Unusual or "Extreme" Beliefs about the Past, Community Identity, and Dealing with the Fringe, in C. Colwell-Chanthaphonh and T. J. Ferguson (eds), *Collaboration in Archaeological Practice: Engaging Descendant Communities*. Lanham, MD: AltaMira Press, pp. 55–86.

6

Heritage Management and Conservation: From Colonization to Globalization

Webber Ndoro and Gamini Wijesuriya

Introduction

It can be argued that the systems and practice of heritage management experienced in parts of Asia and Africa today were imposed in these continents during the colonial period. This has led to the assumption that heritage management did not exist in these parts of the world before colonization. Perhaps surprisingly, the practice and ethos that the colonizing countries imposed in these continents did not in any way disappear with the political withdrawal. Indeed, in many instances, practices initiated during the colonial era have continued in postcolonial Asia and Africa today. In this chapter, we explore some of the challenges and contradictions that arise from the historical impositions of heritage management systems. The colonial heritage management systems appear to have also acquired a strong ally in the international and global institutions that seem to reinforce the heritage definitions, practice, and systems emanating from the colonial period. The globalization of heritage through UNESCO and organizations such as ICCROM, ICOMOS, and IUCN, which began five decades ago, has meant that heritage can only be seen as a technical, standardized, and non-flexible system with very little room for the local entities to contribute (Waterton 2010) or to recognize the context-dependent nature of the heritage discourse (Wijesuriya 2010). This discourse at the international level privileges monumentality and the physical remains at the expense of functionality, meaning, and community connections.

Both Asia and Africa are regions endowed with rich cultural and natural diversity and long heritage legacies (Africa being the cradle of humankind, after all). They also are characterized by complex levels of religious and ethnic diversity and endowed with rich and multifarious intellectual, tangible, and intangible heritage. In Asia, the Buddhist, Hindu, and, to a lesser extent, Confucian worldviews governed how the past and its remains were to be viewed and commemorated. In Africa, traditional religions, Islam, and Christianity likewise had an influence in the way heritage places were looked after (Mazrui 1986). Whilst from the viewpoint of Europe and international

Global Heritage: A Reader, First Edition. Edited by Lynn Meskell.

organizations time is perceived as linear and values as inherent in materials, in most parts of Africa and Asia time is considered cyclical and values are ascribed to both materials and the wisdom or the knowledge that created them (including associated rituals, practices, and festivals), which continue to have a function in contemporary lives. It must also be noted that the historical trajectories of the two regions exhibit many differences and specificities given their cultural diversity and the different historical pathways they have taken, while the various organizations in charge of heritage in these regions continue to strive to enforce very specific definitions of heritage and how its conservation is to be practiced. Most often, such practice is based on the overarching dictates of international organizations; in other words, the general thrust is that of "one size fits all."

Just as discussions of heritage management in many parts of the world have shown, there appears to be a clear distinction between what heritage institutions manage and the wider debate on what they should be protecting (see Harrison 2010; Lowenthal 1998; Smith 2004; Wijesuriya 2010). More recently the work of Emma Waterton (2010) has indicated that discussion concerning the appropriateness of a few experts dominating what is to be managed as heritage is a pervasive debate not confined to former colonies alone (see also Sully 2007). Wijesuriya (2010) highlights how the modern conservation movement, or the conventional conservation approach (CCA), has ignored or overlooked diversity, continuity, and community connections in its work. In an increasingly multicultural world there are demands for a more inclusive definition, practice, and management of heritage. Smith (2004), basing her work on the experience of Australia, discusses how the official definitions and practices of heritage have excluded or marginalized alternative expressions of heritage. It is also noteworthy that countries like China, which have their own specificities in terms of historic and cultural context, have nevertheless dogmatically followed the heritage conservation standards as set by European constructs, at least at the official level (Du Cros and Lee 2007). Very often their emphasis has been on the tangible aspects of the heritage: that is, the "bricks and mortar" concept, aspects of monumentality, and the dictates of such documents as the Venice Charter (Du Cros and Lee 2007).

It has also become clear that heritage management and conservation practice in both Africa and Asia is complex and dynamic. The international discourse as espoused by UNESCO and other international organizations may not necessarily coincide with the interests of the two regions. For example, the issues of indigenous people and human rights have become part of the heritage discourse in Europe, Australia, and North America (Keitumetse 2007; Ruggles and Silverman 2007). The research results of Smith (2004) and Byrne (2008) have shown that archaeological heritage management in settler societies, particularly in the United States and Australia, has largely ignored indigenous people in the governance of their own heritage. In Africa and Asia, this was also largely the practice during colonial times. However, there is a tendency to extend the case of the United States and Australia to the context of Africa and Asia, forgetting that currently the indigenous populations of these regions are by definition the majority in their respective countries, and so govern themselves. In fact, the very concept of indigenous people is far more complex in both Africa and Asia. Whist access to heritage by minority groups is an important issue in many parts of the world, in Asia and Africa even the use of and access to heritage by the majority of the population remains problematic. Moreover, very often the local community's definition and use of heritage is at odds with the precepts of preserving it for the future. Issues of poverty reduction and sustainable development are thus considered critical to the discourses of heritage in these regions.

Heritage and/or Development

The practice of heritage management and conservation in the last several decades has been oriented towards the safeguarding and protection of that which is irreplaceable and that which is threatened by loss, damage, and misuse (Logan and Reeves 2009). It is also informed by the premise that globalization or any modern development threatens the authenticity, the integrity, the localness, and the uniqueness of heritage places (Winter and Daly 2012). It was this which triggered international concern over the construction of the Aswan Dam on the Nile River in the 1960s. The construction of this dam aimed to provide energy and irrigation for the communities along the river, but threated to flood the temples of Abu Simbel and other ancient monuments along the Nile Valley. This prompted UNESCO, together with the governments of Egypt and Sudan, to appeal to the international community for assistance and cooperation to rescue the heritage that would be destroyed. Thus, there was need to document, excavate, and evacuate the monuments that were under threat. Apart from the international cooperation – which was replicated in Asia in the rescues and restorations of archaeological remains at Mohenjo-Daro in Pakistan, the Borobudur temple in Indonesia (Donnacie 2010), and the Cultural Triangle in Sri Lanka – these campaigns signaled the beginning of an uneasy relationship between heritage protection and what was considered to be the needs of development in the two regions.

The rapid growth witnessed in many parts of Asia and the isolated developments in Africa are often considered a major threat to the heritage of these regions. For this reason, international organizations such as UNESCO, IUCN, ICCROM, and ICOMOS have become champions in disseminating information to help protect the fragile and irreplaceable heritage of the world. It is therefore considered that the building of large dams in these regions, for example in Ethiopia, has to be stopped, particularly when in the vicinity of heritage sites and landscapes. In the case of Ethiopia, the dams threaten the ecosystems not only of that country, but also of Kenya and the rest of the world (UNESCO 2014). But it can be argued that the irrigation and electricity that these environmentally negative projects facilitate also address some of the issues articulated in the UN's Millennium Development Goals (MDGs), specifically poverty reduction and economic sustainability for local peoples and the wider state of Ethiopia. A similar conundrum faced China regarding the Three Gorges Dam, one of the largest hydroelectric projects in the world to date. With China's growing energy needs, it has been argued that this project will enable the country to move away from its dependence on coal (Qiang 2003). Writing about dam building in Southeast Asia, Hirsch and Warren (2002) also point out the positive environmental effects of the dams in terms of non-fossil fuel production and carbon reduction. Many countries are thus faced with the contradictory needs to conserve their heritage and to strengthen their infrastructure and economic development, as is the case with the proposal for dam construction along the Three Parallel Rivers in Yunnan, China and the Farakka Dam on the Ganges River in India.

Similarly, managing the impacts of development activities and resource extraction in and around heritage properties in these two continents has also increasingly become a challenge. The issues of mining and development, particularly in Africa, which bedevil the conservation of heritage places today and have dominated many of the World Heritage Committee meetings in the recent past, also demonstrate the uneasiness between heritage and resource exploitation (see UNESCO 2014). The discovery of substantive deposits of minerals, petroleum, and natural gas resources in commercially viable quantities in various parts of Africa near World Heritage properties presents a growing challenge to effective heritage protection, conservation, and management. Yet, for most governments, these discoveries are hailed as the vehicle to escape poverty.

The connection between resource exploitation and archaeological heritage has its origins during the colonial period. In the early years of European conquest, there was massive looting of objects from cultural heritage places. In southern Africa, the activities of the Ancient Ruins Company that was formed by the British South Africa Company to prospect for gold and other valuable antiquities at Zimbabwe-type sites in Rhodesia (Zimbabwe) is a prime example of this connection (Ndoro 2005). The mining activities of the Ancient Ruins Company caused massive damage to the physical fabric and the deposits of sites such as Great Zimbabwe. Spectacular archaeological objects such as the Zimbabwe Birds were all looted, with some of them presented to Cecil John Rhodes as gifts (Matenga 1998). Other objects from heritage sites in Asia and Africa found their way to different destinations such as the British Museum, the Smithsonian, the Louvre Museum, and many other museums in European capitals.

It can therefore be argued that the heritage movement at a global level is premised upon the idea that development must be controlled to ensure that no heritage places are damaged or destroyed. This is clearly demonstrated, as indicated above, by the dominant themes of the conservation reports examined by the UNESCO World Heritage Committee each year. The debate revolves around extraction of minerals, construction of infrastructure, (e.g., dams and roads), and political conflict in or around World Heritage sites. In many of these cases heritage professionals are seen as anti-development officers, given their rigid opposition to "development" projects. Whilst the monuments and sites which the experts have fenced off remain the preserve of a few in terms of visitation, economic benefits, and local empowerment, the new development projects come with attractive packages of employment and economic benefits, albeit short term. But across Africa and Asia, where there are areas of prosperity surrounded by a sea of poverty, there are limited choices between heritage protection and unemployment. These are the unfortunate realities that create more antagonistic attitudes to heritage conservation. Compounding this, often the presentation and governance of heritage is mainly technical and shows no relevance to the everyday life to the general public. It was this debate over mining at World Heritage properties in Canada, the United States, and Australia which alluded to the incompatibility of international environmental standards with national law and institutions, highlighting tensions between state sovereignty and common heritage (Affolder 2007).

The Cultural Triangle of Sri Lanka, as part of the UNESCO campaign mentioned above, started in 1981 with the premise that culture is a gold mine awaiting excavation and focused on the income to be generated from tourism. Questions regarding the contribution of tourism to development have been raised in all spheres, but the drive for an increase in tourism has had a pronounced effect in Asia over the last decades. The rush to inscribe properties on the World Heritage List is also a part of this move towards the intensification of tourism at heritage sites on the continent.

Traditional Management Systems

One of the most commonly held misconceptions is that there was no system of heritage management and conservation in pre-colonial Africa and parts of Asia (Joffroy 2005; Wijesuriya, 2003). And yet, when the Western ways of management were first instituted, both regions were replete with heritage sites and landscapes, most of which were in a sound state of preservation and management already. In some parts there was a system of elders, priests, chiefs, or other custodians who looked after important heritage resources such as sacred groves, temples, and forests. Such a system not only protected cultural heritage; it resulted in the conservation of the natural environment and a balance between nature and culture. In fact, there was a deep sense of community ownership as different sections of communities took part in conserving different sections of the heritage, be it royal palace walls or revered shrines (Wijesuriya 2005). One example of traditional heritage management and conservation is that of the Barotseland in western Zambia. Here, the colonial authorities used the policy of indirect rule that placed a huge responsibility for administration on the traditional authorities. As a result, the Barotse chiefs, or *indunas*, had jurisdiction over site management (Musonda 2005). In Asia, the continuity of traditional management systems can be seen in the ancient Ifugao Rice Terraces of the Philippines. Here the remarkable agricultural system has been maintained through a traditional system for more than 2,000 years (Koohafkan and Altieri 2011).

A regional comparison of traditional heritage management reveals a shared principle of usable and living heritage. Heritage places such as Timbuktu, Aksum, Great Zimbabwe, and Kilwa, among others, were not left to decay, waiting for "discovery" by foreign heritage experts. Many archaeological sites and ruins, for example Anuradhapura in Sri Lanka, Lumbini in Nepal, Bodhgaya in India, and many other sites, are still places of worship and pilgrimage and are considered sacred by millions of Buddhists. These places contain archaeological remains dating back to the third century BCE, but their sacredness adds a different set of values and conservation challenges. Most of these places still play major roles as part of a dynamic cultural landscape whose meaning is derived from its wider social and religious context.

In Timbuktu, Mali, a management system with masons to maintain and alter the mosques had been established by the sixteenth century CE (Sidi and Joffroy 2005). Each family was responsible for specific mosques and would collectively organize the work of maintaining and repairing the structures. The work was a component of their religious and social duties and was conducted as part of a celebration. This allowed the community to own and identify with this place. Each family and mason also tried to leave an imprint on the material fabric of Timbuktu; thus the mosques were subject to numerous alterations and new experimentations.

In Asia, heritage management practice has long existed in diverse forms and is reflected in numerous texts, chronicles, and inscriptions. According to the Great Chronicle Mahavamsa of Sri Lanka (Tunprawat 2009), a ruler of the third century BCE, received from Emperor Asoka of India the gift of a sapling of the tree under which the Lord Buddha was enlightened. The tree still exists and has become one of the most sacred Buddhist places. The ruler even ordered that the pieces of the wooden ship that transported the plant be brought to the city and displayed in a special building for the people to view – thus laying the foundation for the concept of museums (Tunprawat 2009). This careful attention to the preservation of sacred objects can be seen further in the fourth century CE, evidenced by the tooth relic of the Buddha, which was brought from India for protection and is still preserved in a container surrounded by a special building built by the ruler.

The influence of religion led to well-established principles, procedures, and practices in diverse forms of conservation, management, and long-term care for heritage.

For instance, treatises like *Mayamatha* from the sixth century CE devoted chapters providing guidance for the preservation of objects, monuments, and sites in Sri Lanka (Dagen 1985; Wijesuriya 2000):

> Those (temples) whose characteristics are still perceptible in their principal and secondary elements (are to be renovated) with their own materials.
>
> If they are lacking in anything or have some similar type of flaw, the *sage wishing to restore them*, (must proceed in such a way that) they regain their integrity and that they are pleasantly arranged (anew);
>
> this (is to be done) with the dimensions – height and width – which were theirs, with decorations consisting of corner, elongated and other aedicule, without anything being added (to what originally existed)
>
> and always in conformity with the advice of the knowledgeable

There are references to ministers and officers in charge of and specializing in restoration and conservation. High regard was evidently given to the qualities and skills of architects, master builders, and craftsmen, and great emphasis placed on their duties and the need for teamwork. The following excerpts from a ninth-century CE inscription highlight the importance of craftsmen involved in conservation and their duties and obligations (Wijesuriya 2003):

> [There shall be] clever stone-cutters and skillful carpenters in the village devoted to the work of [temple] renewal.
>
> They all ... shall be experts in their [respective] work.
>
> ... shall be granted to the officer who superintends work.
>
> ... his respective duties, shall be recorded in the register.
>
> ... they alone shall be answerable for its correctness.
>
> The limit [of time] for the completion of work is two months and five days.
>
> Blame [shall be attributed to] ... who do not perform it according to arrangement

The construction of stupas, the most dominant architectural feature of Buddhist monasteries, started in the third century BCE and reached unprecedented proportions in Sri Lanka from the second century BCE, during which they rose up to 120 meters in height. Built in burnt bricks and demonstrating great symbolic meanings, the stupas were subjected to damage due to a variety of reasons. Thus continuous renewal of them throughout the centuries using the principles recorded above, and with the use of traditional knowhow, was practiced throughout the history of Sri Lanka.

As in many parts of Asia, in Myanmar the Shwedagon Pagoda (the most revered Buddhist site in the country) had been restored and renovated since 1372, as records indicate (Tunprawat 2009), up until the region's colonization by the British in 1886. Even though the kings led the projects, the local communities took part and were allowed to express their faith at the pagoda. With the arrival of the British, however, all religious activities were halted and the site became a scientific specimen for documentation and study.

The history of both continents clearly indicates that communities have cared for their heritage before the time of colonization. They valued sites and objects and looked after them through traditional systems of care that have also evolved through time and still today have established approaches. In some instances the custodianship and curatorship of culture and nature pre-dates or was parallel to Western methods.

Colonial Heritage Management Systems

The arrival of Europeans in both continents greatly influenced traditional worldviews (Wallerstein 1995). After the political control of the colonies, colonists undertook to study and document the antiquities of the two continents. European presence in Africa started in the late fifteenth century with the colonization of coastal areas, first by the Portuguese and subsequently by the British, French, and (in a limited way and much later) the Germans. Political and economic colonization by its nature brought its own interpretations of Africa and its history, which were largely influenced by the European ideologies of the time that viewed the continent as dark and backward (Maluleke 2010; Mazrui 1986). The demise of pre-colonial African polities defined the basis for heritage practice. The separatist politics in South Africa, especially after 1948, also meant that heritage would be practiced under apartheid influence until 1994 (Meskell 2011).

African nationalism and white resistance to democratizing research greatly affected the practice of protecting and governing heritage places in most parts of Africa, particularly in settler colonies like Kenya, South Africa, and Zimbabwe. Heritage increasingly became a "white" discipline, mostly practiced in land alienated from the natives and in museums that were essentially European institutions designed to showcase ancient cultures and pasts in a very static manner. African archaeological and ethnographic objects were also appropriated in this manner, such that production of knowledge of the past was firmly in the hands of a colonial minority. The issue of preserving heritage to insure that only a few could enjoy and understand it led to the introduction of protected areas. The justification given for this was that the "natives" did not understand their own heritage and that it would be either contaminated or destroyed if left to them. First, the concept of protected areas was applied to nature reserves, where wildlife conservation concepts were introduced, and it was later extended to the cultural heritage field. The concept of protected areas management can be traced back in Africa to the time of colonization and the ideas of Africa as an uncontaminated continent with pristine natural areas: "the True Africa and undamaged and unspoiled image" (Nelson 2003: 71). For example, the creation of the Selous Game reserve in the 1930s was preceded by the removal of large local populations. Protected areas like Kruger National Park, Okavango, Tsavo, Seregate, and Hwange were seen as the best way to serve the natural heritage of Africa and to preserve it from African depredation. In fact, the creation of these protected areas served to alter both animal behavior and botanical development within them. In many countries, such as Zimbabwe and South Africa, cultural heritage places were typically managed by institutions founded on the natural sciences. Similarly, in Asia scientific missions were carried out with the goal of discovering lost ancient civilizations, as at Angkor, which subsequently had to be protected from destruction by the locals (Winter 2007).

The advent of colonialism led to the establishment of institutions to protect, manage, and study cultural heritage in the individual colonies. For instance, the Historical Monuments Commission of Rhodesia was instrumental in identifying and protecting heritage assets in what is now Zimbabwe. At the same time, antiquities departments were established in Kenya, Ghana, and Nigeria, among others.

Across the two regions, the efforts of state antiquities bodies were complemented by those of organizations such as IFAN (Institut Française d'Afrique Noire), which was established in Dakar for the purposes of conducting research in French West Africa, and École Française d'Extrême-Orient (EFEO), which was based in Saigon. The British Institute of Eastern Africa played a similar role in most of southern and eastern Africa. Apart from the establishment of antiquities organizations, a number of legislative regimes were also put in place to protect cultural and natural heritage in the occupied territories.

The colonialization of Africa and Asia therefore signaled the beginnings of Western-style heritage management and conservation, which introduced and enforced values that were at times completely different from traditional ones. For example, unlike the traditional systems before them, the Western systems were run by and intended to serve only a few colonial elites, with no role for the colonized communities. The emphasis was on monumentality and antiquities. The long history of excavations at such places as Great Zimbabwe, Kilwa, the Rift Valley sites in eastern Africa, Jenne–Jenno, Meroe, and Mapungubwe left major scars on the material fabric and landscapes of these archaeological heritage places (Ndoro 2005). Local people were only hired for their labor and knowledge of the local history (Shepherd 2007). Although their knowledge was useful in building interpretations, the local informants were rarely acknowledged. One outcome of the earliest archaeological excavations was the looting of archaeological objects, which in some cases precipitated the establishment of legislation to control the largely destructive excavations, protect the fabric of sites, and stop the trade in cultural objects (Negri 2005). European expansion into other parts of the globe resulted in the partitioning of the vast sub-Saharan latitudes into spheres of influence for different European powers in the late nineteenth century. Southern and eastern Africa was dominated by British colonies, while the French were mostly in west and central Africa. In between the colonies of the British and the French, there were those of other countries such as Belgium and Portugal. The definition of what heritage was, and how it was to be protected, differed from one colonial power to the other. For example in the British colonies the emphasis was largely on archaeological sites whilst in the French areas the emphasis was on the architectural heritage. These colonial biases are very much reflected in the typologies of heritage being currently nominated to the World Heritage List.

Colonial occupation, initially in the maritime provinces of India and Sri Lanka, began in the early sixteenth century. It was in the early nineteenth century that British rule was established in India and Sri Lanka, signaling the start of a new politicization process that would cover all of Sri Lanka and the majority of India. Influenced largely by the personal interests of the colonial administrators who focused largely on archaeological ruins, heritage management became part of the colonial governance systems in the mid-nineteenth century (Lahiri 2001). The British introduced their own systems of conservation, abandoning or disregarding the traditional systems that existed before.

The Archaeological Survey of India, started in 1862, soon became a fully fledged public sector management entity controlled by the central government, and also a place for innovative personalities like Sir Mortimer Wheeler (Kean 2011). On the same basis, the Archaeological Survey of Ceylon was established by the colonial government in 1890 initially with a view to document abandoned ruins. Both these projects later became the central institutions in charge of managing heritage, each with their own legislative frameworks (Wijesuriya 2000). The colonial influence upon these institutions is evident in all their aspects: for example, in the late nineteenth century, the colonial government of Sri Lanka sought the assistance of the Royal Asiatic Society of Great Britain for the restoration of the Buddhist monuments (Wijesuriya 1993).

Despite some small contributions, little or no effort was made to contextualize local or indigenous heritage management discourse within the region. As in Africa, the imposition of Western approaches emphasizing scientific methodologies in conservation and heritage management came at the expense of local and traditional systems in India. This has been demonstrated by the work of the Archaeological Survey of India (Cohn 1996; Mathur 2007; Wallerstein et al. 1995). With the creation of Pakistan and Bangladesh, the Archaeological Survey of India extended the legacy of its system of documentation and management. Nepal too based its archaeological training on similar models from India (also see Daly and Rahmayati 2011 for Indonesia, and Du Cros and Lee 2007 for similar efforts in China).

Postcolonial Heritage Management

In the postcolonial period, there was the need to forge new national identities; in some cases heritage become a convenient vehicle to do so. Ethnic or tribal allegiances and tensions were not easily accommodated in most postcolonial states, as seen in such places as India, Pakistan, Kenya, Zimbabwe, and many other newly independent states. In Zimbabwe at independence, the then prime minister Robert Mugabe could proclaim that "independence will bestow on us ... a new future and perspective and a new past" (quoted in Pwiti 1996: 153). The end of colonial rule offered a new opportunity to foster new trajectories in the development of heritage management. However, in most cases it appears that the postcolonial states were more comfortable continuing with the colonial heritage management practice, given that they were in large parts colonial creations with ethnic and tribal conflicts still to be addressed.

In Africa and Asia, even after fifty years of independence the majority of heritage legislation continues to reflect the management systems introduced during the settler colonial era. It can be argued that the settler land-ownership patterns left a mark on the way heritage was to be managed, and that the protected areas system, despite its weaknesses, continues to define heritage practice, especially in Africa. This is true for Asia as well, despite leaders in modern-day conservation such as Roland Silva having headed ICOMOS consecutively for almost a decade (Wijesuriya, personal communication). Indeed, fundamental legislation and the way sites are conserved and managed still closely resemble the patterns and principles established during the colonial era, which focus primarily on monumental heritage. From a management point of view, the colonial-era system valued Western science and approaches at the expense of local values that were, in most cases, regarded as superstitious and irrelevant to conservation and research (Chirikure and Pwiti 2008). At independence, many countries realized the value of the past in nation-building (Garlake 1982) and the need to restore cultural pride that had been seriously eroded by colonialism. National governments keenly supported heritage conservation legislation by amending some of the colonial legislation to reflect new realities. However, independence did not result in the incorporation of local communities into heritage management and protection. Besides this challenge, postcolonial heritage management is faced with the ever-present problems of lack of capacity, resources, and poor inventory systems (McIntosh 1993).

Most of the official government organizations charged with looking after heritage in Asia and Africa are largely compelled to follow practices that have their roots in colonial times, practices which also tend to be acceptable to international organizations such as ICOMOS and UNESCO. Also, ICCROM, which has served as the training ground for many heritage professionals since early 1960s, trained experts to focus on the Western model of conservation, who on their return to their home countries subsequently strengthened systems that had been propagated under colonial rule. The work of the National Museums and Monuments of Zimbabwe, for example, demonstrates this. Despite the rhetoric of liberation and independence, the governance of heritage places and objects has remained the same as during the colonial days. For instance, the 1972 National Museums and Monuments Act is still the basic legal instrument for heritage management, with no changes made. Thus the majority of places protected under this legislation have not changed.

The obsession with monumentality, observed with the recording and documentation of places such as Kilwa Kisiwani and Great Zimbabwe, was also replicated in most parts of Asia. Colonial administrators in the region were amazed by the rich heritage that had fallen into ruins due to colonial occupation, and these monumental sites continued to dominate the national list of monuments. India still has fewer than 5,000 monuments on its national register, which is very small in proportion to the size and the diversity of its culture heritage. Interestingly, and in high contrast to the case of Africa, Asian countries have started paying attention to colonial creations during the postcolonial period. Indeed, ideas such as mutual heritage/shared heritage (originally called "heritage of dual parentage") were introduced to the world during the postcolonial period by Sri Lanka through a resolution at the ICOMOS General Assembly in 1984. The principle behind this was that the colonial past is part of the nation's history, and so the heritage created during that period stands as testament to the combined works of native and colonizer groups. However, most legal instruments on the protection of heritage still fail to recognize traditional systems of management. African and Asian heritage managers have been slow to correct this shortcoming (Jopelo 2010; Smith 2004).

The protected areas management system in Africa, which has been applied mostly to natural heritage places, might not be suitable for cultural sites and landscapes, given the fact that it removes the cultural practitioners from the area. This therefore creates fossilized areas that are the preserve of only the scientific communities, in the same way that colonial governments created protected areas for the amusement and enjoyment of the settler population. It can be argued that the protected areas system in many ways perpetuates the segregation systems that were prevalent in these former settler colonies.

It could be argued that postcolonial heritage experts have more in common with colonial authorities than with the general population. In some instances, African and Asian local heritage practitioners collaborated with colonial authorities and emerged as crucial links between local people and the colonial administration. In other words, the newly educated elites in most colonial situations simply became instruments in the hands of the colonial authorities. Sometimes, however, they did criticize the colonial authorities on a limited basis and argued for a different understanding of heritage and its preservation (Mahachi and Ndoro 1997).

Global Heritage Management: Africa and Asia

Colonial era definitions of what constitutes heritage, how it is managed, and who should manage it have gained dominance in Asia and Africa, and have been further reinforced by the international organizations such as UNESCO, ICCROM, IUCN, and ICOMOS. The notion of World Heritage made it mandatory for heritage authorities and professionals in the two continents to use so-called doctrines of conservation developed by the Western world. Before the World Heritage system, the acceptance of such doctrines was only voluntary, whereas currently they are imposed upon various nations. Issues such as authenticity and what constitutes "outstanding universal values" continue to be defined based on the 1964 Venice Charter (Cameron 2009). This is despite the fact that the current Operational Guidelines of the 1972 World Heritage Convention are supposed to take into consideration the Nara Document on Authenticity that seeks to incorporate non-Western approaches to heritage management into UNESCO practice.

The Venice Charter came out of a specifically western European historical background and understanding of heritage after World War II. It was based on the concept of the notion of materiality and the assumption of values inherent within any tangible reminder from past events. The Venice Charter also put the compliance and responsibility for safeguarding heritage places squarely on the shoulders of heritage professionals for the benefit of future generations. This already puts this standard-setting international regulatory mechanism on a confrontational path with the customary and traditional systems in most of Asia and Africa, as here heritage places have a daily function in the lives of present generations. In addition to this, traditional and religious practice entail that the community be the custodians of their heritage, not the experts.

The 1994 Nara Document on Authenticity was perhaps the first international declaration that made attempts to include non-Western concepts within the ways in which heritage is dealt with at international levels. Based on the Asian experience, and more specifically Japanese practice, it tried to be critical (Ruggles and Silverman 2009) and at the same time expand the definition of materiality and attention given to context as laid out by the Venice Charter. The Nara Document, in contrast to the Venice Charter, states that the cultural context must be taken into consideration when seeking to understand heritage and its significance. It also suggests going beyond the material fabric of heritage in considering questions of authenticity.

The UNESCO World Heritage site of the Kasubi Tombs, Uganda, illustrates the fact that, despite the general acceptance of the Nara Document by the World Heritage Committee, ICOMOS still uses the Venice Charter to evaluate and define what can be conserved and what can be of "outstanding universal value." The Kasubi Tombs are the burial grounds of the Kabakas, the kings of the Buganda kingdom, renowned for its traditional thatched architecture. Yet practical expedience in the 1970s and 1980s had led to some of the tombs being provided with corrugated iron roofs. This did not in any way affect the value or significance of the tombs to the custodians and the owners. However, the precepts of World Heritage status made sure that the original thatched roof was restored using French and South African experts before nomination, given international convention dictates on material authenticity. Whilst the use of other materials for the building has not in any way affected the use or value of the site to the local community, ICOMOS deems that the thatched roofs are crucial to the Outstanding Universal Value of the site. According to ICOMOS experts, Kasubi was a major example of an architectural achievement in organic materials, principally wood, thatch, and wattle and daub. For the Buganda people nothing could contaminate the burial place of the Kabaka; the value of the place would remain irrespective of what type of roof covers it. Unfortunately the Kasubi Tombs were damaged by fire in 2011. Despite the existence of traditional knowledge from Buganda, its restoration has been delayed because of the apparent need for international expertise and involvement (UNESCO-Africa desk, personal communication).

On the other hand, unlike the Kasubi Tombs, where authenticity seems to be frozen in time, in the case of the Temple of the Tooth Relic of Sri Lanka, the community continues to hold sway in determining its value. For Buddhists in Sri Lanka, the Temple of the Tooth Relic is the most sacred place even in contemporary Sri Lanka. The temple was originally built during the reign of Vimaladhramsuriya II (1687–1707). The site was inscribed to the World Heritage List in 1988. However, the temple was bombed in 1998 by the Tamil terrorist group fighting for a separate state. Unlike the Kasubi case, the restoration of the temple was a negotiated process, during which the community took the driver's seat, not the experts. The results of the restoration were a far cry from the accepted norms of international heritage management bodies and the standards set by the Venice Charter. Rather, it was the traditional custodians of the Tooth Relic Temple who laid down the principles and procedures to be followed by the restorers. The high priests of the Buddhists, the *Malwatte* and *Asgririya*, and the custodians the *Diyawadana Nilame* led the process. The restoration project was completed in nine months with a new copper tile roof replacing the terracotta tiles of a later addition to the complex. New timber and new stone sculptures were also used, thus violating the Venice Charter. However, this did not diminish the value or sacredness of the temple to the Buddhist community in Sri Lanka. The restoration of the Temple of the Tooth Relic was thus more in line with the dictates of the Nara Document on Authenticity. It also clearly demonstrated that cultural heritage is a process and is connected to the daily functions of society (Wijesuriya 2007).

The Operational Guidelines of the World Heritage Convention have subsequently incorporated concepts of the Nara Document on Authenticity. However, the experience from Africa and Asia is that ICOMOS experts dealing with heritage typically have issues with the application of these concepts in practice. For example the nomination of Robben Island to the World Heritage List on the basis of World Heritage criteria vi was resisted, and treatment of the multilayered history of the island had to be added in order to ensure that the relatively insignificant historical remains on the island were given an equal recognition with that of the historic struggles for democracy against apartheid. The subsequent outstanding universal value as crafted by experts reflects the so-called multilayered history of the island and the prison buildings (UNESCO 1999). The fact that this island was only known to the rest of the world and to Africa as the place of banishment and imprisonment for Nelson Mandela and other resistors of apartheid is lost in the language of ICOMOS and UNESCO. Similarly the urgent nomination of Preah Vihear Temple complex was presented as material culture from the past with no wider contemporary cultural and political values. The main emphasis was on its exceptional quality of architecture and curved stone ornamentation. It is important to note that the strong historical and cultural values of this place are sacrificed in the nomination for its "pure" architectural styles (Winter 2007). In particular, no significance was given to the current social connections with its contemporary surroundings. This was despite the fact that the two countries of Cambodia and Thailand almost went to war over the site. UNESCO's idea of heritage being neutral is naive, as demonstrated by the political turmoil that was set in motion after inscription (Silverman 2011). This clearly demonstrated that the values of the site go beyond the outstanding masterpiece of Khmer architecture upon which ICOMOS recommended its inscription.

The disjuncture between global heritage organizations and local communities is demonstrated by the refusal of ICOMOS to include Njelele (a sacred site) as part of the nomination of the Matobo Cultural Landscape in Zimbabwe. For ICOMOS, the rock art found within the Matobo were of far greater value to the world than the rituals and religious values of Njelele, which was considered by some experts as a pagan practice (Makuvaza 2008). This was despite the fact that for Zimbabweans, Matobo *is* Njelele: this is the abode of *Mwari*, the Shona equivalent of God and therefore regarded as the most important heritage place in Zimbabwe (Nyathi and Ndiwini 2005). The condition of inclusion was that the religious leaders and communities had to abide by the rules and regulations of a protected area. No indigenous rituals were to be permitted, and permission for any use had to be authorized by the protected areas management authority and should not threaten the fauna and flora of the area. For the local community, nomination meant a change of ownership of the sacred site from the community at large to National Parks and National Museums and Monuments of Zimbabwe, with the consequence that local community use of the site would be restricted, while at the same time opening the site to tourism (Makuvaza 2008). For local communities the concept of a "protected area" or "monument" has often meant fences, a denial of access, and desecration of sacred places through tourism.

The authorized heritage discourse, as Smith (2004) puts it, of UNESCO's World Heritage system can at one level be seen as a means by which certain interests are imposed over others, especially as it always conflicts with local practices. In Rwanda, the fallout between the government and French authorities over the 1990s genocide has meant that UNESCO and ICOMOS experts have rejected the States Party-proposed Tentative List that predictably contains only sites associated with the genocide. In turn, UNESCO has send ICOMOS experts to assist Rwanda in identifying possible heritage sites to nominate. The UNESCO experts suggest, among others, a list of cathedrals, churches, and archaeological sites as part of a compromise for tentative listing. As far as Rwandans are concerned, no site can have more or greater significance than the sites of genocide that were witness to the wiping out of so many of their compatriots. Despite Rwanda seeking assistance from UNESCO for their own expert findings, the Advisory Bodies have ignored the interest and values of the Rwandans themselves.

The cases of Matobo, Robben Island, Preah Vihear, and Rwanda clearly demonstrate that the international standards set by UNESCO and ICOMOS are often geared towards privileging certain cultural symbols and particular "experts" who are deemed capable of discerning the value, meaning, and significance of any heritage place in the world. The concept of listing and the heritage being defined is clearly Eurocentric or at least based on pro-Western cultural norms.

Conserving the Sacred: Angkor World Heritage Site

The dichotomy of heritage experts and traditional communities is clearly exhibited in Cambodia. Here communities have maintained their links as a place of worship through time, from the Angkorian period (802–1431 CE) to the present. This is despite the fact that they had been denigrated by both the French experts and the new heritage professionals. Despite all the politics of emphasizing the authenticity of material at Angkor, it has always remained a place of worship for the communities (Tunprawat 2009). The Angkor Complex of Monuments is described by UNESCO as "a unique artistic realization, a chef d'oeuvre of the human mind" (UNESCO 2008). It represents the Khmers' ingenuity as a combination of architecture and traditionally managed landscapes, mixed with deep religious traditions. Although traditional conservation had taken place at Angkor for centuries, major modern conservation only started in 1908 with the colonization of Cambodia by the French, when the restorations were undertaken by foreign experts. The work of École Française d'Extreme-Orient continued even after independence in 1940s; however, no training was given to the local population (Winter 2007).

Since the management of the site by the French began, several regulations to govern land use and the behavior of the local communities have also been implemented. Some of the inhabitants from Angkor Wat and Angkor Thom were moved and relocated in the name of insuring conservation and management of these architectural and archaeological resources (Miura 2004). During the war in the 1970s, a large number of artifacts were removed for safekeeping and a number of temples damaged. At the end of the war, in the early 1990s, looting and vandalism were common problems at Angkor (Baillie 2007). In 1992 Angkor was inscribed on the World Heritage List with ICOMOS describing it as one of the most important archaeological sites in Southeast Asia. Although the description does recognize the religious values attached to the place, it is the architectural and archaeological values that are emphasized.

The conservation work resumed in 1999 with national staff being supervised by the International Coordinating Committee (ICC) set up and co-chaired by France and Japan. As Angkor is vast, many countries guided by the international guidelines have volunteered to assist the main contributors (which are Japan, France, Germany, Australia, and the United States). The ICC meets twice a year, during which the main concern is the architectural and archaeological research and conservation of the site. No local communities are represented in the ICC and very little effort is made to understand the sociocultural context of the heritage site (Miura 2004; Winter 2007). The first phase of these restorations was characterized by strict policies and regulations on the original inhabitants – for example, the villagers were banned from rice cultivation within Angkor Thom, collecting forest products in the area, and grazing cattle on the monuments. These activities had been traditional livelihood practices for the communities up to that point. These restrictions on land use in turn led to impoverishment and unemployment (Winter 2007). This obviously has created tension with the authorities. The policy of conserving old pagodas also had a negative effect on the monastic life in Angkor, as the old monastic buildings which were left as picturesque ruins could not attract worshippers. This lack of worship meant fewer donations and no support to traditional religious studies, which in turn hindered the conservation of the spiritual heritage associated with the place (Baillie 2007). Recently efforts made to incorporate the aspirations of the community into the mainstream conservation programs on the site have also met with limited success (Tunprawat 2009; Winter 2007).

Mountain of the Gods: Tsodilo Cultural Landscape

The management of Tsodilo Cultural Landscape in Botswana clearly demonstrates how the concept of protected areas management system influences the governance of World Heritage sites in Africa. The system is taken to be of the highest standard set by UNESCO and its Advisory Bodies. The "mountain of the gods," or Tsodilo Hills, was the first World Heritage site nomination for Botswana in 2001. Before its designation as a place of outstanding universal value, Tsodilo was the ancestral home of the San and the Hambakushe groups of Botswana. They regarded the hills as the abode of the ancestral spirits and conducted many rituals throughout the hills to appease their gods. It was also a grazing area, a hunting ground, and burial place for their community. Also, the Tsodilo Hills, like Motobo in Zimbabwe, was considered to be a place rich with some of the most spectacular rock art in southern Africa.

As a protected area with a rich archaeological heritage, it was asserted that the locals could contaminate the scientific evidence and above all compromise its conservation by hunting and grazing in the hills (Keitumetse and Nthoi 2009; Segadika 2006). This was despite the fact that these groups had lived in the area for thousands of years. Thus, in order to nominate the site, indigenous groups had to be moved at least 3 kilometers away and the site had to be fenced off to prevent encroachment. The two local groups also had to change their hunting practices and stop their ritual practices. New villages were then allocated in areas that would not interfere with the World Heritage site. The places where communities used to live were then earmarked for the development of tourist facilities. These changes then influenced and facilitated the Tsodilo Hills' nomination as Botswana's first World Heritage site. Its management plan, which was based on the concept of the protected areas system, was heralded as a good example to be followed throughout Africa (even though the UNESCO criteria cited for its nomination refers to living traditions). The nomination of Tsodilo and its subsequent management (which emphasizes its archaeological aspects over these living traditions that international organizations supposedly now celebrate) is yet another example of ICOMOS experts in Africa ignoring the thrust of the Nara Document, which was intended to broaden the definition of authenticity as narrowly set out in the Venice Charter to include intangible aspects (Segadika 2006). It similarly exemplifies the "one size fits all" definition of heritage and the application of a natural protected areas concept to places of cultural heritage.

Conclusions

The challenge for local heritage practitioners and experts is how to include non-European views within the concept and processes of World Heritage. Part of the problem is that whilst the definition and standards of management are set at a global (Western) level, the unfortunate scenario is that the day-to-day management is at a local level where the immediate realities of poverty are very present and pressing. The assumption of UNESCO and its Advisory Bodies is that there exists a World Heritage with a uniform set of criteria and heritage values that are intrinsic rather than given by present-day inhabitants. These values are too often bestowed by archaeologists, architects, and other scientists, as Harrison (2010) reminds us in the case of the destruction of the Bamiyan Buddhas. Local voices and aspirations unfortunately do not frequently coincide with the interests of global heritage discourses. As Winter (2007) has put it, "world heritage" invariably does not seem to accommodate local contestations, nationalistic agendas, and the sub-national interests of minority groups.

From the case studies outlined, the practice of heritage is not something fixed, nor is it already constituted. The only consistent thing in heritage is change, which may be historically or context driven. The trajectory it takes is dynamic and cannot be standardized through international instruments that are narrowly constituted from one part of the globe. In most of Africa and Asia, these practices have even marginalized the majority of the population by introducing the protected areas concept into heritage management, which largely stems from the colonial period and its belief that local communities were a threat to their own heritage. Just as in the colonial period, it has been assumed by foreign experts and bodies that the local communities do not value what they have, and thus have be moved, as in the case of the Tsodilo and Angkor World Heritage sites. While even the advocates of protected areas management have sometimes argued that successful conservation and management of heritage places requires local participation (Child 1995; Murombedzi 1992), in reality this has not been forthcoming despite the rhetoric of community engagement and involvement (Chirikure and Pwiti 2008).

Another aspect that heritage professionals have been slow to address is the "community-based systems" that have declined in effectiveness due to the hegemony of state-based systems and modern conservation discourse. This is despite the practical reality, which shows that state-based systems on their own are incapable of providing a holistic and sustainable management of local cultural heritage (Mumma 2005). As Fishman says, the sovereign State is not always the basic unit of "culture" in cultural property: "this State-centric power structure has prompted the observation that local communities may be among the least empowered players in the 'cultural property world' currently in place" (Fishman 2010: 349).

REFERENCES

Affolder, N. (2007) Mining and the World Heritage Convention: Democratic legitimacy and treaty compliance. *Pace Environmental Law Review* 24: 35–66.

Baillie, B. (2007) Conservation of the sacred at Angkor Wat: Further reflections on living heritage. *Conservation and Management of Archaeological Sites* 8: 123–131.

Byrne, D. (2008) Western Hegemony in Archaeological Heritage Management, in G. Fairclough, R. Harrison, J. H. Jameson, and J. Schofield (eds), *The Heritage Reader*. London: Routledge, pp. 229–234.

Cameron, C. (2009) The Evolution of the Concept of Outstanding Universal Value, in N. Stanley-Price and J. King (eds), *Conserving the Authentic: Essays in Honour of Jukka Jokilehto*. Rome: ICCROM, pp. 127–136.

Child, G. (1995) *Wildlife and People: The Zimbabwean Success*. Harare: Wisdom Foundation.

Chirikure, S. and G. Pwiti (2008) Community involvement in archaeology and cultural heritage management: An assessment from case studies in Southern Africa and elsewhere. *Current Anthropology* 49(3): 467–485.

Cohn, B. S. (1996) *Colonialism and Its Forms of Knowledge: The British in India*, Princeton, NJ: Princeton University Press.

Dagen, B. (trans.) (1985) *Mayamatha – an Indian Treatise on Housing, Architecture and Iconography*. New Delhi: Sitaram Bharatiya Institute of Scientific Research.

Daly, P. and Y. Rahmayati (2011) Cultural Heritage and Community Recovery in Post-Tsunami Aceh, in P. Daly, R. M. Feener, and A. Reid (eds), *From the Ground Up: Perspectives of Post Tsunami and Post-Conflict Aceh*. Singapore: ISEAS press, pp. 57–78.

Donnacie, I. (2010) World Heritage, in R. Harrison (ed.), *Understanding the Politics of Heritage*. Manchester: Manchester University Press, pp. 115–153.

Du Cros, H. and Y. S. Lee (2007) *Cultural Heritage Management in China: Preserving the Cities of Pearl River Delta*. London: Routledge.

Fishman, P. J. (2010) Locating the international interest in international cultural disputes. *Yale Journal of International Law* 35: 347–410.
Garlake, P. (1982) *Great Zimbabwe Described and Explained*. Gweru: Mambo Press.
Harrison, R. (2010) The Politics of Heritage, in R. Harrison (ed.), *Understanding the Politics of Heritage*. Manchester: Manchester University Press, pp. 154–173.
Hirsch, P. and C. Warren (2002) *The Politics of Environment in Southeast Asia*: Honolulu: University of Hawaii Press.
Joffroy, T. (2005) *Traditional Conservation Practices in Africa*. Rome: ICCROM.
Jopelo, A. (2010) Traditional Custodianship of Rock Art Sites in Southern Africa: A Case Study from Central Mozambique. M.A. Thesis, University of the Witwatersrand, South Africa.
Kean, J. (2011) *To Cherish and Conserve: The Early Years of Archaeological Survey of India*. New Delhi: Archaeological Survey of India.
Keitumetse, S. (2007) Celebrating or Marketing the Indigenous? International Rights Organisations, National Governments and Tourism Creation, in P. M. Burns and M. Novelli (eds), *Global Frameworks and Local Realities*. Oxford: Elsevier, pp. 109–122.
Keitumetse, S. O. and O. Nthoi (2009) Investigating the impact of World Heritage site tourism on the intangible heritage of a community: Tsodilo Hills World Heritage site, Botswana. *International Journal of Intangible Heritage* 4(10): 144–149.
Koohafkan, P. and M. Altieri (2011) *Globally Important Agricultural Heritage Systems: A Legacy for the Future*. Rome: FAO, pp. 24–26.
Lahiri, N. (2001) Destruction or Conservation? Some Aspects of Monument Policy in India (1899–1905), in R. Layton, P. G. Stone, and J. Thomas (eds), *Destruction and Conservation of Cultural Property*. One World Archaeology Series. London: Routledge, pp. 1–21.
Logan, W. and K. Reeves (2009) *Places of Pain and Shame: Dealing with Difficult Heritage*. London: Routledge.
Lowenthal, D. (1998) *The Heritage Crusade and the Spoils of History*. Cambridge: Cambridge University Press.
Mahachi, G. and W. Ndoro (1997) The Socio-Political Context of Southern African Iron Age Studies with Special Reference to Great Zimbabwe, in G. Pwiti (ed.), *Caves, Monuments and Texts: Zimbabwean Archaeology Today*. Studies in Archaeology, 4. Uppsala: Uppsala University, pp. 89–108.
Makuvaza, S. (2008) Why Njelele, a rainmaking shrine in the Matobo World Heritage Area, Zimbabwe, has not been proclaimed a national monument. *Journal of Heritage Management* 1(2): 63–80.
Maluleke, T. S. (2010) Of Africanised bees and Africanised churches: Ten theses on African Christianity. *Southern African Journal of Missiology* 38(3): 369–379.
Matenga, E. (1998) *The Soapstone Birds of Great Zimbabwe*. Harare: Zimbabwe Publishing Group.
Mathur, S. (2007) *India by Design: Colonial History and Cultural Display*. Berkeley: University of California Press.
Mazrui, A. (1986) The triple heritage of the state in Africa, in *The State in Global Perspective*. Paris: UNESCO, p. 112.
McIntosh, R. (1993) Archaeological heritage management and site inventories in Africa. *Journal of Field Archaeology* 20: 500–504.
Meskell, L. (2011) *The Nature of Heritage: the New South Africa*. Oxford: Wiley Blackwell.
Miura, K. (2004) Contested Heritage: People of Angkor. Ph.D. dissertation, School of Oriental and African Studies, London.
Mumma, A. (2005) The Link between Traditional and Formal Legal Systems, in W. Ndoro and G. Pwiti (eds), *Legal Frameworks for the Protection of Immovable Cultural Property in Africa*. Rome: ICCROM, pp. 22–24.
Murombedzi, J. (1992) *Decentralization or Recentralization: Implementing CAMPFIRE in the Omay Communal Lands of the Nyaminyami District*. CASS NRM Working Paper, no. 2. Harare: Center for Applied Social Sciences.

Musonda, S. (2005) Customary Systems of Heritage Conservation: The Barotseland Experience, Zambia, in W. Ndoro and G. Pwiti (eds *Legal Frameworks for the Protection of Immovable Cultural Property in Africa*. Rome: ICCROM, pp. 25–26.

Ndoro, W. (2005) *The Preservation of Great Zimbabwe: Your Monument, Our Shrine*. Rome: ICCROM.

Negri, V. (2005) An Overview of Formal Legislation on Immovable Cultural Heritage in Africa, in W. Ndoro and G. Pwiti (eds), *Legal Frameworks for the Protection of Immovable Cultural Property in Africa*. Rome: ICCROM, pp. 5–8.

Nelson H. R. (2003) Environmental colonialism, "saving Africa from Africans". *The Independent Review* 3(1): 65–86.

Nyathi, P. and B. Ndiwini (2005) A Living Religious Shrine under Siege: The Njelelle Shrine/King Mzilikazi's Grave and Conflicting Demands on the Matopo Hills area of Zimbabwe, in H. Stovel, N. Stanley-Price, and R. Killick (eds), *Conservation of Living Religious Heritage*. ICCROM Conservation Studies 3. Rome: ICCROM, pp. 58–68.

Pwiti, G. (1996) Let the ancestors rest in peace? New challenges for cultural heritage management in Zimbabwe. *Conservation and management of archaeological sites* 1: 151–160.

Qiang, C. (2003) Archaeology, Cultural Heritage Protection, and Capital Construction in China, in N. Agnew and J. Bridgland (eds), *Of the Past, for the Future: Integrating Archaeology and Conservation*. Los Angeles, CA: GCI.

Ruggles D. F. and H. Silverman (2007) *Cultural Heritage and Human Rights*. New York: Springer.

Segadika, P. (2006) Managing intangible heritage at Tsodilo. *Museum International* 58 (1-2): 31–40.

Senamai, A. (2014) An Un-Inherited Past: Preserving the Khami World Heritage Site, Zimbabwe. Ph.D. dissertation, Deakin University, Australia.

Shepherd, N. (2007) What Does It Mean "To Give the Past back to the People"? Archaeology and Ethics in the Postcolony, in Y. Hamilakis and P. Duke (eds), *Archaeology and Capitalism: From Ethics to Politics*. Walnut Creek: Left Coast Press, pp. 99–114.

Sidi, A. and J. Joffroy (2005) The Conservation of the Grand Mosques of Timbuktu, in T. Joffroy (ed.), *Traditional Conservation Practices in Africa*. Rome: ICCROM, pp. 24–31.

Silverman, H. (2011) Border wars: The ongoing temple dispute between Thailand and Cambodia and UNESCO's World. *International Journal of Heritage Studies* 17(1): 1–21.

Smith, L. (2004) *Archaeological Theory and the Politics of Cultural Heritage*. London: Routledge.

Sully, D. (2007) *Decolonizing Conservation: Caring for Maori Meeting Houses outside New Zealand*. Walnut Creek, CA: Left Coast Press.

Tunprawat, P. (2009) Managing Living Heritage Sites in Mainland Southeast Asia. Ph.D dissertation, University of Silpakorn, Thailand.

UNESCO (1999) Robben Island Nomination Dossier. Available at: http://whc.unesco.org/uploads/nomination/916.pdf. Accessed December 1, 2014.

UNESCO (2008) *World Heritage List*. Available at: http://whc.unesco.org/en/list. Accessed November 19, 2014.

UNESCO (2014) *World Heritage Committee Reports of the 38th Session*. Available at: http://whc.unesco.org/en/sessions/38com. Accessed November 19, 2014.

Wallerstein, I. et al. (eds) (1995) *Open the Social Sciences: Report of the Gulbenkian Commission on Restructuring the Social Sciences*. Stanford, CA: Stanford University Press.

Waterton, E. (2010) *Politics, Policy and the Discourses of Heritage in Britain*. London: Palgrave Macmillan.

Wijesuriya, G. (1993) *Restoration of Buddhist Monuments in Sri Lanka: The Case for an Archaeological Management Strategy*. Colombo: ICOMOS.

Wijesuriya, G. (2000) Conserving the Temple of the Tooth Relic, Sri Lanka. *Public Archaeology* 1(2): 99–109.

Wijesuriya, G. (2003) Are We Reinventing the Wheel? Archaeological Heritage Management under the British Colonial Rule in Sri Lanka, in S. Lawrence (ed.), *Archaeologies of the British: Explorations of Identity in the United Kingdom and Its Colonies 1600–1945*. One World Archaeology Series. London: Routledge, pp. 274–290.

Wijesuriya, G. (2005) Past Is in the Present: Perspectives in Caring for Buddhist Heritage, in H. Stovel, N. Stanley-Price, and R. Killick (eds), *Conservation of Living Religious Heritage*. Rome: ICCROM, pp. 31–43.

Wijesuriya, G. (2007) The Restoration of the Temple of the Tooth Relic in Sri Lanka: A Post-Conflict Cultural Response to Loss of Identity, in N. Stanley-Price and R. Killick (eds), *Cultural Heritage in Postwar Recovery*. ICCROM Conservation Studies 6. Rome: ICCROM, pp. 87–97.

Wijesuriya, G. (2010) Conservation in Context, in M. S. Falser, W. Lipp, and A. Tomaszewski (eds), *Proceedings of the International Conference on Conservation and Preservation – Interaction between Theory and Practice, In Memoriam Alois Riegl (1858–1905)*. Florence: Edizioni Polistampa, pp. 233–248.

Winter, T. (2007) *Post-Conflict Heritage, Post-Colonial Tourism: Culture, Politics and Developments at Angkor*. London and New York: Routledge.

Winter T. and P. Daly (2012) Heritage in Asia: Converging Forces, Conflicting Values, in P. Daly and T. Winter (ed.), *Routledge Handbook of Heritage in Asia*. Oxford: Routledge, pp 1–35.

7

Heritage and Violence

Alfredo González-Ruibal and Martin Hall

Introduction

For a long time, heritage has been associated with positive and productive values: the construction of ideas of community and nation, and even international identities. During the last decade and a half, however, there has been a growing concern with the legacies of violence, the product of a hundred years of global, civil, and ethnic wars, genocides, colonialism, and dictatorship. This is a fast-growing subfield in heritage studies and the deployment of heritage consumption. A variety of descriptors have been proposed: negative, dissonant, painful, dark, difficult (Biran, Poria, and Oren 2011; Dolff-Bonekämper 2002; Logan and Reeves 2008; MacDonald 2009; Meskell 2002; Tunbridge and Ashworth 1996). In parallel, archaeologists and heritage practitioners have been paying closer attention to the conflicts that emerge in cases of apparently peaceful heritage, including classic *lieux de mémoire*. We will not refer to these here, as they will be tackled in other chapters (see De Cesari and Herzfeld in this volume). We will focus on heritage that is directly associated with violence.

A general distinction can be drawn between heritage that is a direct outcome of violence, such as battlefields, concentration camps, memorials, mass graves, and prisons, and heritage that existed before conflict but was touched by it and therefore changed forever. This can include traditional heritage sites (such as Dresden's old town or Canterbury Cathedral), as well as everyday environments such as urban settings or agricultural landscapes. Examples here are the lasting heritage of apartheid and the ways in which this is inscribed on the land, and the killing fields of Cambodia (Hall 2001, 2009a; Totten and Parsons 2012).

The way conflict affects places also varies. Violence can transform places materially, as happened with the National Library of Sarajevo, bombed by the Serbs (Hall 2002; Riedlmayer 1995). Or, traces of violence can be inscribed through association; an example is the train station of Montoire-le-Loir, where Hitler shook hands with Pétain (Dolff-Bonekämper 2002). Monuments can gain new significance through the collateral damage of conflicts, as has been the case with many Mesopotamian

Global Heritage: A Reader, First Edition. Edited by Lynn Meskell.

sites and museums damaged forever by the war in Iraq (Stone and Bayali 2008). Monuments can also become targets in themselves, as happened during the Bosnian War (Bevan 2005; Chapman 1994; Hall 2002) or with the Palestinian villages and olive groves razed by the Israelis (Bardenstein 1999). Increasingly, "landscapes of destruction" are becoming emblematic of heritage in our contemporary world (González-Ruibal 2008).

In this chapter, we will set out some of the prevalent characteristics of legacies of violence and conflict; together, these broadly frame heritage work in this area. We then look at civil conflict and violence perpetrated by the state, and at circumstances where the heritage of violence has an international dimension. Focusing on more detailed cases helps understand the specific dynamics that give this subfield of heritage its distinctiveness. We have chosen state violence across a range of countries in South America and ethnically organized conflict in Sri Lanka; there are of course many other cases that would serve equally well. Finally, we look at issues of engaged practice and "memory work"; aspects of this subfield that, we argue, will be of increasing importance in the future.

On Violence

Before addressing specific case studies and situations, though, is the question of why so much attention is now being paid to violence in heritage studies? In 2014 the European Union opened a call within the Horizon 2020 program which specifically addresses "the cultural heritage of war"; this is only part of the many heritage projects that the EU has funded in recent years dealing with the material and immaterial legacies of violence (civil, ethnic, international). It can be argued that this is consciously related to the Union's image as promoter of peace – it received the Nobel Prize in 2012 – and the troubled recent history of Europe. Yet individual countries, such as the United Kingdom, are also investing important resources in conflict and postconflict studies, in which heritage plays a prominent role.

Heritage, as a product of modernity and capitalism, shows similar expansive, even voracious, qualities. While the modern episteme needs to encompass within its rationality all that is real, capitalism has a long-recognized ability to commodify everything, including cultural production, as Horkheimer and Adorno (2001 [1944]) observed seventy years ago. Although the German philosophers were thinking in terms of popular culture, their insights can be extended to the dynamics of heritage today, which encourage passivity and acceptance in the style of the theme park; indeed, it can be argued that heritage is now part of the experience economy (Harrison 2013: 84–88). As with modernity in general, conventional and mainstream heritage seeks to encompass (and commodify) all that is real.

Today, there are no longer aesthetic or other conventions that define and limit that which heritage can be considered to be, at least in practice. Commodification is not restricted to positive values and goods. It can also embrace pain, disease, trauma, or violence. Consequently, this negativity applies to heritage. Perhaps the most eloquent example of this cannibalization of suffering is the phenomenon of dark tourism (Lennon and Foley 2000), but none the less important is the trivialization of places of trauma through marketing strategies, such as cafés or shops (Shepherd 2013: 236–238). While dark tourism is based on a fascination for violent pasts, the trivialization of painful places often works in an opposite way, eliding the troubling side of history to make places easier to incorporate in the experience economy.

It would be wrong, though, to see the association between violence and heritage as only a commercial strategy of late capitalism. On the one hand, for thousands of years sites of pain have been not only visited, but have also been part of commercial strategies; in pilgrimage, for example, and the selling of relics (Lennon and Foley 2000: 3–4). Fascination with death and disaster clearly pre-dates modernity. On the other hand, to see the evident success of the heritage of violence in our contemporary world as merely economic would be to indulge in a crude reductionism that denies insights into both its complexity and its rationale. In the rest of this chapter, we offer a reading of the heritage of violence that reaches beyond the superficialities of the experience economy for deeper insights into the role that heritage plays in the world today.

To get to these deeper meanings, we have to dig beneath the moralistic veneers of the experience economy; the tendency to empty discourses on abstract values that Levinas called the "humanism of the arrogant" (Levinas 2008: 213): "war against war perpetuates war, stripping it of its bad conscience." Simmons (1999: 90) has expanded this key insight:

> considering the unchanging conditions of man making war on man, the century of genocide in which we live, and the repeated atrocities, is morality not meaningless? According to Levinas, morality can only have meaning when it has its own justification, when it is not absorbed by ontology and politics, when it exists outside of the violence of ontology and politics.

The insistence on simply rejecting war, which is promoted at many heritage sites, serves to negate the political symptoms of conflict and offers to clean the conscience of nations and supranational organizations. In seeking this outcome, commodified heritage obscures the specifics of violence and conflict, transforming every war and every violence to the same war and the same violence. This naturalizes what is in reality historically and culturally specific. Consequently, the heritage of violence, which is potentially subversive and thought provoking, serves to produce the self-satisfying passivity that Horkheimer and Adorno (2001) denounced in popular culture: violence is in human nature, the heritage of conflict testifies to that nature, and therefore we can only contemplate (and enjoy) the heritage of conflict while lamenting the fate of the human race.

Beneath – and despite – this tendency to commodification, though, violence and conflict shape individual and collective memory and leave indelible traces in the material world. Rather than dismissing the heritage of violence as beyond hope, appropriated by the theme parks and memorabilia of the experience economy, we need to look for different approaches. This means examining structural problems in specific contexts and in long-term perspective. For example an important issue that is seldom considered is the problem of how violence shapes subjectivity at a deep level. This troubled both Frantz Fanon (2004 [1961]) and Hannah Arendt (1969); extreme, protracted violence, physical and symbolic, may produce long-term ontological changes in the subject. In this situation, violence becomes so enmeshed in the making of the person that no discourse on peace and reconciliation (including heritage discourses) can effectively excise it.

Fanon and Arendt formulated concepts of violence at much the same time, but in very different contexts: Fanon from within the movement for Algerian liberation; Arendt from the experience and memory of fascism, the rise and repression of the anti-war movement in the United States, and the threat of nuclear Armageddon

(Arendt 1969; Fanon 2004 [1961]). Subsequent work has developed these themes, exploring decolonization in the second part of the twentieth century and the legacy of violence in postcolonial states (Mbembe 2001; Ngugi 1998) and the violence of the "end-time" of late capitalism (Žižek 2008, 2012, 2013). In turn, this work challenges core assumptions of Northern and Western scholarship: the hubris of detached and authoritative interpretation, the assumption that violence is an aberration in the north but an endemic condition of the south (Mignolo 2011). Increasingly, these rich and insightful theoretical strands are informing insights into the relationship between heritage and violence that avoid the seductive trap of the experience economy and its attendant advocates.

Archaeology, then, can be put at work examining how the materiality of history is practically engaged in the production of troubled selves by continuously actualizing past grievances. After all, material things are known for their ability to fix meanings, direct behavior, and stabilize collectives (Hodder 2012; Olsen 2010). Some questions here would be: how can collectives created through violence be destabilized and reassembled? How can we reorder things to change the vicious circle of conflict? How can we do that while escaping the cycle of neutralization and commoditization of pain in the process of unearthing violence (Starzmann 2013)? And how can insights into the meanings of materiality be used in the mediation of conflict situations, averting the use of violence (Hall 2013)?

Legacies of Violence

In considering legacies of violence, then, there are a number of characteristics that will shape the role that heritage plays, irrespective of the location, scale, or specific nature of conflicts.

First, and perhaps most importantly, has conflict ceased? If a conflict is active, the production of heritage will vary accordingly. Conflicts that are denied by those who control the territory, such as in the Armenian Genocide, do not produce heritage *in loco*, but in the diaspora. Ongoing struggles, such as the Colombian or the Israeli–Palestinian conflicts, hamper forms of memorialization and the transformation of places into heritage sites. Another relevant issue is whether a conflict has ended with the victory of a specific side or through international intervention, as this heavily affects the politics of remembrance by introducing a set of values that may be at variance with realities on the ground and local feelings (Viejo Rose 2013).

The two cases that we look at in more detail below present contrasting circumstances in this regard. In South America, legacies of violence are attached to the dictatorships that had come to an end by 1990; as in South Africa, the record of these conflicts is now being taught to students who were not alive in their time. But Sri Lanka's thirty-year civil war only ended in 2009 and the wartime distinctions between Tamil and Sinhalese define both the politics inside the country and its international relations. Conflict remains endemic in our contemporary world (for example, across the Middle East and parts of Africa); increasingly, heritage practitioners will find themselves in situations where conflicts remain open.

This leads immediately to a second key characteristic: is there a shared master narrative (Alexander 2004)? This is evidently unlikely where a conflict remains open and heritage interventions will inevitably be cast as partisan; an example here is the set of positions taken in response to Meskell's comparison of the heritage legacies of Lower Manhattan and Afghanistan's Bamiyan Valley in the immediate aftermath of the 2001 destruction of the World Trade Center in New York (Meskell 2002). Where conflicts have been at least in part settled, a master narrative becomes established. This can be more or less spontaneous, the product of social reconciliation, but it can also be crafted by the state, as in the case of the American Civil War where claims for reconciliation enabled the transformation of battlefields into heritage sites, albeit not free from contention (Sutton 2012).

However, the assumption that there will be a settled master narrative for conflicts that have long been formally resolved may often be unjustified. An example here is Japan's Yasukuni Shrine to those killed in wars between 1861 and 1951; because some of those commemorated at Yasukuni were convicted of war crimes, commemorations regularly provoke protests by Korea, Taiwan, and China (Economist 2013). Haber (2010) argues that an "objectifying" archaeology – that sees narratives as settled – would constitute a "regime of truth" that could itself be a form of repression, an insight that is aligned with Mignolo's general critique of the continuing claims to a normality of non-violence by dominant Northern and Western powers (Mignolo 2011). Challenging these truth claims does not mean the abandonment of analytical rigor and the use of scientific techniques. If anything, engagement with archival evidence, oral recollection, and the complexities of past and present political interests makes the value of archaeological techniques all the more important. When the results of such research may be critical in litigation and tested against the rules of legal evidence, there is no latitude for technical error or unjustified assumptions.

A third factor that, we argue, will shape the nature of heritage work in this area will be the characteristics and extent of state intervention. Legacies of violence range from domestic conflict to eliminationism (following Goldhagen 2009). There is evidently a spectrum here. In Spain, for example, it has been left to relatives of the killed by the dictatorship to remember their dead (Renshaw 2011) and there was no nationwide heritage initiative (such as a museum) after the re-establishment of democracy in 1978 (Monegal 2008).

An example of an intermediate set of circumstances – where heritage and legacy issues are widespread but below the level of explicit state intervention – is the heritage of slavery and colonial appropriation in Cape Town and the treatment and commemoration of burial grounds (Hall 2009a; Shepherd 2007). However, the dynamics of heritage discourse and practice changes appreciably when there is evident state interest. This is the case with Robben Island – off the coast of Cape Town – and the intertwined narratives of political imprisonment, the representation of the African National Congress as a liberation movement and party in government, and the life story of Nelson Mandela (Corsane 2006). State policies vary widely, even within countries. Goebel and Keene (2011: 31–32), for instance, compare the wildly different ways in which the sieges of Leningrad and Stalingrad have been memorialized. Likewise, the same state ideology does not mean a similar behavior towards the cultural heritage of a vanquished enemy. The same authors note the differing ways in which Poles and Russians have dealt with two occupied cities, Breslau and Königsberg. The latter was razed to the ground by the Soviet power, whereas part of the former's history was respected and appropriated by the Polish state (Goebel and Keene 2011: 40–41).

Contemporary conflict heritage may also be transnational in nature, as modern wars are rarely localized in a single country or region. In these circumstances, questions of legacies of violence will be between, rather than within, states. After a conflict is over, a diversity of actors (victims, governments, veterans) may make claims over sites or objects beyond national boundaries that are pivotal in the definition of their individual or collective history, whether they are places of mass extermination (Kouoyomedjian and Siméone 2005), battlefields (Ziino 2012), or stolen works of art (Nicholas 1994). Wars do not only result in destruction – they also produce massive de-localizations of heritage.

Together, the status of conflict (whether it is in the past or continuing), the degree to which there is a shared interpretation of what happened and the scale of the issue (and particularly the level of involvement of the state) will shape legacies of violence as they are expressed through heritage. Together, these factors structure processes of remembrance and commemoration, and engagement with communities and the "memory work" that we discuss at the end of this chapter.

Reconstruction is perhaps the most debated issue in the relationship between conflict and violence, and remembrance and commemoration. Reconstruction has been regarded as an effective way of coping with a traumatic past and achieving reconciliation by nation-states and international agencies (Ibreck 2013). Such approaches, however, often provoke as much conflict as they intend to overcome. In Spain, reconstruction after the Spanish Civil War has been criticized since the dictatorship that emerged from the war used the occasion to redesign villages and towns according to their exclusionary nationalist and imperialist ideals (Muñoz-Rojas 2011; Viejo Rose 2011). In the former Yugoslavia, the European Union has invested heavily in heritage reconstruction (Schwartze 2012). However, the multicultural model espoused by the organization, and by governments such as Bosnia-Herzegovina, has not gained support from local communities (Viejo Rose 2013). The prevalence of these debates and disagreements again makes the point that questions of the heritage and legacies of violence are inherently political and are invariably associated with the dispositions of power – the key point in Arendt's and Fanon's founding formulations of contemporary theories of violence (Arendt 1969; Fanon 2004 [1961]).

A key issue for reconstruction projects is the role of ruins. Here, attitudes change through time, not the least due to the physical processes of ruination, since the materiality of the past cannot be frozen in time and physical processes of decay continue (see González-Ruibal 2013; Olivier 2001: 185–186). While claiming broad benefits for reconstruction and remembrance, policies may privilege the few and use the opportunities offered by large urban refurbishments to raze heritage or reshape it to serve the needs of elites. An example here is the controversial restitution of Beirut (Charlesworth and Nelson 2012).

Civil Conflicts and State Violence

These general characteristics of the heritage of violence may become particularly complex in situations that involve civil conflicts and violence by the state. Damage from conflicts may be extensive and closure and reconciliation difficult to achieve, contentious, and rarely satisfactory to all stakeholders.

Producing a new narrative after civil conflict is often difficult because there will usually be a part of the population that identifies with former perpetrators of violence. While analyses often emphasize the primary distinction between hegemonic, authorized heritage and grassroots or subaltern initiatives (Smith 2006), community groups and social movements are often internally divided. Victims may differ as to how the past should be remembered – if at all. Thus in Argentina, the transformation of a former detention center into a heritage site has provoked intense debates among stakeholders about the activities that should take place in the restored facility, and about the narrative that should be displayed (Hidalgo 2012). Similar debates have characterized consideration of other once-clandestine centers of detention, of mass graves, and of places associated with state terrorism (Zarankin and Salerno 2012).

It is also worth noting that civil conflicts are rarely just that: internecine wars and dictatorships are usually inserted within major, long-term conflicts. In South America some have argued that the dictatorial regimes that ravaged their countries during the second half of the twentieth century should not be seen in isolation, but rather as enmeshed in the long-term history of violence through colonial conquest, slavery, and class conflict (e.g., López Mazz 2015). This requires a comprehensive heritage perspective that integrates slave plantations, sites of genocide, and detention centers within the same program. Such an approach requires the integration of pre-conflict cultural heritage and a critique of interpretations that deploy earlier heritage for the purposes of nationalist narratives (Mire 2011; Rowlands 2008). In general terms, it is a mistake to require, as a criterion for success, that there is unanimity in the processes and outcomes of developing narratives of the past through the heritage of violence and conflict. As Latour notes "things" – here the material traces of the past – may bring people together because they divide them (Latour 2005: 13). Total agreement around "the thing heritage" is neither feasible nor desirable, and much less so in postconflict situations.

Genocides are usually the outcome of extreme civil conflicts and violent state regimes, and have particular challenges for remembrance and commemoration (Totten and Parsons 2012). In considering the implications for the legacies of these kinds of violence and conflict, the broader term "eliminationism" is preferable: a set of phenomena that are directed towards the destruction of particular groups without necessarily implying their total annihilation (Goldhagen 2009). So defined, eliminationist policies have abounded during the last hundred years and have been remembered, or denied recognition, in different ways.

The definitive genocide, the Nazi extermination of the Jews, has been the object of countless studies of memory and heritage, many of which focus on the way Germans have remembered (or forgotten) their criminal history through time (Koshar 2000). The tendency of the state to produce a rather pacified interpretation of the past has been challenged by grassroots initiatives, in which alternative forms of heritage have been produced, most famously the "topography of terror" (Bernbeck and Pollock 2007). The stories portrayed in former extermination camps have varied substantially since 1945. Recent developments include an increasingly comprehensive narrative that includes minorities other than Jewish (such as Roma-Sinti, Poles, Soviet citizens, and homosexuals). There has been an expansion of "dark tourism," which has resulted in problems of trivialization and commodification (Ronson 2004). There is the increasingly pressing question of authenticity (Marrus 1997); as time passes, more conservation work has to be undertaken, replacing most of the original fabric of the genocide sites. In this context, archaeology is reclaiming a more prominent role in the research, management and presentation of the Holocaust (Sturdy Colls 2012; Theune 2010, 2013).

African eliminationist atrocities have begun to receive attention by heritage researchers. In Rwanda, the production of a genocide heritage started soon after the events in 1994 and has been substantially shaped by the new (Tutsi) government. This has included both places related to the massacre, as well as a museum, the Kigali Genocide Memorial Centre. The Rwandan state's master narrative presents colonialism as the root cause of the 1994 massacre and also emphasizes the universal character of genocides; this approach, it has been argued, is intended to facilitate reconciliation among Rwandans and to alleviate national guilt (McKinney 2012). However, the image of a peaceful past only interrupted by colonial intervention may be contradicted by archaeological data, presenting ethical and political issues for archaeologists who find evidence for a less bucolic narrative (Giblin, Clement, and Humphris 2010). A similar contradiction applies in Sierra Leone. Here, and unsurprisingly, a long civil conflict between 1991 and 2002 with eliminationist dimensions has been commemorated in a new master narrative that uses cultural heritage to portray a peaceful co-existence in the past. However, this idealized vision of the past makes it difficult to come to terms with trauma and to understand the political causes of recent troubles (Basu 2008). Again, and more broadly, effective critiques of heritage narratives need to take account of analyses of the deployment of violence in the postcolonial state that build on Fanon's (2004 [1961]) insistence that the ever-present threat of violence defines political relationships (see Mbembe 2001; Ngugi 1998). At the same time, the silencing of violence in postcolonial contexts cannot be understood outside the framework of the coloniality of power (Quijano 2000). Sanitizing and simplifying the legacies of violence in Africa or Latin America suits well the interests of the West, which is always complicit in one way or another with the sources of conflict in former colonized nations.

In Sudan the state has created a decentralized heritage network, with museums in different areas of the country that have been affected by conflict. The aim is to portray the diversity of Sudanese identities and a non-conflictual multiculturalism. Seen from the perspective of Mbeme's analysis of the dynamics of power and violence in Cameroon, though, this looks like a sanitized interpretation of cultural identity that is at odds with historical evidence. Leturcq suggests that, as a counterpoint, the negative aspects of identity should also be represented in heritage narratives and that "diversity" be replaced by the concept of "alterity," in which exchanges between different ethnic groups are emphasized, whether these interactions are conflictive, cultural, or commercial (Leturcq 2009). Of course, as an alternative approach to representing the legacy of violence, this would not be in the interests of the Sudanese state.

Eliminationism is the disposition of state violence at its most extreme, directed at exterminating both people and memory. Consequently, and in order to make a *tabula rasa*, there will be a drive to destroy all material traces of the group targeted for elimination. Again, the Holocaust is the paradigmatic case. More recent campaigns have included the war in Bosnia-Herzegovina, the destruction of the Bamiyan Buddhas in Afghanistan, and the razing of the Babri Masyid in Ayodhya, India (Bernbeck and Pollock 1996; Meskell 2002). There is a mirroring tendency to eradicate the traces, and memory, of perpetrator regimes; in Germany the architectural legacy of the Nazi regime has largely been destroyed. Controversies often emerge around the commemoration of perpetrators (see Burström and Gelderblom 2011; MacDonald 2009; Pinkepank 2011). For example, while Nazi sites may serve an educational function, they may also become places of memory for neo-Nazis (Hansell 2011). It can be argued that the "Spuren des Terrors" – the traces of terror that have been identified and marked out in different German cities (Braun, Hattstein, and Mecke 2002) – can be more effective than the preservation of Nazi architecture. Stolpersteine, bronze cobbles, serve as reminders of the deportation of Jews from a particular place, while fragments from the Berlin Wall are effective as material traces for remembering dark pasts (Klausmeier and Schmidt 2004).

International Conflicts and Heritage

Compared to civil conflicts, dictatorships, and genocides, the heritage of international wars may appear less controversial. Master narratives have been crafted for World Wars I and II that are widely accepted; in the first case based on the idea of sublime but meaningless sacrifice, in the second on the concept of the "good war." Nevertheless, disagreements emerge. One concerns the representation of a multiplicity of voices that have been silenced in formal narratives, ranging from colonial fighters to women sexual slaves. Their stories are rarely represented at heritage sites, memorials, and museums, which are usually male- and Western-oriented.

A further issue is the question of "enclave heritage." Modern wars tend to affect wide areas and involve the displacement of huge numbers of people (as soldiers, volunteers, or refugees). This produces "heritage out of place." Gallipoli is perhaps the best-known case – a place in Turkey that is regarded as national heritage by Australians (Ziino 2012). Other examples abound, especially for World War II (Beaumont 2012). Also characteristic of the legacy of modern warfare are "people out of place." For instance, volunteers who fought for the other side, as with the many SS volunteers from Norway, Denmark, or France, who died fighting for Nazi Germany: how are their remains to be treated? Should they be remembered in any way (Jasinski, Soleim, and Sem 2012: 271)? And how should the Cold War be remembered (Schofield and Cocroft 2009)? While nuclear confrontation never materialized, the proxy wars that were triggered caused untold suffering in what was designated, as part of the ideology of the time, the "Third World."

Issues of enclave heritage also apply to the legacy of colonial conflicts, and to colonialism more generally. Colonial forts, monuments to war heroes, and cemeteries are often allowed to decay, which is not surprising, given the inequities of colonial conquests (Chadha 2006). Colonial nations may or may not reclaim this heritage and their attitudes to it are often ambivalent; individual initiatives may weigh more than those of states (Logan and Than Bìhn 2012). States may deliberately annihilate the heritage of those regions that they occupy, both during war and in peaceful times. An example here is Algeria, where the French destroyed large parts of the Islamic heritage of the country (Le Cour Grandmaison 2005: 104). Indeed, the beginning of this behavior can be traced back to the origins of modernity, with the Spanish razing of indigenous heritage in the Americas during the wars of the sixteenth century.

Heritage and State Violence in South America

Many of the prevalent characteristics of the heritage of conflict and violence are demonstrated in the historiography of heritage and twentieth-century dictatorships in South America. Looking in more detail at this region provides additional insights into the ways in which the need for commemoration and remembrance can intersect with heritage practice.

Between 1920 and 1990, 15 countries in South America had authoritarian regimes in which military juntas usurped civil systems of government, suspended civil rights, and instituted martial law. These regimes depended on methods of repression that included censorship, exile, detention, torture, and murder. At the heart of these technologies was a particular form of terror captured in the neologism "the disappeared" (*los desaparecidos*). When someone had been disappeared, the place and details of detention were unknown (Crossland 2000). Few returned and, since the fact or manner of death remained undisclosed, family, friends, and community were denied any closure (Feitlowitz 1998; Klein 2007). Between 1980 and 1990, these authoritarian regimes began to collapse. Removal of the most overt forms of repression strengthened broad coalitions seeking social justice and redress, increasing in turn the demand for evidence and the desire for a master narrative that could make sense of what had happened (Feitlowitz 1998; Funari, Zarankin, and Salerno 2010). This demand has drawn together a broad alliance of heritage practitioners with expertise in oral and written testimony, forensic research, and archaeology. As a result, it is now acknowledged that this continent-wide system of violence has a distinctive heritage that is inscribed in the materiality of places, buildings, and the apparatus of terror, and is imbricated with testimony and memory. As an instance of heritage violence and postconflict recovery, the story of *los desaparecidos* can be understood as stigmatization, disappearance, and evidence for resistance. A particularly powerful feature of this work has been the direct engagement of former victims in constituting remembrance through their own testimony. And international complicity with South American regimes of terror, particularly by the United States, connects the regional specificity of this heritage work with international regimes of violence (Hall 2010).

Stigmatization was the process of marking out categories of people as opponents to order and stability. In general terms such people were "communists" to be identified by their appearance and choice of dress. Melisa Salerno (2010) has shown how militarized regimes, heavily invested in the symbolism of uniforms and bodily regimentation, claimed contrary appearance and dress as evidence of dissident beliefs and subversion. Through this device, victims could be detained and incarcerated without any explicit knowledge of their political beliefs or actions.

Disappearance lies at the heart of an archaeology of heritage violence because, in the absence of documentary evidence and with only the fragmentary recollection of a few survivors, the material traces of clandestine detention centers offer some hope of substantiating the record of the past, and therefore of attaining closure. Clandestine detention centers were usually set up in existing buildings and identified by code names. Mapping this network and recording the remnants of its detention centers offers the opportunity of grounding the fragmentary recollections of survivors and the occasional documentary source in a substantial system of meaning that recovers memory and defeats the objective of eradicating the lives of the regimes' victims through the processes of disappearance (López Mazz 2010; Zarankin and Niro 2010).

More tenuous, but invaluable in augmenting the system of meaning and memory, is material evidence of resistance to the regime of humiliation, torture, and dehumanization in the detention centers. Examples include evidence for escape attempts, prisoners' craftwork (such as toys made from wood and bone), and graffiti (Biasatti 2011; López Mazz 2010; Navarrete and López 2010; Salerno, Zarankin, and Perosino 2012).

Oral testimony often plays a key role in assembling the heritage of conflict and violence; this is all the more powerful when former victims are directly engaged in the reconstitution of the past (Funari, Zarankin, and Salerno 2010). Here is Claudio Niro writing about his own detention:

> 9 May 1976, I arrived at Vesubio, a clandestine center of detention located at Camino de Cintura and Richieri highway (Mantanza Department). Four individuals following Suárez Mason's orders got me off a Ford Falcon. I was hooded and my hands were tied at my back. Meanwhile, the individuals insulted me and hit me, forcing me into a room. Once inside, they made me stand against a wall with my legs wide open.

> Several torturers kicked my testicles once and again. This procedure was called "ablande". It was intended to intimidate the prisoner before getting him or her into the torture room ... "Cuchas" were small rooms were four or five people stayed hooded, handcuffed and leg-ironed to walls and other prisoners. Once in the "cuchas", kidnappers forced us to take off our clothes and wear brown uniforms they had previously handed us in. This procedure made us lose – along with our clothes – all traces of an exterior life. (Zarankin and Niro 2010: 57)

One consequence of closure – of developing a broadly accepted master narrative as has been the case with the South American dictatorships – is that stories of violence may be objectified as residing "elsewhere," in the past, or in distant and exotic places (Haber 2010). Consequently, a significant dimension of the South American master narrative of repression and torture is the now incontrovertible evidence of complicity by the United States by means of the covert set of agreements known as Operation Condor. Operation Condor provided the South American regimes with advice, communication facilities, intelligence support, and, at times, active assistance with covert operations (Dinges 2004; Feitlowitz 1998; Klein 2007; López Mazz 2010).

> Condor was a Cold War-era covert network of U.S.-backed Latin American military regimes in Argentina, Brazil, Bolivia, Chile, Paraguay, and Uruguay, later joined by Ecuador and Peru in less central roles. The secret Condor apparatus enabled the militaries to share intelligence – and to seize, torture, and execute political opponents across borders. Condor agents also assassinated key opposition leaders around the world. (McSherry 2005: 1)

The discovery of the "terror archives" in Paraguay in 1992 provided evidence of some 50,000 murders, 30,000 disappearances, and 400,000 detentions by the security services of the participating countries. There are evident parallels with present-day covert security operations; connections such as these keep the heritage of conflict and violence relevant to live issues of human rights and social justice.

Conflict and World Heritage in Sri Lanka

In contrast with South America, where the last dictatorship ended more than two decades ago, the experience of conflict and violence is more recent in Sri Lanka. Here, civil war began in 1983 with an insurgency by the Liberation Tigers of Tamil Eelam (the LTTE, or Tamil Tigers), claiming the right to an independent state in the north and eastern part of the island. Conflict continued until a ceasefire in 2001 and a fragile truce that lasted until 2005. The war finally ended in 2009 with a decisive victory by government forces and allegations of extensive human rights violations that remained unresolved five years later (Sri Lanka Government 2011; United Nations 2011; Weiss 2011). It is estimated that between 80,000 and 100,000 people were killed over the full course of the war. While the Sri Lankan conflict is defined in terms of local religious and ethnic identities, its narrative is inseparable from wider claims to rights based on heritage that have been exacerbated by the involvement of UNESCO and the designation of a large region at the heart of the island as a World Heritage site.

There is little evidence for closure here. Gordon Weiss, who reported on the closing stages of the war, has described "a pervasive sense of guilt coated by a collective apathy born of the effort to forget ... unpunished murderers in palm-fringed villages share the streets with the families of their victims, and have done so for decades" (Weiss 2011: 40). Mutual mistrust is rooted in the sharply polarized ethnic identities of Tamil and Sinhalese, with mutual stereotyping. For example after the ceasefire broke down and war resumed in 2005 those living in the north had unrelenting stereotypes of Sri Lanka's south:

> most knew nothing or very little of the Sinhalese-dominated state, other than as an aggressor intent on their destruction. Many of the people who lived in the Vanni had fled from the oppressive occupation of the army in the Jaffna peninsula, where they had seen torture, summary execution and the random killing of civilians in "security incidents". This latent fear was exacerbated by the unremitting sledgehammer propaganda of the Tigers, who erected giant billboards throughout the area featuring gory mosaics of President Rajapaksa killing babies, and Sinhalese soldiers bathed in the blood of Tamil children. Just as in Israel, where Israeli children no longer speak Arabic and have never met a Palestinian, conflict had entailed a total separation of nationalities. Many of the young Tamils who filled the Tiger ranks had never met a Sinhalese. (Weiss 2011: 102)

This ethnic stereotyping, which has defined and given continuing momentum to the conflict and which saturates life in Sri Lanka today, is closely tied into interpretations given to the island's cultural heritage, which provides a continual trace of architecture, monuments, art, and written texts that span more than 2,000 years. The dominant convention, strongly endorsed by the state, is that the country's heritage is a straightforward narrative of successive Buddhist states withstanding external aggression. In this interpretation, the Sinhalese lineage was established in the sixth century BCE when the island's first king was banished there from northern India. The Sinhalese state flourished at Anuradhapura until the fifth century CE, after which its rulers were forced to fend off continual aggression from southern India, retreating eventually to Kandy. After 1505, the Sinhalese were subjected to colonial domination by Portugal, the Netherlands, and Britain, finally achieving independence in 1948 (see, for example, Sri Lanka Tourism Development Authority 2013). The state's heritage narrative, then, is one of proud and persistent defense of religion and civilization against external aggressors; Tamil Sri Lankans are, and always have been, an "enemy within."

However, as has long been pointed out, neither the documentary nor the archaeological evidence supports this straightforward interpretation. Both artistic representations on the remnants of urban architecture and excavations of living areas suggest a considerable degree of syncretism. This is supported by the documentary record, which maps a complex history of alliances, intermarriages, disagreements, and skirmishes with South Indian polities, which is hardly surprising given the proximity of the island to the mainland. "Contrary to the view expressed in classical texts on North Indian elite groups instrumental in introducing advanced institutions to an island largely populated by backward forest dwellers...intrusive techno-cultural elements from South India introduced the earliest recognizable social, economic, political and religious-cultural institutions to different ecological zones in Sri Lanka" (Seneviratne 1996: 311).

Central to both Sri Lanka's nationalist claims to heritage and counter-interpretations of the historical records is the Cultural Triangle, a rich and extensive complex of archaeological sites and religious centers across the center of the island, including the urban complexes of Anuradhapura, Ritigala, Polonnaruva, and Sigiriya. In the late 1970s, and in the face of growing Tamil counter-claims of historically based rights to the land, the

Sri Lankan government lobbied for the designation of places in the Cultural Triangle as a World Heritage site. UNESCO was wooed with a lavish display:

> the first of January 1980 was a full-moon day and one of the most auspicious days of the year. Every effort was made to convince the Director-General of UNESCO to be present on that day to inaugurate the campaign ... there were 3,000 monks at Jetavana monastery in its hey-day and that for the restoration we must have an equal number; 3,000 chairs were provided and we had 4,000 participants. We asked for 10,000 children dressed in white to sit on the stone paving of the upper terrace; this too was done. The full complement of the Cabinet of Ministers was present on the inauguration dais. We hoped that 100,000 persons would attend and there were double the number on the occasion ...The vast upper terrace of the stupa was decorated along its perimeter with two hundred flag poles and a drummer to each pole. Strands of bunting in the colors of the Buddhist flag were draped from the top of the giant stupa to the base of each flag pole. The color and spectacle of the occasion was completed by the procession of dignitaries, accompanied by dancers and drummers, who circumambulated the stupa once before climbing to the top of the three basal terraces and placing there a relic-casket to the chanting of sacred verses by Buddhist monks. (Silva 1993: 179–80)

UNESCO granted World Heritage status to the Cultural Triangle in 1982. Ten years later, this decision was reaffirmed by UNESCO Director-General Federico Mayor:

> [t]he Cultural Triangle project is indeed steering the proper course with its underlying dedication to safeguarding the national cultural heritage in order to foster and strengthen a sense of identity that cannot but contribute to the socio-economic development of the whole nation. Let us seek together the best and most practical means to lead this campaign to a successful and rewarding conclusion. (Mayor 1990)

This emphasis on the dominant Sinhalese identity claims has, in turn, shaped excavation, conservation, and restoration strategies with an emphasis on Buddhist Theravada sites with monumental structures, royal parks, and sculptured art. Monuments belonging to "heterodox" Buddhist sects such as the Mahayanist and Tantrayanist, as well as Hindu monuments, have not been accorded the same degree of importance, contributing further to writing more complex, alternative, histories out of Sri Lanka's prevalent heritage narrative (Seneviratne 2008).

This appropriation of cultural identity in the context of violent and escalating conflict resulted in heritage assets themselves becoming targets in Sri Lanka's war. In 1984, the LTTE carried out two attacks on the Cultural Triangle, killing pilgrims to Anuradhapura and resulting in the requirement for a strong security presence across the Cultural Triangle as a whole. Despite this the LTTE was able to carry out a successful attack on the Temple of the Sacred Tooth Relic in Kandy in 1998, coinciding with the celebrations for Sri Lanka's fiftieth anniversary of independence from British colonial rule. Sixteen people, including three suicide bombers, were killed, with extensive damage to the temple and to surrounding buildings.

But despite this Manichean representation of Sri Lanka's cultural heritage and its endorsement by UNESCO (which continues in the publications distributed at Cultural Triangle sites today) there has still been a persistent counternarrative founded in the research and scholarship of Sri Lanka's rich corpus of texts and surviving material culture. For example Guneratne (2002) has shown how the separate historical lineages of Sinhalese and Tamil were a function of nineteenth-century colonial typologies – now well understood in other contexts – and a contemporary, language-based nationalism.

He, along with others, argues that Sri Lanka's primary historical links are rather with South India, which is not surprising given close geographical proximity. Rajasingham-Senanayake (2002) stresses the significance of cultural hybridity expressed through mixed settlement, intermarriage, and bilingual and bicultural communities in many parts of the country.

The case of Sri Lanka, then, shows both how heritage can be deployed as an artifact of aggression in conflicts and how international agencies, claiming to be "above" politics, can be suborned by partisan positions. Here, indeed, cultural identities and claims to rights based in the past are so closely connected to the determinants of violent conflict that it is difficult to see how there can be lasting reconciliation without first resolving a master narrative of the country's history that is equally acceptable to Tamil and Sinhalese Sri Lankans.

Legacies of Violence and Engaged Practice

The cases from Sri Lanka and South America show that the claim of analytical detachment, whether made in the name of archaeology as science or from an assertion of radical insight, is never justified: heritage practitioners are invariably implicated in the historical and political contexts in which they work. A more appropriate epistemology is Latour's insistence that "word" and "world" are part of a continuum of knowledge creation; a set of translations connected in a chain of "circulating references" that we "pass over" repeatedly and compulsively as we seek to deepen our understanding both by generalizing from particular instances, and by reducing the complexity of individual circumstances to their essential features (Latour 1999). In the context of the heritage of conflict and violence, this process of "packing the world into words" can be chillingly powerful. In Zarankin and Niro's work in Argentina, for example, the chaos and terror of detention and torture are reduced into a survivor's narrative and assembled along with the material traces of the detention center and fragmentary police records as a set of "circulating references" that are evidence for a persistent "technology of power," a syndrome far more substantial than the individual experience.

Another important issue for discussion has to do with the temporality of violence. Memories of conflict tend to blur the duality between the recent and the deep past. It is usually assumed that the closer events are in time, the more they matter to people. Yet this is not necessarily always the case: traumatic events can be extremely resilient to disappear and the stubborn materiality of the past collaborates to this resilience. Remote events can be very important in the present, like the Mughal conquest of India during the sixteenth century, the defeat of Catalonia during the War of Succession (1712–1714), or the Jewish revolts of the first and second centuries CE (Bernbeck and Pollock 1996; Hernández Martínez 2012: 258–260; Kohl 1998: 238; Abu El-Haj 2001: 1, 55, 130). In all these cases, ancient wounds are part of the cultural memory of contemporary communities (Hindus, Catalonians, Jews) and heritage acts as a bridge to unite past and present: the supposed remnants of the temple of Rama, the ruins of the siege of Barcelona in 1714, and the citadel of Masada of the first century CE. They are not less controversial or important for present narratives than the last dictatorship in Argentina.

A strand that runs through much of the heritage work reviewed in this chapter is the relationships with local communities, victims, and other individuals or collectives directly affected by conflict. Communities that have undergone traumatic political experiences are prone to be fractured along different faultlines, more so than in peaceful contexts. Archaeologists and heritage practitioners may be caught in a mesh of contending and incompatible narratives and memory practices (see González-Ruibal, Ayán-Vila, and Ceasar 2015; Renshaw 2011). This may be aggravated when conflicts are ongoing (Goodhand 2000). Intra-community conflicts are usually difficult to navigate and require in-depth knowledge of the situation, which is often hard to acquire in the framework of a conventional archaeological or heritage project involving a team for a limited amount of time. An approach is required that can build trust between local stakeholders, to better understand the intricacies of the political situation (see Meskell 2005). In countries that have been (or are still) ruled by dictatorship, silence toward certain issues is likely to prevail and some questions will be probably asked with standard replies showing compliance with the prevalent order. The community, participatory, or public paradigm of science that may work under liberal regimes is then of limited use, and perhaps even counterproductive. It may thus be necessary to develop new protocols for heritage studies under these sociopolitical circumstances.

In these circumstances, reconciliation is often cast as the primary objective, and is extensively appropriated by international institutions, funding agencies, heritage managers, and scholars (Carman and Sørensen 2009: 23; Colwell-Chanthaphonh 2007; Scham and Yahya 2003). The concept of reconciliation, however, needs closer analysis, as engagement with the long tradition of a critical theory of violence shows. Along with concepts such as "peace," "liberty," the merits of reconciliation seem incontrovertible. Yet, precisely because of this, such terms can become drained of real meaning. Some have criticized an "ideology of reconciliation" which is rather a claim for national unity, forgetting past wrongs, and foregoing justice (Schaap 2008). Despite the work of the Truth and Reconciliation Commission in South Africa, for instance, retributive justice has been elided, narration has superseded conventional juridical procedures, and old structures of inequality and conflict have remained in place (Van der Walt, Franchi, and Stevens 2003). In this context heritage – a form of national narrative – may take center stage, with sanitized and nostalgic displays (Hall 2006; Hall and Bombardella 2005; Meskell 2011; Shepherd 2013). Reconciliation may also be used to stifle dissent; under the pretext of social reconciliation, the government of Rwanda has instituted a law against "divisionism" as a weapon against political opponents (Waldorf 2009).

Partisan closure, however, is by no means the inevitable outcome of the use of heritage to attempt reconciliation after violence and conflict. Museums and heritage sites can rather become places where the political roots of conflicts are dissected and where debates around controversial issues are sparked. Criticizing the concept of reconciliation does not mean that this is not a viable objective: the idea is to develop a notion and a practice of reconciliation that can accommodate justice and dissent simultaneously (Schaap 2008). A good example here is the alternative approach to cultural interpretation, pioneered for Sri Lanka's Cultural Triangle by Seneviratne. Writing in 2003, during the fragile cessation in hostilities, he argued that the kinds of nationalist representations that had been staged at Anuradhapura in 1980 had resulted in a "crisis of education" that had "unleashed violent, anarchic and parochial responses from the next generation that is rapidly developing a bias towards social fascist and fundamentalist ideologies" (Seneviratne 2003: 180). Given this, he made the case for using Sri Lanka's heritage resources for conflict resolution, launching a project at Anuradhapura that presented the diversity of Sri Lanka's history that used the tangible heritage of the site:

> rather than carrying out a monologue with the past, we now carry out a dialogue with the past. We now utilize archaeology and heritage studies as a major instrument of conflict resolution … Unless and until we learn to present the past by incorporating all communities as its stakeholders and develop an unbiased historical explanation of the past, it will only alienate different groups for different reasons. (Seneviratne 2008: 193)

The outcome of approaches such as these can be the restoration of memory. In contrast to a reactionary nostalgia, such as the yearning of military juntas and their civilian supporters for a prelapsarian world of regimented order, a restored memory assists in processes of restitution and redress by insisting on understanding historical sequences of cause, effect, and consequence (Boym 2001; Hall 2013). Documenting complex historical sequences through material evidence has always been, after all, the backbone of archaeology, whose work brings to light not only the glorious but the abject and violent as well. The discipline can thus be put at the service of postconflict societies by promoting a deeper and more complete understanding of the past and by exposing the shortcomings of the simplistic views so cherished by ideologies of exclusion.

REFERENCES

Abu El-Haj, N. (2001) *Facts on the Ground: Archaeological Practice and Territorial Self-Fashioning in Israeli Society*. Chicago, IL: University of Chicago Press.

Alexander, J. C. (2004) Toward a Theory of Cultural Trauma, in J. C. Alexander, R. Eyerman, B. Giesen, N. Smelser, and P. Sztompka (eds), *Cultural Trauma and Collective Identity*. Berkeley: University of California Press, pp. 1–30.

Arendt, H. (1969) *On Violence*. New York: Harcourt.

Bardenstein, C. B. (1999) Trees, Forests, and the Shaping of Palestinian and Israeli Collective Memory, in M. Bal, J. V. Crewe, and L. Spitzer (eds), *Acts of memory: Cultural recall in the present*. Hannover: University Press of New England, pp. 148–168.

Basu, P. (2008) Confronting the past? Negotiating a heritage of conflict in Sierra Leone. *Journal of Material Culture* 13(2): 233–247.

Beaumont, J. (2012) Hellfire Pass Memorial Museum, Thai-Burma Railway, in M. Gegner and B. Ziino (eds), *The Heritage of War*. London: Routledge, pp. 19–40.

Bernbeck, R. and S. Pollock (1996) Ayodhya, archaeology, and identity. *Current Anthropology* 37(1): 138–142.

Bernbeck, R. and S. Pollock (2007) Grabe, wo du stehst! An Archaeology of Perpetrators, in Y. Hamilakis and P. Duke (eds), *Archaeology and Capitalism: From Ethics to Politics*. Walnut Creek, CA: Left Coast Press, pp. 217–234.

Bevan, R. (2005) *The Destruction of Memory: Architecture at War*. London: Reaktion.

Biasatti, S. (2011) Dilución o dilucidación? Usos y usos en torno a las topografías del terror. *Ebre 38: revista internacional de la Guerra Civil, 1936–1939* 6: 203–221.

Biran, A., Y. Poria, and G. Oren (2011) Sought experiences at (dark) heritage sites. *Annals of Tourism Research* 38(3): 820–841.

Boym, S. (2001) *The Future of Nostalgia*. New York: Basic Books.

Braun, M. S., M. Hattstein, and B. Mecke (2002) *Spuren des Terrors: Stätten nationalsozialistischer Gewaltherrschaft in Berlin*. Berlin: Braun.

Burström, M. and B. Gelderblom (2011) Dealing with difficult heritage: The case of Bückeberg, site of the Third Reich Harvest Festival. *Journal of Social Archaeology* 11(3): 266–282.

Carman, J. and M. L. S. Sørensen (2009) Heritage Studies: An Outline, in M. L. S. Sørensen and J. Carman (eds), *Heritage Studies. Methods and Approaches*. London: Routledge, pp. 11–28.

Chadha, A. (2006) Ambivalent heritage between affect and ideology in a colonial cemetery. *Journal of Material Culture* 11(3): 339–363.

Chapman, J. (1994) Destruction of a common heritage: The archaeology of war in Croatia, Bosnia and Hercegovina. *Antiquity* 68: 120–126.

Charlesworth, E. and A. Nelson (2012) Reconstruction as Exclusion: Beirut, in M. Gegner and B. Ziino (eds), *The Heritage of War*. London: Routledge, pp. 234–253.

Colwell-Chanthaphonh, C. (2007) History, Justice, and Reconciliation, in B. J. Little and P. Shackel (eds), *Archaeology as a Tool of Civic Engagement*. Lanham, MD: AltaMira, pp. 23–46.

Corsane, G. (2006) Robben Island: Facing Challenges of Creating a National Museum in a World Heritage Site, in *Re-Mapping the Field: New Approaches in Conflict Archaeology*. Berlin: Westkreuz, pp. 64–71.

Crossland, Z. (2000) Buried lives. Forensic archaeology and the disappeared in Argentina. *Archaeological Dialogues* 7(2): 146–159.

Dinges, J. (2004) *The Condor Years: How Pinochet and His Allies Brought Terrorism to Three Continents*. New York: New Press.

Dolff-Bonekämper, G. (2002) Sites of hurtful memory. *Conservation: The GCI Newsletter* 17(2): 4–10.

Economist (2013) For whom the bell tolls. A visit to the controversial Yasukuni shrine upsets the neighbours. April 27, 2013. Available at: http://www.economist.com/news/asia/21576724-visit-controversial-yasukuni-shrine-upsets-neighbours-whom-bell-tolls?zid=315. Accessed November 20, 2014.

Fanon, F. (2004 [1961]) *The Wretched of the Earth*. New York: Grove.

Feitlowitz, M. (1998) *A Lexicon of Terror: Argentina and the Legacies of Torture*. New York: Oxford University Press.

Funari, P., A. Zarankin, and M. Salerno (2010) Introduction, in P. P. A. Funari, A. Zarankin, and M. Salerno (eds), *Memories from Darkness; Archaeology of Repression and Resistance in Latin America*. New York: Springer, pp. i–xxviii.

Giblin, J. D., A. Clement, and J. Humphris (2010) An Urewe burial in Rwanda: Exchange, health, wealth and violence c. AD 400. *Azania: Archaeological Research in Africa* 45(3): 276–297.

Goebel, S. and D. Keene (2011) Towards a Metropolitan History of Total War: An Introduction, in S. Goebel and D. Keene (eds), *Cities into Battlefields: Metropolitan Scenarios, Experiences and Commemorations of Total War*. London: Ashgate, pp. 1–46.

Goldhagen, D. (2009) *Worse than War. Genocide, Eliminationism, and the Ongoing Assault on Humanity*. New York: PublicAffairs.

González-Ruibal, A. (2008) Time to destroy: An archaeology of supermodernity. *Current Anthropology* 49(2): 247–279.

González-Ruibal, A. (2013) Reclaiming Archaeology, in A. González-Ruibal (ed.), *Reclaiming Archaeology: Beyond the Tropes of Modernity*. London: Routledge, pp. 1–29.

González-Ruibal, A., X. Ayán-Vila, and R. Ceasar (2015) Ethics, Archaeology and Civil Conflict: The Case of Spain, in A. González-Ruibal and G. Moshenska (eds), *Ethics, Archaeology and Violence*. New York: Springer, pp. 113–136.

Goodhand, J. (2000) Research in conflict zones: Ethics and accountability. *Forced Migration Review* 8(4): 12–16.

Guneratne, A. (2002) What's in a Name? Aryans and Dravidians in the Making of Sri Lankan Identities, in N. Silva (ed.), *The Hybrid Island. Culture Crossings and the Invention of Identity in Sri Lanka*. London: Zed Books, pp. 20–40.

Haber, A. (2010) Torture, Truth, Repression, and Archaeology, in P. P. A. Funari, A. Zarankin, and M. Salerno (eds), *Memories from Darkness; Archaeology of Repression and Resistance in Latin America*. New York: Springer, pp. 3–8.

Hall, M. (2001) Cape Town's District Six and the Archaeology of Memory, in R. Layton, P. Stone, and J. Thomas (eds), *The Destruction and Conservation of Cultural Property*. London: Routledge, pp. 298–311.

Hall, M. (2002) Blackbirds and Black Butterflies, in C. Hamilton, V. Harris, J. Taylor, M. Pickover, G. Reid, and R. Saleh (eds), *Refiguring the Archive*. Cape Town: David Philip, pp. 333–361.

Hall, M. (2006) Identity, memory and countermemory; The archaeology of an urban landscape. *Journal of Material Culture* 11(1-2): 189–209.

Hall, M. (2009a) New knowledge and the university. *Anthropology Southern Africa* 32(1-2): 69–86.

Hall, M. (2009b) Proclamation 43, in John Schofield (ed.), *Defining Moments, Dramatic Archaeologies of the Twentieth Century*. Oxford: British Archaeological Reports, pp. 115–122.

Hall, M. (2010) Revealing Memories from Darkness, in P. P. A. Funari, A. Zarankin, and M. Salerno (eds), *Memories from Darkness; Archaeology of Repression and Resistance in Latin America*. New York: Springer, pp. 177–186.

Hall, M. (2013) Milieux de Mémoire, in A. González-Ruibal (ed.), *Reclaiming Archaeology: Beyond the Tropes of Modernity*. New York: Routledge, pp. 355–366.

Hall, M. and P. Bombardella (2005) Las Vegas in Africa. *Journal of Social Archaeology* 5(1): 5–24.

Hansell, F. (2011) Commemorating the Past: The Integration of Nazi Perpetrator Sites into the German Memorial Landscapes, in S. Merrill and L. Schmidt (eds), *A Reader in Uncomfortable Heritage and Dark Tourism*. Cottbus: BTU, pp. 249–268.

Harrison, R. (2013) *Heritage: Critical Approaches*. London: Routledge.

Hernández Martínez, A. (2012) Tres décadas de conservación del patrimonio arqueológico en España (1978–2008). *Pós. Revista do Programa de Pós-Graduação em Arquitetura e Urbanismo da FAUUSP* 19(31): 251–264.

Hidalgo, E. B. (2012) Argentina's former secret detention centres: Between demolition, modification and preservation. *Journal of Material Culture* 17(2): 191–206.

Hodder, I. (2012) *Entangled: An Archaeology of the Relationships between Humans and Things*. Oxford: Wiley.

Horkheimer, M. and T. W. Adorno (2001 [1944]) The Culture Industry: Enlightenment as Mass Deception, in M. G. Durham and D. M. Kellner (eds), *Media and Cultural Studies: Keyworks*. Oxford: Blackwell, pp. 41–72.

Ibreck, R. (2013) International constructions of national memories: The aims and effects of foreign donors' support for genocide remembrance in Rwanda. *Journal of Intervention and Statebuilding* 7(2): 149–169.

Jasinski, M. E., M. N. Soleim, and L. Sem (2012) "Painful Heritage": Cultural Landscapes of the Second World War in Norway: A New Approach, in R. Berge, M. E. Jasinski, and K. Sognnes (eds), *N-TAG TEN. Proceedings of the 10th Nordic TAG Conference at Stiklestad, Norway 2009*. BAR International Series 2399. Oxford: Archaeopress, pp. 263–273.

Klausmeier, A. and L. Schmidt (2004) *Wall Remnants–Wall Traces: The Comprehensive Guide to the Berlin Wall*. Berlin: Westkreuz.

Klein, N. (2007) *The Shock Doctrine: The Rise of Disaster Capitalism*. London: Penguin.

Kohl, P. L. (1998) Nationalism and archaeology: On the constructions of nations and the reconstructions of the remote past. *Annual Review of Anthropology* 27: 223–246.

Koshar, R. (2000) *From Monuments to Traces: Artifacts of German Memory, 1870–1990*. Berkeley: University of California Press.

Kouoyomedjian, B. and C. Siméone (2005) *Deir-es-Zor: Sur les traces du Génocide Arménien de 1915*. Arlès: Actes Sud.

Latour, B., (1999) *Pandora's Hope: Essays on the Reality of Science Studies*. Cambridge, MA: Harvard University Press.

Latour, B. (2005) From Realpolitik to Dingpolitik – or How to Make Things Public, in B. Latour and P. Weibel, (eds), *Making Things Public. Atmospheres of Democracy*. Cambridge: ZKM Center for Art and Media, pp. 4–31.

Le Cour Grandmaison, O. (2005) *Coloniser. Exterminer. Sur la guerre et l'etat colonial*. Paris: Fayard.
Lennon, J. and Foley, M. (2000) *Dark Tourism: The Attraction of Death and Disaster*. London: Continuum.
Leturcq, J. G. (2009) Heritage-making and policies of identity in the "post-conflict reconstruction" of Sudan. *Égypte/Monde Arabe* 5-6: 295–328.
Levinas, E. (2008) *Difícil Libertad: Ensayos sobre el Judaísmo*. Madrid: Caparrós.
Logan, W., and K. Reeves (eds) (2008) *Places of Pain and Shame: Dealing with Difficult Heritage*. London: Routledge.
Logan, W. and N. Than Bình (2012) Victory and Defeat at Đin Biên Ph: Memory and Memorialization in Vietnam and France, in M. Gegner and B. Ziino (eds), *The Heritage of War*. London: Routledge, pp. 41–53.
López Mazz, J. (2010) An Archaeological View of Political Repression in Uruguay (1971–1985), in P. P. A. Funari, A. Zarankin, and M. Salerno (eds), *Memories from Darkness; Archaeology of Repression and Resistance in Latin America*. New York: Springer, pp. 33–45.
López Mazz, J. M. (2015) Archaeology of Historical Conflicts, Colonial Oppression and Political Violence in Uruguay, in A. González-Ruibal and G. Moshenska (eds), *Ethics, Violence and Archaeology*. New York: Springer, pp. 71-87.
MacDonald, S. (2009) *Difficult Heritage: Negotiating the Nazi Past in Nuremberg and Beyond*. London: Routledge.
Marrus, M. R. (1997) The Future of Auschwitz: A Case for the Ruins, in S. D. Denham, I. Kacandes, and J. Petropoulos (eds), *A User's Guide to German Cultural Studies*. Ann Arbor: University of Michigan Press, pp. 357–366.
Mayor, F. (1990) Address by Mr Federico Mayor Director-General of the United Nations Educational, Scientific and Cultural Organization (Unesco) at the Ceremonial Session to mark the Tenth Anniversary of The International Campaign for the Safeguarding of The Cultural Triangle of Sri Lanka Colombo, UNESCO. Available at: http://unesdoc.unesco.org/images/0008/000894/089429eo.pdf. Accessed November 20, 2014.
Mbembe, A. (2001) *On the Postcolony*. Berkeley: University of California Press.
McKinney, S. (2012) Narrating Genocide on the Streets of Kigali, in M. Gegner and B. Ziino (eds), *The Heritage of War*. London: Routledge, pp. 160–176.
McSherry, J. Patrice (2005) The undead ghost of Operation Condor. *Logos* 4(2): 1–10.
Meskell, L. (2002) Negative heritage and past mastering in archaeology. *Anthropological Quarterly* 75(3): 557–574.
Meskell, L. (2005) Archaeological ethnography: Conversations around Kruger National Park. *Archaeologies* 1(1): 81–100.
Meskell, L. (2011) *The Nature of Heritage: The New South Africa*. Oxford: Wiley Blackwell.
Mignolo, W. D. (2011) *The Darker Side of Western Modernity: Global Futures, Decolonial Options*. Durham, NC: Duke University Press.
Mire, S. (2011) The knowledge-centred approach to the Somali cultural emergency and heritage development assistance in Somaliland. *African Archaeological Review* 28(1): 71–91.
Monegal, A. (2008) Exhibiting objects of memory. *Journal of Spanish Cultural Studies* 9(2): 239–251.
Muñoz-Rojas, O. (2011) *Ashes and Granite: Destruction and Reconstruction in the Spanish Civil War and Its Aftermath*. Brighton: Sussex Academic Press.
Navarrete, R. and A. M. López (2010) Scratching Behind the Walls: Graffiti and Symbolic Political Imagination at Cuartel San Carlos (Caracas, Venezuela), in P. P. A. Funari, A. Zarankin, and M. Salerno (eds), *Memories from Darkness; Archaeology of Repression and Resistance in Latin America*. New York: Springer, pp. 105–127.
Ngugi wa Thiong'o (1998) *Penpoints, Gunpoints, and Dreams*. Oxford: Clarendon Press.
Nicholas, L. H. (1994) *The Rape of Europa: the Fate of Europe's Treasures in the Third Reich and the Second World War*. New York: Knopf.
Olivier, L. (2001) The Archaeology of the Contemporary Past, in V. Buchli and G. Lucas (eds), *Archaeologies of the Contemporary Past*. London: Routledge, pp. 175–188.

Olsen, B. (2010) *In Defense of Things. Archaeology and the Ontology of Objects*. Lanham, MD: AltaMira.
Pinkepank, H. (2011) The Uncomfortable Heritage of the KdF-Seaside Resort Prora, in S. Merrill and L. Schmidt (eds), *A Reader in Uncomfortable Heritage and Dark Tourism*. Cottbus: BTU, pp. 232–248.
Quijano, A. (2000) Coloniality of power and Eurocentrism in Latin America. *International Sociology* 15(2): 215–232.
Rajasingham-Senanayake, D. (2002) Identity on the Borderline: Modernity, New Ethnicities, and the Unmaking of Multiculturalism in Sri Lanka, in N. Silva (ed.), *The Hybrid Island. Culture Crossings and the Invention of Identity in Sri Lanka*. London: Zed Books, pp. 41–70.
Renshaw, L. (2011) *Exhuming Loss: Memory, Materiality and Mass Graves of the Spanish Civil War*. Walnut Creek, CA: Left Coast Press.
Riedlmayer, A. (1995) Erasing the past: The destruction of libraries and archives in Bosnia-Herzegovina. *Middle East Studies Association Bulletin* 29(1): 7–11.
Ronson, J. (2004) Hotel Auschwitz. *Journal of Cultural Research* 8(1): 75–90.
Rowlands, M. (2008) Civilization, violence and heritage healing in Liberia. *Journal of Material Culture* 13(2): 135–152.
Salerno, M. (2010) "They Must Have Done Something Wrong..." The Construction of Subversion as a Social Category and the Reshaping of Identities through Body and Dress (Argentina, 1976–1983), in P. P. A. Funari, A. Zarankin, and M. Salerno (eds), *Memories from Darkness; Archaeology of Repression and Resistance in Latin America*. New York: Springer, pp. 81–104.
Salerno, M. A., A. Zarankin, and M. C. Perosino (2012) Arqueologías de la clandestinidad. *Una revisión de los trabajos efectuados en los centros de detención clandestinos de la última dictadura militar en Argentina. Revista Universtaria de Historia Militar* 2: 1–36.
Schaap, A. (2008) Reconciliation as ideology and politics. *Constellations* 15(2): 249–264.
Scham, S. A. and A. Yahya (2003) Heritage and reconciliation. *Journal of Social Archaeology* 3(3): 399–416.
Schofield, J. and W. Cocroft (eds) (2009) *A Fearsome Heritage: Diverse Legacies of the Cold War*. Walnut Creek, CA: Left Coast Press.
Schwartze, F. (2013) Symbols of Reconstruction, Signs of Divisions: The Case of Mitrovica, Kosovo, in M. Gegner and B. Ziino (eds), *The Heritage of War*. London: Routledge, pp. 219–233.
Seneviratne, S. (1996) "Peripheral Regions" and "Marginal Communities": Towards an Alternative Explanation of Early Iron Age Material and Social Formations in Sri Lanka, in R. Champakalakshmi and S. Gopal (eds), *Tradition, Dissent and Ideology. Essays in Honour of Romila Thapar*. Delhi: Oxford University Press, pp. 264–312.
Seneviratne, S. (2003) Knowledge information in multicultural South Asia: redefining education for the next generation. *Ethnic Studies Report* 21(2): 179–205.
Seneviratne, S. (2008) Situating World Heritage Sites in a Multicultural Society: The Ideology of Presentation at the Sacred City of Anuradhapura, Sri Lanka, in M. Liebmann and U. Z. Rizvi (eds), *Archaeology and the Postcolonial Critique*. New York: Altamira, pp. 177–195.
Shepherd, N. (2007) Archaeology dreaming: Post-apartheid urban imaginaries and the bones of the Prestwich Street dead. *Journal of Social Archaeology* 7(1): 3–28.
Shepherd, N. (2013) Ruin memory: A hauntology of Cape Town, in A. González-Ruibal (ed.), *Reclaiming Archaeology: Beyond the Tropes of Modernity*. London: Routledge, pp. 233–243.
Silva, R. (1993) The Cultural Triangle: International Safeguarding Campaign, in A. W. P. Guruge et al. (eds), *The Cultural Triangle of Sri Lanka*. Paris: UNESCO, pp. 176–193.
Simmons, W. P. (1999) The Third. Levinas' theoretical move from an-archical ethics to the realm of justice and politics. *Philosophy and Social Criticism* 25(6): 83–104.
Smith, L. (2006) *Uses of Heritage*. London: Routledge.
Sri Lanka Government (2011) *Report of the Commission of Inquiry on Lessons Learnt and Reconciliation*. Colombo: Ministry of Defence and Urban Development. Available

at: http://www.defence.lk/warcrimes/lessons_learnt_and_reconciliation_commission_final_report.html. Accessed November 20, 2014.

Sri Lanka Tourism Development Authority (2013) *Welcome to Sri Lanka, Wonder of Asia* (home page). Available at: http://www.srilanka.travel. Accessed November 20, 2014.

Starzmann, M. T. (2013) Excavating Tempelhof airfield: Objects of memory and the politics of absence. *Rethinking History: The Journal of Theory and Practice* 18(2): 211–229.

Stone, P. G. and J. F. Bajjaly (eds) (2008) *The Destruction of Cultural Heritage in Iraq*. Rochester, NY: Boydell and Brewer.

Sturdy Colls, C. (2012). Holocaust archaeology: Archaeological approaches to landscapes of Nazi genocide and persecution. *Journal of Conflict Archaeology* 7(2): 70–104.

Sutton, R. K. (2012) Commemorating the American Civil War in National Park Service Battlefields, in M. Gegner and B. Ziino (eds), *The Heritage of War*. London: Routledge, pp. 108–124.

Theune, C. (2010) Historical archaeology in national socialist concentration camps in Central Europe. *Historische Archäologie* 2: 1–14.

Theune, C. (2013) Archaeology and Remembrance: The Contemporary Archaeology of Concentration Camps, Prisoner-of-War Camps and Battlefields, in N. Mehler (ed.), *Historical Archaeology in Central Europe*. Rockville, MD: Society for Historical Archaeology, pp. 241–260.

Totten, S. and W. Parsons (2012) *Centuries of Genocide: Essays and Eyewitness Accounts*. New York: Routledge.

Tunbridge, J. E. and G. J. Ashworth (1996) *Dissonant Heritage: The Management of the Past as a Resource in Conflict*. Oxford: Blackwell.

United Nations (2011) *Report of the Secretary-General's Panel of Experts on Accountability in Sri Lanka*. New York: United Nations. Available at: http://www.un.org/News/dh/infocus/Sri_Lanka/POE_Report_Full.pdf. Accessed November 20, 2014.

Van derl Walt, C., V. Franchi, and G. Stevens (2003) The South African Truth and Reconciliation Commission: "Race", historical compromise and transitional democracy. *International Journal of Intercultural Relations* 27(2): 251–267.

Viejo Rose, D. (2011) *Reconstructing Spain: Cultural Heritage and Memory after Civil War*. Brighton: Sussex Academic Press.

Viejo Rose, D. (2013) Reconstructing heritage in the aftermath of civil war: Re-visioning the nation and the implications of international involvement. *Journal of Intervention and Statebuilding* 7(2): 125–148.

Waldorf, L. (2009) Revisiting Hotel Rwanda: Genocide ideology, reconciliation, and rescuers. *Journal of Genocide Research* 11(1): 101–125.

Weiss, G. (2011) *The Cage*. London: Bodley Head.

Zarankin, A. and C. Niro (2010) The Materialization of Sadism: Archaeology of Architecture in Clandestine Centers of Detention (Argentinean Military Dictatorship, 1976–1983), in P. P. A. Funari, A. Zarankin, and M. Salerno (eds), *Memories from Darkness; Archaeology of Repression and Resistance in Latin America*. New York: Springer, pp. 57–79.

Zarankin, A. and M. Salerno (2012) Todo está guardado en la memoria. Reflexiones sobre los espacios para la memoria de la dictadura en Buenos Aires (Argentina), in A. Zarankin, M. Salerno, and M. C. Perosino (eds), *Historias Desaparecidas. Arqueología, Memoria y Violencia Política*. Cordoba: Brujas, pp. 143–171.

Ziino, B. (2012) We Are Talking about Gallipoli After All: Contested Narratives, Contested Ownership and the Gallipoli Peninsula, in M. Gegner and B. Ziino (eds), *The Heritage of War*. London: Routledge, pp. 142–159.

Žižek, S. (2008) *Violence*. London: Profile.

Žižek, S. (2012) *The Year of Dreaming Dangerously*. London: Verso.

Žižek, S. (2013) Trouble in paradise. *London Review of Books*, July 18, 2013. Available at: http://www.lrb.co.uk/v35/n14/slavoj-zizek/trouble-in-paradise. Accessed November 20, 2014.

8

Urban Heritage and Social Movements

Chiara De Cesari and Michael Herzfeld

Introduction

Critical heritage studies inevitably confront the conflict between the desire for conservation and corresponding processes of demographic elimination.[1] In this chapter, we deploy a position of "engaged anthropology" (Herzfeld 2010) to contest persisting essentialist approaches to heritage and culture – a legacy of nineteenth-century anthropology – that still largely undergird most nationalist and other identitarian discourses and that occasionally, in their extreme form, morph into an excuse for genocide and mass destruction. The same essentialist notion of culture infuses much of the expert discourse on heritage (see, e.g., De Cesari 2010a) and renders it susceptible to political exploitation, even to the point of collusion between scholarship and exclusionary politics.

In the interests of encouraging heritage scholars to subject their own epistemic history to equally ruthless inspection, we argue for trenchantly strengthening the already ongoing re-examination of the assumptions underlying the concept of heritage itself. Such work, including explorations of equivalent terminologies elsewhere in the world, will eventually also illuminate the circumstances under which heritage becomes the victim of, and the pretext for, structural, epistemic, and physical violence against urban communities.

A further epistemological shift addresses the tendency to dichotomize heritage into "formal" and "informal" varieties (see De Cesari 2010b). We hope to reverse this tendency – which partly responds to earlier habits of ignoring whatever did not fit authorized, official, colonial, monumental, or academically respectable models of heritage (see, e.g., Byrne 2014; Harrison 2010; Meskell 2002; Smith 2006) – in favor of more nuanced and grounded distinctions.

We note the intersection of heritage violence with the resistance it engenders over spaces variously defined as domestic, collective, common, and public. Our focus is on urban heritage. Struggles over urban heritage often occur as local actors try to regroup in the face of neoliberal urbanism or other forms of discriminatory and violent spatial planning. We define neoliberal urbanism as a combination of relentless speculation

Global Heritage: A Reader, First Edition. Edited by Lynn Meskell.

and socio-spatial reorganization with a rapid diminution of state and municipal responsibility for social services. Resistance originates in coalitions of residents claiming their "right to the city" (Harvey 2006, 2012; Lefebvre 1968) and to their own heritage – rights, that is, occluded by processes of privatization, alienation, and monumentalization. "Urban regeneration" claims to preserve heritage while improving society. For residents and social critics alike, however, gentrification, Smith's (2002) substitute for euphemistic talk of urban renewal (see also Jacobs 1961), is a far more apt term.

In these processes, bureaucratic and commercial forces force the enclosure of commonly enjoyed spaces and take control of domestic architecture, transforming both into gated communities and security-controlled residences (e.g., Caldeira 2001; Holston 1989). In the recent Gezi Park protests in Istanbul, state, capital, and social movements variously mobilized the concept of heritage to support competing interpretations of the past and, concomitantly, of both urban space and heritage.

Bureaucrats, business tycoons, local merchants and artisans, religious zealots, settlers, archaeologists, heritage consultants, and residents are all involved in these processes. Sometimes radically different understandings of the term "common good" underlie heritage conflicts (see Alonso González 2014; Cellamare 2008; Settis 2010, 2011, 2012). Although struggles over contested religious space usually entail a different language (e.g., Abu El-Haj 2001; Dumper 2014; Hayden 2002; Ratnagar 2004), they, too, revolve around competing interpretations of particular physical spaces and traces.

The heritagization of places (especially, but not exclusively, in nationalistic state practice) often induces radical shifts in the real estate value and social geography of heritagized neighborhoods. This articulation of heritage, commodification, and displacement has long typified both nationalistic and colonial idioms of violence. Forces variously lumped together as "neoliberal" have increasingly co-opted, expanded, and reformulated the violence of those earlier structures of power and inequality. In exploring the impact of historic conservation on the urban social fabric, we conjoin Smith's critique of gentrification with the concept of spatial cleansing as the "social and cultural evacuation of space" (Herzfeld 2006). When urban (and occasionally rural) areas are monumentalized, local populations may be evicted either in the name of heritage or because of the insidious actions of the market with its sudden, massive increases in real estate prices and rents. Spatial cleansing is "an overall pattern whereby theme parks, partially made up of ancient materials but heavily restored and refurbished to suit modern ideas about the past, come to replace densely populated areas and in turn create growing zones of disaffected and displaced people" (Herzfeld 2006: 132). What criteria of selection determine the impact of spatial cleansing and whose interests do they serve?

It is important to avoid unnecessarily reductionist dichotomies between bad heritage (by state and capital) and good heritage (by civic committees and protest movements). Not all state interventions are necessarily misguided; many NGO-directed activities turn out to be self-serving, or, more accurately, serve the interests of neoliberal "government at a distance" (Rose and Miller 1992; see also Ferguson and Gupta 2002; Miller and Rose 2008). As several scholars have noted (e.g., Elyachar 2002; Ferguson 2010; Muehlebach 2009), there are surprising affinities between neoliberal techniques and rhetoric on the one hand and some forms of progressive politics on the other; in particular, conservative neoliberal policymakers and local activists alike mobilize the language of "community involvement" and "participation" for their respective urban heritage policies. Despite this shared language, heritage plays a growing role in both the production of, and resistance to, inequality.

The mobilization of heritage thus serves as a technique of governmentality (Foucault 1991; Miller and Rose 2008). It is deployed to control social classes variously classified as dangerous, disruptive, and embarrassingly lacking in culture. Residents often proudly enjoy those embarrassments as a form of solidarity cast as cultural intimacy (Herzfeld 2005), but their allegedly uncouth behavior too easily plays into their detractors' hands. Moreover, the tactics of power often appropriate seemingly benign actors and concepts (especially NGOs and their rhetoric) to consolidate control over what is thereafter reconstituted as valuable real estate, historic centers, and national heritage. These tactics co-opt the symbolism of national or regional pride, and increasingly also the idiom of cosmopolitan responsibility for a universal heritage, to serve ends that clearly transcend national borders and have more to do with *capital accumulation* than with the symbolic importance of *capital cities*. They also often coincide with exclusionary policies reminiscent of earlier campaigns of spatial cleansing such as the fascist reconstructions of Italian cities under Mussolini and, perhaps most famously, Baron Haussmann's militarization of the Paris street system in response to the 1870 Paris Commune uprising (Lamprakos 2014).

In response to such oppression, residents often also resort to heritage rhetoric. The convergence of nationalist, colonialist, municipal, and financially speculative patterns of violence with community resistance provides an important explanatory backdrop to the various "Occupy" movements. These movements have in turn reappropriated the language of "invasion," often used by authorities as an evocative metaphor for squatting.

More recent research examines ways in which uses of heritage as place-making shift under neoliberal and transnational governmentality. In recalling the diverse social movements that have coalesced around heritage and urban sustainability, we again reject the analytical use of the informal–formal dichotomy because it is itself directly implicated in structural violence. Officials refuse recognition to the often highly regulated self-governance of the communities they contemptuously dismiss as "informal" while also concealing the lawlessness of those settlements they recognize as legal. In considering these dynamics, we will briefly illustrate them with our own work in Bangkok, Palestine/Israel, and Rome.

Learning from Gezi Park

In June 2013, media images of mostly youthful Turks confronting the police to defend a central city park from being built up threatened to undermine the new positive international image of Turkey, booming economically under the Islamic neoliberalism of former Istanbul mayor (and now national president) Tayyip Erdoğan. The protests, aimed at saving an urban heritage site, Gezi Park, escalated into a broadly based revolt against Erdoğan's authoritarianism, exposing competing visions of both democracy and the past in Turkey (Bernardoni et al. 2013).

The government's heritage project sought to replace the early twentieth-century park with a shopping mall to be housed in an on-site reconstruction of the vanished Ottoman barracks, exemplifying the vast program of neoliberal urban transformation framed in the nationalist-neo-Ottomanist rhetoric of the ruling party since 2002 (Eraydin and Taşan-Kok 2013; Nocera 2013). Characteristically sugar-coated as urban regeneration, this rhetoric offered a fusion of traditionalist religion, nostalgia for the imperial past, and unfettered market economics. It sought massive gentrification through the growing commodification, privatization, and heritagization of the urban commons. This policy has triggered radical shifts in social geography, propelled by an alliance of local and national government with national and transnational capital. Its visible results include the transformation of historic inner-city residential quarters into tourist sites and playgrounds for the rich and the expulsion of inhabitants of several generations' standing (see Dinçer 2011; Göktürk, Soysal, and Türeli 2010). Minority groups are especially vulnerable, and it was the resistance in Beyoğlu, historically the home of minorities and artists, that triggered the most recent protest (Nocera 2013).

In Istanbul's periphery, slum clearance – the terminological predecessor of urban regeneration – continues unhindered, with no respect for local (if often more recent) forms of heritage, such as in the case of Ayazma (Bartu Candan and Kolluoğlu 2008). Such is the hegemonic notion of heritage now called "neo-Ottomanism" (Walton 2010), through which the AKP party promotes its project of regional hegemony through ritual enunciations of national aggrandizement, imperial rebirth, and responsible conservation. But the social movements sparked by such interventions tellingly also mobilize notions of heritage – a heritage of neighborly intimacy and multicultural urban practices.

Heritage as Possession and Dispossession

In modern nationalist thought, as Handler (1985, 1988) argues, "having a culture" – or its monumental residue – follows the logic of "possessive individualism" associated with early modern European notions of personhood. Implementing this logic, the authors of state-managed heritage have largely promoted the view of national pasts as having a timeless lien on both territory and culture, often through violent enforcement and the massive reordering of spatial functions. Nation-states – whether the nineteenth-century models or those that came after decolonization – have consequently had a deeply vested interest in promoting the conservation of carefully selected monuments. But national governments are not the only entities that claim possession in this idiom; the dispossessed often react in turn by becoming increasingly state-like in ways that require continual recalibration of the balance between resistance and complaisance.

Nation-states have been the most powerful actors in these conflicts for the past two centuries. State policies have been closely tied to questions of national identity (Smith 2004); the regulation of heritage through historic conservation often aims to reduce a fractious body politic to a single, ostensibly unified, and territorially bounded nation-state (e.g., Hobsbawm and Ranger 1983; Kohl 1998). This use of heritage has, not coincidentally, facilitated the bureaucratic control and regulation of people's daily lives. For example, Herzfeld (1991), writing of the town of Rethemnos on the island of Crete, Greece, has shown how local inhabitants struggled to defend their own homes, their lived space, and "social time" from the state authorities' tight bureaucratic control, a detemporalized past, and a monumental conception of history. While the residents eventually profited from the conservation effort – Rethemnos has weathered the Greek financial crisis of 2009–2014 in relatively good shape, in part because of its well-preserved Venetian and Ottoman domestic architecture – the predominant effect has been to flatten local historical knowledge into an encompassing national narrative.

Such anthropological studies of heritage and nationalism and the reproduction of nation-state power resonate with works published by Marxist historians in the

United Kingdom in the 1980s that were critical of the emerging "heritage industry" (Hewison 1987). Significantly, these historians pilloried the Thatcherite use of a nostalgic heritage as a key tool in the neoliberal campaign of reordering the urban environment to suit anti-welfarist policies (see also Hobsbawm and Ranger 1983; Wright 1985). During this phase and the subsequent increase in interest in the nationalistic uses of archaeology (e.g., Arnold 1990; Diaz-Andreu and Champion 1996; Kohl and Fawcett 1995; Meskell 1998), those who resisted the national and neoliberal heritage models became more nuanced and reflexive about their own expropriation of those discourses. These periods together thus mark the paradoxical emergence of critical heritage studies from the very preoccupations that also nourished early neoliberal uses of the heritage concept. That common origin prompts the concern that, just as neoliberalism coopts the social conscience of volunteers and their organizations in order to devolve authority away from state institutions, it could too easily co-opt critical heritage discourses as a way of delegitimizing whatever obstructed its economic or ideological goals – as in Gezi Park and, in Bangkok, the threatened removal of the Pom Mahakan community (see below).

Awareness of various groups' capacity to generate their own interpretations of the past is both a rejection of orthodox Marxist notions of false consciousness and the product of an increasing body of empirical research with affected populations (Ferguson 1996; Hayden 1995). Thus, Samuel (1994) demonstrated the Foucauldian "strategic reversibility" of the heritage discourse as a means of resistance to state control. Much subsequent work has borne out this insight, mapping out the fundamental "dissonance" and multivocality of heritage as an always-already contested terrain (Tunbridge and Ashworth 1996; see also Graham, Ashworth, and Tunbridge 2000; Lowenthal 1996). While alternative heritages are still silenced in the name of conservation (Silverman 2012, 2013; Trouillot 1995; Whitelam 1996), local populations often adapt official historical narratives, including archaeological chronologies, to their own particular exigencies (Breglia 2006; Brown 1998; Daniel 1996; Hamilakis 2007; Kapferer 1988; Karakasidou 1993; Odermatt 1996; Stewart 2010; Sutton 1996; Watkins 2000; see also Shao 2013). These are the roots of more globalized protest movements today.

Many bureaucracies are animated by a desire to create archaeological "facts on the ground" (see Abu El-Haj 2001), a version of the fallacy of misplaced concreteness according to which material "presencing" of the past (see MacDonald 2013) could pre-empt political liens on the future. National bureaucracies assume and enhance a strict isomorphism among territory, people, and cultural heritage. Paradoxically, a similar "methodological nationalism" that takes the nation for granted as unit of analysis is also a feature of memory and heritage studies (Beck 2000; De Cesari and Rigney 2014; Wimmer and Glick Schiller 2002).

Heritage, then, is a key locus for realizing the nation. In making and destroying heritage, people materialize ethnonational identity, sovereignty, and power claims (Baillie 2013) in ways that belie instrumentalist claims about supposedly neutral heritage (Hamilakis 2007). Often building on approaches foregrounding the centrality of material things to social and political life (Latour 2005; Miller 2005), current interventions reconfigure heritage as a deeply political process by which identities and agencies are performed, produced, and renegotiated (Herscher 2010; see also Dimova 2013). These insights, acknowledging the deep entanglement of people and things (see also Hodder 2012), illuminate the relationship between heritage and ethnic cleansing. Nationalist heritage and archaeology identify present-day populations with past traces by "telescoping" (Vansina 1985) complex histories and creating spatial contiguities (see, e.g., Abu El-Haj 2001; Bernbeck and Pollock 1996). Conversely, destroying an enemy's heritage (Herscher 2010) or even expropriating it (Navaro-Yashin 2009) is not the act of a prior national self but the very production of national subjectivity (see also Daniel 1996). In response, the recovery of heritage provides victims with redress, as happened with the recent mapping of destroyed Palestinian villages in Israel (Davis 2010; Khalidi 1992; Lentin 2010; Pappe 2006).[2]

A key element in nationalism, heritage has also played a vital role in colonialism (see Silberman 1982; Trigger 1984). Nineteenth-century imperialism entailed the theft of other people's pasts for European collections and the selective destruction of cultural heritage in the colonies. Moreover, especially in Egypt, Mesopotamia, Palestine, and Greece, the search for antiquities in locations multiply viewed as "cradles of [Western] civilization" in the nineteenth and even in the twentieth century helped legitimize the colonial projects of those who claim(ed) to be the true heirs and saviors of these great civilizations (see Abu El-Haj 2001; Colla 2007; Hamilakis 2007).

Sometimes the colonizers claimed to have saved a heritage that would otherwise have gone lost thanks to the negligence of uncaring natives.[3] A classic illustration is Lord Elgin's removal of the marbles named after him, but called "the Parthenon Marbles" by Greek officials and archaeologists and still the object of an already decades-long struggle between British and Greek authorities. Greece was not formally a colony, but its crypto-colonial (Herzfeld 2002) status certainly made it relatively easy for the British to keep the marbles after Greece was created out of former Ottoman territory. Nonetheless, the locals may well have been grinding the statuary for mortar, as Elgin's supporters claimed (Jenkyns 1980), while calls to "return" the marbles to Greece represent an antiquarian rendition of the irredentist logic that sought to bring all Greek-speaking people "back" into the Greek national territory (see Voutira 2003). The "Elgin Marbles" ironically symbolize Greece's beholden status precisely because "returning" them continues to represent an official goal of the Greek state.

Nationalist successors to colonial powers continue many of the policies of the former occupiers in the name of national redemption. As the nationalist politics of archaeology and heritage in several postcolonial context demonstrate (see Colla 2007; De Cesari 2008; Maffi 2009), the discourse of links to ancient civilizations has been co-opted into elites' cultural nationalism and resignified as a tool of national liberation and aggrandizement. But "the rot remains" (Stoler 2008: 200): such uses of heritage by anti- and postcolonial elites tend to reproduce the colonial legacy of race- and class-based dispossession and displacement. Such, for example, is the violence perpetrated by the Egyptian state against the villagers of Gurna next to Luxor's Valley of the Kings. Despite their long tradition of livelihood based on closeness to the ancient ruins, they were displaced in favor of a commodified and nationalistic rendition of heritage (Meskell 2005; Mitchell 2002).

The history of heritage is thus indelibly marked by its interplay with nationalism and colonialism. A state successfully blending both projects is Israel, where Zionism harnessed heritage to the task of "returning" the Jews to their biblical homeland. Scholars such as Abu El-Haj (2001) have demonstrated Israeli archaeology's centrality to settler colonialism (see also Ben-Yehuda 2002; Zerubavel 1995). Often allied with the military, archaeology in Israel took on key features of the older colonial science by obliterating the Palestinian historical presence and producing a body of material facts attesting to the ancient Israelite presence. This antiquarian policy gave substance to the ideological idiom of return, and, in a manner startlingly reminiscent of the Greek ideology of Hellenism, retrospectively legitimized the absorption of Palestine into the Zionist *Altneuland* (Herzl 1902) – the "old-new" Jewish state of Israel.

In analyzing the modern state's aspiration of reordering the social world through administrative socio-spatial schemes, Scott (1998) posits two opposed rationalities and two opposed visions of the urban. One, exemplified by Le Corbusier's top-down, functionalist, and modernist architectural philosophy, disregards – and indeed obliterates – what we might (in Scott's terms) call organic urban heritage, that stratified and shifting, living, and locally grounded tangle of human–environment relations. To the modernist model Scott opposes the militancy that Jacobs (1961) based on the idea that this vernacular heritage was the place where creativity and urbanity truly thrive. Jacobs in turn inspires Scott's dichotomy between the selective, simplifying, and utilitarian knowledge of state and *metis*, or local knowledge. Slum clearance and modernist planning have spread across the world, especially between the 1960s and the 1980s, devastating both residents' livelihoods and their heritages. Such destruction continues, not in the name of an ordered and ordering modernity alone, but to make way for the monumental celebration of dominant groups' visions of the past. Spatial cleansing entails "social and cultural evacuation" rather than outright destruction. A form of heritage-led urban regeneration has partly displaced modernist town planning and Hausmannesque slum clearance, while, ironically, modernist architecture is now threatened with demolition as a sign of backwardness or as a reminder of now-embarrassing pasts (as happened with socialist modernist cityscapes; see Schwenkel 2012; for neo-Prussian Berlin, see Cochrane 2013; Colomb 2012).

Heritagization as Urban Governmentality

Slum clearance and large-scale forced relocations accompanied by large-scale destruction of local and inhabited forms of heritage continue to take place. We have focused here on cities, but it is important to note that similar processes have also long affected rural areas (especially to make space for parks and protected conservation areas; Heatherington 2010; Kosek 2006; Meskell 2012). The proponents of both modernization and commodified heritagization are especially skeptical of local claims to be protecting heritage when that heritage only concerns the comparatively recent and largely invisible history of a currently resident community (e.g., Bartu Candan and Kolluoğlu 2008; Harms 2011). Local communities and even individual families have sometimes succeeded in stopping or slowing such processes; tactics of resistance, recalcitrance, and renegotiation can frustrate the toughest planners' intentions (e.g., Zhang 2006, 2010). As a result, the authorities increasingly try to use their own version of heritage to combat such local interests, while wily community leaders develop great skill in identifying their local interests with wider national models of identity.

As a result of such developments, which betray underlying processes of mutual learning between what superficially seem to be implacable foes, official regulation of urban space now tends to greater subtlety. Heritagization becomes a game of mutual co-optation or a struggle to control the practical implications of governmentality. It disguises goals and practices of urban control and capital accumulation, while also reconfiguring purely local interests as common good.

Heritage has long played an important role in the consolidation of national territories. But economic globalization has intensified and distorted those older patterns. Today, turning a historic city district into heritage often causes a precipitous rise in real estate values. Furthermore, heritagization provides authorities with legal, academic, and moral tools, represented as technical and non-political forms of expertise, for intervening in people's daily lives.

Harvey (2012) interprets the city as the new key site of capitalist accumulation and exploitation, thus repositioning struggles over the production of urban space at the heart of contemporary capitalist dynamics and class conflicts; theorists, he argues, must include "those people who produce and reproduce urban life" (Harvey 2013). In this context, capital accumulation works against homogenization by making cities unique and authentic, so as to capture capital and tourist flows. Such shifts in the frontiers of capitalism produce a new urbanism characterized by "the struggle … to accumulate marks of distinctions and collective symbolic capital in a highly competitive world" (Harvey 2012: 106). For Harvey, this process displaces and marginalizes residents who do not conform to the sanitized city culture of those in power; Laurajane Smith (2006) similarly notes how the "authorized heritage discourse" privileges the cultural symbols of the privileged classes. Heritage thus emerges as a crucial device whereby managers and developers create urban distinction and authenticity, branding cities in distinct but globalized, easily recognizable ways. Thompson's (1979) "rubbish theory," showing how objects hitherto regarded as valueless become collectors' items at critical moments of scarcity, illustrates a related process dramatically demonstrated by Singapore's relatively few surviving Chinese shophouses, once despised and neglected but now expensively beautified, gentrified, and socially decontextualized (Yeoh and Kong 1994: 30–32).

These models illustrate the political economy of heritage as added value and heritagization as a motor of capital absorption and accumulation (Franquesa 2013). Anthropologically, such dynamics have been explored by John Collins (2008, 2011a, 2011b) in his analysis of the governmental restoration and patrimonialization of the historic center of Bahia, Brazil since the early 1990s. That project has displaced over 4,000 former residents while turning the center into the capital of a sanitized and racialized Afro-Brazilian culture for global consumers. Under UNESCO's aegis, this is an example of "capital's novel colonization of everyday life through cultural heritage management" (Collins 2011a, 125). Collins points out the complexities of a subjectification triggered by such commodification of buildings and people through "heritage-based reifications of everyday habits as potentially alienable forms of property" (Collins 2011b: 683). In Bahia's Pelourinho, those who did not fit the stereotype of the folkloric subject were evicted, a process legalized by the nationalization of private properties and cultural practices as heritage. Paradoxically, in Bahia a reverse privatization aids capitalization (cf. Alonso González 2014; Settis 2011). There, as in Hebron and Jerusalem (see below), heritagization emerges as a state-legitimated appropriation of land and culture. At the same time, it shapes not only people's self-image but also their avenues of agency.

How do residents react to these phenomena? The cases we present below exemplify how social movements attempt to respond. Such movements appear local but are, in many respects, united by global logics and forces (see also Harvey 2012). Local actors can sometimes turn the tables on heritagized power plays, but their relatively weak economic and political condition usually places them at an enormous disadvantage. At times, while residents understand the violence that threatens them, they often buy into the insidious ideology of beautification according to which an elegant, clean city benefits everyone (see Harms 2012 on Saigon). A gradually percolating and pervasive market logic ultimately obscures all but quantifiable losses; local heritage values are difficult to translate into monetary terms. Some forms of resistance are nonetheless more successful, as when residents of settlements close to a municipal railway line in Karachi, organized as a number of networked NGOs, used statist instruments such as surveys against the state itself (e.g., Hasan 2009).

A significant feature of such newly heritagized landscapes is that those involved include numerous actors of widely varying degrees of power and equally varied ideological orientations. In this complex constellations of actors and forces, allies and enemies are not always distinguishable from each other. NGOs play an important, if sometimes ambivalent, role. As the Palestinian cases discussed below demonstrate, civil society organizations are often "not as 'NG' [non-governmental] as they might wish us to believe" (Ferguson and Gupta 2002: 993). These organizations can be small, grassroots, voluntary groups organizing against state urban projects, as the case of Istanbul shows. But NGOs can be found on both sides of the hypothetical divide. Some even effectively constitute an arm of the state, and the case of Silwan's Jewish settlers discussed below illustrates precisely this point. As examples both of government from below (or "counter-governmentality," Appadurai 2001: 35) and of government from afar, NGOs are subject to donor pressures (Fisher 1997): this sometimes takes the form of heritage claims.

Transnational capital and supranational bodies (such as UNESCO, the World Bank, and the European Union), play a key role in reconfiguring the contours of local urban lives (see Ferguson 2006; Trouillot 2001). Cases such as the parallel heritagization and gentrification of the historic center of Rome exemplify a pattern whereby various powerful actors – real estate speculators, underworld groups, local churches and confraternities, banks, and transnational capital – exploit heritage resources at the expense of local residents, sometimes with the connivance of local authorities and often under the cover of newly neoliberal legislation designed to remove such top-down brakes on runaway speculation as rent control. As a result, residents suddenly find themselves facing eviction – sometimes after several generations of relatively minor rent increases – because they cannot pay the newly inflated prices. At the same time, social movements start as local groupings, but either grow into or build upon transnational networks and alliances. Heritage has thus entered an international pattern fueled by the gradual decay or reconfiguration of the institutions of the welfare state or by forms of austerity triggered by economic crisis (De Cesari n.d.).

That non-governmental and transnational forces increasingly shape both urban and heritage outcomes is not necessarily good news. Public participation and community involvement do not necessarily determine those outcomes (see Ferguson 2010; Valverde 2011: 279). Celebrated as making heritage more democratic and accessible, participation has produced uneven effects, and has sometimes legitimated very different policy projects (McQuarrie 2013; Meskell 2012: 160; see also De Cesari n.d.; Waterton 2010; Waterton and Smith 2011). Comparing urban renewal projects carried out by resistant actors such as Hezbollah in Beirut and an alliance of slum dwellers and squatters in Mumbai, Ananya Roy (2009) analyzes the institutionalization of participation as the making of regimes of "civic governmentality" producing governable spaces and subjects. Urban governance through reform and regeneration do often blur the distinction between radical urban citizenship projects and novel configurations of governmentality.

Governments and municipalities use heritage to connive at the dispossession of a growing part of the urban population worldwide (for a survey of urban heritage, see Ruggles 2012). Pioneering work in countries such as South Africa reveals the ways in which urban heritage planning still produces injustice and exclusion (Meskell 2012; Weiss 2014). While the arts of the poor and their survival tactics are celebrated as a way out of poverty and a model of entrepreneurship in times of crisis (Elyachar 2002, 2012), "informal" settlements and their heritage are rapidly being destroyed while their populations are relocated to inhospitable spaces (see also Nakamura 2014).[4]

The idea of the informal settlement itself serves as a justification for urban planners bent on projects of land grab, forced relocation, and heritage destruction. A paradigmatic case is the demolition of "illegal" Palestinian buildings by Israeli authorities that are themselves illegal, at least according to international law, and that constantly deny building permits to their occupied subjects.[5] Such is the operational logic that guides contemporary planning processes. Recent scholarship on slums oscillates between two different positions. Some writings mark informality in celebratory fashion as a "way of life" (AlSayyad 2004) and the "habitus of the dispossessed" (Bayat 2007: 579), and thus as a site of social and cultural creativity. Certainly, much "heritage" is also unrecognized where states have imposed regimes of "transience" such as refugee camps (Malkki 1992; Sayigh 2007).[6] Critical scholars, however, emphasize instead the necessity of recognizing the discriminatory character of planning that rests on the formal–informal dichotomy (notably Roy 2012). Not only are the "formal" and the "informal" deeply entangled, but "informality" itself may constitute a key technology of colonial, crypto-colonial, and postcolonial governance (Gupta 2013; Herzfeld forthcoming; Hull 2012). Until planners can recognize the extraordinary capacity of many slum dwellers for generating the formal rules of community management, these two groups of people will continue to talk past each other, more and more forms of heritage will disappear forever, and the lives of the urban poor will become increasingly precarious. Generous recognition of slum dwellers' capacity for effective self-governance would, conversely, favor greater security for all. Indeed, housing shortages, often created by monopolistic abuses of the heritage concept, may pose the greatest current threat to global security.

Redevelopment and renewal projects across the world allegedly bring millions in investments and community benefits to degraded, de-developed post-industrial neighborhoods. Heritagization is promoted by local governments and other actors as a way out of de-industrialization and as offering the possibility of a new life for what are held to be urban wastelands (Harrison 2013). But how can such so-called development be viewed as reviving old neighborhoods if the society itself is either evicted in its entirety or regulated out of any possibility of engagement in the mapping of future trajectories?

What is being erased, cleansed in the name of heritage, has at least as much of a claim on the name of heritage as what supersedes it. Heritage without people serves only privileged and often absent elites. A neighborhood exists, not simply as a space on a map, but as the site of complex social and human–environment relationships (Appadurai 2001). Such social entities, which are often of considerable age and historical interest, are too tied to particular spatial configurations to survive the destruction of their built environments. The consequence of eviction is social evisceration – the destruction of a heritage in which the wealthy rarely have any interest, other, perhaps, than a prurient nostalgia.

There is something tragically ironic about this process. It is the world of familiar spaces that people struggle to preserve, even though they may frame that struggle in official-sounding language. While some communities are riven by disputes about whether to accept compensation or to defend their ground, as has happened in the famous Bon Pastor neighborhood of low-cost workers' housing in Barcelona (Lawrence-Zuniga 2012), the fact that the choice occasions such bitter dispute suggests that many actors have cultural reasons – often framed as affect – for staying put. By what logic are those reasons excluded from the category of heritage?

The growing drive to heritagize the urban environment recalls Renato Rosaldo's (1989: 108) formulation of "imperialist nostalgia" as something "often found under imperialism, where people mourn the passing of what they themselves have transformed ... [It] uses a pose of 'innocent yearning' both to capture people's imaginations and to conceal its complicity with often brutal domination" (for acts of conservation-cum-destruction, see also Rabinow 1989 on the "liberal" conservation of Muslim religious architecture by French colonial planners). More generally, nostalgia of any kind is often the expression of inequality (Hill 1992) or loss (Boym 2001; Dimova 2013). When it comes to the lived urban environment, some can afford nostalgia; many others, their lives wrecked by new regimes of precariousness, cannot.

Dispossession and Resistance by Heritage I: Palestine/Israel

Outside the Old City of Jerusalem, parts of the occupied Palestinian neighborhood of Silwan/Wadi Hilwah were recently expropriated and "redeveloped" into an archaeological park-cum-Jewish colony, the City of David. Despite rich archaeological findings dating from prehistory until the early Islamic period and later, only the biblical past is presented. The Israeli parks authority has subcontracted the management of the park to an NGO called Ir David Foundation (commonly abbreviated as El-Ad), a militant group close to the ultranationalist-religious Israeli settlers' movement. Founded by a former commander of an elite military unit, El-Ad is committed to the "preservation and development of the Biblical City of David and its environs," a mission that includes "residential revitalization" – in short, colonization.[7] Daily lives go on unobtrusively amidst the manicured ruins of the park: a Palestinian elderly lady making her way home with her groceries or roaming settlers' children point to the literal presence of the political present in the past. Some residents of the park are more and some are definitely less happy about living with archaeology; some are citizens, others are subjects (see Mamdani 1996), depending on their ethnonational community and their closeness to the version of the biblical past promoted on the site. Along the winding central road, prominent signs bear the biblical harp of David and point to "the house of Aner" and other biblical names. These are not archaeological remains but the homes of present-day Jewish settlers, for whom settlement of the Holy Land is a religious-nationalist mission; they are built in neo-biblical style to blend in with the heritagized environment (Pullan and Gwiazda 2009). The land upon which the park and the new settlers' homes are built has been either expropriated or acquired through contested compulsory purchases from Palestinians, forcing many to leave their ancestral neighborhood.[8]

In Wadi Hilwah/City of David a monolithic and exclusivist narrative of the past has been mobilized to displace Palestinians and their living heritage and urban world in favor of the new settlers. Such is the destructive potential of archaeology: excavation areas in the park encroach upon and besiege Palestinian homes, some of which have partly collapsed because of digging conducted beneath them. Exposed to settlers, border police violence, and the constant threat of demolition or expropriation, the remaining Palestinian residents are forced to live a subjugated and less than urban life in a heavily securitized neo-biblical landscape of ruins and fences, tourists and watchtowers, settlers and CCTV cameras – a landscape no longer their own. Even the name of the main street has been changed from Wadi Hilwah Street into "City of David Ascent."

At the City of David, "securitization goes hand in hand with privatization as a mechanism of control over movement within the park and settlement" (Pullan and Gwiazda 2009: 35). The land is close to the most expensive real estate in Jerusalem; heritagization has contributed to the skyrocketing property values (see Ricca 2007). Created in 1986, El-Ad now owns the majority of the lands of the park, and is expanding it. It has achieved all this thanks to the direct and indirect support of several state institutions and agencies. For example, after decades of neglect of the Palestinian neighborhood, the Israeli-run municipality started a project of "regeneration" incorporating several formerly public Palestinian areas for the settlers. Visitors are thus drawn into complicity with this ongoing process of dispossession and expropriation.

The case of the City of David is not an exception but reproduces a pattern critical to the workings of the Israeli nationalist-colonial project: a form of spatial cleansing that borders on ethnic cleansing. Since the early years of the state, archaeology has played a key function in the Israeli state-building process: it has legitimized colonization by producing the material evidence of the ancient land of Israel, thus substantiating the ideology of return (Abu El-Haj 2001). Here, heritagization works on two levels. Ideologically, archaeology produces spatiotemporal continuity – the past made into an affective and effective present so evidently at work at the City of David – so that Palestinian lands are judaized (Benvenisti 2000; Yiftachel 2012) and absorbed into the national territory. For settlers, this signifies living rightfully on the occupied land: "This is not just a stone; this wall is not just a wall … I feel King David's hand as I put my hand on this stone" (El-Ad spokesperson Doron Spilman, quoted in Greenberg 2009: 43). "Feeling" recurs in responses to the material traces of the past, so that "hundreds of Jewish residents live in the City of David and help form the inspiring new mosaic of the return of the Jewish People to their homeland and eternal capital – Jerusalem" (quoted in Greenberg 2009: 42).

Moreover, such projects turn heritage into a technical means of appropriation. As in the case of Bahia, land grab by heritage (B'Tselem 2002; Weizman 2007) passes through the "nationalization of once privately held properties, ostensibly for the benefit of all" (Collins 2011a: 123), with the state "reclassify[ing] privately owned or incompletely registered lands … as cultural possessions of a collectivity" (124). Unfortunately for Jerusalem's Palestinians, this collectivity does not include them, and their homes and livelihoods – their urban social worlds – are wrecked in the process now known as "urbicide" (see Campbell, Graham, and Monk 2007).

Oddly, the park is not managed by the Israeli national park authority but by an alleged NGO. The state itself, protected from being the immediate agent of violence and dispossession, provides, in part through excavations conducted by the Israel Antiquities Authority, the legal and material infrastructure for El-Ad, while harnessing its benefits after the fact (see Weizman 2014). At the time of this writing, demolition orders have been given for eight Palestinian structures around a plot slated by the Israeli-run municipality to become the new extension of the City of

David.[9] (The municipality considers these Palestinian homes illegal because they are built without its permits; these demolition orders, however, should be read against the fact that, since the Israeli annexation of East Jerusalem, the municipality has not awarded Silwan's Palestinian residents a single building permit.) By thus arbitrarily drawing the line between urban formality and informality, and between heritage and non-heritage, both the local and the national governments, operating within a deeply contested legality, unilaterally set the legal boundaries to their advantage.

In places such as Silwan/the City of David, where the moral and affective force of nationalism and the past are mobilized to efface a brutal colonial reality, heritage emerges as the site of a two-sided dialectic. Colonial ruins may turn into "epicenters of renewed claims ... history in a spirited voice ... sites that animate new possibilities, bids for entitlement, and unexpected political projects" (Stoler 2008: 198). The City of David has become a symbol of non-violent Palestinian resistance against the occupation – even if it has not proved successful – as well as the trigger of some friction within Israeli society thanks to the protest of a small but vocal group of archaeologists, appalled by such misuse of their discipline (they have created an activist organization, Emek Shaveh, which organizes critical tours of the site and regularly publishes updates on its website).[10]

As a counterpoint next to the entrance of the City of David, there is a small stone building covered by a ramshackle roof where a large sign announces the "Wadi Hilwah Information Center – Silwan." The purpose of the center, run by local residents, is to inform people about human rights violations in Silwan and to "ask the people of Israel and the world to support their struggle for the right to live in their village as part of a multi-cultural Jerusalem based on principles of equality and peace."[11] The organization has its own active website that publishes news updates about human rights abuses in the territories, with a special focus on the travails – frequent arrests, home demolitions, and settlers' use of archaeology as a tool of dispossession – of Jerusalemites. The center's website presentation points straight at the politics of heritage:

> We ... do not allow any person to obscure our deep rooted identity which lies in the houses, stones, trees, gardens, springs, and sky of our village [Silwan] ... We are proud of the full history of our village and proud of being the owners of this beautiful legacy. We acknowledge all the civilizations that have passed through the village, those who constructed the village or even those who destroyed it and wreaked havoc.[12]

A similar dialectics of dispossession and resistance through heritage has been unfolding in the Old City of Hebron, the most populous West Bank city after Jerusalem. Hebron is a key historic and religious site, with its traditional Arab-Islamic architecture built around the city's important shrine, the Haram Ibrahimi or Tomb of the Patriarchs, sacred to both Jews and Muslims because it is believed to house the tombs of several biblical patriarchs, including Abraham, the father of both faiths. Since the beginning of the Israeli occupation of the West Bank in 1967, groups of radical religious-nationalist Jewish settlers have occupied a number of buildings throughout the Old City, close to the shrine. For settlers, the Tomb of the Patriarchs is the strongest evidence of their right to the city. As David Wilder, spokesperson for the new Jewish community of Hebron, said in a recent interview:

> People [settlers] who live here [in Old Hebron] of course live here for ideological reasons ... Keep in mind that the Tomb of the Patriarchs down the street is the second holiest site

> for the Jewish people in all the world. So, this is all Jewish land. When I came back here, I did not come back here to conquer and occupy foreign land. I came home. I came back to where Jews had lived.[13]

For settlers, archaeology in its very materiality speaks of their roots in the city and the rightfulness of their presence. Inhabiting the archaeological remains and the Jewish heritage of Hebron and "revitalizing" them through ritual practices, pilgrimages, and festivals transform colonization into the repossession of ancestral lands.

Once again supported by the overwhelming power of the Israeli state, settlers' assertion of their right to the city dispossessed local Palestinians of both homes and heritage and triggered the militarization and segregation of the Old City. Economic life has ceased with the occupation of key urban nodes such as the vegetable market and the bus station and with the closing of the majority of the local stores (B'Tselem 2007); the targets of systemic violence, especially middle-class Palestinians have left the Old City, their number dropping from over 7,500 before 1967 to approximately 400 in the early 1990s. Here, too, heritage provides an example of the strategic reversibility of power since it became the platform for a Palestinian counter-settlement project.

At the time of the Oslo Agreements in 1994, a group of local politicians, architects, and activists created a committee to restore the Old City and to bring Palestinians back to live in the restored old houses so as not to leave them abandoned and thus prey to occupation by the settlers. They set in place the Hebron Rehabilitation Committee (HRC). This organization was clearly the product of the Palestinian strategy at the time, combining negotiations with different forms of resistance designed to strengthen their negotiating position; over the years, however, it turned into something different. The winner of several architectural and heritage prizes – proud to be connected to international heritage expert networks and to speak the language of scientific heritage – HRC continues to work toward the restoration and rehabilitation of Hebron's decaying historic buildings and toward improving the livelihoods of resident Palestinians. By 2013 it had brought back over 6,000 Palestinians to live in the Old City, where gradually, especially in recent years, stores have been reopening and an appearance of normalcy is returning.

Colonization in Hebron continues, but at a slower pace. HRC's focus was at first exclusively on restoring houses in order to stop settlement expansion, but it subsequently moved to a much broader approach targeting the "development" and "revitalization" of the Old City, a mission that includes running a number of socioeconomic development initiatives and a legal center to monitor settlers' violation of human rights, as well as preparing the heritage and tourism master plan for the whole city. In the absence of state structures, and in an area under Israeli military control, this organization has come to run the administration of the Old City in the manner of a department of the municipality, receiving millions of dollars from European and Arab donors (De Cesari 2011). Recently, HRC has begun to prepare the nomination of Hebron's Old City for the World Heritage List, a move that is also intended to strengthen Palestinian claims to local territorial sovereignty.

Similar organizations and initiatives across the West Bank have carried out numerous urban regeneration projects, targeting the restoration and social reuse of the local vernacular architecture (De Cesari 2010b, n.d.). The Israeli occupation has profoundly shaped these heritage projects, all of which fundamentally aim to preserve what Palestinian intellectual and activist Raja Shehadeh (2007) has called a "vanishing landscape," a heritage-rich fabric of human–environment interactions.

In Palestine/Israel, heritage is thus mobilized to transform contested lands and to claim sovereignty and control.

Dispossession and Resistance by Heritage II: Pom Mahakan

The case of Pom Mahakan in Bangkok, Thailand, already well documented (see Herzfeld 2003, 2006, 2013), offers instructive parallels and contrasts. A community of roughly three hundred inhabitants has resisted attempts by the Bangkok Metropolitan Administration (BMA) to evict the entire group from its dwelling area. Over a period of nearly 23 years at the time of writing, the community has played a cat-and-mouse game with the bureaucrats in the courts; engaged the bureaucrats' own tactics of playing for time; faced a possibly violent army onslaught, mostly deflected, on its homes; and developed a rich language of heritage in order to counter the authorities' attacks on its legitimacy with an assumption of expertise and especially of "local knowledge" – this last blazoned on a very official-looking shingle announcing the main function of the rather makeshift community resource museum. Brown and white signs marking items of historical interest at various points in the very small space occupied by the community significantly mimic the style of the official signage outside.

Most community members are fairly recent arrivals; only three families can trace any connection to the original royal settlement of bureaucrats. But that diversity of origins has itself allowed the leaders to claim a part in Thailand's much-vaunted regional diversity. At the same time, the predominantly royalist tone of the leaders' pronouncements about heritage provide a means of suggesting that attacks on the community represent attacks on the very essence of what it means to be Thai. This is especially true of the community's frequent attempts to historicize its vernacular architecture in terms of the reigns of various kings of the present dynasty – a suggestive irony when one considers that one of the persistent complaints about heritage conservation in Thailand is precisely that it fails to respect vernacular traditions (see especially Askew 1996). One of the leaders, asked whether this use of an official discourse might not be identifying the community too closely with the political tradition of the state, showed in his response that he thought that the strategy was working, that the community had no other choice, but that the residents were aware of the dangers of tying their identity too closely to a single narrative. In what he said, there was a further implication, probably dampened by prevailing fears of discussing sensitive political issues: since the threatened eviction was supposed to make way for a park in honor of the Thai queen, only a resolutely royalist stance could work.

Communities in such situations have limited choices. Legally the majority of the residents were considered to be squatters; it is significant that, whereas the BMA accused them of "invading" (*buk luk*) the space, they retorted that it was the BMA that was "invading." (This reciprocal use of insults is characteristic; when BMA officials called them "obstinate" [*doea*], they used the same epithet in response.) Their vision more generally mirrors that of the authorities; they are technically outside the old city wall and of the fortress from which they draw their name, but from their perspective it is the bustling modern city that lies outside their "historical" space – a space from which, in their view, the bureaucrats have alienated themselves by refusing to recognize their value as a "historic" community. In a word, they have taken the official model of historicity and made it their own – to the point, moreover, of treating the various family spirit shrines as shrines to the ancestors of the Thai people in general.

The bureaucrats' plan replaces the community with an empty lawn; this unpeopled vision of heritage was confirmed by a court decision asserting that a "public park," as the space is intended to become, could not contain private houses. Such self-serving logic leads local activists to comment that it is the law, not the community's perspective, that needs fixing. More to the immediate point, it occludes what used to be a crucial part of the Thai national doctrine – that the people, along with the monarchy and the Buddhist religion, were the core of Thainess – in favor of what the planners clearly hope will provided a "civilized" space: a lawn surrounded by a formal white balustrade. Rumors that a MacDonald's would be built on the site proved untrue, or at least premature, but they indicate that the battle lines were being drawn between local community interests and a transnational economic system that demanded immediate profit in a "free" market.

The story of Pom Mahakan is still playing out. The fact that the majority of the residents have remained on the site suggests that the strategy of absorbing and rebroadcasting the rhetoric of monarchical Thainess has served the community well thus far; whether it will continue to do so is unclear and will depend on future political developments at the national level, but also on the leaders' capacity for negotiation in a conflictual space – they are very proud of having escaped serious difficulties as a result of the recent Red–Yellow Shirt confrontations, both factions being represented in the community in an exemplary display of peaceful co-existence.

As with the Palestinian cases, the Pom Mahakan situation partly revolves around conflicting interpretations of law. But here the question of national sovereignty is not at stake. Rather, the underlying issues concern the content of national culture and the extent to which the rule of law guarantees indisputably ethnic Thais the right to decent habitation and permits them to advance an alternative vision – however partial, given current political tensions – of what it means to be Thai and of who should have the responsibility for curating such a potentially important heritage site. As in the Palestinian cases, too, conflicting interpretations of heritage serve the aims of disputants to a territorial conflict; but this territory is important, not because its ultimate national identity is at stake, but because it is used to represent in miniature two conflicting visions of the past and future of the Thai national polity. Heritage discourse can feed interethnic and intranational conflict alike; the reversibility of the "authorized" power play is common to both situations.

Dispossession and Resistance by Heritage III: Rome

The Palestinian and Thai cases both suggest that ethnicized conflict can give the oppressed some chance of at least partial success. That is much more difficult to achieve when conflict involves unclear class distinctions in an otherwise peaceful cultural setting. Especially when residents are renters rather than owners (see also Caftanzoglou 2001 on Athens; cf. Herzfeld 1991), the chances of success are slight. In the Monti district of Rome, one of the last working-class areas in the center of the city, the sheer multiplicity of powerful players and the weakness of divided local communities representing polarizations to left and right have, in combination with the "liberalization" (i.e., abolition) of rent control sapped the capacity of economically weak merchants and artisans (Herzfeld 2009). These residents, lacking collateral, are also unable to borrow funds – except from unscrupulous loan-sharks – to stand against banks, churches, property speculators, and real-estate developers, especially once the formerly despised buildings are reconceptualized as historic. This is a classic clash of the opposed ethical imperatives of the right to housing and the protection of architectural and other forms of heritage, and offers a contrast with the convergence of these concerns in the Pakistani, Palestinian, and Thai cases mentioned here. Imposing *palazzi*, once home to numerous local families but latterly allowed to decay in the hope that rats and peeling walls would force the residents out, are now advertised on line as desirable and expensively furnished rentals, much as the old *hutong* in Beijing have been displaced by newer structures offering a supposedly authentic (but anachronistic) experience with conveniences that were never part of the cramped local living conditions.[14]

Pressures to leave are violent expressions of the standoff between neoliberal and state forces on the one hand and resisting residents, often defined as illegal squatters, on the other. Such pressures include menacing nocturnal telephone calls, cruel enactments of fitting inhabited spaces to new requirements once the present residents have been forced out, and, above all, the use of neglect and – more actively – fires that are far from accidental. Force may be met with force, as Chance (forthcoming) has documented for the reciprocal use of fire in South Africa, while legal delaying tactics are not uniquely the privilege of the powerful. But residents usually have less access to both material and legal resources, so the contest is usually an uneven one. The evidence lies in outcomes around the world.

The violence thus described is a common prelude to spatial cleansing. Fire empties vast spaces and leaves them at the developers' mercy. Neglect that makes habitation untenable achieves the same effect more slowly; ironically, the accumulation of refuse sometimes accelerates the process of spatial cleansing.

The case studies described here show the enormous variety of patterns in the clash between housing and heritage. As anthropological research reveals ever more complex nuance in the invocation of heritage on all sides of such conflicts, especially when these conflicts pit local communities against nationalistic, colonial, and neoliberal juggernauts, the need for a critical examination of heritage discourses, and especially of the politics of the supposedly apolitical forms of relevant expertise, becomes ever more urgent. That examination must be based, as we have suggested here, on the ethnographic exploration of local specificities. To do otherwise is to yield to the generalizing logic and destructive simplification that together now constitute the greatest threats to the survival of cultural diversity as a resource for humanity's future.

NOTES

1 The authors wish to express their gratitude to Sophie van den Elzen for her efficient help in tidying up the bibliography and citations in the final phase of compilation. We also thank Lynn Meskell for presciently proposing our collaboration and for her patience with us as we communicated across five different countries.

2 See also the websites Palestine Remembered, http://www.palestineremembered.com/ and Zochrot, http://zochrot.org/en (accessed November 20, 2014).

3 The imperialist discourse of antiquities is still alive and well today, especially in the rhetoric of those of the museum establishment opposed to the repatriation of colonial spolia; they advance the argument that the "West" has saved these *spolia* from secure destruction (see Cuno 2008). Also in these modern cases, the argument that natives do not care for sites well enough is being used to dispossess rightful owners of their heritage.

4 A related case that has not, to our knowledge, being analyzed thus far in terms of erasure of heritage is that of Roma communities being the target of racist violence by both states and citizens, as well as of ongoing evictions across European countries (on the European Roma and memory, see van Baar 2011; see also Nationalities Blog, http://nationalities.wordpress.com/2010/09/26/huub-van-baar-expulsion-fever-in-europe-the-case-of-the-roma/, accessed November 20,2014).
5 See B'Tselem – The Israeli Information Center for Human Rights in the Occupied Territories, http://www.btselem.org/planning_and_building/statistics; Israeli Committee Against House Demolitions, http://www.icahd.org/ (accessed November 20,2014).
6 See also Palestine Remembered, http://www.palestineremembered.com/ (accessed November 20,2014).
7 The Ir David Foundation, http://www.cityofdavid.org.il/en/The-Ir-David-Foundation (accessed November 20, 2014).
8 See Wadi Hilweh Information Center, "The Story Behind the Tourist Site," http://silwanic.net/docs/WadiHilwahENG.pdf (accessed November 20, 2014); see also Pullan and Gwiazda (2009), Greenberg (2009).
9 See http://www.reuters.com/article/2014/01/29/us-israel-palestinians-archaeology-idUSBREA0S0F520140129 (accessed November 24, 2014).
10 For Emek Shaveh's website, see http://alt-arch.org/en/about-us/ (accessed November 20, 2014).
11 See Wadi Hilweh Information Center, "About Silwan," http://silwanic.net/?page_id=684 (accessed November 20, 2014).
12 See Wadi Hilweh Information Center, "About Silwan," http://silwanic.net/?page_id=684 (accessed November 20, 2014).
13 See FQ TV, "Hebron, 'Lo Stato di Palestina? Sì, ma in Texas,'" http://tv.ilfattoquotidiano.it/2011/08/30/hebron-lo-stato-di-palestina-si-ma-in-texas/154243/ (accessed November 20, 2014).
14 See also Non Arkaraprasertkul (2013) for a comparable perspective on gentrification in Shanghai.

REFERENCES

Abu El-Haj, N. (2001) *Facts on the Ground: Archaeological Practice and Territorial Self-Fashioning in Israeli Society*. Chicago, IL: University of Chicago Press.

Alonso González, P. (2014) From a given to a construct: Heritage as commons. *Cultural Studies* 28(3): 359–390.

AlSayyad, N. (2004) Urban Informality as a Way of Life, in A. Roy and N. AlSayyad (eds), *Urban Informality: Transnational Perspectives from the Middle East, Latin America, and South Asia*. Lanham, MD: Lexington Books, pp. 7–30.

Appadurai, A. (2001) Deep democracy: Urban governmentality and the horizon of politics. *Environment & Urbanization* 13(2): 23–44.

Arkaraprasertkul, N. (2013) Traditionalism as a way of life: The sense of home in a Shanghai alleyway. *Harvard Asia Quarterly* 15(3/4): 15–25.

Arnold, B. (1990) The past as propaganda: Totalitarian archaeology in Nazi Germany. *Antiquity* 64: 464–478.

Askew, M. (1996) The rise of Moradok and the decline of the Yarn: Heritage and cultural construction in urban Thailand. *Sojourn* 11: 183–210.

B'Tselem (2002) *Land Grab: Israel's Settlement Policy in the West Bank*. Jerusalem: B'Tselem. Available at: http://www.btselem.org/publications/fulltext/200205_land_grab. Accessed November 20, 2014.

B'Tselem (2007) *Ghost Town: Israel's Separation Policy and Forced Eviction of Palestinians from the Center of Hebron*. Joint report with the Association for Civil Rights in Israel, May. Jerusalem: B'Tselem. Available at: www.btselem.org/Download/200705_Hebron_eng.pdf. Accessed November 20, 2014.

Baillie, B. (2013) Memorializing the "Martyred City": Negotiating Vukovar's Wartime Past, in W. Pullan and B. Baillie (eds), *Locating Urban Conflicts: Ethnicity, Nationalism and the Everyday*. Basingstoke: Palgrave Macmillan, pp. 115–131.

Bartu Candan, A. and B. Kolluoğlu (2008) Emerging spaces of neoliberalism: A gated town and a public housing project in Istanbul. *New Perspectives on Turkey* 39: 5–46.

Bayat, A. (2007) Radical religion and the habitus of the dispossessed: Does Islamic militancy have an urban ecology? *International Journal of Urban and Regional Research* 31(3): 579–590.

Beck, U. (2000) The cosmopolitan perspective: Sociology of the second age of modernity. *British Journal of Sociology* 51(1): 79–105.

Ben-Yehuda, N. (2002) *Sacrificing Truth: Archaeology and the Myth of Masada*. Amherst, NY: Humanity Books.

Benvenisti, M. (2000) *Sacred Landscape: The Buried History of the Holy Land since 1948*. Berkeley: University of California Press.

Bernardoni, M., F. Mat, P. Maestri, L. Nocera, F. Ruggero, and F. Salomoni (2013) *#GeziPark: Coordinate di una rivolta*. Roma: Edizioni Alegre.

Bernbeck, R. and S. Pollock (1996) Ayodhya, archaeology, and identity. *Current Anthropology* 37(1): S138–S142.

Boym, S. (2001) *The Future of Nostalgia*. New York: Basic Books.

Breglia, L. (2006) *Monumental Ambivalence: The Politics of Heritage*. Austin: University of Texas Press.

Brown, K. (1998) Contests of Heritage and the Politics of Preservation in the Former Yugoslav Republic of Macedonia, in L. Meskell (ed.), *Archaeology under Fire: Culture and Politics in the Eastern Mediterranean*. New York and London: Routledge, pp. 68–86.

Byrne, D. (2014) *Counterheritage: Critical Perspectives on Heritage Conservation in Asia*. New York and London: Routledge.

Caftanzoglou, R. (2001) Shadow of the Sacred Rock: Contrasting Discourses of Place under the Acropolis, in B. Bender and M. Winer (eds), *Contested Landscapes: Movement, Exile and Place*. Oxford: Berg, pp. 21–36.

Caldeira, T. (2001) *City of Walls: Crime, Segregation, and Citizenship in São Paulo*. Berkeley: University of California Press.

Campbell, D., S. Graham, and D. Bertrand Monk (2007) Introduction to urbicide: The killing of cities? *Theory and Event* 10(2): 1–8.

Cellamare, C. (2008) *Fare città: Pratiche urbane e storie di luoghi*. Milan: Elèuthera.

Chance, K. (forthcoming) "Where there is fire, there is politics": Governance and ungovernability in urban South Africa. *Cultural Anthropology*.

Cochrane, A. (2013) Breaking Down the Walls of Heartache: Reflections on the Ordinary Spaces of Division and Unification in Berlin, in W. Pullan and B. Baillie (eds), *Locating Urban Conflicts: Ethnicity, Nationalism and the Everyday*. Basingstoke: Palgrave Macmillan, pp. 214–232.

Colla, E. (2007) *Conflicted Antiquities: Egyptology, Egyptomania, Egyptian Modernity*. Durham, NC: Duke University Press.

Collins, J. (2008) "But what if i should need to defecate in your neighborhood, madame?" Empire, redemption, and the "tradition of the oppressed" in a Brazilian World Heritage site. *Cultural Anthropology* 23(2): 279–328.

Collins, J. (2011a) Culture, content, and the enclosure of human being: UNESCO's "intangible" heritage in the new millennium. *Radical History Review* 109: 120–135.

Collins, J. (2011b) Melted gold and national bodies: The hermeneutics of depth and the value of history in Brazilian racial politics. *American Ethnologist* 38(4): 683–700.

Colomb, C. (2012) *Staging the New Berlin. Place Marketing and the Politics of Urban Reinvention post-1989*. London: Routledge.

Cuno, J. B. (2008) *Who Owns Antiquity?: Museums and the Battle over Our Ancient Heritage*. Princeton, NJ: Princeton University Press.

Daniel, E. V. (1996) *Charred Lullabies: Chapters in an Anthropography of Violence*. Princeton, NJ: Princeton University Press.

Davis, R. D. (2010) *Palestinian Village Histories: Geographies of the Displaced*. Stanford, CA: Stanford University Press.
De Cesari, C. (2008) Cultural Heritage beyond the "State": Palestinian Heritage between Nationalism and Transnationalism. Ph.D. dissertation, Department of Cultural and Social Anthropology, Stanford University, California.
De Cesari, C. (2010a) World heritage and mosaic universalism: A view from Palestine. *Journal of Social Archaeology* 10(3): 299–324.
De Cesari, C. (2010b) Creative heritage: Palestinian heritage NGOs and defiant arts of government. *American Anthropologist* 112(4): 625–637.
De Cesari, C. (2011) *Cultural governmentality: Government through heritage conservation in Old Hebron*. Conflict in Cities Working Papers Series No. 23. Available at: http://www.conflictincities.org/PDFs/WorkingPaper23CorrectVersion.pdf. Accessed November 20, 2014.
De Cesari, C. (n.d.) *Heritage and the Struggle for Palestine*. Book manuscript in progress.
De Cesari, C. and A. Rigney (2014) Introduction, in C. De Cesari and A. Rigney (eds), *Transnational Memory: Circulation, Articulation, Scales*. Berlin: de Gruyter.
Díaz-Andreu, M. and T. Champion (1996) *Nationalism and Archaeology in Europe*. Boulder, CO: Westview.
Dimova, R. (2013) *Ethno-Baroque: Materiality, Aesthetics and Conflict in Modern-Day Macedonia*. New York: Berghahn.
Dinçer, İ. (2011) The Impact of Neoliberal Policies on Historic Urban Space: Areas of Urban Renewal in Istanbul. *International Planning Studies* 16(1): 43–60.
Dumper, M. (2014) *Jerusalem Unbound: Geography, History, and the Future of the Holy City*. New York: Columbia University Press.
Elyachar, J. (2002) Empowerment money: The World Bank, non-governmental organizations, and the value of culture in Egypt. *Public Culture* 14(3): 493–513.
Elyachar, J. (2012) Next practices: Knowledge, infrastructure, and public goods at the bottom of the pyramid. *Public Culture* 24(1): 109–129.
Eraydin, A. and T. Taşan-Kok (2013) State response to contemporary urban movements in Turkey: A critical overview of state entrepreneurialism and authoritarian interventions. *Antipode*, 46(1): 110–129.
Ferguson, J. (2006) Transnational Topographies of Power: Beyond "the State" and "Civil Society" in the Study of African Politics, in *Global Shadows: Africa in the Neoliberal World Order*. Durham, NC: Duke University Press.
Ferguson, J. (2010) The uses of neoliberalism. *Antipode* 41(s1): 166–184.
Ferguson, J. and A. Gupta (2002) Spatializing states: Toward an ethnography of neoliberal governmentality. *American Ethnologist* 29(4): 981–1002.
Ferguson, T. J. (1996) Native Americans and the practice of archaeology. *Annual Review of Anthropology* 25: 63–79.
Fisher, W. (1997) Doing good? The politics and antipolitics of NGO practices. *Annual Review of Anthropology* 26: 439–464.
Foucault, M. (1991) Governmentality, in G. Burchell, C. Gordon, and P. Miller (eds), *The Foucault Effect: Studies in Governmentality*. Chicago, IL: University of Chicago Press, pp. 87–104.
Franquesa, J. (2013) On Keeping and Selling: The Political Economy of Heritage Making in Contemporary Spain. *Current Anthropology* 54(3): 346–369.
Göktürk, D., I. Soysal, and L. Türeli (2010) Introduction, in D. Göktürk, I. Soysal, and L. Türeli (eds), *Orienting Istanbul: Cultural Capital of Europe?* London: Routledge, pp. 1–24.
Graham, B., G. Ashworth, and J. Tunbridge (2000) *A Geography of Heritage: Power, Culture and Economy*. London: Arnold.
Greenberg, R. (2009) Towards an inclusive archaeology in Jerusalem: The case of Silwan/the City of David. *Public Archaeology* 8(1): 35–50.
Gupta, A. (2013) Messy bureaucracies: Comment on Hull, Matthew. 2012. *Government of Paper: The Materiality of Bureaucracy in Urban Pakistan*. Berkeley: University of California Press. *HAU: Journal of Ethnographic Theory* 3(3): 435–440.

Hamilakis, Y. (2007) *The Nation and Its Ruins: Antiquity, Archaeology, and National Imagination in Greece*. Oxford: Oxford University Press.
Handler, R. (1985) On Having a Culture: Nationalism and the Preservation of Quebec's Patrimony, in G. Stocking (ed.), *Objects and Others: Essays on Museums and Material Culture*. Madison: University of Wisconsin Press, pp. 192–217.
Handler, R. (1988) *Nationalism and the Politics of Culture in Quebec*. Madison: University of Wisconsin Press.
Harms, E. (2011) *Saigon's Edge: On the Margins of Ho Chi Minh City*. Minneapolis: University of Minnesota Press.
Harms, E. (2012) Beauty as control in the new Saigon: Eviction, new urban zones, and atomized dissent in a Southeast Asian city. *American Ethnologist* 39(4): 735–750.
Harrison, R. (2010) Heritage as Social Action, in S. West (ed.), *Understanding Heritage in Practice*. Manchester: Manchester University Press, pp. 240–276.
Harrison, R. (2013) *Heritage: Critical Approaches*. London: Routledge.
Harvey, D. (2006) The Right to the City, in R. Scholar (ed.), *Divided Cities: The Oxford Amnesty Lectures 2003*. Oxford: Oxford University Press, pp. 83–103.
Harvey, D. (2012) *Rebel Cities: From the Right to the City to the Urban Revolution*. London: Verso.
Harvey, D. (2013) On Why Struggles over Urban Space Matter: An Interview with David Harvey, by Hiba Bou Akar and Nada Moumtaz. *Jadaliyya*. Available at: http://www.jadaliyya.com/pages/index/15156/on-why-struggles-over-urban-space-matter_an-interv. Accessed November 20, 2014.
Hasan, A. (2009) Land, CBOs and the Karachi Circular Railway. *Environment & Urbanization* 21(2): 331–345.
Hayden, D. (1995) *The Power of Place: Urban Landscapes as Public History*. Cambridge, MA: MIT Press.
Hayden, R. M. (2002) Antagonistic tolerance: Competitive sharing of religious sites in South Asia and the Balkans. *Current Anthropology* 43: 205–231.
Heatherington, T. (2010) *Wild Sardinia: Indigeneity and the Global Dreamtimes of Environmentalism*. Seattle: University of Washington Press.
Herscher, A. (2010) *Violence Taking Place: The Architecture of the Kosovo Conflict*. Stanford, CA: Stanford University Press.
Herzfeld, M. (1991) *A Place in History*. Princeton, NJ: Princeton University Press.
Herzfeld, M. (2002) The absent presence: Discourses of crypto-colonialism. *South Atlantic Quarterly* 101: 899–926.
Herzfeld, M. (2003) Pom Mahakan: Humanity and order in the historic center of Bangkok. *Thailand Human Rights Journal* 1: 101–119.
Herzfeld, M. (2005) Political optics and the occlusion of intimate knowledge. *American Anthropologist* 107(3): 369–376.
Herzfeld, M. (2006) Spatial cleansing: Monumental vacuity and the idea of the West. *Journal of Material Culture*, 11: 127–149.
Herzfeld, M. (2009) *Evicted from Eternity: The Restructuring of Modern Rome*. Chicago, IL: University of Chicago Press.
Herzfeld, M. (2010) Engagement, gentrification, and the neoliberal hijacking of history. *Current Anthropology* 51(S2): 252–267.
Herzfeld, M. (2013) The crypto-colonial dilemmas of Rattanakosin Island. *Journal of the Siam Society* 100: 209–223.
Herzfeld, M. (forthcoming) *Siege of the Spirits: Community and Polity in Bangkok*. Chicago: University of Chicago Press.
Herzl, T. (1902) *Altneuland*. Leipzig: Hermann Seemann Nachfolger.
Hewison, R. (1987) *The Heritage Industry*. London: Methuen.
Hill, J. H. (1992) "Today there is no respect": Nostalgia, "respect" and oppositional discourse in Mexicano (Nahuatl) language ideology. *Pragmatics* 2(3): 263–280.
Hobsbawm, E. and T. Ranger (1983) *The Invention of Tradition*. Cambridge: Cambridge University Press.

Hodder, I. (2012) *Entangled: An Archaeology of the Relationships between Humans and Things*. Oxford: Wiley Blackwell.
Holston, J. (1989) *The Modernist City: An Anthropological Critique of Brasilia*. Chicago, IL: University of Chicago Press.
Hull, M. (2012) *Government of Paper: The Materiality of Bureaucracy in Urban Pakistan*. Berkeley: University of California Press.
Jacobs, J. (1961) *The Death and Life of Great American Cities*. New York: Random House
Jenkyns, R. (1980) *The Victorians and Ancient Greece*. Oxford: Basil Blackwell.
Kapferer, B. (1988) *Legends of People, Myths of State: Violence, Intolerance, and Political Culture in Sri Lanka and Australia*. Washington, DC: Smithsonian Institution Press.
Karakasidou, A. (1993) Politicizing culture: Negating ethnic identity in Greek Macedonia. *Journal of Modern Greek Studies* 11: 1–28.
Khalidi, W. (1992) *All That Remains: The Palestinian Villages Occupied and Depopulated by Israel in 1948*. Washington, DC: Institute for Palestine Studies.
Kohl, P. (1998) Nationalism and archaeology: On the construction of nations and the reconstructions of the remote past. *Annual Review of Anthropology* 27: 223–246.
Kohl, P. and C. Fawcett (1995) *Nationalism, Politics, and the Practice of Archaeology*. Cambridge: Cambridge University Press.
Kosek, J. (2006) *Understories: The Political Life of Forests in New Mexico*. Durham, NC: Duke University Press.
Lamprakos, M. (2014) The idea of the historic city. *Change over Time: An International Journal of Conservation and the Built Environment* 4(1): 8–38.
Latour, B. (2005) *Reassembling the Social: An Introduction to Actor-Network-Theory*. Oxford: Oxford University Press.
Lawrence-Zuniga, D. (2012) Barcelona's *Repensar Bon Pastor*: A collaboration of anthropologists and architects. *American Anthropologist* 114: 526–527.
Lefebvre, H. (1968) *Le droit à la ville* [The Right to the City], 2nd edn. Paris: Anthropos.
Lentin, R. (2010) Zochrot: Nakba Co-Memory as Performance, in *Co-Memory and Melancholia: Israelis Memorialising the Palestinian Nakba*. Manchester: Manchester University Press, pp. 182–219.
Lowenthal, D. (1996) *Possessed by the Past: The Heritage Crusade and the Spoils of History*. New York: Free Press.
MacDonald, S. (2013) *Memorylands: Heritage and Identity in Europe Today*. London: Routledge.
Maffi, I. (2009) The emergence of cultural heritage in Jordan: The itinerary of a colonial invention. *Journal of Social Archaeology* 9(1): 5–34.
Malkki, L. (1992) National geographic: The rooting of peoples and the territorialization of national identity among scholars and refugees. *Cultural Anthropology* 7(1): 24–44.
Mamdani, M. (1996) *Citizen and Subject: Contemporary Africa and the Legacy of Late Colonialism*. Princeton, NJ: Princeton University Press.
McQuarrie, M. (2013) No contest: Participatory technologies and the transformation of urban authority. *Public Culture* 25(1): 143–175.
Meskell, L. (ed.) (1998) *Archaeology under Fire: Nationalism, Politics and Heritage in the Eastern Mediterranean and Middle East*. London: Routledge.
Meskell, L. (2002) Negative heritage and past mastering in archaeology. *Anthropological Quarterly* 75(3): 557–574.
Meskell, L. (2005) Sites of Violence: Terrorism, Tourism, and Heritage in the Archaeological Present, in L. Meskell and P. Pels (eds), *Embedding Ethics*. Oxford: Berg, pp. 123–146.
Meskell, L. (2012) *The Nature of Heritage: The New South Africa*. Oxford: Blackwell.
Miller, D. (ed.) (2005) *Materiality*. Durham, NC: Duke University Press.
Miller, P. and N. Rose (2008) *Governing the Present: Administering Economic, Social and Personal Life*. Cambridge: Polity.
Mitchell, T. (2002) Heritage and Violence, in *Rule of Experts*. Berkeley: University of California Press, pp. 179–206.

Muehlebach, A. (2009) *Complexio oppositorum*: Notes on the left in neoliberal Italy. *Public Culture* 21: 495–515.
Nakamura, C. (2014) Mumbai's quiet histories: Critical intersections of the urban poor, historical struggles, and heritage spaces. *Journal of Social Archaeology* 14(2): 1–25.
Navaro-Yashin, Y. (2009) Affective spaces, melancholic objects: Ruination and the production of anthropological knowledge. *Journal of the Royal Anthropological Institute* 15(1): 1–18.
Nocera, L. (2013) Taksim tra progetti e visioni: Cosa si cela dietro la minaccia del cemento, in M. Bernardoni, F. Mat, P. Maestri, L. Nocera, F. Salomoni, and F. Ruggero (eds), *#GeziPark: Coordinate di una rivolta*. Roma: Edizioni Alegre.
Odermatt, P. (1996) Built heritage and the politics of (re)presentation: Local reactions to the appropriation of the monumental past in Sardinia. With commentary by M. Herzfeld, B. Annis, and O. Löfgren. *Archaeological Dialogues* 3: 95–136.
Pappe, I. (2006) *The Ethnic Cleansing of Palestine*. Oxford: Oneworld.
Pullan, W. and M. Gwiazda (2009) "City of David": Urban design and frontier heritage. *Jerusalem Quarterly* 39: 29–37.
Rabinow, P. (1989) *French Modern: Norms and Forms of the Social Environment*. Cambridge, MA: MIT Press.
Ratnagar, S. (2004) Archaeology at the heart of a political confrontation: The case of Ayodhya. *Current Anthropology* 45: 239–59.
Ricca, S. (2007) *Reinventing Jerusalem: Israel's Reconstruction of the Jewish Quarter after 1967*. London: Tauris.
Rosaldo, R. (1989) Imperialist nostalgia. *Representations* 26: 107–122.
Rose, N. and P. Miller (1992) Political power beyond the state: Problematics of government. *British Journal of Sociology* 43(2): 173–205.
Roy, A. (2009) Civic governmentality: The politics of inclusion in Beirut and Mumbai. *Antipode* 41: 159–79.
Roy, A. (2012) Urban Informality: The Production of Space and Practice of Planning, in R. Crane and R. Weber (eds), *The Oxford Handbook of Urban Planning*. Oxford: Oxford University Press. Available at: http://www.oxfordhandbooks.com/view/10.1093/oxfordhb/9780195374995.001.0001/oxfordhb-9780195374995-e-33. Accessed 20 July 2014.
Ruggles, D. F. (2012) *On Location: Heritage Cities and Sites*. New York: Springer.
Samuel, R. (1994) *Theatres of Memory*. London: Verso.
Sayigh, R. (2007) *Voices: Palestinian Women Narrate Displacement*. Available at: http://almashriq.hiof.no/palestine/300/301/voices/. Accessed November 20, 2014.
Schwenkel, C. (2012) Civilizing the city: Socialist ruins and urban renewal in Central Vietnam. *positions* 20(2): 437–470.
Scott, J. C. (1998) *Seeing Like a State*. New Haven, CT: Yale University Press.
Settis, S. (2010) *Paesaggio costituzione cemento: la battaglia per l'ambiente contro il degrado civile*. Turin: Einaudi.
Settis, S. (2011) We the Citizens, English translation of chapter 7 of *Paesaggio costituzione cemento: la battaglia per l'ambiente contro il degrado civile* (Einaudi, 2010). *California Italian Studies* 2(1). Available at: http://128.48.120.176/uc/item/7c90g6dp. Accessed November 20, 2014.
Settis, S. (2012) *Azione popolare: cittadini per il bene commune*. Turin: Einaudi.
Shao, Q. (2013) *Shanghai Gone: Domicide and Defiance in a Chinese Megacity*. Lanham, MD: Rowman and Littlefield.
Shehadeh, R. (2007) *Palestinian Walks: Notes on a Vanishing Landscape*. London: Profile.
Silberman, N. A. (1982) *Digging for God and Country: Exploration, Archeology, and the Secret Struggle for the Holy Land, 1799–1917*. New York: Knopf.
Silverman, H. (2012) The Space of Heroism in the Historic Center of Cuzco, in D. Fairchild Ruggles (ed.), *On Location: Heritage Cities and Sites*. New York: Springer, pp. 89–113.

Silverman, H. (2013) Cuzcotopia: Imagining and Performing the Incas, in R. Staiff, R. Bushell, and S. Watson (eds), *Heritage and Tourism. Place, Encounter, Engagement*. London: Routledge, pp. 128–151.
Smith, L. (2004) *Archaeological Theory and the Politics of Cultural Heritage*. London: Routledge.
Smith, L. (2006) *Uses of Heritage*. London: Routledge.
Smith, N. (2002) New globalism, new urbanism: Gentrification as global urban strategy. *Antipode*, 34.3: 434–457.
Stewart, C. (2010) Immanent or Eminent Domain? The Contest over Thessaloniki's Rotonda, in A. Stroulia and S. B. Sutton (eds), *Archaeology in Situ: Sites, Archaeology, and Communities in Greece*. Lanham, MD: Lexington Books, pp. 179–200.
Stoler, A. L. (2008) Imperial debris: Reflections on ruins and ruination. *Cultural Anthropology* 23(2): 191–219.
Sutton, D. E. (1996) Explosive debates: Dynamite, tradition, and the state. *Anthropological Quarterly* 69: 66–78.
Thompson, M. (1979) *Rubbish Theory: The Creation and Destruction of Value*. Oxford: Oxford University Press.
Trigger, B. (1984) Alternative archaeologies: Nationalist, colonialist, imperialist. *Man* 19(3): 355–370.
Trouillot, M.-R. (1995) *Silencing the Past: Power and the Production of History*. Boston, MA: Beacon Press.
Trouillot, M.-R. (2001) The anthropology of the state in the age of globalization: Close encounters of the deceptive kind. *Current Anthropology* 42(1): 125–139.
Tunbridge, J. E. and G. J. Ashworth (1996) *Dissonant Heritage: The Management of the Past as a Resource in Conflict*. Chichester: Wiley.
Valverde, M. (2011) Seeing like a city: The dialectic of modern and premodern ways of seeing in urban governance. *Law and Society Review* 45(2): 277–312.
van Baar, H. (2011) The European Roma: Minority Representation, Memory, and the Limits of Transnational Governmentality. Ph.D. dissertation, Universiteit van Amsterdam, the Netherlands.
Vansina, J. (1985) *Oral Tradition as History*. Madison: University of Wisconsin Press.
Voutira, E. (2003) Refugees: Whose Term is it Anyway? Emic and Etic Constructions of "Refugees" in Modern Greek, in J. van Selm, K. Kamanga, J. Morrison, A. Nadig, S. Spoljar Vrzina, and L. van Willigen (eds), *The Refugee Convention at Fifty: A View from Forced Migration Studies*. Lanham, MD: Lexington Books, pp. 65–80.
Walton, J. F. (2010) Neo-Ottomanism and the Pious Aesthetics of Publicness: Making Space and Place Virtuous in Istanbul, in D. Göktürk, I. Soysal, and L. Türeli (eds), *Orienting Istanbul: Cultural Capital of Europe?* London: Routledge, pp. 88–103.
Waterton, E. (2010) *Politics, Policy, and the Discourses of Heritage in Britain*. Basingstoke: Palgrave Macmillan.
Waterton, E. and L. Smith (2011) The recognition and the misrecognition of community heritage. *International Journal of Heritage Studies* 16(1/2): 4–15.
Watkins, J. (2000) *Indigenous Archaeology: American Indian Values and Scientific Practice*. Walnut Creek, CA: Alta Mira Press.
Weiss, L. M. (2014) Informal settlements and urban heritage landscapes in South Africa. *Journal of Social Archaeology* 14(1): 3–25.
Weizman, E. (2007) *Hollow Land: Israel's Architecture of Occupation*. London: Verso.
Weizman, E. (2014) Introduction: Forensis, in *Forensis: The Architecture of Public Truth*. Berlin: Sternberg, pp. 9–32.
Whitelam, K. W. (1996) *The Invention of Ancient Israel: The Silencing of Palestinian History*. New York: Routledge.
Wimmer, A. and N. G. Schiller (2002) Methodological nationalism and beyond: Nation-state building, migration and the social sciences. *Global Networks* 2(4): 301–334.

Wright, P. (1985) *On Living in an Old Country: The National Past in Contemporary Britain*. Oxford: Oxford University Press.

Yeoh, B. S. A. and L. Kong (1994) Reading landscape meanings: State constructions and lived experiences in Singapore's Chinatown. *Habitat International* 18(4): 17–35.

Yiftachel, O. (2012) Between Colonialism and Ethnocracy: "Creeping Apartheid" in Israel/Palestine, in N. Jeena (ed.), *Pretending Democracy: Israel, an Ethnocratic State*. Pretoria: Afro-Middle East Centre AMEC, pp. 95–113.

Zerubavel, Y. (1995) *Recovered Roots: Collective Memory and the Making of Israeli National Tradition*. Chicago, IL: University of Chicago Press.

Zhang, L. (2006) Contesting spatial modernity in late-socialist China. *Current Anthropology* 47: 461–484.

Zhang, L. (2010) *In Search of Paradise: Middle-Class Living in a Chinese Metropolis*. Ithaca, NY: Cornell University Press.

9

Sustainable Development: Heritage, Community, Economics

Sophia Labadi and Peter G. Gould

Introduction

Conceived in the environmental movement of the 1970s, "sustainable development" has come to embody aspects of a panacea – the possibility for social and economic progress in a manner that distributes benefits equitably, uses resources prudently, and conserves what we currently value for the future, all the while improving living standards for the poorest among us. The term encapsulates economic viability, environmental and heritage conservation, and social equity across generations in a manner to which few can object.

In application, however, the phrase "sustainable development" presents more quandaries than answers. Indeed, it has been criticized as a fuzzy, if not paradoxical aggregation (Flipo 2005: 1; Meskell 2012: 27). Frequently, the vagueness of the "sustainable development" concept has been cited as the reason for its appeal. What, for example, is the "development" to be sustained – in the most general sense and particularly in the context of archaeology and heritage? How is "sustainability" to be measured? Whose interests are paramount when sustainability and development conflict? How is any of this to be measured and tracked? And how do heritage professionals fare when trying to pursue sustainable development in practice?

This chapter critically considers the concepts of development and sustainability in the context of heritage in order to explore the theoretical, practical, and ethical issues that are introduced when heritage-related projects are undertaken with sustainable development as an objective. The chapter begins with a close consideration of the notion of "development" – its origins, conflicting interpretations, and emerging conceptions of the term that are moving beyond merely economic considerations. It turns then to the idea of "sustainability," its content and implications. Although neither term is rooted in heritage or cultural matters, we suggest that the concepts are evolving toward definitions that are embedding culture deeply into the discourse around sustainable development as it applies to heritage at the local and international levels. This is occurring even as development agencies are refocusing their efforts on local

Global Heritage: A Reader, First Edition. Edited by Lynn Meskell.

communities where issues of culture and heritage may be paramount. The entangling of community and culture in the sustainability debate highlights the final topic of this chapter. That is the challenge of defining and quantifying the economic and other impacts of sustainable development projects and translating sustainability concepts into practice. To illustrate those issues, the chapter concludes with two case studies, one examining challenges at the very local level, the other considering the experience and limitations of the World Heritage Convention's incorporation of sustainability objectives.

Development

The concept of "development" traces its roots to the Enlightenment and the idea of "progress," which applauded technological changes, the rationalization of economic activity, and the abandonment of traditional culture and values (Condorcet 1795; Du Pisani 2006). However, "development" in its contemporary context is a distinctly post-World War II idea (Sen 1983) whose origins can be traced to the break up of colonial empires starting in the 1940s and the consequent emergence on the international stage of a multitude of new nations. These newly created nations, mostly former colonies, typically lacked competitive industries, functioning financial systems, or experienced administrators. They certainly did not enjoy the standard of economic prosperity experienced after the postwar recovery in Europe or the United States.

Economists and politicians compared the circumstances of the "north" and the "south" at this time and proffered varied prescriptions. However, invariably the economic, political, and social order in Europe and North America was presented as the model to be emulated. It was the task of governments and the emerging roster of international organizations to provide, from the "top down," the political and economic instruments necessary to promote capital formation, harness nature, build infrastructure, and replace small-scale agriculture and commerce with intensive farming and large-scale industry. Labor was to migrate from rural areas to new towns and cities where schools and hospitals were to be widely available, the education system supported, and commercial trade improved (De Senarclens 1988). In other words, development was considered to be a top-down, technocratic set of interventions, leading countries on a linear road from poverty and ignorance to "riches, civilization, democracy and rationality" (Shanin 1997: 67).

This process engaged the economic, social, and cultural organizations of the United Nations, national development agencies, and the global financial infrastructure of the World Bank, the International Monetary Fund, and numerous regional development banks. To all of them, development was to be achieved through universal application of strategies believed to be effective in creating jobs and a diversity of goods and services. Eventually, development projects integrated with the unfolding globalized economy to form the "Washington Consensus" policy (Rodrik 2007), a mix of free trade and investment flows coupled to domestic deregulation and strict fiscal discipline. It is this model that has driven the development assistance strategies of global financial institutions even into the most recent economic crisis.

This approach, modeled on "developed countries," implied as its corollary the notion of "developing countries," those nations, largely located in Asia and the "south" of the globe, to whom the development process was to be applied. For the first decades of this process, faith in neoliberal theories of free-market economics and democracy as the prevailing model for the world was unquestioned among policy makers. There is no doubt that huge gains have been made on a global scale in income, education, life expectancy, and other measures as a result of the postwar development agenda (Bhagwati and Panagariya 2013; Deaton 2013). However, the shortcomings of that process have been pronounced (Herzfeld 2010; Meskell 2009a; Smith 2006; Weiss 2007).

Disappointment and Redefinition

Critics of the process objected that the "developing world" was not an objective reality. Instead, they argued, development agencies defined this "other" space in order to create a market place for goods and products of the developed world and to replace traditional social and cultural values with materialist aspirations to access and consume the goods of the developed world. Illich (1971), who labeled this process "reification," argued that reification has often been accompanied by the "disvalue" of local cultures and associated value systems, due in part to the technocratic and expert vocabularies used by development experts that undermined traditional knowledge and the beliefs underlying them.

Development aid programs have been criticized for undermining entrepreneurial motivation (Moyo 2009) and generating failed outcomes (Easterly 2006; Stiglitz 2003). Several development specialists (Deaton 2013; Easterly 2013; Ferguson 1990; Ovaska 2003; Rapley 2004) have demonstrated how external development programs and technocratic experts have endorsed corrupt and undemocratic nation-state governments at the expense primarily of the poorest citizens, rather than enhancing the lives and capabilities of the people who live in those nations. Some archaeologists likewise have been intensively critical of the inequities and disempowerment of the poor associated with the global development process (Breglia 2009: 205–227; Hodder 2003: 63–64; Meskell 2009a: 11). The high level of disappointment with the results of this process was clearly expressed in the 2012 UN report, *The Future We Want*:

> One in five people on this planet, or over one billion people, still live in extreme poverty, and ... one in seven – or 14 percent – is undernourished, while public health challenges including pandemics and epidemics remain omnipresent threats. (UNCSD 2012: 4)

While some have argued that countries fail to achieve development breakthroughs because they suffer from cultural deficiencies (Harrison and Huntington 2000), others (UNDP 2004) have rejected that view and cite the prosperity achieved by nations built on Buddhist, Islamic, and other traditions. Some have been affronted by the degree to which tangible and intangible evidence of both past and contemporary traditional cultures were being undermined by the "development process" (Douglas 2004). Moreover, and somewhat ironically, those nations in which top-down-driven development projects had the greatest impact in raising living standards and the quality of life of their citizens (such as China, the Asian Tigers, India, or Brazil) followed models for national political and economic governance that bore little or no resemblance to the neoliberal and free-market-oriented structures espoused by the Washington Consensus (see Balassa 1988; or, in the heritage literature, Logan 2002; Winter and Daly 2012). Easterly (2013) laments the sacrifice of individual freedoms, human rights, and democracy associated with this so-called "Asian Model," a process he has labeled "authoritarian development," and has chastised the economists and agencies who have supported it.

As the negative impacts of economic change on existing cultures and values became evident, a few economists and politicians began searching for a different standard for development. For much of the late twentieth century, progress was evaluated based on economic outcomes, most notably measures of gross domestic product per person in the population ("GDP per capita") and related measures of employment, wage levels, and similar exclusively economic metrics. Sen (1999), an early critic of the failures of the development process, has attempted to move the development discourse away from purely economic metrics to broader measures of well-being intended to redirect the goal of development toward enhancing the capacity of individuals to pursue their own objectives and ensuring that they have the freedom and capability to do so (for heritage examples in this vein, see also Hodder 2010; Meskell 2010). Sen contends that this cannot be achieved solely through high rates of growth in GDP per capita. Rather, he has argued that development entails the furtherance of individuals' access to capabilities, including education, health care, and the legal freedom to choose for themselves the cultural life and cultural manifestations that will contribute to their well-being.

Sen thus put culture, considered in this context as dynamic and ever-changing, at the heart of development. Following Sen, Appadurai has argued that "cultural capacity" is at the heart of the development process and insists that the poor be empowered to express their own and unique aspirations, which should form the basis for development policies designed to improve their well-being. In this process, "self-governance, self-mobilization and self-articulation are vital to changing the terms of recognition of the poor" (Appadurai 2004: 81). This broadening definition of "development" is being reflected, to some degree, in economic analysis, and for some analysts (Fabrizio, Snowdon, and Prasad 2000; Rauschmayer, Omann, and Frühmann 2011) it provides a basis for deflecting discussions of sustainability away from purely material measures toward a notion of human needs that embraces social and cultural continuity in the face of change.

Sustainable Development

One consequence of the surge in industrial output in the twentieth century, and especially after World War II, was a growing recognition of the adverse environmental consequences of growth – pollution, wasteful resource use, spoiled rural landscapes, and inhospitable urban environments. The apparent conflict between nature and development gave rise to a drive for "sustainable development." That concept received its iconic treatment in the 1988 report of the World Commission on Economic Development, known as the Brundtland Commission after its chair, Gro Harlem Brundtland, the then prime minister of Norway. The Brundtland commission was the outgrowth of a neo-Malthusian movement that emerged in the 1970s and was led by the Club of Rome, researchers at the Massachusetts Institute of Technology, and others concerned that overpopulation, exploitation of raw materials, and unrelenting pollution of the planet would generate a collapse of the world ecosystem and economy (Kanninen 2013: chapters 1, 2). It was the first of a series of international declarations to express revulsion with the environmental and economic consequence of unbridled global development and to urge the preservation and sustainable use of non-renewable natural resources. Barthel-Bouchier (2013) highlights the close linkages between the movements for environmental conservation and heritage preservation, while Meskell (2012) has commented on the manner in which this discourse about environmental protection and preservation has framed the subsequent parallel discourse about heritage protection, often to the detriment of local and indigenous communities.

The Brundtland commission report provided the now classic definition that growth is sustainable if it "meets the needs of the present without compromising the ability of future generations to meet their own needs" (WCED 1987: Paragraph 27). A succession of international conferences has extended the Brundtland Commission's concept and its focus on the need to reconcile economic development and environmental sustainability. These conferences and associated documents have also increasingly referred to culture and heritage as integral elements of sustainable development. They thus reflect a more comprehensive approach to the definition of sustainable development than the Brundtland report. In particular, discussions initiated at the 1992 Earth Summit in Rio de Janeiro, Brazil, led to the 2004 adoption of the *Agenda 21 for Culture* at a conference of the United Cities and Local Governments. Formally adopted by 1,000 cities, local governments, and other organizations, this statement provides a framework and a tool to consider culture as essential to sustainable urban development (UNLC 2008: 4).

Sustainable Development and Culture

Nonetheless, culture, defined as the complex and constantly changing set of distinctive spiritual, material, intellectual and emotional features that characterize a society or social group, has fared poorly in the global sustainable development discourse. With UNESCO's support, culture was proposed as a fourth pillar of sustainable development (along with social, environmental, and economic sustainability) at the Johannesburg World Summit on Sustainable Development in 2002 (UNESCO and UNEP 2002: 26). This proposal represented the culmination of many initiatives, including the UNESCO "Decade for Culture and Development" (1988–1997) and the World Commission on Culture and Development's report, *Our Creative Diversity* (WCCD 1996), which argued for the central importance of creativity and empowerment of minorities in the sustainable development process. The 1998 Intergovernmental Conference on Cultural Policies for Development was another international event sponsored by UNESCO to encourage governments, inter alia, to make cultural policy a key component of development strategies, promote participation in cultural life, or make more resources available for cultural development (Arizpe 2004: 179–180). However, the change proposed in 2002 was ultimately rejected.

Furthermore, culture and heritage were totally omitted from the Millennium Development Goals (MDGs) adopted by the United Nations in 2000. These goals defined the international agenda for the first 15 years of the twenty-first century by identifying ambitious targets to eradicate extreme poverty; sharply enhance the capabilities of poor people through improved access to education, health care, and political rights; and improve environmental sustainability. The total omission of culture and heritage from the MDGs demonstrates the difficulty that UNESCO and other organizations have had integrating culture and heritage into the international discourse on sustainable development. It may also reflect the reality that sustainable development lacks both clear definition and a coherent theoretical or practical core (Jabareen 2008), two factors to be discussed below.

Sustainable Development and Heritage

Nonetheless, culture and heritage have at least begun to appear in the official sustainable development dialogue. The UN adopted two resolutions in 2010 and 2011 on the importance of culture and development and, in 2013, adopted a third that requests due consideration be given to culture and sustainable development in the development of the plan of work for the post-2015 period. The increasing position of culture within a sustainable development agenda was also reflected in the Rio Plus 20 report, *The Future We Want* (UNCSD 2012). Recent publications further associate heritage and sustainable development in three other, at times contradictory, ways.

The first of these directly enchains environmental sustainability with threats to heritage itself. Barthel-Bouchier (2013) catalogs the diverse ways that climate change and normal environmental stresses threaten archaeological and cultural heritage in all its forms. Barthel-Bouchier also argues that by adopting sustainability as a crusade, the heritage profession has gained for itself a seat at the policy table alongside environmentalists and others, and in this way created new economic opportunities for the profession arising from increasing government funding to support sustainable development projects. Terrill (2008) and Colette (2007) explore the implications of climate change for the World Heritage Convention in particular. Each argues that the complex technical and intergovernmental political issues arising from the climate change problem argue for a limited and domestically focused response to climate threats affecting World Heritage sites, as well as international solidarity. Harmon (2007) argues that combining environmental and cultural heritage conservation into an integrated program may be the most effective path forward for both concerns.

The second linkage is in the impact that sustainability concepts have had on heritage conservation and preservation practice. As but one example, the papers in Teutonico and Matero's (2003) edited volume describe the economic conflicts, social impact, and technical challenges associated with preserving archaeological sites, urban built heritage, and traditional landscapes in the face of pressures for development to accommodate the housing, commercial, and infrastructure needs of growing populations. In many cases those articles also circled back to the tight linkage between environmental sustainability and cultural sustainability.

Third, the growth of global tourism and its increasing economic importance has pitted the heritage community against the tourism industry and the consequences of mass tourism. Mowforth and Munt (2009) are among the most severe critics of the global quest for "sustainable" tourism, which they regard as a concept cynically manipulated by governments, tourism corporations, and conservationists to rationalize a consumerism that has adverse economic and environmental consequences and yields benefits that ultimately fail to profit local communities. Castañeda and Matthews (2013) also argue forcefully that archaeology has become increasingly dependent upon tourism for funding and even for legitimacy. Salazar has explored the complexities of local power dynamics and the tensions that can arise in community-based tourism, while questioning the value of tourism projects that are not firmly embedded in local communities (Salazar 2012a: 130–131).

Sustainable Development and Community

At the same time that heritage and culture have begun to be mentioned in official international discourses, practices in heritage preservation and in economic development have converged on the view that activity at the community level is central to successful sustainable development. Indeed, Keitumetse (2009) has argued that the focus on communities in both Agenda 21 and in numerous subsequent international cultural agreements constitutes a clear point of intersection between cultural heritage management and sustainable development.

Community engagement in a heritage context involves a broad array of activities, ranging from consultation, education, and public presentations with local inhabitants (Moshenska and Dhanjal 2013; Tully 2007) to a relationship in which local communities, especially indigenous peoples, control the process of conserving, managing, researching, and interpreting tangible and intangible heritage (Habu 2008; Marshall 2002; McManamon, Stout, and Barnes 2008; Smith and Waterton 2009). Whatever the form, community engagement has become an ethical obligation for most academics and practitioners in archaeology and heritage. Consultation is widely seen as a means to ensure some degree of social sustainability when development or tourism can disrupt local communities (Labadi 2013; Low 2003). Community-based programs are coming to be seen as essential to sustainably managing the conflicts between cultural heritage and tourism (Landorf 2009; Nasser 2003; Pearce 1992; Walker and Carr 2013), even though the conditions for successful community engagement are complex and involve groups with different values (Lilley 2007; Meskell 2009b) that can be easily frustrated by political action or inaction (Aas, Ladkin, and Fletcher 2005).

Disappointment with top-down economic development has, at the World Bank, generated projects to encourage locally led development initiatives (Binswanger-Mkhize, de Regt, and Spector 2010; Licciardi and Amirtahmasebi 2012) and fueled serious reconsideration among economists about bottom-up alternatives to top-down economic development programs (Cohen and Easterly 2009). Community-based tourism projects have nonetheless been criticized for impacting negatively on the complex sociocultural structures of local communities (Salazar 2009, 2012b). Lafrenz Samuels (2010) has criticized locally led development projects at the World Bank because of the multiplicity of actors, the lack of clarity of the project objectives, or the imposition of global concepts at local levels. The World Bank itself has released evaluations of its own projects which, at times, highlight problems such as the lack of longitudinal data to undertake ex-post economic impact assessments (Throsby 2012: 45) or the gentrification of urban quarters that leads to changes in resident populations, as was the case in the medina of Marrakesh, Morocco (Bigio and Licciardi 2010: 10).

The linkage of community to sustainable development has gained official recognition in the conventions promulgated by UNESCO, which in the 1990s promoted the association of culture with development. The World Heritage Convention only became officially associated with the notion of sustainable development from 2002 onwards. In particular, the Budapest Declaration, adopted in 2002 at the 26th Session of the World Heritage Committee, stresses the need to

> Ensure an appropriate and equitable balance between conservation, sustainability and development, so that World Heritage properties can be protected through appropriate activities contributing to the social and economic development and the quality of life of our communities. (UNESCO 2002a)

This new emphasis is exemplified by UNESCO's choice in 2012 of "World Heritage and Sustainable Development: the Role of Local Communities" as the official theme for the 40th Anniversary of the World Heritage Convention. The Committee's 2011 amendment of the definition of sustainable development in the Operational Guidelines specifies that the proposed uses of World Heritage properties may "contribute to the quality of life of communities concerned" (UNESCO 2011: Paragraph 119). Thus, from the turn of the millennium onward, the notion of development has increasingly been associated with the notion of "sustainability" in the implementation of the World Heritage Convention, and both have been linked to involvement with local communities.

Sustainability, Economy, and the Value of Heritage

In every country today there is intense competition for funding to research and to sustain heritage, for the right to impose regulations and limitations on the use of heritage resources, and for resources and legislation to protect traditional peoples and cultural resources that are under siege by modernization. Throsby (2010) has recently cataloged the numerous tools of public policy – from direct funding to restrictive regulations, from tax incentives to other subsidies – that embed the actual practice of cultural heritage management deep within the political process. Heritage interests are pitted against all other claimants on the public purse and against private interests who may seek to undermine cultural legacies in the pursuit of development projects large and small (Lafrenz Samuels 2008). Such disputes play out in a contest of political wills where results are determined not in the field of abstract values, where heritage may have a moral upper hand, but instead in the realm of economic value, where the tools and concepts at the disposal of heritage practitioners are largely inadequate (Labadi 2011; Mason 2008; Peacock and Rizzo 2008).

In order to justify saving a building, a neighborhood or a landscape, or to convince legislators to finance research programs or impose regulatory controls on the development process, the advocates for heritage must demonstrate the value of that which is to be saved. Typically, these decisions are viewed as investment decisions, where a "return" is expected from an "investment" in culture or heritage. Alternatively, they may become budget decisions, wherein the "benefits" of a program, in terms of income growth or jobs created, are obliged to outweigh the financial costs. The challenge of "valuing" the benefits of culture is not a new one, but for most of modern history the problem was approached as an abstraction (Morris 1877; Riegl 1982 [1928]).

By the late twentieth century, however, economists trained in the neoclassical tradition had developed a full complement of analytical tools designed to place a monetary value on tangible and intangible aspects of culture (Klamer and Zuidhof 1988; O'Brien 2010; Throsby 2001). In a contingent valuation study, for example, the researcher directly asks members of the public to state the amount they would be "willing to pay" to, for example, visit a heritage site or prevent the destruction of one. Another approach, known as "choice modelling," attempts to rank-order consumers' preferences among a set of heritage investments rather than solicit a specific financial value for each one. Hedonic pricing models, typically used in urban settings, compute the increase in market value of surrounding real estate as an estimate of the value generated by preserving or enhancing heritage venues. Some tourism studies interpret the amount tourists will pay to travel to and visit a site as a proxy for the site's value, while other studies consider the total economic "impact" of heritage preservation using "input–output" models that estimate the total income gain to a region from heritage tourism at a particular site. Most of these approaches can be criticized for relying on neoclassical economic assumptions, which have come under fire in recent years especially from behavioral economists, and each is subject to specific technical challenges or limitations.

The larger issue, recognized by some scholars, is that these economic measures do not capture the full contribution of cultural and heritage resources to the lives of people (De la Torre 2002; Kim, Wong, and Cho 2007; Klamer 2002: chapter 4, 2004; Throsby 2001). Numerous efforts have been undertaken to define and quantify better and broader metrics for the value and sustainability of development in entire economies. In 2008, the French government sponsored an effort under the leadership of economists Joseph Stiglitz, Amartya Sen, and Jean-Paul Fitoussi (2009: 12–16) to define a set of metrics for sustainable development more appropriate than traditional economic statistics. Reflecting Sen's capability approach, the French report explicitly sought to introduce measures that could assess current well-being, both measured in current economic and quality of life terms, and measures intended to evaluate the potential for those outcomes to "last over time." These economists recognized the need, when analyzing economic well-being, to consider the distribution of household income, consumption, and wealth, as well as the need to consider key non-material dimensions of well-being such as health, education, personal activities (including work, political voice, and governance), social connections and relationships, present and future environmental conditions, and economic as well as physical insecurity. Nonetheless, while Sen in particular has recognized that culture is at the heart of a people-centered approach to development, this report did not include or suggest ways to measure culture per se as an important dimension.

Other attempts to do so also have been made. Zancheti and Hidaka (Zancheti 2011; Zancheti and Hidaka 2012) have presented a comprehensive, if theoretical, report on UNESCO efforts to develop metrics to measure the state of urban heritage preservation, and efforts have been made to develop measures of sustainable development at the local community level (Choi and Sirakaya 2006; Valentin and Spangenberg 2000). The use of quantitative indicators and benchmarks has been advocated and increasingly used in the evaluation of sustainable development projects involving heritage conservation. This is the case, for instance, for all projects funded by the Heritage Lottery Fund, ranging from museums, buildings, and monuments to conservation areas in the United Kingdom (HLF 2012). In a number of cases, such evaluations have revealed a severe lack of data at the local level or cited changes over time in the coverage or content of national-level data (Reeve and Shipley 2013).

Since 2009, UNESCO has attempted to create a suite of indicators to measure the contribution of culture to development at the national level. Nothing has yet been released. One of the authors of this chapter (Labadi) contributed to this project in its first stages and found that existing national statistics were too poor to measure meaningfully the contribution of culture to development. Indeed, no measure of the contribution of heritage to national development was proposed in this project. Statistics focused on the number of protected sites rather than on their social or economic impacts. At this juncture, all of these efforts to define sustainable development metrics remain academic exercises. Definitions are not settled and national governments are not collecting the data necessary to support national or cross-national analysis of culturally embedded sustainable development.

Case Studies

The argument in this chapter is that sustainable development is gaining rhetorical prominence in the management of heritage, and that heritage and culture are receiving attention as important policy considerations at least in the context of international relations. That increased visibility has not, however, translated into clear changes in the behavior of nation-states or other parties as they address such issues as the impact of climate change on the physical integrity of heritage resources, or the consequences for both tangible and intangible cultural heritage of the physical and social stress from mass tourism. Moreover, the increasing prominence of sustainability concepts in the rhetoric of cultural heritage management has made the shortcomings more visible in the definition of sustainable development, in the identification of sustainability metrics, and in the limitations of cultural economics as an influence on the actual behavior of public officials.

Several authors have produced books in recent years that incorporate case studies relating to sustainable heritage. Considering just recent volumes, Teutonico and Matero (2003) enumerate numerous challenges to sustainable conservation of tangible heritage. Barthel-Bouchier (2013) addresses environmental threats. Galla's (2012) edited volume for UNESCO offers an upbeat compendium of the results of numerous projects from around the world that have attempted to meld economic development and sustainable heritage. Walker and Carr (2013) provide a case-based critical overview of the interaction of tourism and archaeology. Recent Ph.D. theses by one of the present authors (Gould 2014) and by Burtenshaw (2013) have explored the community-level attitudes and institutions that may be associated with sustainable heritage projects.

We have chosen here to focus on two specific cases that illuminate the central issues raised in this chapter. These two case studies address the issues of sustainable development from "top-down" and "bottom-up" perspectives. The first considers development issues from the bottom up, focusing on a community-level project in Italy that introduces political and economic considerations that lie at the heart of sustainable heritage projects. The second addresses the effectiveness of global initiatives to preserve and protect archaeology and heritage through the World Heritage Convention system, first though an evaluation of the management of an important world heritage site in India and then through consideration of the World Heritage system's engagement with communities.

Case 1: Sustainable development in a community-based setting

Small, local archaeological and heritage sites, those that primarily benefit local communities, constitute the vast majority of heritage venues across the globe. These sites may be integral to local community identity or peripheral and related to a distant and unvalued past. They may be important parts of a regional tourist market, or ignored and inaccessible to any but the most intrepid traveler. In any event, small heritage sites present their own special challenges of economic impact and political governance. An intriguing example of the practical economic and political challenges faced by community-based heritage sites is the recent history of a system of natural and archaeological sites, the Parchi della Val di Cornia, located in the vicinity of Piombino in the Tuscany region of Italy. Paterlini, in collaboration with one of the authors (Gould), has studied this system in detail. Her study illuminates both the challenges and the opportunities for economic development in community-based heritage management (Paterlini 2012; Paterlini and Gould 2013).

The Val di Cornia is a valley in the southern part of the province of Livorno in Tuscany. The hilly terrain is rich in mineral wealth that was mined by the Etruscans, became a substantial source of medieval Tuscan wealth, and reached its peak in the mid-nineteenth century with the growing importance of the steel industry. By the mid-1970s, however, mines in the area had closed and the region entered a period of economic decline. What remained was a landscape rich in both archaeological and natural resources. The idea for a park system to support the local economy was conceived by archaeologist Ricardo Frankovich, who envisioned and ultimately brought to life in 1993 a network that today consists of two important Etruscan and medieval archaeological sites, three museums, one documentation center, three beach-front parks and one forest park. Castles, mining sites, and numerous other venerable buildings were restored and repurposed to serve as restaurants, meeting spaces, museums, and other park facilities. The entire network operates through a jointly owned company, the Parchi della Val di Cornia, S.p.A., that is owned by five neighboring municipalities (*comune* in Italy) of Piombino, San Vincenzo, Campiglia Marittima, Suvereto, and Sassetta.

Clusters of related tourist sites have long been recognized as potentially valuable ways to generate visitation and revenues to support heritage and benefit the local community. Networks encourage the development of related businesses, such as hotels and restaurants, that channel tourist dollars into local economies, increase local demand for goods and services, and make the entire region attractive for government support (Michael 2003; Porter 1998). Some (Morrison, Lynch, and Johns 2004; Saxena 2005) have argued that networks of tourist sites both have practical business benefits and can generate increased cohesion within the communities involved, even to the extent of mitigating local conflicts and empowering the engagement of local residents in the management of local resources.

In the case of the Val di Cornia park system, the concept of the park as a network of sites was based on the assumption that each *comune* had some potential to attract tourists, which would benefit the other parks and *comunes* in the system. In practice, the value of the multisite network was well documented in Paterlini's study. The park system as a whole was host to nearly 90,000 visitors per year in 2011. Visitors stayed an average of 12 days in the Tuscany region, and 70 percent of those interviewed stayed in the Val di Cornia itself. Nearly three-quarters of the visitors interviewed by Paterlini were aware of the park system and nearly half said they had vacationed in the region because it offered a combination of recreational and cultural sites and museums. Over three-quarters of visitors purchased tickets that enabled them to visit multiple park locations, rather than just one, and nearly 80 percent of visitors visited at least two sites in the system (data from Paterlini 2012: chapter 4).

Capital funding to construct the park facilities was provided by the European Union and various national and regional Italian authorities. Initially, the five *comunes* were to have equal stakes in the park corporation. Revenues from admission tickets and parking revenues were intended to cover costs. As matters unfolded, however, shortfalls in the level of tourist visitation in the early years produced operating losses that were covered by the leading *comune* in the system, Piombino. In return, over time Piombino came to own a controlling share of the corporation, over 60 percent. The business of the entire network eventually did increase, and by 2007 the park system was substantially self-sufficient, requiring only modest subsidies from the *comunes* who contributed in proportion to their individual populations.

The income stream to the Parchi had been dominated by parking fees, which made up over 40 percent of the park's revenues and were largely derived from parks located in Piombino. The *comune* of Piombino collected parking revenues on behalf of the system and forwarded those funds to the corporation annually. With the onset of the economic crisis in 2008, however, funding from national sources to support local government activities was drastically reduced in Italy. As austerity programs in

Italy began to erode national funding for local programs, the parking revenues became a tempting source of funding for Piombino's leaders to use in support of other municipal activities. After the park's losses began to rise again in 2011, the shareholding *comunes* called for personnel and spending reductions in the park corporation. Nonetheless, losses continued. Finally, in 2012, the political leadership of Piombino threatened to withhold parking revenues from the park system and to use the monies for local purposes.

As a potential means to staunch the financial losses, Paterlini conducted a contingent valuation study to determine whether tourists would be willing to pay additional entrance fees to the parks. While the limitations of such studies have been widely acknowledged, economists still accept them as the best available technique for many purposes (Bakhshi, Reeman, and Hitchen 2009; O'Brien 2010; Throsby 2001). This study asked visitors how much more they would be willing to pay in entrance fees to the site they had just visited, offering them a menu of potential alternative fees. The study, which was conducted with the involvement of park authorities, was intended to determine whether price increases could prevent further staff and spending cuts, or even the possible break up of the network if Piombino's government elected to withhold the parking fees for its own use.

Paterlini's results were highly encouraging (Paterlini 2012: chapter 4). Across the entire system, the visitors surveyed were willing to pay a median price increase of €3, or 9.2 percent, an amount sufficient in 2012 to make the park fully self-sufficient if Piombino in fact transferred parking fees to the park system. Moreover, the average interviewee was willing to pay an increase of €6, or 18.4 percent, while 70 percent of the beach visitors were willing to pay a fee to use the beaches (which otherwise were free) as long as the charge to park cars close to the beaches was included in the price. Furthermore, the study identified a large potential market – tourists who pass through Piombino en route to vacations on the nearby island of Elba – that the *comune* had not successfully tapped for stays on the mainland. The study vividly illustrated the potential of this sort of research to illuminate strategies for heritage sites that otherwise may not be visible to heritage managers.

The economic results, which were presented to officials and to a public meeting in Piombino, did not change the political calculus, however. Entrance fees were not increased, Piombino elected to retain the parking revenues, and contributions by the five *comunes* were effectively reduced, requiring the elimination of four additional staff positions (A. Paterlini, personal communication, 2014). Today the Parchi della Val di Cornia continues to operate, but its financial and operational future is problematic and heavily dependent on local politics. The fate of the park system highlights the vulnerability of the entire structure to economic events and political forces, national and international as well as local, that can undermine sustainability in any community-based venture (Aas, Ladkin, and Fletcher 2005).

Case 2: Sustainable development in the World Heritage process

The World Heritage Convention (WHC), adopted in 1972, addresses heritage resources at the opposite end of the spectrum from the locally oriented sites of Val di Cornia, representing instead an international effort to protect cultural and natural places of "outstanding universal value." However, increasingly, as will be discussed below, it mandates engagement with local communities. While the convention itself does not explicitly mention the notion of sustainable development, which only emerged 16 years later in the aforementioned Brundtland Report, this document can be considered as one of the initial international texts that paved the way for the Brundtland Report (Bandarin and Labadi 2007: 28–29). Indeed, the WHC, which was partly developed for the 1972 United Nations Conference on the Human Environment held in Stockholm, clearly prefigured Brundlandt's objections to the consequences of development. The preamble to the WHC, for example, stresses that:

> The cultural heritage and the natural heritage are increasingly threatened with destruction ... by changing social and economic conditions which aggravate the situation with even more formidable phenomena of damage or destruction. (UNESCO 1972)

This preamble reflects UNESCO's concern, inter alia, over the destruction of a number of heritage sites such as the man-made flooding in the 1960s of the Nubian monuments of the Upper Nile valley. This calamity, the consequence of Egypt's decision to build the Aswan Dam, spawned an international campaign led by UNESCO to save these archaeological treasures (Batisse and Bolla 2005). The WHC was thus developed to protect natural and cultural heritage of outstanding universal value in the face of development pressures.

World Heritage and Mass Tourism

Due to the prominence of World Heritage sites, management of mass tourism and associated infrastructure development should be at the heart of any sustainable approach to World Heritage. These are, arguably, the main threats confronting these internationally recognized heritage sites. Both the form to nominate sites for inclusion on the World Heritage List and UNESCO's suggested format for drafting management plans refer to conventional tools to control tourism and infrastructure development, such as evaluation of carrying capacity or zoning (Pedersen 2002: 57). However, the concept of sustainable development and its associated tools are very difficult to translate and implement at the site level (Labadi 2013) and governments and local authorities do not routinely collect the data necessary to evaluate the success of management efforts. This problem is well illustrated by the management of tourism and infrastructure development at the Mahabodhi Temple Complex at Bodh Gaya in India (Government of India 2002; HUDC 2006; UNESCO 2010: 140–142).

Inscribed on the World Heritage List in 2002 under all of the World Heritage Convention's criteria except criterion v, the Mahabodhi Temple Complex has direct associations with the life of the Lord Buddha. It is the place where, in 531 BCE, he is believed to have attained the supreme and perfect insight while seated under the Bodhi Tree (UNESCO 2002b). The present temple dates from the late Gupta period, the fifth or sixth centuries, and is one of the earliest Buddhist temples built entirely in brick that is still standing in India. At the time of this site's inscription on the World Heritage List in 2002, the World Heritage Committee noted the lack of a management plan and expressed concern that no tourism monitoring policy was in place. A management plan, also addressing tourism issues, was subsequently adopted and integrated into a larger development plan for the period 2005–2031 (HUDC 2006).

Despite the adoption of this management and development plan, two important issues remain unresolved at the site. The first concerns tourism management. The recent opening of the Gaya International Airport "has been a major catalyst for increasing the number of pilgrims coming from Bangkok, Sri Lanka, Nepal, Burma, and Bhutan" (Geary 2008: 13). This increase will certainly continue in the short- to medium-term, fueled by a boom in regional tourism (Winter 2010: 117–129). This is well exemplified by the peak of 300,000 pilgrims who visited this site within a mere 15 days on the occasion of the Kalachakra Initiation, held at the beginning of 2012. The 2010 state of conservation report for the Mahabodhi Temple laments the continued lack of information on managing the increased flow of visitors (UNESCO 2010: 140). Such lack of information might reflect a lack of visitor management and control. Sustainable development tools, such as carrying capacity, do not seem to have been applied to manage visitation, increasing the risk that uncontrolled and increasing levels of tourism and pilgrimage might lead to long-term damage to the site.

The second unresolved issue concerns new construction. In recent World Heritage State of Conservation reports, the government of India reported that all development activities in Bodh Gaya are now guided by the management plan. That plan stipulates that no new construction should take place within the World Heritage property, and that very limited development related to religious and related usage can be allowed in the buffer zone (HUDC 2006: 100). However, the commitment of the authorities to enforce this ban on construction is open to question and information on the extent of development and its controls is lacking (UNESCO 2010: 141). Pressures arise to circumvent the ban because the increased visitor levels require more hotels and residential facilities. In addition, foreign countries have acquired land around the temple to build religious structures, monasteries, and residential accommodation for their visiting pilgrims (Government of India 2002). The Indian government has not provided information on how new construction is being controlled, raising the prospect that uncontrolled tourism and construction will impact negatively upon the "peaceful atmosphere of this revered site" (Government of India 2002: 27). These developments have been implemented without establishing a threshold of acceptable change, a concept at the heart of sustainable development, as it aims to ensure that present changes do not undermine the key values of the site.

The situation at the Mahabodhi Temple Complex at Bodh Gaya illustrates the challenges presented by the activities, facilities, and patterns of visits by tourists to World Heritage sites and the potential physical, environmental, and cultural impacts or benefits of their visits. The lack of information on these activities makes it difficult in practice to determine measures for ensuring the sustainability of a property and associated benefits. This is due primarily to the multiplicity of local, national, or international actors; the paucity of regulations and the failure to implement those that are in place; and the lack of official standards, principles, and agreed-upon metrics regarding sustainable activities and facilities at World Heritage sites. This situation in Bodh Gaya also illustrates the difficulty of setting up benchmarks and thresholds due to the competing values of the site, including religious, economic, or historical, which all have impacts upon the management and conservation of the site.

World Heritage and Communities

The recent push for the inclusion of community engagement in the World Heritage inscription and management process has also experienced challenges and disappointments. As discussed above, communities are increasingly seen to be at the heart of sustainable development. At its 31st Session in Christchurch, New Zealand, in 2007, the World Heritage Committee decided to add, as one of its strategic objectives, "to enhance the role of communities in the implementation of the World Heritage Convention" (UNESCO 2007: 7). In addition, Paragraph 12 of the latest version of the Operational Guidelines recognizes clearly the importance of community participation in World Heritage processes (UNESCO 2011). However, these initiatives cannot conceal a real ambivalence towards local populations, as highlighted, for instance, by the short lived World Heritage Indigenous Peoples Council of Experts (Meskell 2013). This ambivalence is clearly expressed in the official form for the nomination of sites for inclusion on the World Heritage List, which still presents local communities as threats to nominated properties (Labadi 2013). Numerous threats arising from local communities have been cited in these nomination dossiers: the growth of the local population in the region where the site is located, the danger and/or reality of encroachment by private properties onto the World Heritage site, the need to expropriate private properties from the owners, vehicle circulation and pollution, and vandalism or graffiti. Only a minority of the dossiers analyzed by Labadi interpreted the presence of the population on the site and its renewal as one of the site's fundamental and indispensable features.

There are three possible reasons for this continuing ambivalent attitude toward local communities. First, the mention of local communities as threats in the official form used to nominate sites for inclusion on the World Heritage List may be related to the traditional view within the heritage profession that local communities "are a nuisance and are normally blamed for vandalizing places of heritage due to their perceived limited appreciation of the resources" (Taruvinga and Ndoro 2003: 3, see also Timothy and Boyd 2003: 244). A second reason might relate to the reluctance of international and national experts to share their power with local communities and implement bottom-up strategies. A third reason might be that the outstanding universal value of the site, which is the central concept of the WHC, is considered to be unrelated to and to supersede the concern and legitimate interests of local communities. Regardless, the fact is that the World Heritage process itself contributes to the marginalization of communities that live on or adjacent to World Heritage sites.

In short, sustainable development has not yet been integrated effectively within the processes of the World Heritage Convention. To fill this gap, at its 36th Session in St. Petersburg in 2012, the World Heritage Committee requested the preparation of a specific policy to integrate sustainable development into the processes of the Convention (UNESCO 2012: 6). A working group was formed in 2013 to develop such policy, and one of the authors of this chapter (Labadi) is part of this initiative. Such efforts aside, however, there remains a significant gap between the aspiration for and the implementation of sustainable development concepts in the context of the World Heritage system.

Conclusion

This chapter has explored the connections among three concepts that have acquired a certain saliency in heritage management: sustainable development, community, and economics. While there is no doubt that these concepts are interconnected, and no doubt that they are involved increasingly in the discourse surrounding heritage management, we have attempted in this chapter, particularly through the two case studies presented, to illustrate the long distance that must be travelled before these are more than abstract ideals with little practical application.

The discussion of the World Heritage Convention, and especially the case of the Mahabodhi Temple Complex, has illustrated that the implementation of sustainability concepts in practice can encounter conceptual objections, along with serious bureaucratic and political obstacles, that can undermine sustainable outcomes for communities despite the best intentions of international compacts. The Val di Cornia case illustrates both the substantial potential for economic rebirth that can accrue from heritage resources and the obstacles that practical economic and political pressures can pose, even in small communities, for heritage enterprises seeking to achieve a measure of sustainability. In other words, bureaucratic inertia, a lack of data and metrics, outside economic forces, or local political conflict can lead to outcomes, such as community disempowerment or economic failure, that are the opposite of sustainability.

Confronting these issues will require a different agenda in archaeology and heritage management. Practicing archaeologists and heritage managers need to work assiduously to identify the problems, analyze them objectively with valid data, and then labor to correct practices that lead to undesirable consequences. They must do so even if the consequences include a degree of political or social estrangement from global and national elites, and even if doing so requires archaeologists to change their own practices and priorities or to suspend their political predispositions. Academic training should prepare emerging scholars and heritage professionals not only to engage with the archaeological record or local communities, but also with the global and national economic and political forces that ultimately are shaping the future of heritage sustainability. Increasingly it will become impossible to work in the field without being closely attuned to and conversant in these external factors. To facilitate these efforts, cultural economists need to abandon theoretical abstractions in favor of a political economy that creates usable tools and meaningful institutional models that can be used in practice. In short, heritage practitioners must be equipped – both emotionally and with the necessary skill sets and tools – to turn to a degree of advocacy and political engagement that, while uncomfortable, may be essential if archaeology is actually to uplift the lives of people on a sustainable foundation.

REFERENCES

Aas, C., A. Ladkin, and J. Fletcher (2005) Stakeholder collaboration and heritage management. *Annals of Tourism Research* 32: 28–48.

Appadurai, A. (2004) The Capacity to Aspire: Culture and the Terms of Recognition, in V. Rao and M. Walton (eds), *Culture and Public Action*. Stanford, CA: Stanford Social Sciences, pp. 59–84.

Arizpe, L. (2004) The Intellectual History of Culture and Development Institutions, in V. Rao and M. Walton (eds), *Culture and Public Action*. Stanford, CA: Stanford Social Sciences, pp. 163–185.

Bakhshi, H., A. Reeman, and G. Hitchen (2009) *Measuring intrinsic value--how to stop worrying and love economics. Mission Money Models* web publication. Available at: http://mpra.ub.uni-muenchen.de/14902/. Accessed November 24, 2014.

Balassa, B. (1988) The lessons of East Asian development: An overview. *Economic Development and Cultural Change* 36: S273–S290.

Bandarin, F. and S. Labadi (eds) (2007) *World Heritage: Challenges for the Millennium*. Paris: World Heritage Center.

Barthel-Bouchier, D. (2013) *Cultural Heritage and the Challenge of Sustainability*. Walnut Creek, CA: Left Coast Press.

Batisse, M. and G. Bolla (2005) *The Invention of "World Heritage."* Club Histoire. History Papers 2. Paris: Association des Anciens Fonctionnaires de l'UNESCO (AAFU).
Bhagwati, J. and A. Panagariya (2013) *Why Growth Matters*. New York: PublicAffairs.
Bigio, A. and G. Licciardi (2010) *The Urban Regeneration of Medinas: The World Bank Experience in the Middle East and North Africa*. Washington, DC: The World Bank.
Binswanger-Mkhize, H. P., J. P. de Regt, and S. Spector (2010) *Local and Community Driven Development*. Washington, DC: The World Bank.
Breglia, L. (2009) When Patrimonies Collide: The Case of Chunchucmil, Yucatán, in L. Mortenson and J. Hollowell (eds), *Ethnographies and Archaeologies*. Gainesville: University Press of Florida, pp. 55–70.
Burtenshaw, P. (2013) The Economic Capital of Archaeology: Measurement and Management. Ph.D. dissertation, University College London, United Kingdom.
Castañeda, Q. and J. P. Mathews (2013) Archaeology Meccas of Tourism: Exploration, Protection, and Exploitation, in C. Walker and N. Carr (eds), *Tourism and Archaeology*. Walnut Creek, CA: Left Coast Press, pp. 37–64.
Choi, H. C. and E. Sirakaya (2006) Sustainability indicators for managing community tourism. *Tourism Management* 27: 1274–1289.
Cohen, J. and W. Easterly (2009) *What Works in Development? Thinking Big and Thinking Small*. Washington, DC: The Brookings Institution.
Colette, A. (2007) Climate Change and World Heritage: Report on Predicting and Managing the Impacts of Climate Change on World Heritage and Strategy to Assist States Parties to Implement Appropriate Management Responses. Paris: UNESCO World Heritage Center.
Condorcet, N. (1795) *Outlines of an Historical View of the Progress of the Human Mind*. London.
Deaton, A. (2013) *The Great Escape: Health, Wealth and the Origins of Inequality*. Princeton, NJ and Oxford: Princeton University Press.
de la Torre, M. (2002) *Assessing the Values of Cultural Heritage*. Los Angeles, CA: Getty Conservation Institute.
de Senarclens, P. (1988) *La Crise des Nations Unies*. Paris: Presses Universitaires de France.
Douglas, M. (2004) Traditional Culture – Let's Hear No More About It, in V. Rao and M. Walton (eds), *Culture and Public Action*. Stanford, CA: Stanford Social Sciences, pp. 85–114.
Du Pisani, J. A. (2006) Sustainable development – historical roots of the concept. *Environmental Sciences* 3: 83–96.
Easterly, W. (2006) *The White Man's Burden: Why the West's Efforts to Aid the Rest Have Done So Much Ill and So Little Good*. New York: Penguin.
Easterly, W. (2013) *The Tyranny of Experts: Economists, Dictators and the Forgotten Rights of the Poor*. New York: Basic Books.
Fabrizio, C., P. Snowdon, and N. Prasad (2000) *Change in Continuity: Concepts and Tools for a Cultural Approach to Development*. Paris: UNESCO.
Ferguson, J. (1990) *The Anti-Politics Machine: "Development," Depoliticization and Bureaucratic Power in Lesotho*. Cambridge: Cambridge University Press.
Flipo, F. (2005) Les tensions constitutives du "développement durable". *Développement durable et territoires: Dossier de séance*. Paris: DATAR, pp. 1–6.
Galla, A. (ed.) (2012) *World Heritage: Benefits Beyond Borders*. Cambridge: Cambridge University Press.
Geary, D. (2008) Destination enlightenment: Branding Buddhism and spiritual tourism in Bodhgaya, Bihar. *Anthropology Today* 24: 11–14.
Gould, P. G. (2014) Putting the Past to Work: Archaeology, Community and Economic Development. Ph.D. dissertation, University College London, United Kingdom.
Government of India (2002) Nomination of the Mahabodhi Temple Complex at Bodh Gaya, for inclusion on the World Heritage List.
Habu, J. (ed.) (2008) *Evaluating Multiple Narratives: Beyond Nationalist, Colonialist, Imperialist Archaeologies*. New York: Springer Science + Business Media.

Harmon, D. (2007) A bridge over the chasm: Finding ways to achieve integrated natural and cultural heritage conservation. *International Journal of Heritage Studies* 13: 380–392.
Harrison, L. and S. P. Huntington (2000) *Culture Matters: How Values Shape Human Progress*. New York: Basic Books.
Herzfeld, M. (2010) Engagement, gentrification and the neoliberal hijacking of history. *Current Anthropology* 51: S259–S267.
HLF (2012) *Evaluation: Good Practice Guidance*. London: Heritage Lottery Fund.
Hodder, I. (2003) Archaeological reflexivity and the "local" voice. *Anthropological Quarterly* 76: 55–69.
Hodder, I. (2010) Cultural heritage rights: From ownership and descent to justice and well-being. *Anthropological Quarterly* 83: 861–882.
HUDC (2006) *City Development Plan for Bodhgaya under the JNNURM*. Bodhgaya: Housing and Urban Development Corporation.
Illich, I. (1971) *Celebration of Awareness*. London: Marion Boyars.
Jabareen, Y. (2008) A new conceptual framework for sustainable development. *Environment, Development and Sustainability* 10: 179–192.
Kanninen, T. (2013) *Crisis of Global Sustainability*. London and New York: Routledge.
Keitumetse, S. O. (2009) Sustainable development and cultural heritage management in Botswana: Towards sustainable communities. *Sustainable Development* 19: 49–59.
Kim, S. S., K. K. F. Wong, and M. Cho (2007) Assessing the economic value of a world heritage site and willingness-to-pay determinants: A case of Changdeok Palace. *Tourism Management* 28: 317–322.
Klamer, A. (2002) Accounting for social and cultural values. *De Economist* 150: 453–473.
Klamer, A. (2004) Cultural Goods Are Good for More than Their Economic Value, in V. Rao and M. Walton (eds), *Culture and Public Action*. Stanford, CA: Stanford Social Sciences, pp. 138–162.
Klamer, A. and P.-W. Zuidhof (1988) The Values of Cultural Heritage: Merging Economic and Cultural Appraisals, in M. de la Torre and R. Mason (eds), *Economics and Heritage Conservation*. Los Angeles, CA: Getty Conservation Institute.
Labadi, S. (2011) *Evaluating the Socio-Economic Impacts of Selected Regenerated Heritage Sites in Europe*. Amsterdam: European Cultural Foundation.
Labadi, S. (2013) *UNESCO, Cultural Heritage and Outstanding Universal Value*. Plymouth, MA: AltaMira.
Lafrenz Samuels, K. (2008) Value and significance in archaeology. *Archaeological Dialogues* 15: 71–97.
Lafrenz Samuels, K. (2010) Material Heritage and Poverty Reduction, in S. Labadi and C. Long (eds), *Heritage and Globalisation*. New York: Routledge, pp. 202–217.
Landorf, C. (2009) Managing for sustainable tourism: A review of six cultural World Heritage sites. *Journal of Sustainable Tourism* 17: 53–70.
Licciardi, G. and E. Amirtahmasebi (eds) (2012) *The Economics of Uniqueness: Investing in Historic City Cores and Cultural Heritage Assets for Sustainable Development*. Washington, DC: World Bank.
Lilley, I. (ed.) (2007) *Native Title and the Transformation of Archaeology in the Postcolonial World*. Walnut Creek, CA: Left Coast Press.
Logan, W. (2002) *The Disappearing "Asian" City: Protecting Asia's Urban Heritage in a Globalizing World*. Hong Kong: OUP.
Low, S. (2003) Social Sustainability: People, History, Values, in J. M. Teutonico and F. Matero (eds), *Managing Change: Sustainable Approaches to the Conservation of the Built Environment*. Los Angeles, CA: Getty Conservation Institute, pp. 47–64.
Marshall, Y. (2002) What is community archaeology? *World Archaeology* 34: 211–219.
Mason, R. (2008) Be interested and beware: Joining economic valuation and heritage conservation. *International Journal of Heritage Studies* 14: 303–318.
McManamon, F. P., A. Stout, and J. A. Barnes (eds) (2008) *Managing Archaeological Resources*. Walnut Creek, CA: Left Coast Press.

Meskell, L. (2009a) Introduction: Cosmopolitan Heritage Ethics, in L. Meskell (ed.), *Cosmopolitan Archaeologies*. Durham, NC: Duke University Press, pp. 1–27.

Meskell, L. (2009b) The Nature of Culture in Kruger National Park, in L. Meskell (ed.), *Cosmopolitan Archaeologies*. Durham, NC: Duke University Press, pp. 89–112.

Meskell, L. (2010) Human rights and heritage ethics. *Anthropological Quarterly* 83: 839–859.

Meskell, L. (2012) *The Nature of Heritage: The New South Africa*. Oxford: Wiley Blackwell.

Meskell, L. (2013) UNESCO and the fate of the World Heritage Indigenous People's Council of Experts. *International Journal of Cultural Property* 20: 155–174.

Michael, E. J. (2003) Tourism micro-clusters. *Tourism Economics* 9: 133–145.

Morris, W. (1877) *Manifesto of the Society for the Protection of Ancient Buildings*. London: Society for the Preservation of Ancient Buildings.

Morrison, A., P. Lynch, and N. Johns (2004) International tourism networks. *International Journal of Contemporary Hospitality Management* 16: 197–202.

Moshenska, G. and S. Dhanjal (eds) (2013) *Community Archaeology: Themes, Methods and Practices*. Oxford: Oxbow Books.

Mowforth, M. and I. Munt (2009) *Tourism and Sustainability*. New York: Routledge.

Moyo, D. (2009) *Dead Aid: Why Aid Is Not Working and How There Is a Better Way for Africa*. New York: Farrar, Straus and Giroux.

Nasser, N. (2003) Planning for urban heritage places: Reconciling conservation, tourism, and sustainable development. *Journal of Planning Literature* 17: 467–479.

O'Brien, D. (2010) *Measuring the Value of Culture*. London: UK Department for Culture, Media and Sport.

Ovaska, T. (2003) The failure of development aid. *Cato Journal* 23: 175–188.

Paterlini, A. (2012) Sustainable Archaeology for All in the Crisis Ridden 21st Century. M.A. thesis, University College London, United Kingdom.

Paterlini, A. and P. Gould (2013) Parchi della Val di Cornia, a sustainable community-owned park network in Tuscany. World Archaeological Congress, Dead Sea, Jordan, January 13–18.

Peacock, A. and I. Rizzo (2008) *The Heritage Game: Economics, Policy and Practice*. New York and Oxford: Oxford University Press.

Pearce, D. G. (1992) Alternative Tourism: Concepts, Classifications and Questions, in V. L. Smith and W. R. Eadington (eds), *Tourism Alternatives: Potentials and Problems in the Development of Tourism*. Philadelphia: University of Pennsylvania Press, pp. 15–30.

Pedersen, A. (2002) *Managing Tourism at World Heritage Sites: A Practical Manual for World Heritage Site Managers*. Paris: UNESCO.

Porter, M. E. (1998) Clusters and the new economics of competition. *Harvard Business Review*, pp. 77–90.

Rapley, J. (2004) Development studies and the post-development critique. *Progress in Development Studies* 4: 350–354.

Rauschmayer, F., I. Omann, and J. Frühmann (2011) Needs, Capabilities and Quality of Life, in F. Rauschmayer, I. Omann, and J. Frühmann (eds), *Sustainable Development: Capabilities, Needs and Well-Being*. London and New York: Routledge, pp. 1–24.

Reeve, A. and R. Shipley (2013) *Townscape Heritage Initiative Schemes Evaluation: Ten Year Review Report / Final Report*. Oxford: Department of Planning, Oxford Brookes University.

Riegl, A. (1982 [1928]). The modern cult of monuments: Its character and its origins. *Oppostions* 25.

Rodrik, D. (2007) *One Economics, Many Recipies: Globalization, Institutions and Economic Growth*. Princeton, NJ and Oxford: Princeton University Press.

Salazar, N. (2009) Imaged or imagined? Cultural representations and the "tourismification" of peoples and places. *Cahiers d'Etudes Africaines* 49: 49–71.

Salazar, N. (2012a) Community-based cultural tourism: Issues, threats and opportunities. *Journal of Sustainable Tourism* 20: 9–22.

Salazar, N. (2012b) The Globalisation of Heritage through Tourism: Balancing Standardisation and Differentiation, in S. Labadi and C. Long (eds), *Heritage and Globalisation*. Abingdon and New York: Routledge.

Saxena, G. (2005) Relationships, networks and the learning regions: Case evidence from the Peak District National Park. *Tourism Management* 26: 277–289.

Sen, A. (1983) Development: Which way now? *The Economic Journal* 93: 745–762.

Sen, A. (1999) *Development as Freedom*. New York: Alfred A. Knopf.

Shanin, T. (1997) The Idea of Progress, in M. Rahnema and V. Bawtree (eds), *The Post-Development Reader*. London: Zed Books, pp. 65–72.

Smith, L. and E. Waterton (2009) *Heritage, Community and Archaeology*. London: Duckworth.

Smith, N. (2006) Gentrification Generalized: From Local Anomaly to Urban "Regeneration" as Global Urban Strategy, in M. Fisher and G. Downey (eds), *Frontiers of Capital: Ethnographic Reflections on the New Economy*. Durham, NC: Duke University Press, pp. 191–208.

Stiglitz, J. (2003) *Globalization and its Discontents*. New York: W.W. Norton.

Stiglitz, J. E., A. Sen, and J.-P. Fitoussi (2009) *Report of the Commission on the Measurement of Economic Performance and Social Progress*. Paris: Government of France.

Taruvinga, P. and W. Ndoro (2003) The vandalism of the Domboshava rock painting site, Zimbabwe: Some reflections on approaches to heritage management. *Conservation and Management of Archaeological Sites* 6: 3–10.

Terrill, G. (2008) Climate change: How should the World Heritage Convention respond? *International Journal of Heritage Studies* 14: 388–404.

Teutonico, J. M. and F. Matero (eds) (2003) *Managing Change: Sustainable Approaches to the Conservation of the Built Environment*. Los Angeles, CA: Getty Conservation Institute.

Throsby, D. (2001) *Economics and Culture*. Cambridge: Cambridge University Press.

Throsby, D. (2010) *The Economics of Cultural Policy*. Cambridge: Cambridge University Press.

Throsby, D. (2012) Investment in urban heritage: Economic impacts of cultural heritage projects in FYR Macedonia and Georgia. *Urban Development Series Knowledge Papers 16*. Washington, DC: World Bank.

Timothy, D. J. and S. Boyd (2003) *Heritage Tourism*. London: Prentice Hall.

Tully, G. (2007) Community archaeology: General methods and standards of practice. *Public Archaeology* 6: 155–187.

UNCSD (2012) *The Future We Want*. Rio de Janeiro: United Nations. Available at: http://www.uncsd2012.org/content/documents/727The%20Future%20We%20Want%2019%20June%201230pm.pdf. Accessed November 24, 2014.

UNDP (2004) *Cultural Liberty in Today's Diverse World*. New York: United Nations Development Programme.

UNESCO (1972) *Convention Concerning the Protection of the World Cultural and Natural Heritage*. Paris: UNESCO.

UNESCO (2002a) *Budapest Declaration on World Heritage*. Paris: UNESCO. Available at: http://whc.unesco.org/archive/02budapest-decl.htm. Accessed November 24, 2014.

UNESCO (2002b) *Decisions Adopted by the 26th Session of the World Heritage Committee, 24–29 June 2002, WHC-02/CONF.202/25*. Paris: UNESCO.

UNESCO (2007) Item 13 of the provisional agenda: Evaluation of the results of the implementation of the committee's strategic objectives. Proposal for a "Fifth C" to be added to the Strategic Objectives. *Convention Concerning the Protection of the World Cultural and Natural Heritage – World Heritage Committee – Thirty-first session (23 June–2 July)*. Available at: http://whc.unesco.org/archive/2007/whc07-31com-13be.pdf. Accessed November 24, 2014.

UNESCO (2010) Item 7B of the provisional agenda: State of conservation of World Heritage properties inscribed on the World Heritage List. *Convention Concerning the Protection of the World Cultural and Natural Heritage – World Heritage Committee – Thirty-fourth session (25 July–3 August)*. Paris: UNESCO. Available at: http://whc.unesco.org/archive/2010/whc10-34com-7Be.pdf. Accessed November 24, 2014.

UNESCO (2011) *Operational Guidelines for the Implementation of the World Heritage Convention*. Paris: UNESCO.

UNESCO (2012) *Decisons Adopted by the World Heritage Committee at its 36th Session (St. Petersburg) WHC-12/36.COM/19*. Paris: UNESCO. Available at: http://whc.unesco.org/archive/2012/whc12-36com-19e.pdf. Accessed November 24, 2014.

UNESCO AND UNEP (2002) *Cultural Diversity and Biodiversity for Sustainable Development*. A jointly convened UNESCO and UNEP high-level Roundtable held on 3 September 2002 in Johannesburg during the World Summit on Sustainable Development. Available at: unesdoc.unesco.org/images/0013/001322/132262e.pdf. Accessed November 24, 2014.

UNLC (2008) *Agenda 21 for Culture*. Barcelona: United Cities and Local Governments.

Valentin, A. and J. H. Spangenberg (2000) A guide to community sustainability indicators. *Environmental Impact Assessment Review* 20: 381–392.

Walker, C. and N. Carr (eds) (2013) *Tourism and Archaeology*. Walnut Creek, CA: Left Coast Press.

WCCD (1996) *Our Creative Diversity*. New York: World Commission on Culture and Development.

WCED (1987) Our common future: From one earth to one world. *Report of the World Commission on Environment and Development: Our Common Future*. New York: United Nations.

Weiss, L. (2007) Heritage-making and political identity. *Journal of Social Archaeology* 7: 413–431.

Winter, T. (2010) Heritage Tourism: Dawn of a New Era?, in S. Labadi and C. Long (eds), *Heritage and Globalization*. New York: Routledge, pp. 117–129.

Winter, T. and P. Daly (2012) Heritage in Asia: Converging Forces, Conflicting Values, in P. Daly and T. Winter (eds), *Handbook of Heritage in Asia*. Abingdon and Oxford: Routledge, pp. 1–36.

Zancheti, S. (2011) Measuring urban heritage conservation: Theory and structure (part 1). *Journal of Cultural Heritage Management and Sustainable Development* 1: 96–108.

Zancheti, S. M. and L. T. F. Hidaka (2012) Measuring urban heritage conservation: Indicator, weights and instruments (part 2). *Journal of Cultural Heritage Management and Sustainable Development* 2: 15–26.

10

Transnationalism and Heritage Development

Kathryn Lafrenz Samuels and Ian Lilley

Introduction

Cultural heritage bears a foundational relationship to globalization. It acts as a lynchpin, honoring diversity and difference while also feeding the norming bent of international cooperation. More than a mere symptom of the increased rapidity and intensity of global relations, heritage structures interactions that reach beyond local contexts. It offers a way to organize diversity within a global community. In this chapter we address the ways in which heritage has "gone global" in the past few decades, highlighting the key role played by economic development in bringing heritage to the international stage.

It was within an international setting that the term "cultural heritage" gained salience and became a transportable concept: through the international legal regime of UNESCO conventions that seek to protect cultural resources for their transmission to future generations (Forrest 2010). Indeed cultural heritage in its international context can be primarily understood through the work of UNESCO and its associated Advisory Bodies – ICOMOS, ICCROM, and IUCN – discussed further below, as well as through important court cases that developed within international legal regimes built up around the UNESCO conventions (see Bauer 2015). The chapter in this volume by Meskell and Brumann addresses this international sphere of influence, while the chapter by Labadi and Gould considers issues for heritage practitioners in relation to the UN's Millennium Development Goals (MDGs).

However, the international context of heritage is not the only realm of activity at the global level, and it is useful to define some terms that are typically used by political scientists and political philosophers, among others, working on social and political activities that span the globe. In this respect we follow the definitions provided by Thomas Hale and David Held (2011). "International," strictly speaking, refers to "state-to-state interactions in which one sovereign country deals with another" (Hale and Held 2011: 4), and so it is through UNESCO and the international legal system that we see states interacting with one another over matters of cultural heritage. As discussed, it is here in state-to-state relations that the concept of cultural heritage first

Global Heritage: A Reader, First Edition. Edited by Lynn Meskell.

gained grip, and was envisioned as a common responsibility for the international community. But since the rise of the international heritage system under UNESCO in the 1960s and 1970s, cultural heritage has been mobilized in a variety of other global contexts, crossing national boundaries, which fall outside state-to-state relations. "Transnational" refers to this area of interaction.

While the international heritage work of UNESCO and its Advisory Bodies tends to be associated with conservation, the transnational side of heritage activities is strongly interconnected with the use of cultural heritage resources for economic development (Lafrenz Samuels forthcoming). It is important to note, however, that just as conservation and development represent two sides of the same coin in heritage management, the international and transnational dimensions of heritage activity often work in concert and are not easily separated from one another. For example, one of the first large-scale heritage development projects, in Fez, Morocco, was initiated at the behest of the UNESCO World Heritage Centre. Also, national governments frequently nominate sites for inscription on the World Heritage List in the hope of attracting private investment and boosting tourism revenue.

In the following, we first map out the central actors involved in heritage internationalism, and then turn to the relationships being forged between international development and cultural heritage. These relationships include the involvement of archaeological research and heritage management in compliance work required for meeting the social and environmental safeguards set by multilateral development banks and private corporations, what we could call international compliance archaeology or "heritage in development." Another area of important activity is "heritage as development," or simply "heritage development," where cultural heritage is targeted as a resource to be developed for economic growth. This work is often undertaken by the same actors as those setting safeguards – that is, multilateral development banks and private corporations – but also includes a range of other transnational actors such as NGOs, global cultural resource management firms, and professional networks. We then illustrate the growing importance of cultural heritage in international development through several case studies.

The Main Players

The three major clusters of organizations with which practitioners should be familiar are (1) the United Nations system, (2) multilateral development banks and other lenders, and (3) global corporations.[1]

The United Nations

The United Nations system is large and complicated. This chapter complements treatment of the UN elsewhere in this volume. It concentrates on what might be thought of as adjuncts to the UN, namely the statutory Advisory Bodies to UNESCO on World Heritage: ICOMOS, IUCN, and ICCROM, with an emphasis on the IUCN.

UN heritage work is routed primarily through the United Nations Organization for Education, Science and Culture (UNESCO). The UNESCO body of most importance to heritage managers is the World Heritage Centre (WHC), established under the 1972 World Heritage Convention. The WHC directs World Heritage nomination processes and generates policy and procedure concerning World Heritage management. The Convention also assists countries to strengthen their broader national cultural heritage management capabilities.

The World Heritage Center is assisted by three independent statutory Advisory Bodies (see Meskell and Brumann this volume). The one responsible for cultural heritage is the International Council on Monuments and Sites (ICOMOS), based in Paris. Although its permanent Secretariat is small and relatively poorly resourced, ICOMOS has national committees in many countries and numerous International Scientific Committees or (ISCs) to help carry out its technical functions The other Advisory Bodies are the International Centre for the Study of the Preservation and Restoration of Cultural Property (ICCROM), based in Rome, and the International Union for the Conservation of Nature (IUCN), headquartered in Gland, Switzerland. ICCROM is largely a training group. Its members are individual nation-states, rather than individual people as in ICOMOS, and it has over 130 such state members. ICCROM runs courses in the conservation and preservation of heritage items and materials, maintains a major library, provides technical advice, and facilitates conferences and technical meetings.

In comparison with ICCROM and especially ICOMOS, the IUCN is a vast and very well-resourced organization, with about 1,000 permanent employees around the world. Like ICCROM, its membership comprises nation-states but also includes institutions and organizations such as government agencies, non-governmental and intergovernmental organizations and political/economic integration organizations. There are currently over 1,200 such members. In place of ICOMOS's committees, the IUCN has six Commissions and myriad other groupings dealing with a vast array of matters including cultural heritage. Individuals can be members of the IUCN through membership in one or more of the six Commissions. There are presently some 11,000 individual Commission members.

Although technically concerned with nature conservation and natural heritage, the IUCN has a clear and growing interest in cultural matters. In contrast to the more European approach of ICOMOS, which is deeply influenced by architecture and, to a lesser degree, art history, the IUCN approaches cultural questions from a strongly North American anthropological standpoint, with substantial involvement of indigenous, native, and local community representatives and supporters. The IUCN's perspective on cultural heritage is clear in its work on "sacred natural sites."[2] This is not to say, however, that the IUCN is strongly focused on culture or cultural heritage in any concrete way at the institution level. Although the organization has resolved to incorporate culture in its policies and programing, no formal steps have been taken to do so, and the area is not seen as a funding priority (Lilley 2013b). This situation may reflect a concern at the executive level of the IUCN not to overlap in a formal way with the work of ICOMOS. These two Advisory Bodies have historically not communicated effectively, yet they are now developing stronger links since both understand that cultural and natural heritage are best managed when integrated.[3]

Other UN bodies with interests in cultural heritage include the International Labour Organization (ILO), the World Intellectual Property Organization (WIPO), the UN Permanent Forum on Indigenous Issues (UNPFII), and the Convention on Biological Diversity (CBD). Although focused on labor rights, the ILO supports development programs that overlap with policies and programs entailing heritage as a "driver of development."[4] WIPO programs cover cultural heritage, indigenous intellectual property, museum collections, and other matters of importance to heritage managers.[5]

UNPFII staunchly criticizes the World Heritage system for disregarding indigenous perspectives and concerns (cf. Logan 2013; Meskell 2013).[6] In 2013 the nomination of the aboriginal Pimachiowin Aki property in Canada was deferred by the World Heritage Committee because the nomination dossier did not adequately integrate World Heritage policies and procedures with First Nations' holistic approaches to their heritage.[7] This has brought UNPFII's issues with World Heritage as a concept and a process under renewed focus.

The Secretariat of the Convention on Biological Diversity is housed within the UN Environment Programme (UNEP).[8] Although principally concerned with the natural world, the CBD acknowledges the role of people and culture in the protection of biodiversity.[9] In addition, the CBD's *Akwé: Kon Guidelines* for environmental impact assessments on indigenous and local community lands specifically cover cultural heritage.[10] The UNEP itself, as well as the related UN Development Program (UNDP), oversees various other programs relevant to heritage management, such as the Community Management of Protected Areas Conservation Programme.[11]

There is significant interest in cultural heritage on the part of international agencies and organizations whose remit is technically focused on the natural world. Typically, however, archaeologists and cultural heritage managers remain unaware of this interest or are hostile towards it and are thus unable to build strategic partnerships of mutual benefit to both "sides" of heritage management. This is shortsighted at a time when indigenous and other local communities are advocating for heritage managers to merge nature and culture more effectively in their policies and procedures.

Multilateral development banks and other lenders

Multilateral development banks include the World Bank and regional organizations such as the African Development Bank, Asian Development Bank, European Bank for Reconstruction and Development, and Inter-American Development Bank. All have social and environmental impact or "safeguard" policies, but only the World Bank has a policy expressly concerning cultural heritage, known in the Bank as "physical cultural resources."[12] Intangible cultural heritage, also called "cultural resources" by the Bank but primarily meaning intellectual property, is the preserve of the safeguard covering Indigenous people.[13]

On the ground, the Bank generally leaves heritage impact assessment and management to "local country systems." The latter are ostensibly required to come up to international standards, or be strengthened with the Bank's help until they do. In reality, the Bank usually remains at arm's length. Indeed, despite the supposed requirement for cultural heritage to be considered in Bank-funded projects, abundant anecdotal evidence indicates that it is often to be disregarded entirely or dealt with perfunctorily at best. All safeguards are presently under review.[14]

The International Finance Corporation (IFC) is part of the wider World Bank Group but lends to the private sector (e.g., mining companies), not countries. The IFC used the Bank's safeguard policies before creating its own Performance Standards (PS), and the two are closely aligned. PS8 deals with cultural heritage and PS7 with Indigenous people; the two overlap to some degree.[15] Some 78 commercial banks and financial institutions subscribe to the Equator Principles.[16] These principles are framed as risk-management guidance for financiers of development projects likely to have social and environmental impacts. They mention cultural heritage but link to the IFC's Performance Standards for more detail.

Global corporations

All major corporations engaged in development have social and environmental policies and procedures, often glossed as corporate social responsibility (CSR). Action regarding heritage is often dismissed as "bluewash," or the manipulation of

UN-related concerns such as heritage or human rights to cover up corporate greed and malpractice. Others acknowledge that commercial entities can have genuine social consciences or at least that CSR frameworks provide internally generated standards to which transnational corporations can be held accountable by threat to their legal and social licenses to operate. Fortuitously for those taking action against corporate wrongdoing, such licenses often apply more strongly in the Western nations where such corporations are headquartered than in the regions in which they operate. This means corporations can be sued or have their reputations severely damaged in the West for actions they have perpetrated elsewhere, where the rule of law and issues of social standing may not be as much of an issue.

Regardless of how one interprets the motivation behind its CSR initiatives, Rio Tinto is at the global forefront with regard to concrete action on cultural heritage. The company recently formulated internal guidance on "why cultural heritage matters."[17] This guidance applies throughout the company wherever it operates, even in cases where national or local legislation, policy, and procedure do not require heritage work to the same standard.

It is not only individual transnational corporations that invest in CSR, it is also the bodies that represent the various sectors of industry activity. For instance, the International Council on Mining and Metals (ICCM) is the mining sector's umbrella body. The ICMM's 10 Principles do not mention heritage, yet Principle 3 pertaining to culture covers the topic.[18] The oil and gas equivalent is the International Association of Oil and Gas Producers (OGP).[19] Although its 2002 publication *Key Questions in Managing Social Issues in Oil & Gas Projects*[20] is dated, it includes a summary of cultural heritage issues that follows early World Bank definitions and approaches. The oil and gas industry also has the Global Oil and Gas Industry Association for Environmental and Social Issues (IPIECA).[21] Its guidance documents expressly discuss cultural heritage in relation to development impacts on Indigenous people (deferring to IFC Performance Standards 7 and 8).

Safeguards and Compliance Archaeology

Impact on the discipline

The web of compliance policies and practices described above has had a profound effect on the practice of archaeology and cultural heritage management. One obvious sign of this is the fact that the vast majority of archaeologists around the world are directly or indirectly employed by the compliance industry, whether in civil-society and non-government organizations, as private- and public-sector archaeologists and heritage managers or as trainers, including university staff who teach heritage management.

Indeed, in many parts of the world there is no such thing as "pure" academic archaeology, and has not been for decades. This is because national, provincial, and local government compliance regimes aligned with UN and other international perspectives, policies, and procedures often closely govern the heritage management dimensions of academic research. This can take the form of restrictions on how much of a site can be dug, for example, or requirements for ancillary work, such as additional site recording, that is not entailed in the academic project itself, or rules specifying which excavated material can be analyzed by what technique (e.g., non-destructive versus destructive) and whether material can leave the country in which the site is located or must be returned in a certain way on a specified schedule. Even where such regulatory frameworks do not exist or are not enforced, practitioners mindful of "best practice" elsewhere can impose similar restrictions on themselves, or indeed have them imposed by other interested parties such as global corporations like Rio Tinto that maintain their own standards.

Archaeologists have begun exploring the conceptual and practical ramifications of "compliance culture" for the discipline, in relation to both the impacts of private-sector development such as mining and oil and gas (e.g., MacEachern 2010), public-sector (or public–private partnership) development such as dams (e.g., King and Nic Eoin 2014), and public-sector activity such as World Heritage listing and other heritage management work that explicitly or implicitly situates heritage as a "driver of development" (e.g., Breen 2007; Lafrenz Samuels 2009). As discussed in this volume by Labadi and Gould, the UN General Assembly is now integrating heritage into the Millennium Development Goals. It was in that context that the matter formed the focus of the 2011 ICOMOS General Assembly Symposium in Paris.

In terms of development and compliance, MacEachern (2010) has described the relationship between Exxon and archaeology on the Chad Export Project, a major development in Africa in which the World Bank was also involved. Although not the focus of the paper, an important background dimension of the discussion concerns the interdigitated, but usually unintegrated, nature of the global heritage compliance regime on the ground. In this case, a major global corporate with its internal compliance policies and procedures was part of the same project as a multilateral lender with its own safeguards but the two never met up in any effective way over cultural heritage.

MacEachern's work expands on anthropologist James Ferguson's (2005) insights into the formation of externally owned and managed resource-extraction enclaves that are largely sealed off from the surrounding countryside and its inhabitants. MacEachern's contention is that even excellent archaeological and heritage work in such situations does little to advance archaeology and heritage knowledge or to strengthen research and management capacities beyond the project's lifetime and its physical footprint. Although MacEachern refers to Africa, and, like Ferguson, especially to the ill-governed and so-called "unusable" parts of the continent, such enclaves exist all over the world, including in places such as Australia.

In essence all enclave-based projects have a similar impact on archaeology and heritage management, namely making little or no contribution to archaeology and heritage management beyond the spatial and temporal boundaries of the enclave itself. MacEachern wants us to ask ourselves whether we want to be part of such projects when the ways in which their compliance protocols are operationalized not only under-delivers for archaeology and heritage management but also – and more importantly, from a broader ethical perspective – facilitates "the exploitation and mismanagement of [natural] resources" with no discernible benefit to the bulk of the population (MacEachern 2010: 263; cf. Welch and Lilley 2013).

Archaeologists King and Nic Eoin consider similar issues in relation to intangible cultural heritage. They argue (2014: 196) that developer perspectives "[dissociate] intangibles from their material correlates, and … [transform] landscape experiences by dissolving and reconstituting boundaries and 'resources.'" Their brief was to "preserve by recording" the intangible cultural heritage in an area in Lesotho, Africa, to be flooded by a dam. Overall, the project made a concerted effort to overcome well-described "endemic problems of development scheme" (2014: 197), and indeed is one of the only projects in Africa to consider intangible heritage at all. Yet because of the way intangible heritage is conceived by the developer, the replacement of the local landscape by a dam will result in "trauma on the part of landscape inhabitants and irreplaceable loss" (2014: 216), regardless of the quality of the heritage work that is done according to the developer's outlook, even when that outlook is relatively nuanced and sympathetic to heritage issues.

Although ostensibly concerned to protect archaeological and other cultural property – and often developed and implemented with the best of intentions, commercial imperatives notwithstanding – global compliance protocols frequently fail to do what archaeologists and heritage managers think such policies and procedures should or could do, either for the cultural heritage in question or the populations whose heritage is at stake.

If one traces the conceptual genealogies of the global compliance policies and procedures described earlier, it is clear they all ultimately rest on definitions of culture and heritage originally formulated under UN auspices. It is therefore of interest to think about what sort of culture and, by extension, heritage the UN seeks to support through such mechanisms. Nielsen (2011: 279) asserts that the UN bureaucracy works to shape and project a progressivist "'correct' meaning of culture [that] refers to tolerance, dialogue, democracy, participation, choice and openness." On this basis, he maintains "UNESCO decides in what way people should be civilized" (2011: 288). Following Nielsen's argument, archaeologists and heritage managers working in accordance with compliance protocols based explicitly or implicitly on UN definitions and outlooks risk promoting injustice by mistaking serious social and political rifts as desirable multicultural color, and thus not seeing or attempting to diminish inequalities in resource distribution created by such divisions (Nielsen 2011: 287; cf. Elliott and Schmutz 2012). As King and Nic Eoin (2014: 197) note, in such circumstances "heritage emerges as a weapon as much as an asset."

Other matters we would like to consider here coalesce around what Stirrat (2000) calls "cultures of consultancy." His contention is that although development consultants – and we include archaeologists and heritage managers in this group – are supposedly employed to make professional interventions in the development process, analysis of their output indicates that its value is assessed on aesthetic rather than practical grounds: on form rather than function. The form in question is directly connected with what Nielsen (2011) a decade later called the "right" kind of culture, namely adherence to "a particular vision of modernity" (Stirrat 2000: 31) which in this case values objectivity, rationality, and legitimacy. On these ground, he states (2000: 43), "what consultants do is a cultural activity," the aim of which is to produce reports with certain characteristics, not to have "a direct and predictable impact on the real world."

Stirrat's position is provocative, although it may resonate with those involved in consultancy or contract work. Even if consultants fervently believe in what they are doing, there is no doubt that reports have to follow a particular format to be acceptable to clients and compliance agencies. Indeed, some organizations have report templates to ensure a minimal level of compliance in terms of format if not content details (e.g., World Bank, ICOMOS).

In Australia it is common to find lengthy, standardized, and often unnecessary blocks of text "front-ended" into heritage consultancy reports. Without such padding, many reports would be very short and without sufficient weight to be taken seriously, or to be seen as value for money, regardless of the strength of the project-specific content. Acceptability is thus to varying degrees a matter of "quantity not quality." Whether and to what extent one's reports are then acted upon clearly depends upon how "serious" they, and by extension the consultant, are seen to be. Whether a developer or a compliance agency, the client may have a considerable and disproportionate say over what is presented in a report and in what way, even if the consultant resists any attempts to modify the project-specific content to suit the client's purposes (including one-size-fits-all heritage management approaches of compliance agencies).

Allied to this question is one that concerns what Green (2012) calls "anticipatory development." By this she means the ways in which aspiring consultants and contactors adopt postures to break into the consulting scene and gain access to often very substantial funding. Echoing Stirrat, Green argues "this is mostly concerned with adopting the appropriate form, which enables recognition … and potentially capacity for funding." This "emphasis on form," Green writes, "is a shortcut to legitimacy" (2012: 322). Aspiring participants must "talk the talk" before clients are likely to give them a chance to "walk the talk." But the language is that of the client, namely the developer or compliance agency, rather than the archaeologist or cultural heritage manager on the ground.

The discipline's response (and lack of impact) on the international context

How have archaeologists and heritage managers reacted to the foregoing situation? How have they attempted to improve the perspectives, policies, and procedures of the UN system, lenders, or developers? What have they done to inject their insights gained while trying to put global compliance protocols into practice "at the coalface" (sometimes literally, in mining regions)? From the foregoing discussion it is obvious they are writing about it in academic books and journals. They are also talking about it amongst themselves online and at conferences and "trade" meetings, but what are they *actually doing* to effect change in a concrete way? Some specific examples are discussed below in a case study. Suffice to say that while archaeologists and heritage managers are involved in international efforts on many fronts, the scene remains highly fragmented and, in comparison with nature conservation, disorganized and ineffectual.

Some international and regional professional organizations periodically act in concert to send letters to governments or each other about this or that archaeological or heritage issue. The impact of such activity is variable but almost always slight. It is noteworthy that no archaeological or cultural heritage organization or consortium thereof has ever joined the World Bank's biannual Civil Society Forum.[22] This is where practitioners could have a direct impact on World Bank policy and procedure. To our knowledge only a few archaeological or cultural heritage bodies are involved in the current review of the World Bank safeguards. When it was first proposed that the IFC have its own performance standards separate from World Bank safeguards, the only mention of cultural heritage in the invited civil society interventions was in relation to traditional knowledge and the Convention on Biological Diversity.[23] There was no external archaeological or cultural heritage management input.

In 2000 renowned international heritage lawyer Patrick O'Keefe observed that archaeology and cultural heritage are simply not on the international radar screen, at least not in any manner that matters when major changes are occurring in global policy and procedure, even if those shifts directly affect archaeological and cultural heritage interests right around the world. Nothing has changed in the intervening 15 years, though there are emerging glimmers of hope, as the first case study below makes clear.

Heritage Development

From the preceding discussion, we see that cultural heritage occupies a significant place in the safeguards established to manage the risks and lessen the potentially deleterious social impacts of international development. Further, the rise of international safeguards has had real effects on the discipline of archaeology and heritage management, but with limited influence in the other direction.

However, the *relevance* of cultural heritage to development agendas has changed dramatically on account of the establishment of safeguards and the international compliance archaeology built up around them. This is because an in-house expertise in heritage was cultivated within the large development banks through experience with the safeguards. Archaeological finds were appearing in the course of large infrastructure projects that move earth, such as dams and pipelines, and the safeguards provided an institutional mechanism for addressing these finds in a socially responsible way.

The same was true for historic buildings in the context of urban development. Suddenly, because of the safeguards, the material past was seen to have value. It was only a matter of time before the cultural heritage that was once perceived as a nuisance in the way of development underwent a radical makeover, and became the means to development. This heretofore under-utilized resource was the perfect frontier for economic development, and arrived on the development scene at a timely moment (Lafrenz Samuels forthcoming).

International development in the 1980s and 1990s was under intense criticism from many quarters, including anthropologists (Escobar 1995; Ferguson 1990; Scott 1998). Anthropological critiques of development documented the harsh effects of structural adjustment policies, which were written into the terms of loans and required borrower countries to undertake fiscal reforms in line with neoliberal rationalities: decentralization, privatization, trade liberalization, and the withdrawal of the state from social provisioning (Harvey 2005). Anthropologists such as James Ferguson (1990) pointed to the widespread failure of development projects to meet their intended results, at the same time that development required this failure, indeed fed on it, as failed projects provided the impetus for further development projects. By and large, international development was characterized as out of touch with the communities these projects were meant to benefit and among which the projects were being implemented. The projects failed without the support of local communities, with no sustainability after the project period ended. Moreover, development experts lacked the proper indicators to account for what precisely economic improvement was, or was meant to be doing. Anthropologists emphasized the cultural specificity of conceptions of "the good life," and the fact that rising economic growth might not figure in local cultural priorities, especially as economic growth meant rising affluence for some and not others, promoting widening inequality even as GNP rose (Horowitz 1996).

It was within this context that cultural heritage was embraced by the largest multilateral development banks such as the World Bank and Inter-American Development Bank (Edelman and Haugerud 2005; Goldman 2005; Hibou 2000). Development experts were accustomed to incorporating criticism into new development initiatives, and so the turn to a gentler "good governance" paradigm replaced the structural adjustment model. Required economic reforms were replaced by economic targets, and the external top-down imposition of neoliberal policies was replaced by the – more philosophically acceptable to neoliberalism – internal mechanisms of self-monitoring, on the part of the state and especially by directing responsibility downwards to the community level (Anders 2005; Mosse 2005). Cultural heritage offered an ideal lynchpin between bottom-up community development and the large-scale integrated development approach favored by development agencies and organizations (Hackenberg 2002). More importantly, heritage usefully represented the cultural context that development banks had been criticized for ignoring, and was seen as offering a more sustainable approach to development.

Sustainability, participation, and human capabilities

Sustainability arose as the new paradigm of development in the early 1990s, and the term encompassed social, economic, and environmental sustainability. Culture went from being a denigrated term in development circles, as impeding development, to a celebrated cornerstone of development. Securing social sustainability required the promotion of social inclusion and diversity. The importance of culture to development was promulgated especially by UNESCO, which through a series of important conferences and publications helped shape the idea of sustainable development and the centrality of culture to such an approach. The term "human development" was adopted by the United Nations Development Programme (UNDP). In the key document on sustainability, *Our Creative Diversity* (UNESCO 1995), the World Commission on Culture and Development defined culture as "the whole complex of distinctive spiritual, material, intellectual, and emotional features that characterize a society or social group," building on definitions of culture established at the 1982 World Conference on Cultural Policies held in Mexico City. Another important arena was the Intergovernmental Conference on Cultural Policies for Development, held in Stockholm in 1998, which advocated for states to "design and establish cultural policies or review existing ones in such a way that they become one of the key components of endogenous and sustainable development" (UNESCO and Government of Italy 2000: 275).

Development practice was shaped into sustainable development through attention to social inclusion, identity, cultural expression, and cultural diversity. The emphasis on diversity mirrored environmental understandings of sustainability. Indeed, the management of cultural and natural resources shared conceptual space under sustainable development, with the "intergenerational equity principle" and the "precautionary principle" applying to both natural and cultural resource management. Intergenerational equity provides for the needs of the present generation without compromising the capacity of future generations to meet their own needs (a definition going back to the foundational *Our Common Future* report, UNESCO 1987a), and the precautionary principle advocates a risk-averse approach where irreversible consequences of loss are possible (Rypkema 2010; Throsby 2003, 2005, 2012). These principles of sustainable development apply to both natural and cultural resources because they represent resources that have been inherited from previous generations, and require care in order to be passed down to following generations lest the resources deteriorate.

Under sustainable development, cultural heritage became the creative adaptation of traditional resources to new income-generating industries, and it is this reworking of past endowments for present purposes that differentiates heritage development from the conservation mission of international heritage work, pursued for example through the state-to-state relations of UNESCO World Heritage and its advisory bodies. However, the World Bank adopted and adapted the original vision of sustainable development offered by UNESCO at the Stockholm conference (Duer 1999). "Culture" at the World Bank was understood to include both material and intangible forms, such as communal practices and creative expression (e.g., oral history, language, literature, performing arts, fine arts, and crafts). Culture was also presented as one of the only resources available to the poor, lacking other resources, and therefore provided a basis upon which to generate income. Most directly, this rationale encouraged the development of traditional resources, both tangible and intangible, through such industries as handicraft production, tourism, and historic building rehabilitation in urban regeneration projects. It was in the latter two cases – tourism and urban regeneration – that the World Bank had the most experience. It ran urban development projects in Lahore in India and in Tunis and Fez in North Africa (these latter projects are discussed further below), as well as tourism projects in Bethlehem in Israel, Split/Kastela Bay in Croatia, and country-wide in Jordan, Turkey, Ethiopia, and Lebanon.

Cultural heritage became a central strategy of sustainable development at leading multilateral development banks such as the World Bank and the Inter-American Development Bank. Today development work at the World Bank built around cultural heritage continues to center on urban heritage conservation and revitalization of historic urban cores (Bigio and Licciardi 2010; Licciardi and Amirtahmasebi 2012), and sustainable tourism (Endresen et al. 1999; Hawkins and Mann 2007; World Bank 2009a, 2009b, 2009c). A concern with fostering participation has also figured prominently, in addition to capacity-building of national heritage management sectors and at the local level. Capacity-building means institutional strengthening. It involves activities such as training in conservation methods and management practices, administrative reorganization, establishing and strengthening heritage laws, and has philosophical affinity with the human capability approach in development (i.e., Nussbaum 1997; Sen 1999).

Overall, the World Bank has led the growth of heritage development, establishing best practices and supporting regular expert meetings to discuss new tools, approaches, and case studies. The Inter-American Development Bank (IDB) has also been very active in building expertise in heritage development, particularly in historic city cores, and sharing the results of its efforts (Deruyterre 2006; Galvani 2007a, 2007b; Rojas 1999, 2007; Rojas and de Moura Castro 1999). Furthermore, heritage development activities have seen a marked increase due to transnational actors such as heritage consulting firms, NGOs, and private investors following the lead of the World Bank and IDB. This emerging sphere of heritage development, working alongside and beyond the auspices of the large development banks, is discussed further below.

However, the growth of heritage development has not lived up to its hype in promising a more sustainable and socially attuned foundation for economic growth. Overreaching modernist fantasies still plague development thinking as before, and urban regeneration slides too easily into gentrification (Lafrenz Samuels 2010a), while tourism revenue tends to exacerbate rather than narrow existing social and economic inequalities (Adams 2015). The central role of participation and capacity-building in heritage development also encourages the sort of internal self-regulation that mimics neoliberal market mechanisms, and directs blame for project failure downward to local government and community levels (Cooke and Kothari 2001; Mosse 2005). However, there is the feeling that heritage development is still in its infancy and the kinks remaining to be worked out are not insurmountable. Perhaps hope remains that heritage development will be more closely adapted to the needs of specific projects, with the growing diversity of transnational actors other than the large multilateral development banks becoming involved in heritage development.

Heritage and Development in Action

The past is prologue: Heritage development and the World Bank in North Africa

> The past is prologue. The patrimony is both foundation for the present and a building block for developments in the future. Forthcoming generations are entitled to receive their ancestors' cultural heritage well safeguarded and to fully enjoy it.
>
> Michael Cernea (2001a: 86)

In the past 25 years, the World Bank has positioned itself as a global leader in developing heritage. The region of North Africa has been central to this project, as a global case study of sorts on the promise of cultural heritage for economic growth and poverty reduction. The key role of North Africa, and the Middle East and North Africa (MENA) region more broadly, is showcased in the foundational document *Cultural Heritage and Development: A Framework for Action in the Middle East and North Africa*, written by one of the leading anthropologists at the World Bank, Michael Cernea (2001a). The publication was a rallying cry for developing the World Bank's expertise in heritage, with its MENA regional office leading the way and setting the standard for the other regional offices. Within the MENA region, and North Africa in particular, the World Bank's expertise in heritage development was built through a progression of projects starting in the early 1990s and becoming ever more ambitious in size and scope (Lafrenz Samuels 2009, 2010a, 2010b).

Why North Africa? What conditions made the development of its heritage resources a good idea? Several intersecting factors explain the sudden relevance of heritage development to improving the socioeconomic lot of the region's inhabitants. The MENA region embodies a distinctive set of concerns for development experts, including issues of security, terrorism, failed states, and fragile democracies, which experts believed could be overcome through economic growth. However, investment in the region was low: total net flows of Foreign Direct Investment (FDI) from 1975 to 2000 were barely 1 percent, where FDI is a measure of integration into the world economy. Cultural heritage was thus seen as a way to integrate MENA into the world both economically and socially through cultural tourism: by attracting foreign investment for tourism infrastructure (e.g., hotels, tour companies) and encouraging the kinds of face-to-face interactions of MENA residents with foreign visitors that tourism brings. Ultimately, economic reform in the MENA region was pursued to effect political reform (Bush 2007; Harrigan, Wang, and El-Said 2006). Much of the archaeological heritage being developed was also of Western origin – the material legacy of the Roman empire – and so it was believed would further attract Western tourism.

The World Bank's first heritage development project – with heritage as the focus – was the Fez Medina Rehabilitation Project (1998–2005) in Fez, Morocco. This project was modeled after an earlier project of urban rehabilitation in the Tunis medina, Tunisia, that took place in the early 1980s (Akrout Yaïche 2002; Bahri-Meddeb and Binous 1994;

Serageldin 1999; World Bank Harvard University Graduate School of Design Unit for Housing and Urbanization, and Association Sauvegarde de la Médina de Tunis 1999). Called the Third Urban Development Project, the project was also known more colloquially as the Oukalas Project, after the Tunisian word for unsafe and overcrowded housing caused by structural changes to houses through repeated subdivisions (the process is referred to as *oukalization*) (Escher and Schepers 2008; McGuinness 2005). This project, moreover, built on a previous UNESCO urban rehabilitation project in the Tunis medina (UNESCO 1974) and several other urban projects dating back to the 1940s. The historic character of the Tunis medina was not the focus of development, however, but rather addressing the unsafe living conditions brought about by *oukalization*.

The Fez medina was the first site in Morocco to be inscribed to the World Heritage List, in 1981, and it is known as the best preserved historic center in the MENA region. Four years after the medina's inscription, UNESCO launched a campaign to conserve the deteriorating urban fabric of the city. Initially the project was concerned with the provision of services (e.g., sanitation, plumbing, and emergency services) that were hampered by the narrow winding streets of the medina. The project was fraught, as the first feasibility study cut wide swathes through the historic buildings of the medina, to which UNESCO objected, and additional issues with funding led UNESCO to the World Bank to ask for assistance in implementing the project (Hardouin 1983; Lanchet 2003; Navez-Bouchanine, Lahbil, and Fejjal 1995; UNDP 1992a, 1992b; UNESCO 1987b, 1992; World Bank 1997, 1998). The Fez medina is also home to entrenched poverty, and the World Bank's scoping work during 1993–1997 was key to building competence at the World Bank in developing heritage under its then-new brand of socially inclusive, sustainable development.

Together with the government of Morocco, the World Bank prepared a new urban improvement plan with the shared goals of historic rehabilitation and reduction of poverty. Poverty reduction was envisioned through job creation, rising property values, and pollution reduction. Though the project was triumphantly forecast to generate 10,000 jobs (Cernea 2001a, 2001b), most of them were temporary, informal construction jobs (Serageldin 2001: 242). The Bank would later characterize the project as having failed in its objectives (World Bank 2006). A number of factors contributed to this result (Lafrenz Samuels 2010a). First, a dangerous slippage was imagined between rehabilitating buildings and reducing poverty, whereby the residents of the medina became lost in the equation and instead wealthier inhabitants were sought through gentrification. Focusing poverty reduction efforts on buildings, not people, affixed poverty to the built fabric of the city itself, with residents to blame for the deteriorating conditions of the buildings. Further, Moroccan municipal and national agencies were expected to follow Western norms of private property and governance, so that property regimes (e.g., religious endowments, *habous*) falling outside such norms were deemed intransigent obstacles. The Fez Medina Project underlines the importance of working through local solutions for addressing poverty (such as *habous* institutions), and the danger of fetishizing the built environment at the expense of concern for local residents.

Despite its failings, the Fez Medina Project was certainly the first of its kind, and the heritage focus would be transferred to future urban development projects implemented in Yemen and Lebanon (Cernea 2001a: 72). The Tunisia Cultural Heritage Project (TCHP, 2001–2011) also represented an ambitious scaling-up for heritage development by adopting a sector-wide focus (i.e. capacity-building) in order to foster growth in tourism revenues (Lafrenz Samuels 2010b, 2015). The project's objectives were to "assist the Borrower [government of Tunisia] in its efforts to ensure the sustainable management of the country's cultural heritage with a view to developing cultural tourism" (World Bank 2001). They were thus aimed at institutional strengthening, including reorganization and reform of the heritage sector in Tunisia, employee recruitment and training, and policy development. Like the Fez Medina Project, the US$ 25.3 million TCHP also built on experience gained in the Third Urban Development Project (Oukalas Project), as well as a 1973 Tunisia Tourism Infrastructure Project. While capacity-building was envisioned as providing the foundation for the work, other project goals included market development of cultural tourism (e.g., signage, communications, marketing tools), and improved site development and management at six "emblematic" (World Bank 2012) archaeological and historical sites: Carthage, the Bardo Museum, Kairouan, Sousse, Djerba Island, and Oudhna.

However, the grand designs of the TCHP had to be scaled back dramatically, and activity under the financing agreement focused mainly on renovation and expansion of the Bardo, Kairouan, and Sousse museums, as well as some training in mosaic conservation and management skills. The political context of Tunisia's increasingly repressive regime under former president Ben Ali meant the kinds of institutional and policy reform involved in capacity-building were unwelcome. The TCHP is an interesting case because it overlapped with the final decade of Ben Ali's rule, and was wrapped up in 2011, after the Revolution. Therefore, much of the retrospective analysis in the final report of the project predictably points to the difficulties inherent in trying to enact institutional changes under such conditions (World Bank 2012). At the same time, the drive to effect political reform through economic reform is always going to face pushback from governments, whether repressive or otherwise, and stakeholder consultation in World Bank heritage development projects remains very low, meaning the political reform being proffered is not particularly representative or inclusive.

The final report also notes lessons learned and a response from the Tunisian government. From the World Bank's perspective, lessons learned from the project included that "investment in cultural heritage is a complex process that requires a combination of lending instruments and technical support" and further that "economic benefits can be very high for cultural heritage investments...The project was a first of a generation" (World Bank 2012: 21). This final sentiment is echoed in the government's response, which emphasizes the project as a pilot initiative in response to the World Bank's rating of the project design as "moderately unsatisfactory" (World Bank 2012: 35). Further, the Tunisian government emphasizes that World Bank financing was specifically chosen over other alternative sources because of the Bank's expertise in cultural heritage and tourism. In sum, the Fez Medina Project and TCHP were both significant as being the first of their kind in heritage development at the World Bank. Both faced sustained challenges, but optimism remains that large urban rehabilitation and heritage sector capacity-building projects offer real promise in reducing poverty and encouraging economic growth. Following the TCHP, World Bank heritage development projects have been initiated in China, Bhutan, Ethiopia, Jordan, Lebanon, and Russia.

Transnational futures in heritage development: Public–private partnerships

While heritage development continues apace around the world, transnational efforts in compliance archaeology – heritage *in* development – are also expanding, particularly through PPPs, or public–private partnerships, which are also known as "cross-sectoral" partnerships.

To date, the most comprehensive attempt to develop a global compliance regime that refers to but stands independently of intergovernmental international frameworks is Rio Tinto's aforementioned project on "why cultural heritage matters." The project saw the mining company approach the Centre for Social Responsibility in Mining (CSRM) at the University of Queensland in Australia to develop a resource guide for integrating cultural heritage management into "communities" work at Rio Tinto. The objective was to create a single global set of corporate standards and values concerning heritage that remained flexible enough to encompass "the unique needs and aspirations of the communities that host … [Rio Tinto] operations" (Rio Tinto n.d.: 2).

The project brought together Rio staff from various parts of the organization, including in-house anthropologists and archaeologists, as well as an external review panel comprising archaeologists and anthropologists from around the world, including members of ICOMOS. One of us (Lilley) was Specialist Advisor to CSRM on the project, and in that capacity worked closely with CSRM staff to develop the text, in regular consultation with the international external review panel that he had helped bring together.

The resulting publication comprises three parts. The first is mostly corporate and other front matter but also introduces basic concepts in cultural heritage. This last is critical, as the guide is aimed at people who have little if any training in cultural heritage but who are required to initiate, oversee, or in other capacities engage with heritage work. The second part is a how-to guide. It opens with a section on inclusive engagement, then discusses cultural heritage work in language consonant with terminology used across the corporation: "know and understand," "plan and implement," "monitor, evaluate and improve," and finally "report and communicate." This approach does not simplify heritage discourse, but is rather an exercise in translation to maximize effectiveness (Lilley 2013c). Part two also includes 13 brief case studies from Rio operations around the world, though five are from Australia. This reflects the seminal role of Rio's experiences in that country, especially in relation to questions surrounding indigenous cultural heritage.

The final part of the resource guide is a background reader. It expands upon key heritage concepts, outlines the business case for the inclusion of heritage in mining operations (primarily in terms of Rio's social license to operate), outlines how mining can impact on heritage, and provides pointers to international heritage protocols and standards. In many respects this section is also an exercise in translation that attempts to convey critical information in terms the target audiences will understand. It should be noted that the guide has also been literally translated as well. In addition to the English original, versions are now available in various other major languages, such as French, Portuguese, and Spanish.

Rio Tinto and other transnational organizations are involved in a wide variety of PPPs, ranging from the relatively small scale, such as the cultural heritage guide just discussed, to massive projects that can have very substantial heritage spin-offs. One such project is Rio's vast Oyu Tolgoi operation in Mongolia, which is a joint venture between the company and the government of Mongolia. Mongolia's heritage management capacity was very limited when Rio became involved in the project (which was initially developed by another company), and so, in line with the principles articulated in the "why cultural heritage matters" guide, Rio set out to strengthen the country's heritage management capacities (the Mongolian national who headed the Oyu Tolgoi Cultural Heritage Programme was on the external review panel for the guide). Rio did not do this capacity-strengthening in house, but rather engaged a consortium of independent cultural heritage consultants to work with Mongolian heritage authorities. Exceptional progress was being made until recently, when the heritage work was wound back in the shadow of a major dispute between Rio Tinto and Mongolia concerning project management and financing.

While the advances being made on heritage issues with and through transnational corporations such as Rio Tinto can be cast in a very positive light, especially in relation to the ways in which such organizations previously behaved – and in some cases still do – they are not universally acclaimed. Indeed, a large and vocal subset of the archaeological and heritage management community (not to mention of the natural heritage community as well) decries any involvement with transnational corporations and especially the resource extraction sector. This is clear in the response of some to attempts to bring Rio Tinto and the World Archaeological Congress together to explore areas of mutual benefit (Shepherd and Haber 2011; cf. Smith 2011). Meskell (2012) also discusses the pros and cons of PPPs in South Africa, and her insights are apt here. As she observes, cross-sectoral efforts at their worst are vehicles for corruption and despoliation. At their best, though, PPPs can be invaluable adjuncts to – and even replacements for – government action.

We would add that this last applies not only in developing contexts such as Mongolia or South Africa, where government capacity is severely constrained by a lack of resources. In wealthy jurisdictions such as the United States, government capacity to intervene in what cultural heritage practitioners would regard as poor behavior on the part of private interests is limited not by the sort of factors prevalent in developing countries, but by laws protecting private property and freedom of individual and corporate action. In such cases, global guidelines such as those developed by Rio Tinto are invaluable. This is because they can force recalcitrant elements within or linked to transnational corporations (e.g., as subcontractors) to adhere to acceptable standards. This is no small thing, and should not be dismissed in a country where private interests can loot archaeological sites with impunity on private property.

Transnational futures in heritage development: Global climate change

While multilateral development banks such as the World Bank and IDB have been pivotal to the rise of international heritage development, a range of transnational entities have been following in their footsteps. The wellspring of actors involved in heritage development mirrors broader trends in transnational governance, which are seeing the merging of domestic and international politics; an increased role of non-state actors (e.g., individuals, firms, NGOs) providing technical expertise, monitoring, lobbying, and enforcement in global politics; new mechanisms of compliance ("naming and shaming," capacity-building, persuasion, transparency, and dissemination of best practices); and private governance schemes, for example, corporate social responsibility and the Equator Principles (Hale and Held 2011: 6–12; see also Lafrenz Samuels forthcoming).

This sphere of transnational activity articulates with heritage development financed by the multilateral development banks, so, for example, one of the "comparative advantages" of working with the World Bank is its ability to marshal and coordinate a range of NGOs and private investment. However, this sphere also wields substantial agency in choosing to support specific projects and effect particular outcomes. It is oftentimes more connected to community and stakeholder interests, and therefore can transcend the "big project" top-down mentality of development banks. Increasingly, public–private partnerships and private investment will mark the future of heritage development, suggesting the need for a private labeling schemes or ratings (resembling eco-labels for food and appliances, but now for heritage sites and resources), for example in promoting social equity.

Meanwhile, the treaty-based international system (for example, of UNESCO World Heritage) is ill equipped to face what is perhaps the greatest challenge of cultural heritage in the twenty-first century and on. Global climate change will require transnational solutions as the older system of international state-to-state relations is failing to address climate change mitigation and adaptation needs. Mass migration, rising sea levels, and changing weather patterns (especially increasing drought, humidity, and flooding) will impact much of the world's cultural heritage and historic urban cores. The collapse of the West Antarctic ice sheet means that rising sea levels are no longer a question of "if" but "when," with at least a 10–13 feet (3–4 meter) rise in the next 200–1,000 years (more likely 200–500 years) (Joughin, Smith, and Medley 2014; Rignot et al. 2014). Taking into account that much of the world's built heritage is concentrated near coastlines, this sea level rise will profoundly change the global landscape of cultural heritage as we know it today (Hansen 2009; Marzeion and Levermann 2014).

One region to watch for the unfolding interplay between transnational heritage development and global climate change is the Arctic. In many ways the Arctic is the "canary in the coalmine" for global climate change, warming at a rate two to four times the global average (Screen and Simmonds 2010), and as a result undergoing dramatic ecosystem change, including melting glaciers, collapsing permafrost, erosion, and ocean acidification (ACIA 2004). Demonstrating the key drivers and effects of climate change through coordinated monitoring, mitigation, and adaptation efforts, the region promises important lessons not just in the environmental (physical and biological) mechanisms of climate change, but political and economic dimensions as well, for example, in the effectiveness of policy responses and economic incentives to address changing environmental conditions and lifeways of Arctic communities.

The Arctic is also "good to think with" for understanding the transnational dimensions of cultural heritage, being a geopolitical space with deep legal and intellectual roots to the "common heritage of mankind" principle introduced into international treaties governing Antarctica, the global sea bed, the moon, and outer space (Joyner 1986; Strati 1991). While the "common heritage of mankind" laid the basis for the World Heritage concept established by the 1972 UNESCO convention, there are important distinctions between the two. World Heritage works strictly within a national and international (state-to-state) framework, whereas the "common heritage of mankind" applies to spaces owned by no nation, lying outside national jurisdictions, where economic development and access become the key issues of interest and negotiation.

Climate change in the Arctic is changing the terms of development and access in the region as melting ice caps, migrating fish stocks, and increasing tourist numbers present new opportunities for resource exploitation. In the Arctic, cultural heritage is becoming a "product" of climate change in two senses of the word: as a result of climate change with the rapidly changing lifeways it is effecting, and as a resource to be developed and marketed for economic growth. Heritage development in the Arctic is particularly visible in the surging cruise tourism industry and investment in the cultural sector by oil and gas companies. Increased public perception and understanding of global climate change has led to increased tourism (primarily cruise tourism) to polar regions in a phenomenon known as "last chance" tourism (Hall and Saarinen 2010; Lemelin, Dawson, and Stewart 2012; Lück, Maher, and Stewart 2010; Maher, Stewart, and Lück. 2011). Cultural heritage is variously integrated into cruise tourism across the Arctic, for example performed through dress and dance for cruise tourists during brief visits to communities (Shackel 2011), or experienced through touring archaeological and historic sites, which comprise the majority of shore visits in Svalbard, an archipelago in the Norwegian Arctic (Roura 2011). Cultural heritage has also become a key area for "greenwashing" the reputation of oil and gas companies. This is done in a bid to gloss over the complicity of fossil fuels in causing global heating, as the leading source of increasing atmospheric CO_2 levels (Heede 2014; IPCC 2013). Multinational corporations in the petroleum industry are now routinely sponsoring cultural festivals and community events, as well as donating to museums and commissioning corporate histories.

Heritage development can offer sustainable alternatives in the pursuit of low-carbon economic growth, but the cruise tourism industry will have to follow suit. The petroleum industry's embrace of heritage positions the past as an active ground for debate about how to mitigate and respond to climate change. The enduring vestiges of cultural heritage will provide sanctuary and a sense of stability in an increasingly volatile world, but must be adapted to constant change in a rapidly changing environment, for which the former paradigm of preservation will seem quixotically old-fashioned.

NOTES

1 This section draws heavily on "The International Context," detailed in Lilley (2013a).
2 IUCN, *Sacred Natural Sites: Guidelines for Protected Areas Managers*. Ed. R. Wild and C. Macleod. Available at: http://cmsdata.iucn.org/downloads/pa_guidelines_016_sacred_natural_sites.pdf. Accessed November 26, 2014.
3 E.g., Cultural management capacity and enhanced biocultural resilience in high-value landscapes. Available at: https://portals.iucn.org/2012forum/?q=0092. Accessed November 26, 2014.
4 International Labour Organization, http://www.ilo.org/global/lang--en/index.htm. Accessed November 26, 2014.
5 World Intellectual Property Organization, http://www.wipo.int/portal/en/index.html. Accessed November 26, 2014.
6 UN Permanent Forum on Indigenous Issues, http://undesadspd.org/IndigenousPeoples.aspx. Accessed November 26, 2014.
7 Pimachiowin Aki World Heritage Project, http://www.pimachiowinaki.org/. Accessed November 26, 2014.
8 United Nations Environment Programme, http://www.unep.org/. Accessed November 26, 2014.
9 Convention on Biological Diversity, http://www.cbd.int/. Accessed November 26, 2014.
10 *Akwé: Kon Guidelines*. Available at: https://www.cbd.int/doc/publications/akwe-brochure-en.pdf. Accessed November 26, 2014.
11 UNDP, The GEF Small Grants Programme, https://sgp.undp.org/index.php?option=com_content&view=article&id=103&Itemid=165#.UpQTMMRkOs8. Accessed November 26, 2014.
12 World Bank, *BP 4.11 – Physical Cultural Resources*. Available at: http://go.worldbank.org/5SLEKEUDY0. Accessed November 26, 2014.
13 World Bank, *BP 4.10 – Indigenous Peoples*. Available at: http://go.worldbank.org/PG4KQSUDI0. Accessed November 26, 2014.

14 World Bank, *Review and Update of the World Bank Safeguard Policies*. Available at: http://consultations.worldbank.org/consultation/review-and-update-world-bank-safeguard-policies. Accessed November 26, 2014.
15 International Finance Corporation, *Environmental and Social Performance Standards and Guidance Notes*. Available at: http://www.ifc.org/wps/wcm/connect/topics_ext_content/ifc_external_corporate_site/ifc+sustainability/our+approach/risk+management/performance+standards/environmental+and+social+performance+standards+and+guidance+notes. Accessed December 3, 2014.
16 Equator Principles, http://www.equator-principles.com/. Accessed November 26, 2014.
17 *Rio Tinto in Australia*. Available at: http://www.riotinto.com.au/documents/Rio_Tinto_Cultural_Heritage_Guide.pdf. Accessed November 26, 2014.
18 International Council on Mining and Metals, *10 Principles*. Available at: http://www.icmm.com/our-work/sustainable-development-framework/10-principles. Accessed November 26, 2014.
19 International Association of Oil & Gas Producers, http://www.ogp.org.uk/. Accessed November 26, 2014.
20 International Association of Oil & Gas Producers, *Key Questions in Managing Social Issues in Oil & Gas Projects*. Available at: http://www.ogp.org.uk/pubs/332.pdf. Accessed November 26, 2014.
21 Global Oil and Gas Industry Association for Environmental and Social Issues, http://www.ipieca.org/. Accessed November 26, 2014.
22 World Bank Civil Society Forum, http://go.worldbank.org/G7NNVSLX30. Accessed November 26, 2014.
23 Bretton Woods Project, IFC consultation with civil society on the safeguard review. Available at: http://www.brettonwoodsproject.org/2005/04/art-194337/. Accessed November 26, 2014.

REFERENCES

ACIA (Arctic Climate Impact Assessment) (2004) *Impacts of a Warming Arctic*. Cambridge: Cambridge University Press.

Adams, J. (2015) Polestar or Pretense? International Archaeological Tourism Development in "Less Developed Countries," in K. Lafrenz Samuels and T. Rico (eds), *Heritage Keywords: Rhetoric and Redescription in Cultural Heritage*. Boulder: University Press of Colorado.

Akrout Yaïche, S. (2002) Local involvement in urban management: The experience of the city of Tunis. *International Social Science Journal* 54: 247–252.

Anders, G. (2005) Good Governance as Technology: Towards an Ethnography of the Bretton Woods Institutions, in D. Mosse and D. Lewis (eds), *The Aid Effect: Giving and Governing in International Development*. London: Pluto, pp. 37–60.

Bahri-Meddeb, A. and J. Binous (1994) Tunis – Hafsia, in J. Jokilehto and T. Marasovic (eds), *Guidelines for the Rehabilitation of Mediterranean Historic Settlements. Volume II: Case Studies*. Split: Priority Actions Programme, pp. 56–65.

Bauer, A. (2015) Building Communities of Stewardship beyond Nationalism and Internationalism, in K. Lafrenz Samuels and T. Rico (eds), *Heritage Keywords: Rhetoric and Redescription in Cultural Heritage*. Boulder: University Press of Colorado.

Bigio, A. and G. Licciardi (2010) *The Urban Rehabilitation of Medinas: The World Bank Experience in the Middle East and North Africa*. Washington DC: World Bank.

Breen, C. (2007) Advocacy, international development and World Heritage Sites in sub-Saharan Africa. *World Archaeology* 39: 355–370.

Bush, R. (2007) *Poverty and Neoliberalism: Persistence and Reproduction in the Global South*. London/Ann Arbor, MI: Pluto Press.

Cernea, M. M. (2001a) *Cultural Heritage and Development: A Framework for Action in the Middle East and North Africa*. Washington, DC: World Bank.

Cernea, M. M. (2001b) At the Cutting Edge: Cultural Patrimony Protection through Development Projects, in I. Serageldin, E. Shluger, and J. Martin-Brown (eds), *Historic Cities and Sacred Sites: Cultural Roots for Urban Futures*. Washington, DC: World Bank, pp. 67–88.

Cooke, B. and U. Kothari (2001) *Participation: The New Tyranny?* New York: Zed Books.

Deruyterre, A. (2006) Development with Identity: Mobilizing the Potential of Indigenous Peoples' Natural Resources and Cultural Heritage, in Inter-American Development Bank (ed.), *Sustaining Development for All: Expanding Access to Economic Activity and Social Services*. Washington, DC: Inter-American Development Bank, pp. 89–96.

Duer, K. (1999) *Culture and Sustainable Development: A Framework for Action*. Environmentally and Socially Sustainable Development Working Paper Series. Washington, DC: World Bank.

Edelman, M. and A. Haugerud (2005) Introduction: The Anthropology of Development and Globalization, in M. Edelman and A. Haugerud (eds), *The Anthropology of Development and Globalization: From Classical Political Economy to Contemporary Neoliberalism*. Malden, MA: Blackwell, pp. 1–74.

Elliott, M. and V. Schmutz (2012) World Heritage: Constructing a universal cultural order. *Poetics* 40: 256–277.

Endresen, K., A. Molstad, K. Lindberg, D. E. Hawkins, and W. Jamieson (1999) *Sustainable Tourism and Cultural Heritage: A Review of Development Assistance and Its Potential to Promote Sustainability*. Washington, DC: World Bank.

Escher, A. and M. Schepers (2008) Revitalizing the medina of Tunis as a national symbol. *Erdkunde* 62: 129–141.

Escobar, A. (1995) *Encountering Development: The Making and Unmaking of the Third World*. Princeton, NJ: Princeton University Press.

Ferguson, J. (1990) *Anti-Politics Machine: "Development," Depoliticization, and Bureaucratic Power in Lesotho*. Minneapolis: University of Minnesota Press.

Ferguson, J. (2005) Seeing like an oil company: Space, security, and global capital in neoliberal Africa. *American Anthropologist* 107: 377–382.

Forrest, C. (2010) *International Law and the Protection of Cultural Heritage*. Abingdon: Routledge.

Galvani, M. (2007a) *Thinking Outside the Box: Arguments for IADB's Involvement in the Preservation and Development of Heritage*. Washington, DC: Inter-American Development Bank.

Galvani, M. (2007b) *Thinking Outside the Box: Strategies and Examples for in the Preservation and Development of Heritage*. Washington, DC: Inter-American Development Bank.

Green, M. (2012) Anticipatory development: Mobilizing civil society in Tanzania. *Critique of Anthropology* 32: 309–333.

Goldman, M. (2005) *Imperial Nature: The World Bank and Struggles for Social Justice in the Age of Globalization*. New Haven, CT: Yale University Press.

Hackenberg, R. A. (2002) Closing the gap between anthropology and public policy: The route through cultural heritage development. *Human Organization* 61: 288–298.

Hale, T. and D. Held (2011) *Handbook of Transnational Governance: Institutions and Innovations*. Cambridge, MA: Polity Press.

Hall, C. M. and J. Saarinen (eds) (2010) *Tourism and Change in Polar Regions: Climate, Environment and Experience*. Abingdon: Routledge.

Hansen, J. (2009) *Storms of My Grandchildren*. New York: Bloomsbury.

Hardouin, J. (1983) *Bilan de la Campagne Internationale Pour la Sauvegarde de Fes*. Paris: UNESCO.

Harrigan, J., C. Wang, and H. El-Said (2006) The Politics of IMF and World Bank Lending: Will It Backfire in the Middle East and North Africa? in A. Paloni and M. Zanardi (eds), *The IMF, World Bank and Policy Reform*. London/New York: Routledge, pp. 64–99.

Harvey, D. (2005) *A Brief History of Neoliberalism*. Oxford: Oxford University Press.

Hawkins, D. E. and S. Mann (2007) The World Bank's role in tourism development. *Annals of Tourism Research* 34: 348–363.

Heede, R. (2014) Tracing anthropogenic carbon dioxide and methane emissions to fossil fuel and cement producers, 1854–2010. *Climatic Change* 122: 229-241.

Hibou, B. (2000) The political economy of the World Bank's discourse from economic catechism to missionary deeds and misdeeds. Trans. J. Roitman. *Les Etudes du CERI* 39.

Horowitz, M.M. (1996) On not offending the borrower: (Self?)-ghettoization of anthropology at the World Bank. *Development Anthropologist* 14: 1–12.

IPCC (2013) *Climate Change 2013: The Physical Science Basis. Contribution of Working Group I to the Fifth Assessment Report of the Intergovernmental Panel on Climate Change.* Ed. T. F. Stocker, D. Qin, G-K. Plattner, M. Tignor, S. K. Allen, J. Boschung, A. Nauels, Y. Xia, V. Bex, and P. M. Midgley. Cambridge: Cambridge University Press.

Joughin, I., B. E. Smith, and B. Medley (2014) Marine ice sheet collapse potentially under way for the Thwaites Glacier Basin, West Antarctica. *Science* 344(6185): 735–738.

Joyner, C. C. (1986) Legal implications of the concept of the common heritage of mankind. *The International and Comparative Law Quarterly* 35(1): 190–199.

King, R. and L. Nic Eoin (2014) Before the flood: Loss of place, mnemonics, and "resources" ahead of the Metolong Dam, Lesotho. *Journal of Social Archaeology* 14: 196–223.

Lafrenz Samuels, K. (2009) Trajectories of development: International heritage management of archaeology in the Middle East and North Africa. *Archaeologies: Journal of the World Archaeological Congress* 5: 68–91.

Lafrenz Samuels, K. (2010a) Heritage Management and Poverty Reduction, in S. Labadi and C. Long (eds), *Heritage and Globalisation.* London/New York: Routledge, pp. 200–215.

Lafrenz Samuels, K. (2010b) Mobilizing Heritage in the Maghrib: Rights, Development, and Transnational Archaeologies. Ph.D. dissertation, Department of Anthropology, Stanford University, California.

Lafrenz Samuels, K. (2015) Heritage Rights and the Rhetoric of Reality in Pre-Revolution Tunisia, in K. Lafrenz Samuels and T. Rico (eds), *Heritage Keywords: Rhetoric and Redescription in Cultural Heritage.* Boulder: University Press of Colorado.

Lafrenz Samuels, K. (forthcoming) *In Heritage: Roots, Development, Justice.*

Lanchet, W. (2003) Le ville entre concepteurs et usagers: problématique de la sauvegarde appliquée au cas de la médina de Fès (Maroc). Ph.D. dissertation, Université Françoise Rabelais, France.

Lemelin, R. H., J. Dawson, and E. J. Stewart (eds) (2012) *Last Chance Tourism: Adapting Tourism Opportunities in a Changing World.* Abingdon: Routledge.

Licciardi, G. and R. Amirtahmasebi (2012) *The Economics of Uniqueness: Investing in Historic City Cores and Cultural Heritage Assets for Sustainable Development.* Urban Development Series. Washington, DC: World Bank.

Lilley, I. (2008) Archaeology, Human Rights and Postcolonial Politics, in U. Rizvi and M. Liebmann (eds), *Postcolonialism and Archaeology.* Walnut Creek, CA: AltaMira, pp. 141–164.

Lilley, I. (2013a) Beyond the Equator (Principles): The international context. *International Journal of Cultural Property* 20: 474–479.

Lilley, I. (2013b) Nature and Culture in World Heritage Management: A View from the Asia-Pacific (or, Never Waste a Good Crisis!), in S. Brockwell, S. O'Connor, and D. Byrne (eds), *Transcending the Culture–Nature Divide in Cultural Heritage: Views from the Asia-Pacific Region.* Canberra: Australian National University Press.

Lilley, I. (2013c) Translation/indigenization. *World Archaeological Congress Encyclopaedia of Global Archaeology.* New York: Springer Reference.

Logan, W. (2013) Australia, indigenous peoples and World Heritage from Kakadu to Cape York: State Party behaviour under the World Heritage Convention. *Journal of Social Archaeology* 13(2): 153–176.

Lück, M., P. T. Maher, and E. J. Stewart (eds) (2010) *Cruise Tourism in Polar Regions: Promoting Environmental and Social Sustainability?* London: Earthscan.

MacEachern, S. (2010) Seeing like an oil company's CHM programme: Exxon and archaeology on the Chad Export Project. *Journal of Social Archaeology* 10: 347–366.

Maher, P. T., E. J. Stewart, and M. Lück (eds) (2011) *Polar Tourism: Human, Environmental and Governance Dimensions*. Putnam Valley, NY: Cognizant Communication.

Marzeion, B. and A. Levermann (2014) Loss of cultural World Heritage and currently inhabited places to sea-level rise. *Environmental Research Letters* 9: 1–7.

McGuinness, J. (2005) A textual enactment of community: On discourse analysis, the news media and a social housing project in Tunisia in the 1990s. *The Journal of North African Studies* 10: 1–18.

Meskell, L. (2012) *The Nature of Culture. The New South Africa*. Malden, MA: Wiley Blackwell.

Meskell, L. (2013) UNESCO and the fate of the World Heritage Indigenous Peoples Council of Experts (WHIPCOE). *International journal of cultural property* 20(2): 155–174.

Mosse, D. (2005) *Cultivating Development: An Ethnography of Aid Policy and Practice*. London: Pluto.

Navez-Bouchanine, F., N. Lahbil, and A. Fejjal (1995) *Evaluation sociale. Projet de Sauvegarde de la Médina de Fes. Rapport de synthèse*. Washington, DC/Rabat: World Bank/Préfecture Fès Medina.

Nielsen, B. (2011) UNESCO and the "right" kind of culture: Bureaucratic production and articulation. *Critique of Anthropology* 31: 273–292.

Nussbaum, M. (1997) Capabilities and human rights. *Fordham Law Review* 66: 273-300.

O'Keefe, P. (2000) Archaeology and human rights. *Public Archaeology* 1(3): 181–194.

Rignot, E., J. Mouginot, M. Morlighem, H. Seroussi, and B. Scheuchi (2014) Widespread, rapid grounding line retreat of Pine Island, Thwaites, Smith, and Kohler glaciers, West Antarctica, from 1992 to 2011. *Geophysical Research Letters* 41(10): 3502–3509.

Rio Tinto (n.d.) *Why Cultural Heritage Matters: A Resource Guide for Integrating Cultural Heritage Management into Communities Work at Rio Tinto*. Available at: http://www.riotinto.com/documents/ReportsPublications/Rio_Tinto_Cultural_Heritage_Guide.pdf. Accessed November 26, 2014.

Rojas, E. (1999) *Old Cities, New Assets: Preserving Latin America's Urban Heritage*. Washington, DC: Inter-American Development Bank.

Rojas, E. (2007) The conservation and development of the urban heritage: A task for all social actors. *City and Time* 3: 41–47.

Rojas, E. and C. de Moura Castro (1999) *Lending for Urban Heritage Conservation: Issues and Opportunities*. Washington, DC: Inter-American Development Bank.

Roura, R.M. (2011) *The Footprint of Polar Tourism: Tourist Behavior at Cultural Heritage Sites in Antarctica and Svalbard*. Circumpolar Studies 7. Groningen: University of Groningen Arctic Center.

Rypkema, D. (2010) The Role of Heritage Conservation in a Sustainable Economy, in M. Mälkki and K. Schmidt-Thomé (eds), *Integrating Aims: Built Heritage in Social and Economic Development*. Aalto: Aalto University, School for Science and Technology, Centre for Urban and Regional Studies, pp. 195–210.

Scott, J. C. (1998) *Seeing Like a State: How Certain Schemes to Improve the Human Condition Have Failed*. New Haven, CT: Yale University Press.

Screen, J. and I. Simmonds (2010) The central role of diminishing sea ice in recent Arctic temperature amplification. *Nature* 464: 1334–1335.

Sen, A. (1999) *Development as Freedom*. New York: Knopf.

Serageldin, I. (1999) *Very Special Places: The Architecture and Economics of Intervening in Historic Cities*. Washington, DC: World Bank.

Serageldin, M. (2001) Preserving a Historic City: Economic and Social Transformation of Fez, in I. Serageldin, E. Shluger and J. Martin-Brown (eds), *Historic Cities and Sacred Sites: Cultural Roots for Urban Futures*. Washington, DC: World Bank, pp. 237–244.

Shackel, P. (2011) A snapshot of tourism in Greenland. *International Journal of Heritage Studies* 17(1): 81–88.

Shepherd, N. and A. Haber (2011) What's up with WAC? Archaeology and "engagement" in a globalized world. *Public Archaeology* 10: 96–115.

Smith, C. (2011) Errors of fact and errors of representation: Response to Shepherd and Haber's critique of the World Archaeological Congress. *Public Archaeology* 10: 223–234.

Stirrat, R. (2000) Cultures of consultancy. *Critique of Anthropology* 20: 31–46.

Strati, A. (1991) Deep seabed cultural property and the common heritage of mankind. *The International and Comparative Law Quarterly* 40(4): 859–894.

Throsby, D. (2003) Sustainability in the Conservation of the Built Environment: An Economist's Perspective, in J-M. Teutonico and F. Matero (eds), *Managing Change: Sustainable Approaches to the Conservation of the Built Environment*. Los Angeles, CA: Getty Conservation Institute, pp. 3–10.

Throsby, D. (2005) *On the Sustainability of Cultural Capital*. Department of Economics Research Paper No. 10/200. Sydney: Macquarie University.

Throsby, D. (2012) Heritage Economics: A Conceptual Framework, in G. Licciardi and R. Amirtahmasebi (eds), *The Economics of Uniqueness: Investing in Historic City Cores and Cultural Heritage Assets for Sustainable Development*. Washington, DC: World Bank, pp. 45–74.

UNDP (United Nations Development Programme) (1992a) *Sauvegarde de la ville de Fès: Synthèse*. Paris: UNDP/UNESCO.

UNDP (1992b) *Sauvegarde de la ville de Fès, tome II: Activités, environnement, patrimoine, institutions*. Paris: UNDP/UNESCO.

UNESCO (1974) *Sauvegarde et mise en valeur de la Médina de Tunis*. Paris: UNESCO.

UNESCO (1987a) *Our Common Future*. Paris: UNESCO.

UNESCO (1987b) *Campagne de Sauvegarde de Fès: Résultats et recommandations du projet*. Paris: UNESCO.

UNESCO (1992) *Sauvegarde de la ville de Fès: Rapport patrimoine historique*. Paris/Rabat: UNESCO/Ministère de l'Intérieur.

UNESCO (1995) *Our Creative Diversity*. Paris: UNESCO.

UNESCO and Government of Italy (2000) Towards New Strategies for Culture in Sustainable Development, in World Bank (ed.), *Culture Counts: Financing, Resources, and the Economics of Culture in Sustainable Development. Proceedings of the Conference held in Florence, Italy (October 4–7, 1999)*. Washington, DC: World Bank, pp. 274–284.

Welch, J. and I. Lilley (2013) Beyond the Equator (Principles): A forum on community benefit sharing in relation to major land alteration projects and associated intellectual property issues in cultural heritage. *International Journal of Cultural Property* 20: 467–474.

World Bank (1997) *Project Information Document for Fez Rehabilitation Project (Report No. PIC877)*. Washington, DC: World Bank.

World Bank (1998) *Project Appraisal Document for Fez Medina Rehabilitation Project (Report No. 18462-MOR)*. Washington, DC: World Bank.

World Bank (2001) *Tunisia Cultural Heritage Project: Loan Agreement (7059-TUN)*. Washington, DC: World Bank.

World Bank (2006) *Implementation Completion Report for Fez Medina Rehabilitation Project (Report No. 35074)*. Washington, DC: World Bank.

World Bank (2009a) *Partnership for Development Strategies Based on Cultural Heritage and Sustainable Tourism: Concept Note*. Washington, DC: World Bank.

World Bank (2009b) *Diversifying Investments to Stimulate Economic Growth: Promoting Cultural Heritage and Sustainable Tourism*. Washington, DC: World Bank.

World Bank (2009c) *Stimulating the Economy by Increasing Investment in Cultural Heritage and Sustainable Tourism*. Washington, DC: World Bank.

World Bank (2012) *Tunisia – Cultural Heritage Project*. Washington, DC: World Bank.

World Bank, Harvard University Graduate School of Design Unit for Housing and Urbanization, and Association Sauvegarde de la Médina de Tunis (1999) *The Rehabilitation of the Hafsia Quarter of the Medina of Tunis: Project Assessment 1994 Summary*. Washington, DC: World Bank.

11

Heritage and Tourism

Noel B. Salazar and Yujie Zhu

Introduction

Given the pervasiveness and local particularity of heritage, heritage tourism is among those tourism niches that is growing most rapidly (Timothy and Boyd 2006). Private and public sectors, whether or not in collaboration, are converting heritage resources across the globe into destinations and attractions in a bid to obtain a piece of the lucrative tourism pie. The money visitors spend on admission fees, souvenirs, transport, food, and accommodation contributes billions every year to the global economy and employs millions of people directly and indirectly (Timothy and Boyd 2003). In 2012, international tourist arrivals exceeded the 1 billion mark, international tourism receipts reached US$ 1,075 billion worldwide, with 1 in 11 jobs being related to tourism (UNWTO 2013: 3). An estimated one-third of all international tourism is related to visiting cultural heritage sites, monuments, and landscapes (UNWTO 2009). The mounting struggles over who controls heritage tourism thus reflect its (economic) growth and success (Porter and Salazar 2005; Salazar and Porter 2004).

Some argue that the globalization of heritage through tourism has led to a greater respect for (both material and living) culture than previously existed. However, the transformation of heritage properties into destinations and cultural expressions into performances is seldom straightforward. The interface between heritage and tourism is extremely complex. In a tourism setting, heritage can be (mis)used in a variety of ways for a variety of purposes by a variety of stakeholders. This chapter critically analyzes some of the key issues at stake in the multifaceted relation between heritage and tourism, in particular the positive and negative effects in relation to local communities, but also issues such as authenticity, the role of social imaginaries, and the special tourism status of World Heritage properties. Given the limited space, the focus here is on cultural heritage only, although many of the topics discussed equally apply to natural or "mixed" heritage (a UNESCO term denoting properties containing elements of both cultural and natural significance).

Global Heritage: A Reader, First Edition. Edited by Lynn Meskell.

Heritage (in Global Tourism)

As a representation of the past, heritage is a value-laden concept (Lowenthal 1998). Graham, Ashworth, and Tunbridge (2000: 6) define it as what contemporary society chooses to inherit and to pass on. Moreover, heritage indicates a connection with the present and the future. As Tunbridge and Ashworth (1996: 6) note, "the present selects an inheritance from an imagined past for current use and decides what should be passed on to an imagined future." This indicates that heritage is not history, but produced in the present and in relation to our current experience. Heritage creates and strengthens social relations, values, and meanings about people's past and present. No wonder it is employed by nations as a powerful instrument to reinforce national identity. Heritage enables people to develop a sense of collective belonging to a nation, as an "imagined political community" (Anderson 1983). As such, it can become enmeshed in a nation's attempts to establish social, political, and religious norms to control its citizens (Harrison 2010). The result is, as Smith (2006) argues, that a hegemonic discourse about heritage is created, based on the knowledge of technical and aesthetic experts, and institutionalized in state agencies and amenity societies. This has an impact on the way heritage is managed, presented, and understood. Emerging from different academic disciplines, critical heritage studies have recently challenged this way of thinking about and "doing" heritage.

What does heritage mean from a tourism perspective? It can refer to cultural traditions that embody the "authentic" past (Hitchcock, King, and Parnwell 1993) or to the natural environment, molded in a particular way for tourists. Timothy and Boyd (2003) argue that heritage is a conscious creation of the present, with history being interpreted and packaged mainly to serve the purposes of tourism. Ashworth and Larkham (1994) deconstruct and identify heritage as a dynamic and multiple purpose resource that can be conflictual when it concerns sensitive questions such as memory and identity. In sum, heritage involves a highly politicized project that is contested and transformed by global actors, including representatives of international organizations such as UNESCO, researchers, businesspeople, and those involved in tourism (Smith 2006). These various stakeholders and their (conflicting) interests point to the multilayered core of heritage. While acknowledging this complexity, we discuss in this chapter how heritage tourism in particular illustrates the interactive and dynamic nature of the concept of heritage.

In recent decades, heritage has been regarded as one of the most significant and fastest growing components of tourism; some even call heritage "the essence of tourism" (Timothy 1997: 751). Heritage tourism can be defined, broadly, as the harnessing of cultural, historical, and ethnic components of a society or place as resources to attract tourists (Chang 1999). In this sense, heritage tourism can refer to religious tourism, diaspora tourism, living culture, historic cities and built heritage, archaeological sites, and ancient monuments. As "heritage and tourism are collaborative industries, heritage … [converts] locations into destinations" (Kirshenblatt-Gimblett 1998: 151). Global tourism to heritage sites is increasing around 10 per cent per year on average, with many (but certainly not all) properties doubling or tripling in visitation and revenues every ten years (UNWTO 2009, 2013). It is no exaggeration to say that, throughout the world, heritage and tourism have become inextricably linked and mutually dependent upon each other (Di Giovine 2008).

From a tourism perspective, heritage provides ample opportunities for different ways of seeing and valuing the past (Boniface and Fowler 1993). While both cultural and nature heritage have the potential to create a foundation for tourism's growth, tourism itself has the power to generate funds that make preservation possible (NWHO 1999). In reality, however, these funds may be used by the authorities or private stakeholders, and not directly benefit local communities. Besides its role in economic development, heritage tourism has also been accepted widely as an effective way to achieve the (cultural) educational function of tourism (UNESCO 1965). It enables tourists to become more interested in distant cultures and societies (and in their safeguarding). In addition, heritage tourism is often promoted to build nationalism and patriotism at the domestic level and to spread propaganda among international visitors (Timothy and Boyd 2006). Sometimes, heritage tourism provides a means of establishing local pride because it emphasizes presenting and acknowledging local value and cultural memory while allowing local communities to connect with the wider world (Edson 2004). At the same time, the outcome can be much less positive when local communities are displaced, for example, in order to make room for heritage tourism infrastructure.

The development of ecomuseums is an overall positive example of the relation between heritage and tourism (Howard 2002). Ecomuseums originated in France in the 1970s. The term refers to a holistic interpretation of cultural heritage (versus the specialized focus of traditional museums). The stress in these museums lies on the identity of a place, local participation, and the development of local communities (precisely avoiding relocation or museumization). In other words, heritage is seen here as central to economic innovation and development, particularly in regions that have suffered serious reverses of fortune (e.g., rural or formerly industrial areas). Ecomuseums, as a new form of museology, are usually interactive, hereby satisfying the demand for more experiential tourism. There are currently over four hundred ecomuseums across the globe (Davis 2008). While the majority is based in Europe, the concept has spread across the globe and is particularly popular in China. In 1997, the China Society of Museum Studies, Guizhou Cultural Heritage Bureau, and the Norwegian government launched the Sino-Norwegian Ecomuseum Program. Since then, a nationwide wave of ecomuseums has surged in China. For instance, with the involvement of provincial and local governments, as well as tourism agencies, the Suoga Miao Ecomuseum was established in Guizhou Province in 1998. In this project, the collective memory of Miao people is documented through oral recordings in their own language. The branding of the Suoga village as "ecomuseum" assigned cultural landscapes and traditions not only a value for preservation but also for consumption through tourism development.

The creation of ecomuseums is often complicated through processes of localization, whereby multiple actors with competing agendas interact. Some of the key concerns related to the implementation of ecomuseology revolve around how local needs can be met, how a participatory community approach can be effectively implemented, and how the authority over the management of heritage and practices of development can be constituted and negotiated (Nitzky 2012). Once again, converting heritage into tourism products and activities does not only have positive effects but also negative ones (Chang 1999). The relationship between heritage and tourism is frequently characterized by contradictions whereby "conservationists" perceive tourism activities as compromising conservation goals for economic profit (Nuryanti 1996).

Although heritage tourism is described in many different ways, it is important to remember that, in the end, it is a consumerist practice (Garrod and Fyall 2001). The danger that tourism is promoted before preservation is great when stakeholders regard heritage primarily as an economic resource. The commercialization of heritage often focuses on the interests of tourists and tourism service providers. Since the Mount Emei Scenic Area in China was inscribed in 1996 as a mixed heritage site on the UNESCO World Heritage list (because of its beautiful natural landscape and rich Buddhist culture), it has become one of most popular destinations in China for both domestic and international tourists. The local government established a company for tourism promotion, development, and marketing (Zhu and Li 2013). Since then, the admission fee has increased several times, from US$ 10 to US$ 80. The local heritage management office has also strategically used Buddhist culture to attract more tourists by establishing a new giant Buddha statue on the top of Mount Emei.

When heritage is designed and objectified based on certain political and economic agendas, it can also become a battlefield of power that results in conflicts among various interest groups (Porter and Salazar 2005). The Dresden Elbe Valley, a former World Heritage property in Germany, was listed as a cultural landscape, passing through the Dresden Basin and the city of Dresden. The World Heritage Committee decided to remove it from the World Heritage List in 2009 because the city council intended to build a four-lane road bridge in the core area of the cultural landscape (Pendlebury, Short, and While 2009). While even local authorities had different opinions about the bridge project, a majority of local residents indicated that they wanted to go ahead with this project even if this would mean losing the World Heritage title. The loss of UNESCO recognition, however, has not reduced tourism revenue. Dresden reported a record growth of nearly 7 percent in 2010, the year after it lost its "World Heritage" status.

Another reason for the lack of sufficient safeguards to protect the values of heritage properties is to be found in an underdeveloped understanding, and therefore lack of appreciation, of the heritage value of precious cultural or natural resources by both local communities and tourists (Salazar 2012b). This is particularly an issue in developing countries, where tourism is often considered the primary source for economic growth and the reduction of poverty. However, as Musitelli (2002: 311) argues, "nothing would be served by enacting unrealistic prohibitions or placing blame on poor countries. They are simply adapting to a growing consumer demand for 'exotic heritages.'" If managed badly, heritage tourism can lead to a rise in the price of land or admission fees, the processes of use replacement, and gentrification. Egypt, for instance, has regarded tourism as a means to modernization, and has transformed its heritage into profit-making tourism products. In the Valley of the Nobles (near Luxor), for instance, government officials succeeded in removing about thirteen hundred local families who lived on top of the tombs, a major tourism attraction. The local community endured both real and symbolic violence, and this in the name of their own heritage (Meskell 2005).

Tourists (Encountering Heritage)

Since its inception, tourism studies has witnessed "a shift from homogenizing portrayals of the tourist as a general type to pluralizing depictions that capture the multiplicity of the experience" (Uriely 2005: 200). Research has shown that visitors to heritage sites are usually better educated, bigger spenders, travel in groups, and have average or higher than average incomes (Herbert, Prentice, and Thomas 1989). According to MacCannell (1976), tourists general can be classified by their motivations. They search for "authenticity" in the past (historical sites), in nature (natural parks), in the lives of "primitive" peoples (ethnic tourism), or in faraway exotic destinations that are different from home. Cohen (1979) proposes a fivefold phenomenological typology of tourist experiences. Three of the proposed modes – namely the experiential, experimental, and existential – are closely related to heritage tourism.

The issue of authenticity appears as a central point of scholarly discussion on heritage tourism (e.g., Wang 1999). The highly ambiguous concept is used mainly to understand tourist motivations and experiences. Tourists are believed to search for "authenticity," a quest that reflects the desire for genuine and credible cultural construction and representation in diverse heritage contexts (Zhu 2012a). Indeed, many tourists are eagerly looking for "authentic" heritage, which can be as varied as untouched nature, a traditional indigenous performance, or a private community space or ethnic festival. However, authenticity means different things to different people. The desire for authentic experiences can conflict with expert and professional understandings of what it means to be authentic, especially because tourists may not always wish to be confronted with the reality on the ground (McKercher and Du Cros 2002).

The motivation of "authenticity seekers" leads tourism service providers to stage something as "authentic" (MacCannell 1976) to match the imaginaries of tourists (Salazar and Graburn 2014). Heritage sites are being commercialized and transformed as a consumable production to enhance tourist experience, which is criticized as resulting in the loss of meaning and of authenticity. Festivals, for example, which were traditionally exclusively celebrated by local people without outsider participation, have become a means of symbolic construction to increase popularity for the purpose of tourism (Richards 2007). This is the case in the well-documented Alarde celebration in Fuenterrabia, Spain. According to Greenwood (1989), the Alarde celebrations partially lost their appeal for the local community after the municipal government arranged the celebrations twice a day to attract more visitors. Cohen (1988), on the contrary, argues that commodification does not necessarily destroy the meaning of heritage. He asserts that tourism-oriented products frequently acquire new meanings for locals, as they become a diacritical mark of their ethnic or cultural identity, a vehicle of self-representation before an external public. Furthermore, cultural forms of consumption can sometimes even actively enhance and enliven local communities.

Tourists usually remain unaware of the broader political, economic, and sociocultural context in which heritage tourism is embedded. In East Africa, for instance, tourists are exposed to various types of Maasai heritage and culture (Salazar 2010a). It already starts at the door of their lodge or hotel, where Maasai "warriors" guarantee the safety of the property and its visitors. At a Maasai museum along the safari circuit, the (non-Maasai) museum guide dressed as a warrior takes visitors through the exhibition. Tourists usually do not realize that most of the "authentic" Maasai settlements they visit were specifically built for tourism purposes. Only the disproportionately large souvenir stalls somehow mark them as tourism places. These tourism *boma* were built by Maasai who live in neighboring homesteads. In order to spread the tourism revenues more equally, some Maasai communities have worked out a rotating scheme determining who can stay when at the *boma*. Visits in the area along the safari highway often start with intense negotiations between Maasai and drivers or tour guides about the entrance fee.

The Berlin Wall in Germany serves as a different example of the thorny issue of authenticity in heritage tourism. The Wall was widely regarded as a demonstration of the failure of the German Democratic Republic and later as the symbol of the postwar division of Europe. The remaining parts of the Wall have been firmly established as a tourism attraction, including organized tour itineraries throughout the city. The Wall Museum at Checkpoint Charlie offered an exhibition of Wall victims, comprising a small replica of the dismantled Wall and a display of stories of more than a thousand victims. However, none of the people showed in the exhibition had actually died at the border crossing checkpoint (Frank 2006). Nevertheless, the Wall museum has become a "sacred site" for both international and German tourists.

The academic debate about authenticity still continues. In heritage tourism, the meaning of authenticity is neither simply embedded in an objective reality nor dependent on the symbolic projection of social construction (Zhu 2012a). Rather, authenticity becomes a key issue of tourist experiences. It illustrates the asymmetrical power relations between hosts, brokers, and guests (Salazar 2010a). Tourists arrive at the heritage encounter with their own agendas, contexts, and imaginaries based on personal interests, previous experience, and knowledge (McIntosh and Prentice 1999). Since the marketing, presenting, and developing of heritage tourism targets tourists instead of locals, tourism strengthens the asymmetrical relationship, which often leads to social and cultural conflicts (Porter and Salazar 2005).

The critical analysis of tourism imaginaries can help us understand the dynamics of this asymmetrical relationship. Salazar defines imaginaries as "socially transmitted representational assemblages that interact with people's personal imaginings are used as meaning make and world shaping devices" (2012c: 864). The tourism sector and local authorities are not the only agents in building tourism imaginaries. Tourists harness their purchasing power to feed their imagination and their consumption preferences back into the production of the heritage landscape and, thus, they contribute to the ways in which places are represented and constituted. In his study of the Taj Mahal of India, Edensor (1998) metaphorically regards tourism as a performance and the heritage as a stage on which tourists are directed and rehearsed but also able to improvise their own cultural rituals. In this sense, tourists at heritage attractions assist in the production of their own experiences through their imaginaries (Salazar and Graburn 2014), and they imbue heritage with their own personal meaning (McIntosh and Prentice 1999).

The historic trade center of Lijiang, China is a good example to illustrate the dynamics of imaginaries built by heritage tourism. In the late 1980s and early 1990s, Lijiang started to market itself as an international tourism destination. Since then, the town has attracted large numbers of tourists from around the world. Western backpackers are fascinated by this remote place. After being included in the World Heritage List by UNESCO in 1997, Lijiang has become one of the most popular destinations for both inbound and domestic tourists in China. The local culture has become eroticized, romanticized, and ethnicized through tourism imaginaries collaboratively produced by the local government, tourism practitioners, and the local community. Shifting from a historic trade town to a commercial heritage site, Lijiang has now acquired a new connotation as a "town of romance" (Zhu 2012b).

Besides hunting for ethnic or authentic cultures, tourists also have other motivations to visit heritage properties. For instance, tourism motivated by a desire to visit places of death, atrocity, disaster, and other forms of human suffering is growing in popularity. Millions of people visit memorials, former concentration camps, prisons, or places where natural disasters have occurred. The Genbaku Dome in Hiroshima, Japan, has become an important destination and a World Heritage site. Alongside education, propaganda, and political expedience, the peace park of Hiroshima is now a gathering place for various tourists: officials, monks, pilgrims, anti-nuclear protesters, and artists. Another, increasingly popular, way to connect tourism and heritage is through trails or routes. Argentina, for example, developed the Yerba Mate Trail. Activities along the route vary from agritourism to guided tours of industrial plants and museums. For tourists, trips link the production of yerba mate with local history, culture, and inhabitants (UNWTO 2012: 31). The above examples only hint at the manifold ways in which tourists encounter heritage, in all its forms, structures, and expressions.

World Heritage Tourism

Forty years have passed since the adoption of the Convention concerning the Protection of the World Cultural and Natural Heritage by the General Conference of UNESCO in 1972 (UNESCO 1972). Since then, World Heritage properties have become the centerpiece of global heritage tourism (Shackley 1998). Once a property is inscribed on the World Heritage List, it can become an important destination and it can have a great impact for local economic development.

The expansion of World Heritage properties since the first designations on the List in 1978 clearly coincided with the growth of global tourism as a major form of economic and sociocultural development (Salazar 2010b). Although it is hard to think of World Heritage without considering tourism, the convention text does not mention tourism at all. The original 1977 Operational Guidelines for the Implementation of the World Heritage Convention (UNESCO 1977) do not tackle tourism either. While subsequent versions of the guidelines only mention tourism as a potential "threat" to heritage, linked to poor management and mounting visitor pressure, the latest versions are progressively recognizing the importance of tourism for heritage.[1] This is also true for more recent heritage-related policies, such as the 2003 Convention for the Safeguarding of Intangible Cultural Heritage.

While UNESCO was relatively late to integrate tourism into its heritage work, its advisory bodies and other international organizations developed instruments to connect heritage and tourism at a much earlier stage. For example, ICOMOS launched a Charter of Cultural Tourism in 1976, with 18 international organizations as signatories (Drost 1996). The charter aims to encourage safeguarding and to ensure the conservation and promotion of heritage, taking into account the positive as well as negative effects of tourism development across the world. Drawing on the concept of "sustainable tourism," jointly launched by the World Tourism Organization and the United Nations Environment Programme in 1982, international organizations recognize the serious damage by mass tourism, and they encourage the development of guidelines and recommendations for tourism development. For example, the UN Foundation ran the World Heritage Alliance for Sustainable Tourism between 2006 and 2010. About fifty members from the tourism sector, governments, and conservation sector joined forces to preserve more than twenty World Heritage sites in seven countries. During the same period, Friends of World Heritage, an initiative of the UN Foundation, the World Heritage Center, and Expedia, was a program dedicated to raising awareness about the importance of protecting World Heritage, promoting sustainable development, and offering ways to explore the properties through sustainable travel.[2] Although "sustainable tourism" has been widely accepted by international organizations, governments, NGOs, and the tourism sector, some stakeholders may not clearly understand this concept. Others instead abuse it as a strategy to fulfill their own economic and political agendas.

Although international organizations have developed policies on heritage tourism through inter-agency cooperation and guidelines, World Heritage inscription at most properties has had serious sociocultural and economic impacts. First, heritage inscription "is increasingly becoming an integral part of site or destination marketing campaigns" (Leask and Fyall 2006: 287). World Heritage status was never intended as a tourism marketing device, but it increasingly works that way, acting as a global top brand, and perhaps also as a collectable set to be ticked off on a tourist's to-do list – "been there, done that." Consequently, World Heritage designation has become a "highly appreciated accolade" (Smith 2002: 137) in the tourism world and has also emerged as one of the major promotional tools as the World Heritage list serves "as a selection of display of top heritage tourism sites" (Boniface 2001: 74). Countries deliberately make use of "their" World Heritage in national tourism image and branding campaigns. Particularly cultural sites seem to be drawing on the World Heritage label (Hall and Piggin 2001). While UNESCO never intended the World Heritage list to become an ever-expanding tourist's guide to hundreds of wonders in the modern world, "in reality, however, world heritage sites and 'wonders' have become just that – 'must see' symbolic attractions in cultural tours, itineraries, tour operator and tourist board marketing, with World Heritage site award the equivalent of a Michelin Guide 3-star rating" (Evans 2004: 316).

Besides the marketing effects of World Heritage tourism, many nomination files are handed in these days because the proposing governments hope that the World Heritage "brand" (Ryan and Silvanto 2009) will drastically increase visitor rates and thus economic revenue. Apart from a lack of understanding of what the designation is all about, there is an erroneous assumption in much of the world that inscription on the World Heritage List will inevitably result in increased income generation. Many countries see tourism as a major tool to develop, and in the eyes of those in power the idea of development often equals erasing local, traditional cultural practices.[3] At some World Heritage sites, local governments have become interest groups with their own entrepreneurial pursuit and policy agenda. For local authorities, heritage tourism is not only the object of regulation, but a means of profit making (Zhu and Li 2013).

For instance, Xi'an, the former capital of 13 dynasties in China, is regarded as the cradle of Chinese civilization and an important component in the formation of Chinese identity. Located in Xi'an, the Mausoleum of the First Qin Emperor was listed as World Heritage in 1987. In response to national policies of promoting tourism as one of the pillar industries, Xi'an capitalizes on its historic heritage as cultural resources for tourism consumption. Heritage tourism has become the direct means to achieve the goal of modernization and globalization of Xi'an city. In 2005, the Xi'an municipal government initiated the Tang Imperial City Plan, with a total investment of 23 billion *yuan* (Feighery 2011). This project aims to transform the densely populated areas of the inner city into a functioning replica of the Tang Imperial City from 2005 to 2050. The project also strives for the regeneration of urban space through a convergence of commercial interests associated with the tourism and the real estate industries. Guided by the project plan, a large number of buildings in the inner city of Xi'an were demolished and local residents were relocated to other districts of the city. Meanwhile, historic monuments and Buddhist temples in this area were gradually transformed into cultural theme parks, such as the Tang Paradise Park. Mosques became tourism attractions in surroundings of newly built "Islamic" souvenir stalls. Antique markets and high-end residential houses were built to attract investors and middle-class residents from other cities of China. Imagined symbols and decor of the Tang dynasty are purposely applied to adorn windows and roofs to beautify these new buildings. These projects indeed have little in common with heritage conservation as it is recommended, for example, in the 1964 Venice Charter for the Conservation and Restoration of Monuments and Sites. The reinvention of a historic image of the Tang dynasty attracts tourists in search of a nostalgic past or "staged authenticity" (MacCannell 1973), an alternative form of local distinctiveness through representation and reinterpretation of heritage values.

The case of Prambanan in Indonesia, however, illustrates that economic motivations in heritage tourism do not always prevail over cultural ones. The Prambanan Temple Compounds were designated as World Heritage in 1991. The people of Prambanan village have always referred to the main structure as *Candi Rara* (or *Loro*) *Jonggrang* (Javanese for "temple of the slender virgin"). According to local beliefs, the statue in the north chamber of the central Shiva shrine does not represent the Hindu goddess Durga but Loro Jonggrang. The on-site guides prefer this cultural interpretation of the temple complex over the officially sanctioned version (which is reproduced in tour guide books and other tourism materials). Clearly, different heritage stakeholders at Prambanan use naming in different ways and for different purposes (Salazar 2015). The tensions around the name recently intensified when, in accordance with Article 268 of UNESCO's Operational Guidelines for the Implementation of the World Heritage Convention (UNESCO 2013), the text "Candi Rara Jonggrang" on a newly erected signboard was replaced by "Candi Prambanan."

Global Standards versus Local Distinctiveness

In *The Tourist Gaze*, Urry (2002) discusses the influence of globalization on tourism by addressing the rise of the heritage tourism industry and modern consumption in the late twentieth century. The debate on commercialization and destruction of local uniqueness offers valuable insights about globalization being the supposed cause of cultural homogenization. As we described above, international organizations play a significant role in standardizing heritage tourism. They have developed policies, ethnic codes, and "heritage tourism products" to create global standards. However, the consequences of globalization of heritage and tourism should be viewed as multidimensional, comprising a complex mixture of global standardization and local distinctiveness (Salazar 2010a). Heritage destinations worldwide may be adapting themselves to the homogenizing trends of global tourism. But, at the same time, they have to commoditize their local distinctiveness in order to compete with other destinations (cf. Chang 1999). After all, it is the local particularity of heritage (sometimes branded as "national") that tourists are most interested in witnessing and experiencing (Salazar 2005, 2006).

It is important to point out that there are significant economic, social, political, management, conservation, and interpretation differences between developed and developing countries in terms of heritage tourism. Especially poor countries have a hard time achieving the international standards set by the tourism sector (Salazar 2010a). There are many issues in developing countries that create everyday obstacles to the sustainable development and management of heritage, including the role of local communities in decision making, sharing in the benefits of tourism development, empowerment and power, ownership of historic places and artifacts, lack of funding and skills, and forced displacement to accommodate tourism growth (Hampton 2005).

The promise of sustainable heritage tourism becomes all the more difficult to realize if we take account of the fact that low-income nations, such as Tanzania, Nepal, and Cambodia, receive only a fraction of global tourism revenue (UNWTO 2013).

To assist the development of local and regional distinctiveness, many UNESCO-related and regional organizations have emerged in recent decades. They translate the global concepts of heritage tourism management to address local conditions in varied cultural, political, and historical circumstances (Hitchcock, King, and Parnwell 1993). In the period 1998–2001, the UNESCO Regional Office for Asia and the Pacific, in cooperation with the Nordic World Heritage Foundation, ran the Cultural Heritage Management and Tourism: Model for Co-operation Among Stakeholders Project (Aas, Ladkin, and Fletcher 2005). It used Southeast Asian World Heritage towns as case studies. The project's objective was to support tourism by creating an arena for dialogue among the different stakeholders in each pilot site, whether within tourism or the local communities, and to strengthen the competence, capacity, and economic basis of the latter for handling the preservation and maintenance of their heritage resources. Reconciling the differences in opinion between the local tourism sector and the heritage managers presented a serious barrier towards collaboration between the two groups (Aas, Ladkin, and Fletcher 2005: 44). In 2004, the UNESCO Regional Office for Culture in Latin America and the Caribbean set up a similar long-term training program focusing on cultural heritage management, entitled the Caribbean Capacity Building Program (CCBP) for World Heritage (Núñez Fernández 2008).

Many countries have become aware of the political, cultural, and economic value of heritage, and have initiated their own national or regional heritage tourism development projects. For example, "Incredible India" is a widely influential campaign by the Indian Ministry of Tourism to present the country as an attractive destination, showcasing different unique images of cultural and natural heritage. Besides tourism promotion, the campaign also aims at educating local communities to behave well when dealing with foreign tourists and making people aware of the effects of tourism and the significance of heritage preservation, cleanliness, and hospitality.

Another form of differentiation of heritage management comes from the critics of Western approaches. Although it is widely stated that heritage conservation, as both a practice and a theory, is rooted in seventeenth- and eighteenth-century Europe, and that the West is regarded as the sole originator of material culture conservation, there are many emerging non-Western alliances and bodies that stand out to (re) create cultural Otherness and unique regional identities. For instance, The Aga Khan Trust for Culture (AKTC) focuses on the physical, social, cultural, and economic revitalization of communities in the Muslim world. The Islamic Educational, Scientific, and Cultural Organization (ISESCO) produces "'Islamic-centric' or occidental forms of cultural governance" by establishing numerous cultural heritage programs and related polices (Winter 2013: 13). Similarly, since the Caribbean region was earmarked as being underrepresented by UNESCO in terms of the wealth and diversity of its natural and cultural heritage, the CARICOM (Caribbean Community and Common Market) has developed different projects to promote heritage tourism related to local intangible heritage such as music, art, crafts, and fashion (Jordan and Jolliffe 2013).

Local considerations have given rise to unique outcomes in the form of specialized heritage themes, the division of roles between local agencies, and the varied motives served by heritage enhancement (Chang et al. 1996). In the meantime, the global process of "tourismification" of heritage confronts local stakeholders and affected communities with a whole set of complex issues, including authenticity, interpretation, heritage contestation, social exclusion, contested space, personal heritage, control, and preservation (McKercher and Du Cros 2002; Timothy and Prideaux 2004). Consider, for instance, Angkor and Petra, two World Heritage properties often cited in relation to tourist-carrying capacity problems.

Angkor, Cambodia was on the List of World Heritage in Danger from 1992 (the year of its inscription) until 2004. Western-focused policies have inadequately restrained an explosion in facility construction principally aimed at a tourism market from Northeast Asia (Winter 2007). Since the site gained World Heritage status in 1992, the number of visitors has leapt from fewer than 10,000 to more than 2.5 million a year. A sprawling town has grown up to serve the hordes of tourists that arrive daily. Local hotels have been extracting water from underground reserves, threatening to undermine the temples themselves. Local villagers have been excluded from the property or marginalized by various authorities in the name of both conservation and tourism promotion. At the same time, the arrival of a permanent presence has served as a defense against vandalism and pillage (Musitelli 2002: 332).

The inscription of Petra, Jordan in 1985 was part of a government strategy to capitalize on the country's rich archaeological and biblical sites in order to attract large numbers of Western tourists and Christian pilgrims who come to Jordan as part of "Holy Land" tours. To be fair, tourism was already an issue at Petra before the World Heritage designation. The inevitable sociocultural conflict between the tourism sector and local inhabitants challenges the tourism development process of larger projects, such as the World Bank-sponsored Jordan Cultural Heritage, Tourism and Urban Development Project, which aim at poverty alleviation through tourism. Ironically, the community members who find the least benefit from such projects are also among the poorest (Comer 2011).

Challenges and Trends

As the cases above illustrate, the development of heritage tourism across the globe shares similar challenges in terms of planning, management, and interpretation. In response to these issues, heritage tourism has adapted to emerging technological, economic, demographic, environmental, and social trends. Over the years, many efforts have been made worldwide to achieve an equilibrium between preservation and visitation, and this from different perspectives such as visitor management, heritage destination planning, and the interpretation of heritage (all the while taking into account pricing issues, community development, and marketing) (Li, Wu, and Cai 2008).

One major challenge involves the impact of tourism on local communities. Tourism can create new job opportunities and bring economic benefits. Heritage properties such as the Taj Mahal in India and Borobudur in Indonesia generate direct local employment and economic activities. For instance, tourism provides different employment in Borobudur. Locals work as small-scale entrepreneurs, as vendors of souvenirs, as guides, and in art galleries and guest houses that surround the site (Nuryanti 1996). However, in many developing countries, most of the value added in the tourism industry tends to be captured by foreign investors, international tour operators, and foreign airline companies, while only limited benefits flow to the local poor community. Evidence suggests that only between one-fifth and one-third of total tourism expenditure actually stays in local communities (Ashley 2006).

Apart from economic benefits, other issues are of a more ethical nature, such as land ownership, dramatic change of lifestyle, property rights, and the interaction between social structures and expectations leading to misunderstandings and conflicts. For instance, after the emergence of heritage tourism in Lijiang, the town has experienced rapid changes in social environment and commercial development. Han Chinese from outside Lijiang have dominated the tourism business rather than local people. Guesthouses formerly owned by local Naxi have been replaced by luxury hotels that are run by the so-called "new Lijiang people," namely Han businesspeople. Their wealth, education, business skills, and interregional associations have made them a predominant force in the tourism market. As a result, local Naxi, as original "locals" of the place, are increasingly leaving their homes to tourists and businesspeople (Salazar and Zhang 2013). Social solidarities which are built upon community ties, memory, and culture are rapidly eroding, despite residents' resistance to the mechanism of capital accumulation (Su 2012).

Heritage management can be another challenge. Tourism-oriented infrastructure developments can make site managers and other authorities hesitant to place any restrictions on site access or to take preservation measures. In many countries, problems associated with heritage tourism take the form of planning difficulties such as building demolitions, overcrowding, traffic management, and parking problems (Tunbridge and Ashworth 1996). Uncontrolled tourism development at heritage properties is often related to visitor problems such as the invasion of public spaces by outdoor cafes, noise or light pollution, property degradation due to visitors, and seasonal variation in visitor numbers (Hall and Piggin 2001). Moreover, developing countries face the challenge of limited funding resources and inadequate institutional capabilities. In certain countries in Africa, Asia, and Latin America, it is difficult to rouse interest in heritage conservation. For example, the beautiful image promoted by the "Incredible India" campaign does not reflect the challenges at many Indian heritage sites, such as the lack of hotel rooms, inadequate infrastructure, political indifference, poverty, and violent crime. The key dilemma is that it seems difficult to balance the development of tourism with preservation, often creating a tension or conflict between the large number of stakeholders involved (Harrison and Hitchcock 2005). Each of the stakeholder groups is likely to hold conflicting agendas and priorities, resulting in difficulties arriving at a consensus of opinion on heritage management, interpretation, and appropriation (Porter and Salazar 2005; Salazar and Porter 2004).

Unfortunately, there are no universal solutions. However, better management strategies and useful new technologies have been developed. As mentioned above, international organizations have started to integrate the idea of sustainable tourism into heritage management planning and conservation. In 2001, UNESCO World Heritage Committee authorized the World Heritage Center to develop a decade-long Sustainable Tourism Program, in cooperation with its advisory bodies (ICOMOS, IUCN, and ICCROM) and UNWTO, UNEP, and the UN Foundation.[4] The goal of the program was to enhance the quality and effectiveness of the management of sustainable tourism at World Heritage properties through practical instruments, capacity-building activities, and pilot demonstration projects to identify good practices. This resulted, among other things, in a *World Heritage Paper* on tourism management (Pedersen 2002) and a *World Heritage Review* special on sustainable tourism (WHC 2010). A second World Heritage Sustainable Tourism Program was adopted by the World Heritage Committee at its 36th session in June 2012. The new program further established "an international framework for the cooperative and coordinated achievement of shared and sustainable outcome related at World Heritage Sites" (WHC 2013). As part of the program, a joint project on tourism management in World Heritage sites of Portuguese origin was launched in January 2013 by the World Heritage Center and Turismo de Portugal (the Portuguese Tourism Authority). The latter project has involved site managers and experts from over 14 countries worldwide.

New ways of collaboration and social networking have become a global trend in tourism. The implications of the increasing significance of social networks and the rise of networked organizations and individuals are profound. Since 2009, the World Heritage Center has an agreement with TripAdvisor.[5] The traveller website provides technological and financial assistance and develops an online outreach and awareness-building campaign focusing on conservation and community involvement at World Heritage destinations. TripAdvisor asks its 45 million monthly visitors to contribute reviews and opinions about the condition of World Heritage across the globe, to vote on the places they want to protect most, and to encourage donations. While the World Tourism Organization had already chosen "Preserving World Heritage for the New Millennium" as theme for its 1999 World Tourism Day, more recently it established a strategic partnership with the World Heritage Center (UNWTO 2009). In 2012, UNESCO launched the "People Protecting Places" campaign, a "new travel and tourism movement to help these irreplaceable treasures continue to inspire future generations," in partnership with National Geographic and Intercontinental Hotels and Resorts.[6] However, it is difficult to measure the effectiveness of these big collaborative projects. Long term ethnographic research is thus needed to better understand the specific dynamics and effects of these projects on the ground. The traditional anthropological research method can cast new light on the global dynamics of heritage tourism and provide fresh perspectives for heritage tourism practices (e.g., Breglia 2006).

Heritage interpretation has become another key strategy to successful management policy. As a platform for enhanced visitor management, heritage interpretation links heritage and tourism in reconstructing the past in the present. Interpretation does not function as a simple description of the facts of heritage, but "moves into the realms of spiritual truth, emotional response, deeper meaning and understanding" (Nuryanti 1996: 253). By helping tourists understand the significance of heritage, its environmental setting, historical meanings, and social values, interpretation plays a significant role to mediate heritage and tourism through education, marketing, and managing. Heritage interpretation offers both tourists and the local community conservation awareness. It can also be an effective management tool in directing visitors away from sensitive areas of the sites (Millar 1989). Since 2005, the UNESCO office in Bangkok and the UNESCO-ICCROM Asian Academy for Heritage Management have developed a special training program for tour guides working at World Heritage properties (UNESCO 2005). By building a framework through collaboration among ministries of tourism, training institutions, national tourism organizations, and the UNESCO regional office, the program aims to strengthen the guiding skills of the trainees to educate tourists about heritage conservation issues and codes of responsible conduct. This program has already been implemented in Thailand, India, Malaysia, Laos, and Indonesia. For instance, the program was launched in the My Son Sanctuary and Hoi An Ancient Town World Heritage properties in Vietnam in 2011. More than twenty participants attended the training courses on local history, culture, archaeology, and heritage conservation. The local authorities stated that the training would become compulsory for all guides at heritage sites in the Vietnamese province of Quang Nam.[7]

Finally, it is important to stress that heritage tourism also targets intangible heritage. The UN World Tourism Organization presented a global study on the links between tourism and intangible cultural heritage (UNWTO 2012). Besides exploring major challenges, risks, and opportunities for tourism development related to intangible cultural heritage, it further discusses practical steps for the elaboration, management, and marketing of intangible cultural heritage-based tourism products. Through an extensive compendium of case studies and good practices drawn from across five continents, this research offers in-depth information on and analysis of government-led actions, public–private partnerships, and community initiatives. Not surprisingly, UNWTO stresses the positive aspects: intangible cultural heritage tourism can provide new employment opportunities, help alleviate poverty, curb rural migration flight among the young and marginally employed, and nurture a sense of pride amongst community members. At the same time, the organization recognizes the fragility of intangible heritage and the fact that true partnerships between communities and the tourism and heritage sectors can only occur if all sides develop a genuine appreciation for each other's aspirations and values.

Tourism scholars are paying more and more attention to the intersecting development of heritage and tourism (McKercher and Du Cros 2002; Prentice 1993; Nuryanti 1997; Timothy and Boyd 2003). Several journals, such as the *Journal of Heritage Tourism*, were created to research and review current trends and issues in the field, while established outlets too, such as the *International Journal of Heritage Studies*, are paying increasing attention to tourism. The interdisciplinary UNESCO-UNITWIN Network "Culture, Tourism and Development," made up of about thirty partner universities throughout the world, is since 2002 focused on studying the theoretical as well as practical aspects of heritage tourism.[8] The establishment of the Association of Critical Heritage Studies in 2012 has encouraged the further study and disentanglement of the politics and practices of heritage tourism.[9]

Conclusion

While conservationists argue for the need to "place preservation ahead of tourism" (Comer 2011: 186), the reality is that tourism cannot be neglected as an unwanted negative side-effect. As this chapter has illustrated, the tourism development of heritage is both an opportunity and a risk, and which requires careful consideration, planning, implementation, and management. Sustainable tourism development entails the adoption of planning strategies to mitigate the negative impact of tourism without sacrificing its benefits (Drost 1996). Accepting that tourism is a central component of heritage, more directed efforts are required for properties to "reduce leakages and improve economic benefits to be derived from tourism and to the local community" (Leask and Fyall 2006: 287). Sustainable tourism development requires a long-term partnership with local stakeholders (Salazar 2012a). There is an urgent need for new ideas and concepts that reconcile tourism and preservation with the need for sustainable development. Besides this, more attention needs to be paid to ethical issues, in particular the involvement of local communities, ethical codes of tourism (such as the UNWTO Global Code for Ethics in Tourism), the moral implications of cultural heritage, the responsibilities of museums, and the question of who has the power to own and interpret heritage.

The current situation is "forcing a search for methods of balancing conservation with the livelihood needs of local people and the right of tourists to enjoy such places" (Leask and Fyall 2006: 98). International agencies concerned with the preservation and tourism promotion of heritage sites are increasingly aware of the mistake made in the past of overemphasizing the protection of monuments and sites and the promotion of quality tourism, without paying sufficient attention to the living practices of local inhabitants and their knowledge. As global tourism continues to expand, heritage sites will be the source of historically unprecedented numbers of tourists. Most indicators suggest there will be a huge increase in tourism worldwide over the next ten years, virtually doubling the current numbers. It is estimated that China alone will send out over 125 million outbound tourists by 2021 (WTTC 2011: 27). Interestingly, a large amount of the increased travel for leisure will be intraregional (rather than global). At any rate, the predicted growth of intraregional tourism – 1.2 billion intraregional arrivals per year by 2020 (WTO 2001) – will seriously change the global tourism landscape. While the management of heritage is usually the responsibility of a particular community or custodian group, the protection, conservation, interpretation and (re) presentation of the cultural diversity of any particular place or people are important challenges for us all.

NOTES

1 *The Operational Guidelines for the Implementation of the World Heritage Convention.* Available at: http://whc.unesco.org/en/guidelines/. Accessed November 28, 2014.
2 Friends of World Heritage, http://www.friendsofworldheritage.org/about_us.htm. Accessed November 28, 2014.
3 Until the 1970s, such ideas and practices were common in the Western world as well. The all-pervasive ideology of modernization equated traditional societies with underdevelopment and an inferior phase prior to full-blown development.
4 While this was the first concerted effort to tackle tourism, there had been earlier collaborations. In 1993, for example, the World Tourism Organization and ICOMOS published together a manual for World Heritage site managers (Garfield 1993). That handbook underscored the assumption that conservation must precede tourism.
5 See http://www.tripadvisor.co.nz/PressCenter-i3307-c1-Press_Releases.html. Accessed January 5, 2015.
6 UNESCO, *People Protecting Places*, http://www.peopleprotectingplaces.org/. Accessed November 28, 2014.
7 UNESCO OFFICE in Ha Noi, UNESCO Heritage Guide training enhances professional skills of guides at My Son World Heritage site, http://www.unesco.org/new/en/hanoi/about-this-office/single-view/news/unesco_heritage_guide_training_enhances_professional_skills_of_guides_at_my_son_world_heritage_site/. Accessed November 28, 2014.
8 Universit‘ Paris 1, Réseau UNITWIN / UNESCO “Culture, Tourisme, Développement,” http://www.univ-paris1.fr/ufr/irest/reseau-unitwin-unesco-culture-tourisme-developpement/. Accessed November 28, 2014.
9 Australian National University, School of Archaeology and Anthropology, Association of Critical Heritage Studies, http://archanth.anu.edu.au/heritage-museum-studies/association-critical-heritage-studies. Accessed November 28, 2014.

REFERENCES

Aas, C., A. Ladkin, and J. Fletcher (2005) Stakeholder collaboration and heritage management. *Annals of Tourism Research* 32(1): 28–48.

Anderson, B. R. (1983) *Imagined Communities: Reflections on the Origin and Spread of Nationalism*. London: Verso.

Ashley, C. (2006) *How Can Governments Boost the Local Economic Impacts of Tourism? Options and Tools*. London: Overseas Development Institute.

Ashworth, G. J. and P. J. Larkham (eds) (1994) *Building a New Heritage: Tourism, Culture, and Identity in the New Europe*. London: Routledge.

Boniface, P. (2001) Touring world heritage in AD 2000. *Tourism Recreation Research* 26(1): 73–79.

Boniface, P. and P. Fowler (1993) *Heritage and Tourism in "the Global Village."* London: Routledge.

Breglia, L. (2006) *Monumental Ambivalence: The Politics of Heritage*. Austin: University of Texas Press.

Chang, T. C. (1999) Local uniqueness in the global village: Heritage tourism in Singapore. *Professional Geographer* 51(1): 91–103.

Chang, T. C., S. Milne, D. Fallon, and C. Pohlmann (1996) Urban heritage tourism: The global–local nexus. *Annals of Tourism Research* 23(2): 284–305.

Cohen, E. (1979) A phenomenology of tourist experiences. *Sociology* 13(2): 179–201.

Cohen, E. (1988) Authenticity and commoditization in tourism. *Annals of Tourism Research* 15(3): 371–386.

Comer, D. C. (2011) *Tourism and Archaeological Heritage Management at Petra*. New York: Springer.

Davis, P. (2008) New Museologies and the Ecomuseum, in B. J. Graham and P. Howard (eds), *The Ashgate Research Companion to Heritage and Identity*. Burlington, VT: Ashgate.

Di Giovine, M. A. (2008) *The Heritage-Scape: UNESCO, World Heritage, and Tourism*. Lanham, MD: Lexington.

Drost, A. (1996) Developing sustainable tourism for World Heritage sites. *Annals of Tourism Research* 23(2): 479–492.

Edensor, T. (1998) *Tourists at the Taj: Performance and Meaning at a Symbolic Site*. London: Routledge.

Edson, G. (2004) Heritage: Pride or passion, product or service? *International Journal of Heritage Studies* 10(4): 333–348.

Evans, G. (2004) Mundo Maya: From Cancún to city of culture. World Heritage in post-colonial Mesoamerica. *Current Issues in Tourism* 7(4-5): 315–329.

Feighery, W. (2011) Contested heritage in the ancient city of peace. *Historic Environment* 23(1): 38–47.

Frank, S. (2006) Communist Heritage Tourism and its Local (Dis)Contents at Checkpoint Charlie, Berlin, in H. Berking (ed.), *Negotiating Urban Conflicts: Interaction, Space, and Control*. Bielefeld: Transcript, pp. 195–207.

Garfield, D. (1993) *Tourism at World Heritage Cultural Sites: The Site Manager's Handbook*. Madrid: World Tourism Organization.

Garrod, B. and A. Fyall (2001) Heritage tourism: A question of definition. *Annals of Tourism Research* 28(4): 1049–1052.

GHF (2010) *Saving Our Vanishing Heritage: Safeguarding Endangered Cultural Heritage Sites in the Developing World*. Palo Alto, CA: Global Heritage Fund.

Graham, B., G. J. Ashworth, and J. E. Tunbridge (2000) *A Geography of Heritage: Power, Culture, and Economy*. London: Arnold.

Greenwood, D. J. (1989) Culture by the Pound: An Anthropological Perspective on Tourism as Cultural Commoditization, in V. L. Smith (ed.), *Hosts and Guests: The Anthropology of Tourism*. Philadelphia: University of Pennsylvania Press, pp. 171–186.

Hall, C. M. and R. Piggin (2001) Tourism and World Heritage in OECD countries. *Tourism Recreation Research* 26(1): 103–105.

Hampton, M. P. (2005) Heritage, local communities and economic development. *Annals of Tourism Research* 32(3): 735–759.

Harrison, D. and M. Hitchcock (eds) (2005) *The Politics of World Heritage: Negotiating Tourism and Conservation (Current Themes in Tourism)*. Clevedon: Channel View.

Harrison, R. (ed.) (2010) *Understanding the Politics of Heritage, Understanding Global Heritage*. Manchester: Manchester University Press.

Herbert, D. T., R. Prentice, and C. J. Thomas (eds) (1989) *Heritage Sites: Strategies for Marketing and Development*. Aldershot: Avebury.

Hitchcock, M., V. T. King, and M. Parnwell (eds) (1993) *Tourism in South-East Asia*. London: Routledge.

Howard, P. (2002) The eco-museum: Innovation that risks the future. *International Journal of Heritage Studies* 8(1): 63–72.

Jordan, L.-A. and L. Jolliffe (2013) Heritage tourism in the Caribbean: Current themes and challenges. *Journal of Heritage Tourism* 8(1): 1–8.

Kirshenblatt-Gimblett, B (1998) *Destination Culture: Tourism, Museums, and Heritage*. Berkeley: University of California Press.

Leask, A. and A. Fyall (eds) (2006) *Managing World Heritage Sites*. Oxford: Butterworth-Heinemann.

Li, M., B. Wu, and L. Cai (2008) Tourism development of World Heritage sites in China: A geographic perspective. *Tourism Management* 29(2): 308–319.

Lowenthal, D. (1998) *The Heritage Crusade and the Spoils of History*. Cambridge: Cambridge University Press.

MacCannell, D. (1973) Staged authenticity: Arrangements of social space in tourist settings. *American Journal of Sociology* 79(3): 589–603.

MacCannell, D. (1976) *The Tourist: A New Theory of the Leisure Class*. New York: Schocken.

McIntosh, A. J. and R. C. Prentice (1999) Affirming authenticity: Consuming cultural heritage. *Annals of tourism research* 26(3): 589–612.

McKercher, B. and H. Du Cros (2002) *Cultural Tourism: The Partnership between Tourism and Cultural Heritage Management*. New York: Haworth Hospitality Press.

Meskell, L. (2005) Sites of Violence: Terrorism, Tourism and Heritage in the Archaeological Present, in L. Meskell and P. Pels (eds), *Embedding Ethics*. Oxford: Berg, pp. 123–146.

Millar, S. (1989) Heritage management for heritage tourism. *Tourism Management* 10(1): 9–14.

Musitelli, J. (2002) World heritage, between universalism and globalization. *International Journal of Cultural Property* 11(2): 323–336.

Nitzky, W. (2012) Mediating heritage preservation and rural development: Ecomuseum development in China. *Urban Anthropology* 41(2–4): 367–417.

Núñez Fernández, R. (2008) *Management of Tourism in Heritage Sites*. Havana: UNESCO La Habana.

Nuryanti, W. (1996) Heritage and postmodern tourism. *Annals of Tourism Research* 23(2): 249–260.

Nuryanti, W. (ed.) (1997) *Tourism and Heritage Management*. Yogyakarta: Gadjah Mada University Press.

NWHO (1999) *Sustainable Tourism and Cultural Heritage: A Review of Development Assistance and its Potential to Promote Sustainability*. Oslo: Nordic World Heritage Office.

Pedersen, A. (2002) *Managing Tourism at World Heritage Sites: A Practical Manual for World Heritage Site Managers*. World Heritage Manuals. Paris: UNESCO World Heritage Center.

Pendlebury, J., M. Short, and A. While (2009) Urban World Heritage Sites and the problem of authenticity. *Cities* 26(6): 349–358.

Porter, B. W. and N. B. Salazar (2005) Heritage tourism, conflict, and the public interest: An introduction. *International Journal of Heritage Studies* 11(5): 361–370.

Prentice, R. (1993) *Tourism and Heritage Attractions*. Issues in Tourism Series. London: Routledge.

Richards, G. (ed.) (2007) *Cultural Tourism: Global and Local Perspectives*. New York: Haworth Hospitality Press.

Ryan, J. and S. Silvanto (2009) The World Heritage List: The making and management of a brand. *Place Branding and Public Diplomacy* 5(4): 290–300.

Salazar, N. B. (2005) Tourism and glocalization: "Local" tour guiding. *Annals of Tourism Research* 32(3): 628–646.

Salazar, N. B. (2006) Touristifying Tanzania: Global discourse, local guides. *Annals of Tourism Research* 33(3): 833–852.

Salazar, N. B. (2010a) *Envisioning Eden: Mobilizing Imaginaries in Tourism and Beyond*. Oxford: Berghahn.

Salazar, N. B. (2010b) The Glocalisation of Heritage through Tourism: Balancing Standardisation and Differentiation, in S. Labadi and C. Long (eds), *Heritage and Globalisation*. London: Routledge, pp. 130–147.

Salazar, N. B. (2012a) Community-based cultural tourism: Issues, threats and opportunities. *Journal of Sustainable Tourism* 20(1): 9–22.

Salazar, N. B. (2012b) Shifting Values and Meanings of Heritage: From Cultural Appropriation to Tourism Interpretation and Back, in S. M. Lyon and C. E. Wells (eds), *Global Tourism: Cultural Heritage and Economic Encounters*. Lanham, MD: Altamira, pp. 21–41.

Salazar, N. B. (2012c) Tourism imaginaries: A conceptual approach. *Annals of Tourism Research* 39(2): 863–882.

Salazar, N. B. (2015) One List, a World of Difference? The Dynamics of Global Heritage at Two Neighbouring Properties, in C. Brumann and D. Berliner (eds), *World Heritage on the Ground*. Oxford: Berghahn.

Salazar, N. B. and N. H. H. Graburn (eds) (2014) *Tourism Imaginaries: Anthropological Approaches*. Oxford: Berghahn.

Salazar, N. B. and B. W. Porter (2004) Cultural heritage and tourism: A public interest approach – Introduction. *Anthropology in Action* 11(2/3): 2–8.

Salazar, N. B. and Y. Zhang (2013) Seasonal lifestyle tourism: The case of Chinese elites. *Annals of Tourism Research* 43(4): 81–99.

Shackley, M. L. (ed.) (1998) *Visitor Management: Case Studies from World Heritage Sites*. Oxford: Butterworth-Heinemann.

Smith, L. (2006) *Uses of Heritage*. New York: Routledge.

Smith, M. (2002) A critical evaluation of the global accolade: The significance of World Heritage site status for Maritime Greenwich. *International Journal of Heritage Studies* 8(2): 137–151.

Su, X. (2012) "It is my home. I will die here": Tourism development and the politics of place in Lijiang, China. *Geografiska Annaler: Series B, Human Geography* 94(1): 31–45.

Timothy, D. J. (1997) Tourism and the personal heritage experience. *Annals of Tourism Research* 24(3): 751–754.

Timothy, D. J. and S. W. Boyd (2003) *Heritage Tourism*. Harlow: Prentice Hall.

Timothy, D. J. and S. W. Boyd (2006) Heritage tourism in the 21st century: Valued traditions and new perspectives. *Journal of Heritage Tourism* 1(1): 1–16.

Timothy, D. J. and B. Prideaux (2004) Issues in heritage and culture in the Asia Pacific region. *Asia Pacific Journal of Tourism Research* 9(3): 213–223.

Tunbridge, J. E. and G. J. Ashworth (1996) *Dissonant Heritage: The Management of the Past as a Resource in Conflict*. Chichester: Wiley.

UNESCO (1965) Monuments in peril: A world campaign to protect our cultural heritage. *The UNESCO Courier* 18(1): 4–6.

UNESCO (1972) *Convention Concerning the Protection of the World Cultural and Natural Heritage*. Paris: UNESCO.

UNESCO (1977) *Operational Guidelines for the World Heritage Committee*. Paris: UNESCO World Heritage Center.

UNESCO (2005) *Heritage Tour Guide Training and Certification for UNESCO World Heritage Sites*. Bangkok: UNESCO Bangkok Office.

UNESCO (2013) *Operational Guidelines for the Implementation of the World Heritage Convention*. Paris: World Heritage Center.

UNWTO (2009) *Sustainable Tourism Management at World Heritage Sites: Enhancing Inter-Agency and Stakeholder Coordination for Joint Action*. Madrid: UNWTO.

UNWTO (2012) *Tourism and Intangible Cultural Heritage*. Madrid: World Tourism Organization.

UNWTO (2013) *UNWTO Tourism Highlights. 2013 Edition*. Madrid: United Nations World Tourism Organization.

Uriely, N. (2005) The tourist experience: Conceptual developments. *Annals of Tourism Research* 32(1): 199–216.

Urry, J. (2002) *The Tourist Gaze*, 2nd edn. London: Sage.

Wang, N. (1999) Rethinking authenticity in tourism experience. *Annals of Tourism Research* 26(2): 349–370.

WHC (2010) *Sustainable Tourism: Part Threat, Part Hope*. Vol. 58, *World Heritage Review*. Paris: World Heritage Center.

Winter, T. (2007) *Post-Conflict Heritage, Postcolonial Tourism: Culture, Politics and Development at Angkor*. Routledge Studies in Asia's Transformations. London: Routledge.

Winter, T. (2013) Heritage studies and the privileging of theory. *International Journal of Heritage Studies* 20(5): 556–572.

WTO (2001) *Tourism 2020 Vision*. Madrid: World Tourism Organization.

WTTC (2011) *Travel & Tourism 2011*. London: World Travel and Tourism Council.

Zhu, Y. (2012a) Performing heritage: Rethinking authenticity in global tourism. *Annals of Tourism Research* 39(3): 1495–1513.

Zhu, Y. (2012b) When the global meets the local in tourism – cultural performances in Lijiang as case studies. *Journal of China Tourism Research* 8(3): 302–319.

Zhu, Y. and N. Li (2013) Groping for Stones to Cross the River: Governing Heritage in Emei, in T. Blumenfield and H. Silverman (eds), *Cultural Heritage Politics in China*. New York: Springer, pp. 51–71.

Index

Global Heritage: A Reader, First Edition. Edited by Lynn Meskell.